CIVIL WAR CHICAGO

CIVIL WAR CHICAGO

Eyewitness to History

~

EDITED BY THEODORE J. KARAMANSKI
AND EILEEN M. MCMAHON

Ohio University Press

Athens

Ohio University Press, Athens, Ohio 45701
ohioswallow.com
© 2014 by Ohio University Press
All rights reserved

Printed in the United States of America
Ohio University Press books are printed on acid-free paper ⊗ ™

24 23 22 21 20 19 18 17 16 15 14   5 4 3 2 1

Library of Congress Cataloging-in-Publication Data

Civil War Chicago : eyewitness to history / edited by Theodore J.
Karamanski and Eileen M. McMahon.
    pages cm
    Includes bibliographical references and index.
    ISBN 978-0-8214-2084-3 (pb : alk. paper) — ISBN 978-0-8214-4481-8 (pdf)
    1. Chicago (Ill.)—History—Civil War, 1861–1865—Sources. I. Karamanski,
Theodore J., 1953– editor of compilation, author. II. McMahon, Eileen M., 1957–
editor of compilation, author.
    F548.4.C55 2014
    977.3'1103—dc23

                                                        2014012486

To

Katherine McMahon

Our Sister Who Will Never Be Forgotten

Contents

One

A Divided City: Chicago and the Crisis of the Union   6

Two

The War Spirit: Chicagoans and the Call to Arms   47

Three

Ties between the Home Front and the Battlefield   68

Four

Confined Confederates: Camp Douglas and Chicago   88

Five

The Politics of War   111

Six

The Business and Politics of War   157

Seven

The War in the Wards   202

Eight

The Long Shadow of War   235

Nine

A Guide to Civil War Chicago Sites 270

Illustrations

Editors' Note

The documents presented in this volume were chosen to reflect the fears, aspirations, and challenges of Chicago-area men and women caught up in a sweeping revolutionary era. This collection represents the way powerful opinion shapers in the press tried to cast the conflict as well as the way ordinary Americans responded to the buffeting winds of Civil War. We have tried to present their words with as few changes as possible from the way they were written, and hence we have edited with a light hand. The words they used, while sometimes strange and occasionally offensive to our ears, are preserved from the original texts. In the interests of brevity we have compressed longer texts through the use of ellipses, but always with an awareness of our responsibility not to distort the author's original intent.

Acknowledgments

Nineteenth-century Chicago was a remarkably dynamic place. "Would that I were able to suggest in prose the throb and urge and sting of my first days in Chicago," wrote the young novelist Theodore Dreiser. It is the goal of this book to capture in eyewitness accounts some of the drama and energy that surged through the streets of Chicago during the era of the Civil War. In attempting to do so we have battled the legacy of the Chicago Fire, which destroyed many of the letters and diaries that normally make the American Civil War a joy to research. Fortunately, a handful of institutions have preserved a portion of Chicago's literary legacy from the war. We are particularly grateful to the staff of the Chicago History Museum Research Center, especially Ellen Keith, Lesley Martin, and Debbie Vaughan. At the Newberry Library, we are grateful for the knowledgeable assistance we received from Jo Ellen McKillop Dickie and Maggie Grossman of the Special Collections Department. We also received wonderful assistance from the great staff of archivists at the National Archives, Great Lakes Branch, beginning with Director Douglas Bicknese and Senior Archivist Scott Forsythe, as well as Glenn Longacre, Katie Dishman, Gwen Podeschi and Jane Ehrenhart. We also wish to acknowledge the help of the staffs of the Illinois State Archives regional depository for Chicago, Loyola University Chicago's Cudahy Library, the Abraham Lincoln Presidential Library, and Brother Paul French Learning Resource Center of Lewis University. David Keller and the Camp Douglas Restoration Foundation shared with us some of their ever-growing documentation on Chicago's Civil War prison camp.

At Ohio University Press we are grateful for the patience and guidance of Director Gillian Berchowitz. Beth Pratt designed and typeset the pages. Sally Bennett Boyington copyedited much of the manuscript, and Nancy Basmajian helped keep the production on track. Thanks to them and to all who helped proofread the many documents that make up this volume.

On a more personal level, we have benefited from long association with fellow Civil War scholars Mary Abroe, Brother John Vietoris, and Robert I. Giradi. Joseph Karamanski helped with the difficult but not thankless job of transcribing nineteenth-century newspaper accounts. Over the years several Loyola University Public History students have shared in the research of this subject. We wish to thank Marc Dlugar, Ariel Orlov, Janice Slupski, and Laura Johns. While the list of individual names would be too long for inclusion we also would like to thank the many scholars from across the country who have over the years participated in the Chicago Civil War Symposium for broadening our knowledge of the field. We have also appreciated our always pleasant and beneficial association with the many

Civil War Roundtables in the Chicago area and all they have done to keep alive the memory of the war. We are ever grateful to the administration and alumni of our home institutions, Loyola University Chicago and Lewis University, for providing a stimulating and supportive environment for scholarship, both public and academic.

Introduction

$\mathcal{T}$HIS BOOK IS about the intersection of two of nineteenth-century America's most remarkable phenomena: the appalling creative destruction of the American Civil War and the emergence of the dynamic city of Chicago, which in two generations blossomed from the seedbed of a fur-trading post to the full flower of major metropolitan status. Chicago in the 1860s was a chaotic, bursting-at-the-seams burg that was a magnet for people, commerce, and industry. One resident described the city on the eve of the Civil War as "alive to the tips of her fingers and the core of her heart and brain" and observed that there was a challenge "in the strong and headstrong life" that demanded a response. Impressed by Chicago's "marvelous growth," an English visitor confessed, "Well, she beats her own brag!" Otto von Bismarck, while in the midst of remaking the map of Europe, observed, "I wish I could go to America, if only to see that Chicago." In this volume, that dramatic story of urban growth is blended with America's most tragic chapter—its bloody Civil War. That conflict brought the young nation to the brink of destruction yet in the end lifted the curse of slavery and manhandled America onto the path of modernity. Chicago illustrates in microcosm the trauma of the challenges and changes wrought by war. Chicagoans played a critical role in the awful sectional contest, and the four years of war were formative in the growth of the metropolis.[1]

The Civil War solidified Chicago's standing as the capital of the emerging Upper Great Lakes region in the Midwest. As a transportation hub, it provided a critical link between East and West, North and South. Poised on Great Lakes shipping routes and access to New York via the Erie Canal, connected by waterways to the Mississippi River valley via the Illinois and Michigan Canal and by train links to all parts of the country, Chicago was able to harvest the region's agricultural bounty and turn its natural resources into steel, lumber, and other manufactured products to supply Northern armies. The Civil War helped make Chicago, and Chicago helped save the Union.

While few cities can be said to be made by war, throughout history war has served as a stimulus for urban development. Chicago during the American Civil War is an example of this phenomenon. The conflict's impact on Chicago, however, is not a simple story of economic development or population growth. Rather, the relationship between the city and the Civil War is also cultural, social, and political but most of all reciprocal. The Civil War shaped Chicago, but Chicagoans also fundamentally shaped war. Through eyewitness accounts of the war years, this book hopes to bring to life that dynamic era in Chicago and national history.

~

On the eve of the Civil War, Chicago was just two generations removed from its days as a fur-trading post on the edge of an unsettled wilderness. After the war it became known, in Carl Sandberg's inimitable words, as "Hog Butcher, Tool Maker, Stacker of Wheat, Player with Railroads and Freight Handler to the Nation." The experience of war played a critical role in this transformation. While nineteenth-century Chicago was famously dubbed by historian William Cronon as "Nature's Metropolis," the city's ability to improve upon nature is what proved key to its explosive growth and to its commitment to the Union.[2]

In 1848 Chicago became the link between the Great Lakes waterway and the Mississippi River system because a congressional land grant made possible the building of the Illinois and Michigan Canal. By 1860 the city had become the busiest port on the Great Lakes in part because a penurious Congress that had refused to help develop safe harbors for other emerging lake cities nonetheless spent over $200,000 on Chicago's facilities. Not that Chicagoans simply relied on federal largess; at times they took matters into their own hands, as they did in 1854 when Secretary of War Jefferson Davis refused to allow army engineers to clear a sandbar blocking Chicago's harbor. The citizens seized the army's dredge and did the job themselves.[3]

When the Civil War started and military forces plied the Mississippi and Ohio Rivers, Chicago solidified its position as the emerging capital of the Midwest and Great Lakes. The war circumscribed the southern hinterlands of competing cities such as St. Louis and Cincinnati at a time when Chicago was able to expand its reach to the north and west. More important, Chicago offered transportation links between West and East that were superior to those of both its Mississippi valley rivals, as well as to its Great Lakes rivals. Chicago's advantages were not simply a gift of nature—they were a product of national politics.[4]

~

The city's ties to the federal union also helped it to emerge as a metropolis. In 1860 it was the terminus for the world's longest railroad, the Illinois Central, built because of a 2.6 million-acre federal land grant. In many ways, the nation began its march to Civil War because Chicago's most prominent citizen, Senator Stephen Douglas, was determined that Chicago be the point of origin for the even-longer Pacific railroad. The 1854 Kansas-Nebraska Act that Douglas ushered through Congress to build that railroad eventually gave birth to the Republican Party and sectional combat.

For a city far removed from both "Bleeding Kansas" and the later battlefields of the Civil War, Chicago understood its stake in the crisis and exerted considerable influence over events. It was in Chicago, in part because of the maneuvers of the city's politicos, where Abraham Lincoln was nominated to the presidency. Lincoln's chief rival for the White House in 1860 was Stephen Douglas, the first Chicagoan to run for the highest office in the land. When Lincoln was elected president, Chicago ministers hectored him to abolish slavery; yet once he issued the Emancipation Proclamation, the city's leading newspaper pilloried the president's "mania for blood in the cause of negro emancipation." In 1864, after four years of carnage and seeming stalemate, Chicago hosted the Democratic Party's national convention, which, egged on by the city's influential peace advocates, branded Lincoln and his war effort a "failure" and pushed for recognition of the Confederacy.[5]

Like many other midwestern communities, Chicago's response to the Civil War was complex and at times contradictory. Before 1861 Southerners routinely denounced the city as a "nigger lovin' town" and a "sink hole of abolitionism" because of the lax local enforcement of the Fugitive Slave Law. Yet when the Civil War came, Chicago was decried as a "hotbed of Copperheadism." The *Chicago Times* was one of the most outspoken anti-Lincoln newspapers, and its opposition to the administration's war effort eventually led to its suppression at bayonet point in the summer of 1863. A handful of Chicagoans became so incensed by Lincoln's attempt at a "new birth of freedom" that they acted in concert with Confederate agents in the "Northwest Conspiracy."[6]

Yet Lincoln once described Chicago as second only to Boston in urging an aggressive war. Chicagoans sent more than fifteen thousand soldiers to the front, and the city acted as a major supply hub for the far-ranging armies of the western theater of operations. As early as the summer of 1862, the city cheered the convicted war criminal General John B. Turchin and called for a "hard war" on the Southern populace. In 1864 the Chicago Board of Trade actually passed a resolution demanding that the rations of rebel prisoners at Camp Douglas on the city's south side be cut so that the men might "suffer more." Thousands of Southern soldiers did indeed suffer in the Chicago prisoner of war camp, and today more than four thousand lie on the city's south side in the largest mass grave in the United States.[7]

The Civil War divided Chicago not as violently as it divided the nation but in ways that were significant and enduring. For more than a hundred years, a special tension existed between Irish Americans and African Americans in Chicago. It was born in bare-knuckle confrontations on the docks of Civil War Chicago's waterfront, where unskilled Irish immigrants fought to prevent desperate African American workers from displacing them as stevedores. While some Chicagoans risked their lives to win equality for all Americans, many of their fellow citizens scorned the Union cause and condemned emancipation. In keeping with these sentiments, the Chicago City Council acted in 1864 to legally segregate the races. These years saw the foundation for the persistent racial polarization that led Chicago in the twentieth century to be characterized as one of the most racially segregated cities in the United States.

During the Civil War, class emerged as a factor even more important than race dividing Chicagoans. Industrialization with its increased scale of production, combined with wartime labor shortages and inflation, increased tensions between employers and their workers. For wage earners, the ethnic and religious differences that had loomed large in 1850s Chicago began to blur for men and women who saw themselves locked into the same economic circumstances. During the war, women took jobs as shop clerks and in the garment industry. Men formed the city's first labor hall and founded its first unions. Alliances formed in 1864 between native-born and immigrant workers laid the foundation for the eight-hour-day movement and the violent conflict between capital and labor that would be later played out in the Haymarket Square Riot of 1886 and in the Pullman Strike in 1894.[8]

While thousands of its most productive citizens left the city to fight the Confederacy, Chicago's rapid growth continued unabated. Between 1860 and 1870 the population nearly tripled, rising from 109,260 to 298,977. Many of those who eschewed military service grew fat on war contracts. Young men of military age with a nose for business avoided service at the front and laid the foundation for Gilded Age fortunes. George Pullman began his railroad car works after avoiding military service by purchasing a substitute to join the ranks in his place. Richard Teller Crane also avoided military service, and his small brass foundry expanded three times during the war. It eventually became the world's leading manufacturer of valves and fittings. Marshall Field, likewise of military age, stayed home and exploited wartime prosperity to cement his dominance in retail sales and real estate.

The Civil War built industrial Chicago not because it brought new business particular to military needs but because wartime spending nourished the city's nascent and natural industries. The Union army rode iron rails to victory. Even before the war, Chicago was the nation's railroad center. The need to replace rails and rolling stock increased tremendously during the war, laying the foundation for car works plants and steel production. The city's inland waterway connections made it a natural meeting place for southern Illinois coal and northern Michigan iron ore. During the conflict, miles upon miles of iron rails were spit out of the city's rolling mills and played a key role in maintaining the efficiency of the nation's all-important railroad network. Throughout the war, at the North Chicago Rolling Mill on the banks of the Chicago River, experiments were made with the new blast furnace technology that could produce steel. Finally, in May 1865, Chicago produced the first steel rail made in the United States. The plant that succeeded in this innovation later became a cornerstone for the United States Steel Corporation. For this heartland metropolis, food processing was a natural avenue of industrial opportunity. Already the nation's leading grain distribution and beef packing center, during the Civil War Chicago celebrated its acquisition of the title "Porkopolis," which it stole from Cincinnati. On Christmas Day 1865, the Union Stockyards were founded in the wake of the huge number of beef and pigs that arrived in the city to supply the Union's hungry troops.

Finance, along with railroads and food processing, was a third key to Chicago's Civil War–era industrial growth. In 1861, Chicago banks were shaky and untrustworthy. Less than $150,000 was on deposit in the city. The Lincoln administration stabilized the financial system by ushering in national banking. Nowhere else in the country did the federally chartered banks catch on as enthusiastically as Chicago; by the end of the Civil War there were thirteen national banks in the city, with deposits approaching $30 million. This was the critical capital foundation that made possible large-scale investment in industrialization. Little wonder that during the decade of the 1860s the number of factories in Chicago tripled.

When Chicagoans think of the nineteenth-century city, they think of the Great Chicago Fire of 1871 or the splendid 1893 World's Columbian Exposition. Both events are symbolically honored with stars on the city's official flag. The fire not only destroyed more than three square miles of the city but also erased much of the city's memory of the Civil War. Hundreds of letters, diaries, and artifacts brought home from the war were destroyed by the fire, including an original copy of the Emancipation Proclamation Lincoln gave for auction to the Sanitary Commission. Elites made rich by the war chose to emphasize that a new city was reborn from the ashes of the old.[9] However, the men and women who sacrificed lives and loved ones to create "a more perfect union" refused to let the memory of the war die. They created an elaborate memorial landscape to be their time capsule for future generations. One hundred and fifty years later, the city's people recreate in giant parks named for Lincoln and Ulysses Grant. There is a statue of Grant in Lincoln Park and statues of Lincoln in Grant Park and a score of other places in the city. Chicagoans drive down boulevards named after generals in cars with "Land of Lincoln" emblazoned on their plates as they look out at Beaux-Arts sculptures of Civil War heroes. In the obvious tension of Chicago's racially divided communities, in the bustle of its business district, in its striking economic inequality, in the stars and stripes that wave over a city and a nation, the hand of the Civil War generation still rests upon Chicago's shoulder.[10]

ONE

A Divided City

Chicago and the Crisis of the Union

N THE EVE of the Civil War, Chicago was a city of 110,000 people. It was still village enough that most of its citizens lived within the sound of the courthouse bell. For many Chicagoans, social life had a small-town feel—Sunday school, ice cream socials, winter sleigh rides, and summer picnics. Yet the foreshadowing of a more complex city was evident by the contrast between the marble-facaded row houses on Michigan Avenue inhabited by the business and professional elite with the dark, ramshackle wooden houses of the working class in industrial districts. Muddy streets and pine plank sidewalks gave the city a makeshift feel, while at the same time, the city rushed to embrace the high culture of theater, opera, and symphonic concerts that befitted its emergence as one of the ten largest cities in the United States. For visitors from the hinterland, such as Abraham Lincoln, a poor farmer's son who grew up to become a successful railroad attorney, a trip to Chicago was a chance to taste a cosmopolitan life unimagined in a frontier youth.[1]

Although it was a raw, brash upstart of a city, Chicago played center stage in the unfolding sectional debate over the fate of the country. The city had bargained its geographic position to acquire a harbor, a canal, and railroads to become a critical link in the young nation's westward expansion. By 1860 these internal improvements allowed Chicago to reap the harvest of the quickly multiplying farms of the prairie heartland of Illinois, Iowa, Wisconsin, and Indiana. The tallest structures in the city were its grain elevators that lined the banks of the Chicago River. These towering, steam-powered, vertical grain warehouses were the basis for much of the city's wealth. "Chicago," wrote the English novelist Anthony Trollope in 1861, "may be called the metropolis of American corn—the favorite city haunt of the American Ceres." The canals and railroads funneled millions of bushels of wheat and corn into the city. Chicago's middlemen weighed, graded, valued, stored, and finally shipped to the world the fruit of the farmer's labor. The movement of this grain onto schooners for shipment across the Great Lakes to eastern and European markets made the city's harbor the busiest on the lakes and soon to be the busiest in the United States. During the shipping season, hundreds of white-winged sailing ships entered and exited the harbor. They carried not just the

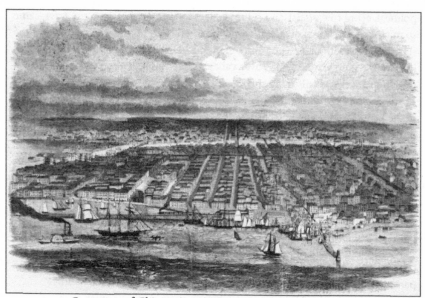

FIGURE 1. Panorama of Chicago in 1860. From *Harper's Weekly*, May 12, 1860.

prosperity of Chicago's Board of Trade but the economic fortunes of a vast inland agricultural region.[2]

Transporting the heartland's harvest to the East Coast provoked powerful political controversy over what the pundits of the day called "internal improvements." Sailing the lakes was a deadly business because there were few natural harbors and few navigation aids for storm-tossed vessels. The lack of ports hindered the development of trade in lumber and iron, as well as agricultural products, for Chicago and the region. Harbors had to be created by dredging the mouths of streams like the sluggish Chicago River. In 1833 Congress made its first appropriation to create a Chicago harbor, and by 1848 it had spent over $200,000 on the project. The harbor, however, demanded regular dredging to maintain its depth. Despite the vast revenues generated by the grain trade and continued western settlement, Chicagoans found themselves trapped in a sectional competition for federal aid for internal improvements with a Southern-dominated federal government. Southern politicians cited notions of limited government to justify withholding improvement money from the West knowing that as the Great Lakes became a major commercial highway the West would become increasingly tied to the Northeast and not to the South.[3]

As eastern Yankee migrants and European immigrants flocked to Chicago via northern water routes, a fundamental divide developed in the state between the northern and southern half of the state. This settlement pattern had profound political, economic, social, and cultural effects on Illinois that, in many ways, came to mirror the sectional divide of the nation. Southern Illinois, the first part of the state that was settled, boasted a population from the upland South who came to the Prairie State via the Ohio River valley. While some were strongly antislavery, this population was culturally and ideologically more in harmony with the people of the South. During the 1850s when sectional tensions became more prominent in the United States, the northern region tended to favor Free-Soilers and later Republican candidates while the southern portion of the state maintained its support for the Democratic Party. This left two swing areas of Illinois that determined the outcome of statewide political contests. One was central Illinois, particularly Sangamon County, the home of Abraham Lincoln, who was one of the founders of the Republican Party in the state. The other was Chicago. Although it was located in the northern portion of the state, Chicago had a large immigrant population that was strongly supportive of the Democratic Party. Chicago was the political base of Stephen Douglas, one of the nation's most important and powerful politicians of the pre–Civil War era. Political events in 1850s Chicago were extremely partisan, deeply engaging to the population, and significant to the nation.

Political and cultural divisions in Chicago were more complex than a simple North-South or Democrat-Republican divide. More than half the residents of the city were foreign born, most of them refugees from the famine in Ireland or political unrest in central Europe. The largest group were the German-born, numbering 22,230 or 20 percent of the city's population in 1860.[4] While Germans could be found in all parts of the city, they so dominated the area north of the Chicago River that it was often referred to as the "Nord Seite." Many were "forty-eighters" who fled the German states when republican revolutions were crushed by monarchs and aristocrats. They came with hands skilled in a variety of useful crafts and minds attuned to reformist politics. Their neighborhoods consisted of small, wood-frame cottages erected on soggy ground near the city limits. Community anchors were either Lutheran or Catholic churches, inevitably ministered in the language of the old country with beer gardens and Turner athletic clubs providing diversion from work.

The Irish were the next-largest immigrant group in Chicago, numbering 19,889 or 18 percent of the city's population in 1860.[5] While scattered throughout the city, the Irish dominated the area along the South Branch of the Chicago River. Many came as diggers for the Illinois and Michigan Canal and settled in Bridgeport, the neighborhood where the waterway began. While the German immigrant community featured professionals, artisans, and shopkeepers, as well as laborers, the Irish tended to make their living in unskilled labor. They worked in what were often "rough" seasonal occupations such as stevedores, teamsters, and sailors and in the growing number of slaughterhouses and meatpacking plants that congregated on

FIGURE 2. Lake Street in Chicago. This picture illustrates the sidewalks and build-ings more than six feet higher than the adjacent street surface. In 1858 city officials officially raised the surface grade to enable installation of a sewer system. It was up to individual property owners to raise their buildings, and some never did. Walking in Civil War–era Chicago therefore required literally walking up and down the side-walks. Courtesy of the Chicago History Museum.

the city's south and west sides.[6] Community stability came from Catholic parishes, which sprouted like clover wherever the Irish settled. Catholic schools and parish associations abetted stable families seeking a better life for the next generation. Corner saloons were magnets for young males and served as the hub of political organization. Chicago's worst slum was the Irish neighborhood known as Kilgub-bin, a dank, depressing place overrun with crime, substance abuse, and poverty.

To many native-born Chicagoans, the shabby, priest-ridden Irish and the clannish, guttural sounding Germans were "the other." Also in that category were smaller, less politically active communities of Scandinavians, with 1,313 Norwe-gians, 816 Swedes, and 150 Danes on the north side and approximately 85 Bohe-mian families west of the river.[7]

During the 1850s the American Party, better known as the Know-Nothings, helped to crystallize political and social unease about the foreign born into a na-tional anti-Catholic, anti-immigrant political movement. In 1855 that tide washed over Chicago and swept Levi Boone, a descendant of the famous pioneer hunter, into the mayor's office. Boone was a cultural conservative who sought to assert social control over the immigrant masses. He tripled the size of a new profession-alized city police force and then sent the men in blue out to enforce a new Chicago City Council ordinance designed to close most Irish taverns and German beer gar-dens. What the Know-Nothings, inspired by Protestant evangelical fervor, saw as moral degradation, immigrants enjoyed as the exercise of individual recreational choice. The result was Chicago's largest civil disturbance to date—the Lager Beer Riot of April 1855. The dispute resulted in one death and numerous arrests. More important, it mobilized the city's ethnic voters for the first time, and thereafter they vanquished the Know-Nothings from the city's politics. For a time the Democratic Party was able to unify immigrant voters behind their candidates, but after 1856 the Republican Party pried middle-class Germans away from the Democrats by appealing to their economic aspirations and their political liberalism. The Republican press, led by the *Chicago Tribune*, was careful to praise the industry of the German immigrants and ridicule the Irish as ignorant, impoverished inebriants.[8]

Political partisanship also affected Chicagoans' dreams of capitalizing on western expansion. Historian Christopher Clark has noted that the Democratic Party, with its aggressive support for Texas annexation and war with Mexico, stood for "extensive development" of the nation, while the Whig Party and later the Republicans advocated "intensive development," such as internal transportation improvements. Chicago, situated between the East and the western frontier, wanted both types of development, and this desire played a role in the evolution of its politics between 1850 and 1860. The politician who more than any other managed to satisfy Chicago's ideologically contradictory desires was Stephen Douglas. When Douglas moved to Chicago in 1847, he had already served as a state's attorney, judge, and congressman. That year he was chosen for the U.S. Senate, where he quickly became the most prominent spokesman for the nation's aggressive "Young America" movement. Young America was idealistic, energetic, and most of all expansionistic. Through direct democracy and vigorous nationalism, Douglas promised white Americans a future of free homesteads spread over the open prairie and industrial cities linked by expanding lines of steel rails. Douglas accelerated Chicago's rise by making it the terminus for the Illinois Central Railroad—the nation's first land grant railroad—and he plotted to anchor the long-dreamed-of Pacific railroad there as well. Unfortunately, Douglas and Young America carried a heavy burden on their march to political power—slavery. For Douglas and his young Democrats to achieve their ambition, they needed a political party united, north, south, east, and west. Unfortunately, throughout the 1850s the issue of slavery increasingly divided the nation along sectional lines.[9]

The five-foot-four-inch senator from Chicago became the "Little Giant" of American politics in 1850 when he forestalled the threat of Southern secession over the question of slavery's expansion into the territories conquered during the Mexican-American War. Where the giants of the Senate—Henry Clay, Daniel Webster, and John C. Calhoun—had failed to craft a plan that could save the Union, Douglas engineered the famed "Compromise of 1850." In an attempt to defuse tension, Douglas applied the pragmatic Young America principle of "popular

FIGURE 3. *Stephen A. Douglas*, by Matthew Brady. Courtesy of the Library of Congress.

sovereignty"—let the people of those territories vote yes or no on whether slavery would be allowed in these new possessions. He mistakenly thought that popular sovereignty would solve this issue of slavery as a divisive force in American life.

On that faulty assumption, Douglas decided in 1854 to realize his dream to make Chicago the beginning point of a transcontinental railroad to the California gold fields. To win Southern support, Douglas pushed for the Kansas-Nebraska Act, which would allow the principle of popular sovereignty in states formed in the unorganized federal lands north and west of Missouri. It seemed a simple solution to Douglas, who viewed democracy in overly optimistic terms and did not see slavery as a moral issue. However, the Kansas-Nebraska Act tore up the revered "Compromise of 1820," which forbade any slave state north of the southern boundary of Missouri. The act was immediately unpopular across the North. Ordinary white people saw it as a threat to the opportunity of free men to profit from the development of the nation's western territories. Thousands of voters in the North abandoned the Democratic Party and, together with members of the failed Whig and American Parties, founded what became the Republican Party. Douglas's blunder likely cost him the 1856 Democratic presidential nomination.[10]

It was against this backdrop that a frustrated politician and successful lawyer chose to challenge Douglas's reelection to the Senate in 1858. Abraham Lincoln had largely focused on his legal career after an undistinguished term in Congress from 1846 to 1848. He was spurred back into the fray by Douglas's Kansas-Nebraska Act, which he saw as an open invitation for slavery to expand across the vast expanse of America's trans-Mississippi territories. That impression was further strengthened by the Supreme Court's *Dred Scott* decision of 1857, which seemed to overthrow popular sovereignty and opened Chicago's Great Plains hinterland to slaveholders. Up to this time Douglas was the champion of Chicago's westward ambitions, but the rise of the slavery issue threatened those credentials. Lincoln launched his challenge against the "Little Giant" in stunning fashion with his famous "House Divided" speech in Springfield, Illinois, in June 1858. That provocative address foretold a great conflict between slavery and freedom for the future of not just the West but the nation and alleged that Douglas was a knowing ally of the Slave Power.[11]

By making the Illinois Senate race a contest about the future of slavery in America, Lincoln ensured that he would garner a national audience. The renowned Lincoln-Douglas debates elevated Lincoln from a local to a national figure among Republicans. The genesis of those debates was a political encounter between the two candidates in Chicago on July 9, 1858. On that occasion Stephen Douglas addressed a crowd of supporters from the balcony of the Tremont House Hotel. Lincoln was seated near the senator and offered an implicit challenge to the combative Douglas. The "Little Giant" directly attacked Lincoln's "House Divided" rhetoric as leading the country toward a dangerous and violent conflict. Douglas claimed to be the voice of moderation and reason and the better candidate to promote sectional reconciliation and democratic procedures. Lincoln responded by inviting the audience to return the next night for his reply to Douglas. On July 10, before another large crowd, Lincoln defended his contention that slavery was a moral evil that was dividing America and that the institution's geographic spread had to be immediately halted, as the first step toward its elimination. In the wake of this exchange, the *Chicago Tribune* suggested, and the two candidates agreed to participate in, a series of seven debates in various congressional districts across the state. These famous debates, however, largely recapitulated the exchange that had initially taken place in Chicago.[12]

In the end, Douglas retained his Senate seat (although Lincoln won a larger share of the votes by citizens in the 1858 polling), because senators were chosen by the Illinois General Assembly, where the Democrats held a narrow majority. The "Little Giant" was returned to Washington. Despite a rain-soaked election day in Chicago that depressed voter turnout, Lincoln bested Douglas there. With strong help from the rural portions of the county, Republican candidates won by more than a 1,500-vote margin in the northern Illinois district that included Chicago. This revealed that the recently formed Republicans had he emerged as a major force in Chicago politics, where they also retained the mayor's office. The Republican Party had successfully shed the image of its Know-Nothing predecessor as being anti-immigrant and established a clear principle of opposing slavery's expansion. The great attention that the nation devoted to the race rebounded to the benefit of each of the candidates. Stephen Douglas was able to reclaim his position as the chief spokesman of the Democrats across the North. Lincoln won praise as an able articulator of Republican principles. The Senate race, therefore, went far to setting each man on the road to the White House.[13]

In 1860 it was Douglas's bad luck that to secure his party's presidential nomination he would have to succeed in Charleston, South Carolina, where the national convention was scheduled. There a minority of rabid proslavery advocates walked out of the convention rather than accede to Douglas's nomination. Two months later the Democrats met again in Baltimore, and proslavery advocates refused to support Douglas unless he forsook his principle of "popular sovereignty" and agreed that slavery should be extended to all western territories regardless of the wishes of the citizenry. When he refused to accept this, they again walked out and the remaining Democrats nominated Douglas—now the candidate of a fatally divided political party.[14]

Thanks to the labors of his friend Norman B. Judd, the head of the Illinois Republican Party, Lincoln had the good fortune that the Republicans held their 1860 national convention in Chicago. The city edged out St. Louis for the honor in part because of its forty-two hotels and in part because Illinois was a critical swing state. Lincoln's supporters in the city, with a conscious eye on influencing the delegates, built one of the largest public halls in the country so they could pack it to the rafters with vocal Lincoln supporters. The Wigwam, as it was known, was capable of holding 1,200 people. Highly touted candidates for the nomination, William Seward of New York and Simon Cameron of Pennsylvania, sent hundreds of streetwise supporters to the Chicago convention in anticipation that strong vocal support from the galleries might stampede the delegates to support the "dark-horse" candidate from Illinois. The Chicagoans, however, outmaneuvered them by printing duplicate tickets and by other means to get the Lincoln supporters seated while their opponents were left outside, mumbling invectives in the muddy street. More important, Lincoln's lieutenants worked cleverly to secure second ballot commitments from supporters of Ohio's Salmon P. Chase and Missouri's Edward Bates, should their candidates falter. Therefore, when on the day of the voting William Seward narrowly missed securing a first-ballot nomination, Lincoln was able to build "irrepressible" momentum in the convention hall. By the third ballot, Lincoln had won enough votes to upset his better-known rival and secure the presidential nomination, and the Wigwam erupted into celebrations that quickly spread across the city.[15]

Chicago reveled in the major party nomination of two "favorite sons" to the White House. Unfortunately for Stephen Douglas, his prospects were dimmed by the presence of two other candidates in the race: John C. Breckenridge, the sitting vice president, was the candidate of the splinter Southern Democrats; and former senator John Bell was nominated by the hastily formed Constitutional-Union Party. Both of these candidates cut into Douglas's natural conservative electoral base. Faced with this unprecedented challenge, Douglas responded in a manner that was typically energetic but otherwise unprecedented. Dating back to the example set by George Washington, no presidential candidate before 1860 actually campaigned for office. Candidates left the majority of the speechmaking and handshaking to be done by their supporters. For that reason neither Stephen Douglas nor Abraham Lincoln had even been present at the national conventions at which they were nominated. After the convention Lincoln respected the tradition of not campaigning for votes. Douglas did not have this luxury. His party was divided by Southern radicals who threatened secession if the Republicans prevailed. Stephen Douglas waged a heroic campaign of personal appearances warning both North and South of the dangers of civil war. From New England to the shores of the Great Lakes, from old Virginia to Mobile Bay, Douglas addressed crowds large and small warning of radicalism and disunion. Unfortunately, Douglas used large doses of antiblack racism to try to build a bridge between white working men, particularly the poor immigrant Irish, and Southern planters; one legacy of his campaign was a Democratic Party that was virulently racist. By the fall of 1860, however, despite his exertions, the Little Giant's cause was clearly doomed. His voice, overly strained from repeated orations, was a mere croak, his once-confident stride reduced to a limp after an accident on the campaign trail, Douglas ended his efforts on election day looking, as friend recalled, "more hopeless that I had ever before seen him."[16]

Chicago exploded in celebrations when news was flashed that Lincoln was elected. Douglas's personal popularity and his long record of accomplishments for the city were not enough to prevent a slim majority of voters in his hometown from supporting Lincoln. The returns showed Lincoln with 10,697 and Douglas with 8,094 votes. Shortly after the bonfires and fireworks debris were cleared from the streets, Lincoln made what would turn out to be his last visit to Chicago.[17] He touched base with some of the Chicago Republicans who had played a role in making his nomination possible, including the influential newspaper publishers Charles Wilson of the *Chicago Daily Journal* and Joseph Medill of the *Chicago Tribune.* During this visit, Lincoln also sat for what would be a famous photograph. He had just begun to grow what would become his trademark beard, and the image captured the youthful, confident, prairie politician with the first wisps of whiskers on his chin.[18]

Unknown to the public, the president-elect used his trip to Chicago to meet secretly with several confidants from the South. In addition to hoping he might be able to place a Southerner in a prominent role in his administration, he was interested in gauging the attitude of the Southern people. Within days of his election, the Southern states of South Carolina, Alabama, and Mississippi had called for conventions to decide the question of secession from the Union. Determined not to give the secessionists any provocation, Lincoln eventually took an action that had a profound effect on Chicago's African American population. In April 1861, less than a week after his inauguration, he ordered federal marshals to strictly enforce the controversial Fugitive Slave Act of 1850. Although warning of the marshals' sweep of Chicago's runaway slave community was leaked in advance, a panicked flight was nonetheless set off. Chicago and Illinois had never been a welcoming haven for African Americans. During the 1850s, the Democratic-dominated legislature passed laws that all but excluded their entry into Illinois. Now with the country teetering on the edge of civil war, abolitionists and black leaders in the city were forced to organize an exodus from Chicago. They chartered a special train, and more than 100 refugees out of an estimated black population of 955 were loaded onto boxcars for Canada. On the very eve of the Civil War, the peculiar institution of the South still had the power to reach into Chicago and uproot lives on the shores of Lake Michigan.[19]

The painful African American flight from Chicago did little to impress secessionists, who by that time had united the Deep South into the so-called Confederate

States of America and had selected Jefferson Davis as their president. The secession crisis, coming on the heels of the divisive presidential election of 1860, found the North divided and unsure how to respond. Those uncertainties dissipated, however, when the secessionists attacked the U.S. troops at Fort Sumter in Charleston, South Carolina. Upon hearing of the attack, Stephen Douglas immediately offered his support to President Lincoln. Douglas played a large role in unifying Democratic Party support in Illinois for a military response to the attack. Back in Chicago, before a Wigwam packed with longtime supporters and recent enthusiasts, Douglas thundered that it was time for Republicans and Democrats to close ranks: "There can be no neutrals in this war: *only patriots—or traitors."*[20]

The impassioned speech before friends, neighbors, and former opponents was the climax of Douglas's tumultuous career. The next day he collapsed, weak with fever and wracked with muscle spasms. Over several weeks a succession of physicians could not prevent his deterioration into delirium and finally death. Public buildings in Chicago were draped in black crape, and the body of the forty-eight-year-old senator was laid in state for two days before a funeral procession wound its way south of the city to a meadow near Lake Michigan. Hundreds of uniformed volunteers were among those who escorted Douglas to his graveside. The fresh-faced boys in blue then departed for the front, where all too many of them would find their own graves.[21]

THE CHICAGO RIVER AND HARBOR CONVENTION MEETS TO SECURE FEDERAL FUNDS TO MAKE THE CITY THE GREAT LAKES SHIPPING CENTER

In July 1847 Chicago hosted its first national political gathering. According to Horace Greeley of the New York Herald, *the more than four thousand attendees made it the largest such gathering up to that time in American history. Called the River and Harbor Convention, it brought together both Whigs and Democrats to protest President James K. Polk's veto of a bill appropriating federal funds for Great Lake harbor construction and improving navigation on western rivers. At the time there was only one harbor, Chicago, on more than 1,600 miles of Lake Michigan shoreline. Great Lake harbor improvements and western railroad construction were critical to Chicago's aspirations for growth. The unity of interest expressed by northern and western states on this issue and the strong opposition of southern states (as expressed below) presaged the economic interests that together with the slavery issue would lead to the formation of the Republican Party and the Civil War.*

THE CHICAGO CONVENTION

This was a convention . . . assembled at Chicago in the state of Illinois, of the 5th of the present month—its avowed object, the embodiment of public opinion,

FIGURE 4. Chicago lakefront, 1860. Chicago's river harbor was one of the busiest in the United States. With the city's rail network it tied Chicago's economy to New York and the northeast. Federal support for harbor and navigation improvements on the Great Lakes and the city's desire for railroad expansion across the Great Plains were key sources of tension between Chicago and Southern politicians. Alfred Andreas, *History of Chicago* (Chicago: A. T. Andreas, 1884), 2:128.

irrespective of party, in favor of the improvement of northern and western lakes and rivers. We are opposed to such conventions; they are seldom productive of practical results. They savor of the spirit of humbuggery, and are generally controlled by interested and designing men. They are hot-beds for hucksters and speculators in river town-lots and lake harbors, where nature has located neither site for a city, nor defense for shipping. We do not say that such was the *materiel* of the Chicago gathering. But judging from the published proceedings, we conclude there was not a little humbuggery about it. . . . A string of resolutions which go to the whole figure for the improvement of the lakes and navigable rivers was adopted. No exception is made with respect to the lakes, and none to rivers, but the word *navigable* is prefixed to the latter. All the rivers and lakes in all the States and Territories are embraced in the comprehensive term, "Internal Lakes and Rivers," and all alike are declared worthy of national patronage in the "promotion of the general welfare and the regulation of commerce among the States and with the Indian tribes." In a word, the resolutions promulgate doctrines which would not leave a vestige of constitutional barrier to a scale of internal improvements without limitation, except in the will of Congress.

The Mississippian (Jackson, MS), July 23, 1847.

RESOLUTION REGARDING THE FUGITIVE SLAVE ACT

The Compromise of 1850 prevented a civil war, but it included a new Fugitive Slave Law that forced local authorities in the free slates to help Southern masters recover their runaway slaves. Like many other Northern communities, Chicago was outraged by the notion that it would become part of the systematic enslavement of other people. Chicago's champion, Senator Douglas, was one of the authors of the great compromise, and in October of 1850 he personally pressured the city council to support the law. However, when he returned to Washington, the council reasserted its antislavery position. In 1850 there were only 323 African Americans officially (not counting runaways) in the city, whose population was 29,289. Note how Chicago's officials balanced their rejection of the new federal law with concern for more federal funds for harbor and railroad projects.

November 29, 1850
Whereas the Fugitive Slave Act, recently passed by Congress, is revolting to our moral sense, and an outrage upon our feelings of justice and humanity, because it disregards all the securities which the Constitution and Laws have thrown around personal liberties, and its direct tendency is to alienate the people from their love and reverence for the Government and Institutions of our Country—therefore;

> Resolved, That as the Supreme Court of the United States has solemnly adjudged that State Officers are under no obligations to fulfill duties imposed upon them, as such Officers, by any Act of Congress, we do not therefore consider it a part of our duty, or the duty of the City Officers of the City of Chicago, to aid or assist in the arrest of fugitives from oppression;—and by withholding such aid or assisstance we do not believe that our "Harbour appropriations would be withheld," "our Rail Roads injured," or "our Commerce destroyed"—or "treason would be committed against our Government."

Chicago City Council Proceedings, Illinois State Archives Regional Depository, Chicago.

1855 MAYOR LEVI BOONE'S INAUGURAL ADDRESS

In 1855 the great-nephew of pioneer Daniel Boone was elected mayor of Chicago. The Kentucky-born physician was a well-respected citizen with an ambitious reform agenda. His new administration restricted the foreign born from city jobs. He also used city license fees to drive most liquor vendors out of the city and stop all alcohol sales on Sundays—the only day most working people were free of their jobs. His overt hostility to immigrants divided the city and sparked the Lager Beer Riot of April 21, 1855. The riot marked the end of Know-Nothing influence in Chicago, although immigrant suspicion of other "reform" parties like the Republicans helped keep many

immigrants in league with the Democratic Party. In this portion of his long inaugural
address, Boone makes clear his distrust of the Catholic Church and the foreign born.

My opponents, and almost the entire public press of this city, volunteered to place
me and the gentlemen associated with me in an antagonistic position to our fellow
citizens of foreign birth. This issue was made not by us, but by our opponents. So
far as I was concerned, no paper in the city was authorized to announce my name
as a candidate much less to define my position upon any subject. Since, however, it
has been done, and I have been publicly denominated and denounced as the "Know
Nothing" candidate for the Mayoralty, and as a portion of my fellow citizens on this
very account, and on account of my supposed hostility to them, have thought it
necessary to engage in a series of measures for my defeat, unprecedented probably,
in the annals of this or any other city, I deem it right in this place distinctly to define
my position on the questions involved in this issue. First of all, then, let me say, that
I should feel it beneath me as a man, much more so as a public officer, to make any
distinction either in my personal or official treatment of my fellow-citizens, on the
single ground of their nationality. As a man I have only to discover the broad seal of
our common humanity, to make him who wears it my brother, and to make me his
friend. As an officer, I have only to see one of the great brotherhood seeking a home
in our city and the protection of our laws, and I rejoice to bid him welcome and to
proffer him the boon of liberty and equal justice, which he here seeks.

When, however, I come to count the true friends of our country, and those to
whom our institutions may be safely committed, I am frank to confess, gentlemen, and I know many, both of native and foreign birth, who think with me,
I cannot be blind to the existence in our midst of a powerful politico-religious
organization, all its members owning, and its chief officers bound under an oath
of allegiance to the temporal, as well at the spiritual supremacy of a foreign des-
pot, bolding [sic] avowing the purpose of universal dominion over this land, and
asserting the monstrous doctrine, that this is an end to be gained, if not by other
means, by coercion and at the cost of blood itself. Against such doctrines and such
schemes, gentlemen, I wish to be known as taking my stand, and to their defeat I
must cheerfully consecrate my talents, my property, and if need be my life.

And, finally, on this subject and in a word, I ask all classes of persons, foreign
as well as native, as a general principle of public policy, to whom can the affairs
of this country, the administration of its laws, its liberties and its constitution, be
so properly committed, in whose hands can it be hoped they will be so safe as in
those of the men who were born under their shadows, whose first vital breath was
drawn in their atmosphere, whose youth as well as manhood has drank into their
spirit, whose fathers planted, and whose father's blood nourished them into life?

Daily Democratic Press (Chicago), March 4, 1855.

LINCOLN AND DOUGLAS DEBATE IN CHICAGO

The famous Lincoln and Douglas debates grew in part out of a political exchange in Chicago. Unlike the formal debates that followed in small towns across the state, the Chicago debate stretched over two days (July 9–10), with Douglas speaking the first evening and Lincoln speaking the next. These two speeches encapsulated the themes that would highlight the formal debates that would follow. Lincoln emphasized the incompatibility of American democratic freedom with slavery, an institution he identified with the aristocratic societies of the Old World's dark past. Douglas attacked Lincoln's rhetoric as destructive of the republic of Washington and Jefferson and implied that his opponent favored black and white equality.

HOMECOMING SPEECH AT CHICAGO

MR. CHAIRMAN AND FELLOW CITIZENS: I can find no language which can adequately express my profound gratitude for the magnificent welcome which you have extended to me on this occasion. This vast sea of human faces indicates how deep an interest is felt by our people in the great questions which agitate the public mind, and which underlie the foundations of our free institutions. A reception like this, so great in numbers that no human voice can be heard to its countless thousands—so enthusiastic that no one individual can be the object of such enthusiasm—clearly shows that there is some great principle which sinks deep in the hearts of the masses, and involves the rights and liberties of a whole people, that has brought you together with unanimity and a cordiality never before excelled, if, indeed, equaled on any occasion. I have not the vanity to believe that it is any personal compliment to me.

It is an expression of your devotion to the great principle of self-government, to which my life for many years past has been, and in the future will be, devoted. If there is any one principle dearer and more sacred than all the others in free government, it is that which asserts the exclusive right of a free people to form and adopt their own fundamental law, and to manage and regular their own internal affairs and domestic institutions. . . .

I regard the great principle of popular sovereignty, as having been vindicated and made triumphant in this land, as a permanent rule of public policy in the organization of Territories and the admission of new States. . . .

Hence what was my duty in 1854, when it became necessary to bring forward a bill for the organization of the Territories of Kansas and Nebraska? Was it not my duty, in obedience to the Illinois platform, to your standing instructions to your Senators, adopted with almost entire unanimity, to incorporate in the bill the great principle of self-government, declaring that it was "the true intent and meaning of the act not to legislate slavery into any State or Territory, or to exclude

FIGURE 5. A rare 1858 photograph of a homecoming parade kicking off Stephen A. Douglas's 1858 senatorial campaign against Abraham Lincoln. Several hours later Douglas addressed his Chicago supporters from the Tremont Hotel. Courtesy of the Chicago History Museum.

it there from, but to leave the people thereof perfectly free to form and regulate their domestic institutions in their own way, subject only to the Constitution of the United States?" I did incorporate that principle in the Kansas-Nebraska bill, and perhaps I did as much as any living man in the enactment of that bill, this establishing the doctrine in the public policy of the country. I then defended that principle against assaults from one section of the Union. During this last winter it became my duty to vindicate it against assaults from the other section of the Union. I vindicated it boldly and fearlessly, as the people of Chicago can bear witness, when it was assailed by Freesoilers; and during this winter I vindicated and defended it as boldly and fearlessly when it was attempted to be violated by the almost united South. . . .

. . . I deny the right of Congress to force a slaveholding State upon an unwilling people. I deny their right to force a free State upon an unwilling people. . . .

In connection with this subject, perhaps, it will not be improper for me on this occasion to allude to the position of those who have chosen to arraign my conduct on this same subject, I have observed from the public prints, that but a few days ago the Republican party of the State of Illinois assembled in Convention at Springfield, and I not only laid down their platform, but nominated a candidate for the United States Senate, as my successor. I take great pleasure in saying that I have known, personally and intimately, for about a quarter of a century, the worthy gentleman who has been nominated for my place, and I will say that I regard him as a kind, amiable, and intelligent gentleman and a good citizen and an honorable opponent; and whatever issue I may have with him will be of principle and not involving personalities. Mr. Lincoln made a speech evidently well prepared and carefully written—in which he states the basis upon which he proposes to carry on the campaign during this summer. In it he lays down two distinct propositions which I shall notice, and upon which I shall take a direct and bold issue with him.

His first and main proposition I will give in his own language, scripture quotations and all [laughter]; I give his exact language. "A house divided against itself cannot stand." I believe this government cannot endure, permanently, half *slave* and half *free*. I do not expect the union to be *dissolved*. I do not expect the house to *fall*; but I do expect it to cease to be divided. It will become *all* one thing or *all* the other. . . ."

From this view of the case, my friends I am driven irresistibly to the conclusion that diversity, dissimilarity, variety in all our local and domestic institutions, is the great safeguard of our liberties; and that the framers of our institutions were, wise, sagacious, and patriotic, when they made this government a confederation of sovereign States, with a Legislature for each, and conferred upon each Legislature the power to make all local and domestic institutions to suit the people it represented, without interference from any other State or from the general Congress of the Union. If we expect to maintain our liberties, we must preserve the rights and sovereignty of the States. . . .

This you see, my fellow citizens, that the issues between Mr. Lincoln and myself, as respective candidates for the U.S. Senate, as made up are direct, unequivocal, and irreconcilable. He goes for uniformity in our domestic institutions for a war of sections, until one or the other shall be subdued. I go for the great principle of the Kansas-Nebraska bill, the right of the people for them to decide for themselves.

On the other point, Mr. Lincoln goes for warfare upon the Supreme Court of the United States, because of their judicial decision in the Dred Scott case. I yield obedience to the decisions in that court—to the final determination of the highest judicial tribunal known to our constitution. He objects to the Dred Scott decision because it does not put the negro in the possession of the rights of citizenship on an equality with the white man. I am opposed to negro equality. I repeat that this nation is a nation of white people—a people composed of European descendants—a people that have established this government for themselves and their posterity, and I am in favor of preserving not only the purity of the blood, but the purity of the government from any mixture or amalgamation of white men and Indians and negroes; we have seen it in Mexico, in Central America, in South America, and in all the Spanish-American States, and its result has been degeneration, demoralization, and degradation below the capacity for self-government.

I am opposed to taking any steps that recognizes the negro man or the Indian as the equal of the white man. I am opposed to giving him a voice in the administration of the government. I would extend to the negro, and the Indian, and to all dependent races every right, every privilege, and every immunity consistent with the safety and welfare of the white race; but equality they never should have, either political or social, or in any other respect whatever. . . .

My friends, I have exhausted myself, and I certainly have fatigued you, in the long and desultory remarks which I have made. . . . In conclusion, I must again say to you, justice to my own feelings demands it, that my gratitude for the welcome you have extended to me on this occasion knows no bounds, and can be described by no language which I can command. I see that I am literally at home when among my constituents. This welcome has amply repaid me for every effort that I have made in the public service during nearly twenty-five years that I have held office at your hands. It not only compensates me for the past, but it furnishes an inducement and incentive for the future effort which no man, no matter how patriotic, can feel who has not witnessed the magnificent reception you have extended to me tonight on my return.

Abraham Lincoln, *Political Debates between Abraham Lincoln and Stephen A. Douglas* (Cleveland, 1897).

LINCOLN ARGUES FOR REPUBLICAN "FREE LABOR" IDEOLOGY

Lincoln both attacks Douglas's reliance on the doctrine of popular sovereignty and articulates the principles of the Republican's "free labor" ideology. Lincoln does this by equating the slave system of the South with the despotism of European kings, something all too many immigrants to Chicago were familiar with. This was an important way for Republicans to appeal to the city's urban workers.

SPEECH AT CHICAGO, ILLINOIS

My Fellow Citizens:—On yesterday evening, upon the occasion of the reception given to Senator Douglas, I was furnished with a seat very convenient for hearing him, and was otherwise very courteously treated by him and his friends, and for which I thank him and them. During the course of his remarks my name was mentioned in such a way, as I suppose renders it at least not improper that I should make some sort of reply to him. I shall not attempt to follow him in the precise order in which he addressed the assembled multitude upon that occasion, though I shall perhaps do so in the main.

What Is Popular Sovereignty?

Popular sovereignty! Everlasting popular sovereignty [laughter and continued cheers.] Let us for a moment inquire into this vast matter of popular sovereignty. What is popular sovereignty? We recollect that at an early period in the history of this struggle, there was another name for this same thing—Squatter Sovereignty. It was not exactly Popular Sovereignty but Squatter Sovereignty. What do those terms mean? What do those terms mean when used now? And vast credit is taken by our friend, the Judge, in regard to his support of it, when he declares the last years of his life have been, and all the future years of his life shall be, devoted to this matter of popular sovereignty. . . .

Now I wish you to mark. What has become of that Squatter Sovereignty? What has become of it? Can you get anybody to tell you now that the people of a territory have any authority to govern themselves, in regard to this mooted question of Slavery, before they form a State Constitution? No such thing at all. . . . No more than a year ago it was decided by the Supreme Court of the United States [*Dred Scott* case], and is insisted upon to-day, that people of a territory, all the rest of the people have no rights to keep them out. This being so, and this decision being made one of the points that the Judge approved, and one in the approval of which he says he means to keep me down—put me down I should not say, for I have never been up. He says he is in favor of it, and sticks to it, and expects to win his battle on that decision, which says that there is no such thing as Squatter Sovereignty; but that any one man may take slaves into a territory, and all the other men in the territory may be opposed to it, and yet by reason of the constitution they cannot prohibit it. When that is so, how much is left of this vast matter of Squatter Sovereignty. I should like to know?—(a voice)—"it has all gone." . . .

Judge Douglas made two points upon my recent speech at Springfield. He says they are to be the issues of this campaign. The first one of these points he bases upon the language in a speech which I delivered at Springfield, which I believe I can quote correctly from memory. I said there that "we are not far into the fifth year since a policy was instituted for the avowed object and with the confident promise of putting an end to slavery agitation; under the operation of that policy, that agitation had only not ceased, but has constantly augmented."—(a voice)—"That's the very language." "I believe it will not cease until a crisis shall have been reached and passed. A house divided against itself cannot stand. I believe this government cannot endure permanently half slave and half free." [Applause.] "I do not expect the Union to be dissolved." I am quoting from my speech—"I do not expect the house to fall, but I do expect it will cease to be divided. It will become all one thing or the other. Either the opponents of slavery will arrest the spread of it, and place it where the public mind shall rest in the belief that it is in the course of ultimate extinction, or its advocates will push it forward until it shall become lawful in all States, North as well as South." [Good, good.]

In this paragraph which I have quoted in your hearing, and to which I ask the attention of all, Judge Douglas thinks he discovers great political heresy. . . . He says I am in favor of making all the States of the Union uniform in all their internal regulations, that in all their domestic concerns I am in favor of making them entirely uniform. . . . He says that I am in favor of making war by the North upon the South for the extinction of slavery; that I am also in favor of inviting (as if he expresses it) the South to a war upon the North, for the purpose of nationalizing slavery. Now, it is singular enough, if you will carefully read upon the North, for the purpose of nationalizing slavery. Now, it is singular enough, if you will carefully read that passage over, that I did not say that I was in favor of anything in it. I only said what I expected would take place. I made a prediction only—it may have been a foolish one perhaps. I did not even say that I desired that slavery should be put in course of ultimate extinction. I do say so now, however, [great applause] so there need be no longer any difficulty about that. It may be written down in the great speech. [Applause and laughter.] . . .

I am not, in the first place, unaware that this Government has endured eighty-two years, half slave and half free. I know that. I am tolerably well acquainted with the history of the country, and I know that it has endured eighty-two years, half slave and half free. I believe—and that is what I meant to allude to there—I believe it has endured because, during all that time, until the introduction of the Nebraska Bill, the public mind did rest, all the time, in the belief that slavery was in course of ultimate extinction. ["Good!" "Good!" and applause.] That was what gave us the rest that we had through that period of eighty-two years; at least, so I believe. I have always hated slavery, I think as much as any Abolitionist. [Applause.] I have been an Old Line Whig. I have hated it, but I have always been quiet about it until this new era of the introduction of the Nebraska Bill began. I always believed that everybody was against it, and that it was in course of ultimate extinction. . . .

The adoption of the Constitution and its attendant history led the people to believe so; and that such was the belief of the framers of the Constitution itself. Why did those old men, about the time of the adoption of the Constitution decree that Slavery should not go into the new territory, where it had not already gone? Why declare that within twenty years the African Slave Trade, by which slaves are supplied, might be cut off by Congress? Why were all these acts? I might enumerate more of these acts—but enough. What were they but a clear indication that the framers of the Constitution intended and expected the ultimate extinction of that institution [Cheers.] And now, when I say, as I said in my speech that Judge Douglas quoted from, when I say I think the opponents of slavery will resist the farther spread of it, and place it where the public mind shall rest with the belief that it is in course of ultimate extinction, I only mean to say, that they will place it where the founders of this Government originally placed it. . . .

Now in relation to his interference that I am in favor of a general consolidation of all the local institutions of the various States. . . . I have said that at all times. I have said, as illustrations, that I do not believe in the right of Illinois to interfere with the cranberry laws of Indiana, the oyster laws of Virginia, or the Liquor Laws of Maine. I have said these things over and over again, and I repeat them here as my sentiments.

. . . I suppose there might be one thing that at least enabled him to draw such an interference that would not be true with me or with many others, that is, because he looks upon all this matter of slavery as an exceedingly little thing—this matter of keeping one-sixth of the population of the whole nation in a state of oppression and tyranny unequalled in the world. He looks upon it as being an exceedingly little thing—only equal to the question of the cranberry laws of Indiana—as something having no moral questions in it—as something on a par with the question of whether a man shall pasture his land with cattle, or plant it with tobacco—so little and so small a thing, that he concludes if I could desire that anything should be done to bring about the ultimate extinction of that little thing, I must be in favor of bringing about an amalgamation of all the other little things in the Union. Now, it so happens—and there, I presume, is the foundation of this mistake—that the Judge thinks thus; and it so very happens that there is a vast portion of the American people that do not look upon that matter as being this very little thing. They look upon it as a vast moral evil; they can prove it is such by writings of those who gave us the blessings of liberty which we enjoy, and that they so looked upon it, and not as an evil merely confining itself to the States which we enjoy, and that they so looked upon it, and not as an evil merely confining itself to the states where it is situated; and while we agree that, by the Constitution we assented to, in the States where it exists we have no right to interfere with it because it is in the Constitution and we are by both duty and inclination to stick by that Constitution in all its letter and spirit from beginning to end. [Great applause.] . . .

We were often—more than once at least—in the course of Judge Douglas' speech last night, reminded that this government was made for white men—that he believed it was made for white men. Well, that is putting it into a shape in which no one wants to deny it, but the Judge then goes into his passion for drawing interferences that are not warranted. I protest, now and forever, against that counterfeit logic which presumes that because I do not want a negro woman for a slave, I do necessarily want her for a wife. [Laughter and cheers.] My understanding is that I need not have her for either, but as God made us separate, we can leave one another alone and do one another much good thereby. There are white men enough to marry all the white women, and enough black men to marry all the black women, and in God's name let them be so married. The Judge regales us with the terrible enormities that take place by the mixture of races; that the inferior race bears the superior down. Why, Judge, if we do not let them get together in the Territories they won't mix there. [Immense applause.]

A voice—"Three cheers for Lincoln." [The cheers were given with a hearty good will.]

Mr. Lincoln—I should say at least that that is a self evident truth.

Now, it happens that we meet together once every year, sometimes about the 4th of July, for some reason or other. These 4th of July gatherings I suppose have their uses. If you will indulge me, I will state what I suppose to be some of them. . . . We run our memory back over the pages of history for about eighty-two years and we discover that we were then a very small people in point of numbers, vastly inferior to what we are now, with a vastly less extent of country,—with vastly less of everything we deem desirable among men,—we look upon the change as exceedingly advantageous to us and to our posterity, and we fix upon something that happened away back, as in some way or other being connected with this ride of prosperity. We find a race of men living in that day whom we claim as our fathers and grandfathers; they were iron men, they fought for principle that they were contending for; and we understood that by what they then did it has followed that the degree of prosperity that we now enjoy has come to us. We hold this annual celebration to remind ourselves of all the food done in this process of time of how it was done and who did it, and how we are historically connected with it; and we go from these meetings in better humor with ourselves—we feel more attached the one to the other and more firmly bound to the country we inhabit. In every way we are better men in the age, and race, and country in which we live for these celebrations. But after we have done all this we have not yet reached the whole. There is something else connected with it. We have besides these men—descended by blood from our ancestors—among us perhaps half our people who are not descendants at all of these men, they are men who have come from Europe—German, Irish, French and Scandinavian—men that have come from Europe themselves, or whose ancestors have come hither and settled here, finding themselves our equals in all things. If they look back through this history to trace their connections with those days by blood, they find they have none, they cannot carry themselves back into that glorious epoch and make themselves feel that they are part of us, but when they look through that old Declaration of Independence they find that those old men say that "We hold these truths to be self-evident, that all men are created equal." And then they feel that that moral sentiment taught in that day evidences their relation to those men, that it is the father of all moral principle in them, and that they have a right to claim it as though they were blood of the blood, and flesh of the flesh of the men who wrote that Declaration (loud and long continued applause) and so they are.

That is the electric cord in that Declaration that links the hearts of patriotic and liberty-loving men together, that will link those patriotic hearts as long as the love of freedom exists in the minds of men throughout the world. [Applause.]

Now, sirs, for the purpose of squaring things with the idea of "don't care if slavery is voted up or voted down," for sustaining the Dred Scott decision [A voice—"Hit him again"], for holding that the Declaration of Independence did not mean anything at all, we have Judge Douglas giving his exposition of what the Declaration of Independence means. . . . Those arguments that are made, that the inferior race are to be treated with as much allowance as they are capable of enjoying; that as much is to be done for them as their condition will allow. What are these arguments? They are the arguments that kings have made for enslaving the people in all ages of the world. You will find that all the arguments in favor of king-craft were of this class; they always bestrode the necks of the people, not that they wanted to do it, but because the people were better off for being ridden. That is their argument, and this argument of the Judge is the same old serpent that says you work and I eat, you toil and I will enjoy the fruits of it. Turn in whatever way you will—whether it come from the mouth of a King, an excuse for enslaving the people of his country, or from the mouth of men of one race as a reason for enslaving the men of another race, it is all the same old serpent, and I hold if that course of argumentation is made for the purpose of convincing the public mind that we should not care about this, should be granted, it does not stop with the negro. I should like to know if taking this old Declaration of Independence, which declares that all men are equal upon principle and making exceptions to it where will it stop. If one man says it does not mean a negro, why not another say it does not mean some other man? . . .

It may be argued that there are certain conditions that make necessities and impose them upon us, and to the extent that a necessity is imposed upon a man he must submit to it. I think that was the condition in which we found ourselves when we established this government. We had slavery among us, we could not get our constitution unless we permitted them to remain in slavery, we could not secure the good we did secure if we grasped for more, and having by necessity submitted to that much, it does not destroy the principle that is the charter of our liberties. Let that charter stand as our standard.

My friend has said to me that I am a poor hand for quote Scripture. I will try it again, however. It is said in one of the admonitions of the Lord, "As your Father in Heaven is perfect, be ye also perfect." The Savior, I suppose, did not expect that any human creature could be as perfect as the Father in Heaven; but He said, "As your Father in Heaven is perfect, be ye also perfect." He set that up as a standard, and he who did most towards reaching that standard, attained the highest degree of moral perfection. So I say in relation to the principle that all men are created equal, let it be as nearly reached as we can. If we cannot give freedom to every creature, let us do nothing that will impose slavery upon any other creature. [Applause.] Let us then turn this government back into the channel in which the framers of the Constitution originally placed it. Let us stand firmly by each other. If we do not do so we are turning in the contrary direction, that our friend Judge Douglas proposes—not intentionally—as working in the traces tend to make this one universal slave nation. [A voice—"that is so."] He is one that runs in that direction, and as such I resist him.

Abraham Lincoln, *Political Debates between Abraham Lincoln and Stephen A. Douglas* (Cleveland, 1897), http://www.bartleby.com/251/1002.html, n.p.

THE REPUBLICAN CONVENTION COMES TO
CHICAGO AND NOMINATES LINCOLN

The fact that Chicago was the site of the 1860 Republican National Convention played an important role in the nomination of Abraham Lincoln for the presidency. Murat Halstead, a journalist for the Cincinnati Commercial, *provided detailed coverage of the four major political conventions of 1860. Halstead was a strong supporter of William Seward who managed to suppress his disappointment with Lincoln's nomination in his account of the climactic balloting on the convention's third day.*

FIGURE 6. The Republican Wigwam, 1860. Courtesy of the Chicago History Museum.

FIRE THE SALUTE. ABE LINCOLN IS NOMINATED.

The city of Chicago is attending to this Convention in magnificent style. It is a great place for large hotels, and all have their capacity for accommodation tested. The great feature is the *Wigwam*, erected within the past month, expressly for the use of the Convention, by the Republicans of Chicago, at a cost of seven thousand dollars. It is a small edition of the New York Crystal Palace, built of boards, and will hold ten thousand persons comfortably—and is admirable for its acoustic excellence. An ordinary voice can be heard through the whole structure with ease. . . .

While this [the third] ballot was taken amid excitement that tested the nerves, the fatal defection from Seward in New England still further appeared—four votes going over from Seward to Lincoln in Massachusetts. The latter received four additional votes from Pennsylvania and fifteen additional votes from Ohio. It was whispered about—"Lincoln's the coming man—will be nominated this ballot." . . . The number of votes necessary to a choice were two hundred and thirty-three, and I saw under my pencil as the Lincoln column was completed, the figures 231 1/2—one vote and a half to give him the nomination. In a moment the fact was whispered about. . . . The news went over the house wonderfully, and there was a pause. There are always men anxious to distinguish themselves on such occasions. There is nothing that politicians like better than a crisis. I looked up to see who would be the man to give the decisive vote. . . . In about ten ticks of a watch, [David K.] Cartter of Ohio was up. I had imagined Ohio would be slippery enough for the crisis. And sure enough! Every eye was on Cartter, and every body who understood the matter at all knew what he was about to do. He is a large man with rather striking features, a shock of bristling black hair, large and shining eyes, and is terribly marked with the small-pox. He has also an impediment in his speech, which amounts to a stutter. . . . He had been quite noisy during the sessions of the Convention, but had never commanded, when mounting his chair, such attention as now. He said, "I rise (eh), Mr. Chairman (eh), to announce the change of four votes of Ohio from Mr. Chase to Mr. Lincoln." The deed was done. There was a moment's silence. The nerves of the thousands, which through the hours of suspense had been subjected to terrible tension, relaxed and as deep breaths of relief were taken, there was a noise in the wigwam like the rush of a great wind, in the van of a storm—and in another breath, the storm was there. There were thousands cheering with the energy of insanity.

A man who had been on the roof, and was engaged in communicating the re-sults of the balloting to the mighty mass of outsiders, now demanded by gestures at the sky-light over the stage, to know what had happened. One of the Secretaries, with a tally sheet in his hands, shouted—"Fire the Salute! Abe Lincoln is nomi-nated!" As the cheering inside the wigwam subsided, we could hear that outside,

FIGURE 7. The interior of the Wigwam. *Harper's Weekly*, May 19, 1860.

where the news of the nomination had just been announced and the roar, like the breaking up of the fountains of the great deep that was heard, gave a new impulse to the enthusiasm inside. Then the thunder of the salute rose above the din, and the shouting was repeated with such tremendous fury that some discharges of the cannon were absolutely not heard by those on the stage. Puffs of smoke, drifting by the open door, and the smell of gunpowder, told what was going on. . . .

. . . The town was full of the news of Lincoln's nomination, and could hardly contain itself. There were bands of music playing and processions marching, and joyous cries heard on every hand, from the army of trumpeters for Lincoln of Illinois, and the thousands who are always enthusiastic on the winning side. But hundreds of men who had been in the wigwam were so prostrated by the excitement they had endured, and their exertions in shrieking for Seward or Lincoln, that they were hardly able to walk to their hotels. There were men who had not tasted liquor, who staggered about like drunkards, unable to manage themselves. The Seward men were terribly stricken down. They were mortified beyond all expression, and walked thoughtfully and silently away from the slaughterhouse, more ashamed than embittered. They acquiesced in the nomination, but did not pretend to be pleased with it; and the tone of their conversations, as to the prospect of electing the candidate, was not hopeful. It was their funeral, and they would not make merry.

A Lincoln man who could hardly believe that the "Old Abe" of his adoration was really the Republican nominee for the Presidency, took a chair at the dinner-table at the Tremont House, and began talking to those around him, with none of whom he was acquainted, of the greatness of the events of that day. One of his expressions was, "Talk of your money and bring on your bullies with you!—the immortal principles of the everlasting people are with Abe Lincoln, of the people, by —." A servant approached the eloquent patriot and asked what he would have to eat. Being recalled to temporal things he glared scornfully at the servant and roared out, "Go to the devil—and what do I want to eat for? Abe Lincoln is nominated, G—d— it; and I'm going to live on air—the air of Liberty by —." But in a moment he inquired for the bill of the fare, and then ordered "a great deal of every thing"—saying if he must eat he might as well eat "the whole bill." He swore he felt as if he could "devour and digest an Illinois prairie." And this was one of thousands. . . .

The city was wild with delight. The "Old Abe" men formed processions, and bore rails through the streets. Torrents of liquor were poured down the hoarse throats of the multitude. A hundred guns were fired from the top of the Tremont House. The Chicago Press and Tribune office was illuminated. That paper says:

"On each side of the counting-room door stood a *rail*—out of the three thousand split by 'honest Old Abe' thirty years ago on the Sangamon River bottoms. On the inside were two more, brilliantly hung with tapers."

I left the city on the night train on the Fort Wayne and Chicago road. The train consisted of eleven cars, every seat full and people standing in the aisles and corners. I never before saw a company of persons so prostrated by continued excitement. The Lincoln men were not able to respond to the cheers which went up along the road for "old Abe." They had not only done their duty in that respect, but exhausted their capacity. At every station where there was a village, until after two o'clock, there were tar barrels burning, drums beating, boys carrying rails; and guns, great and small, banging away. The weary passengers were allowed no rest, but plagued by the thundering jar of cannon, the clamor of drums, the glare of bonfires, and the whooping of the boys, who were delighted with the idea of a candidate for the Presidency, who thirty years ago split rails on the Sangamon River—classic stream now and for evermore—and whose neighbors named him "honest."

Murat Halstead, *Caucuses of 1860: A History of the National Political Conventions of the Current Presidential Campaign* (Columbus, OH: Follet, Foster and Company, 1860), 161–77.

THE REPUBLICAN PARTY PLATFORM LAYS
THE FOUNDATION FOR CHICAGO'S FUTURE GROWTH

The 1860 election was dominated by the issues of slavery and disunion. Those issues are reflected in the first eleven resolutions approved by the Republicans in Chicago. The Chicago convention, however, also marked the emergence of the Republican Party as a progressive force in American economic development. The final six resolutions all dealt with issues critical to Chicago's future, from the protection of immigrant rights to harbor development to the offer of free homesteads in the West to the protection of American industries from foreign competition to the building of a Pacific railroad—all measures that were enacted and all of which helped fuel Chicago's phenomenal growth in the decade that followed.

PLATFORM OF THE NATIONAL REPUBLICAN
CONVENTION HELD IN CHICAGO, MAY 7, 1860

Resolved, That we, the delegated representatives of the Republican electors of the United States, in convention assembled, in discharge of the duty we owe to our constituents and our country, unite in the following declarations:

1. That the history of the nation during the last four years has fully established the propriety and necessity of the organization and perpetuation of the Republican party, and that the causes which called it into existence are permanent in their nature, and now more than ever before demand its peaceful and constitutional triumph.

2. That the maintenance of the principles promulgated in the Declaration of Independence and embodied in the Federal Constitution, "That all men are created equal; that they are endowed by their Creator with certain inalienable rights; that among these are life, liberty, and the pursuit of happiness; that to secure these rights, governments are instituted among men, deriving their just powers from the consent of the governed," is essential to the preservation of our Republican institutions; and that the Federal Constitution, the rights of the states, and the Union of the states, must and shall be preserved.

3. That to the Union of the States this nation owes its unprecedented increase in population; its surprising development of material resources; its rapid augmentation of wealth; its happiness at home and its honor abroad; and we hold in abhorrence all schemes for disunion, come from whatever source they may; and we congratulate the country that no republican member of congress has uttered or countenanced the threats of disunion so often made by democratic members, without rebuke and with applause from their political associates; and we denounce those threats of disunion, in case of a popular overthrow of their ascendancy, as denying the vital principles of a free government, and as an avowal of contemplated treason, which it is the imperative duty of an indignant people sternly to rebuke and forever silence.

4. That the maintenance inviolate of the rights of the states, and especially the right of each state, to order and control its own domestic institutions according to its own judgment exclusively, is essential to that balance of power on which the perfection and endurance of our political fabric depends, and we denounce the lawless invasion by armed force of the soil of any state or territory, no matter under what pretext, as among the gravest of crimes.

5. That the present Democratic Administration has far exceeded our worst apprehension in its measureless subserviency to the exactions of a sectional interest, as is especially evident in its desperate exertions to force the infamous Lecompton constitution upon the protesting people of Kansas—in construing the personal relation between master and servant to involve an unqualified property in persons—in its attempted enforcement everywhere, on land and sea, through the intervention of congress and of the federal courts, of the extreme pretensions of a purely local interest, and in its general and unvarying abuse of the power entrusted to it by a confiding people.

6. That the people justly view with alarm the reckless extravagance which pervades every department of the Federal Government; that a return to rigid economy and accountability is indispensable to arrest the systematic

plunder of the public treasury by favored partisans; while the recent startling developments of frauds and corruptions at the federal metropolis, show that an entire change of Administration is imperatively demanded.

7. That the new dogma that the Constitution of its own force carries slavery into any or all of the territories of the United States, is a dangerous political heresy, at variance with the explicit provisions of that instrument itself, with cotemporaneous exposition, and with legislative and judicial precedent, is revolutionary in its tendency and subversive of the peace and harmony of the country.

8. That the normal condition of all the territory of the United States is that of freedom; that as our republican fathers, when they had abolished slavery in all our national territory, ordained that no "person should be deprived of life, liberty or property, without due process of law," it becomes our duty, by legislation, whenever such legislation is necessary, to maintain this provision of the constitution against all attempts to violate it; and we deny the authority of congress, of a territorial legislature, or of any individuals, to give legal existence to slavery in any territory of the United States.

9. That we brand the recent re-opening of the African Slave Trade, under the cover of our national flag, aided by perversions of judicial power, as a crime against humanity, and a burning shame to our country and age, and we call upon congress to take prompt and efficient measures for the total and final suppression of that execrable traffic.

10. That in the recent vetoes by the federal governors of the acts of the Legislatures of Kansas and Nebraska, prohibiting slavery in those territories, we find a practical illustration of the boasted democratic principle of non-intervention and popular sovereignty, embodied in the Kansas-Nebraska bill, and a demonstration of the deception and fraud involved therein.

11. That Kansas should of right be immediately admitted as a state, under the constitution recently formed and adopted by her people, and accepted by the House of Representatives.

12. That while providing revenue for the support of the general government by duties upon imports, sound policy requires such an adjustment of these imposts as to encourage the development of the industrial interests of the whole country, and we commend that policy of national exchanges which secures to the workingmen liberal wages, to agriculture remunerating prices, to mechanics and manufacturers an adequate reward for their skill, labor and enterprise, and to the nation commercial prosperity and independence.

13. That we protest against any sale or alienation to others of the public lands held by actual settlers, and against any view of the free homestead policy which regards the settlers as paupers or suppliants for public bounty, and we demand the passage by congress of the complete and satisfactory homestead measure which has already passed the house.

14. That the Republican Party is opposed to any change in our naturalization laws, or any state legislation by which the rights of citizenship hitherto accorded by emigrants from foreign lands shall be abridged or impaired; and in favor of giving a full and efficient protection to the rights of all classes of citizens, whether native or naturalized, both at home and abroad.

15. That appropriation by Congress for river and harbor improvements of a National character, required for the accommodation and security of an existing commerce, are authorized by the constitution and justified by the obligation of Government to protect the lives and property of its citizens.

16. That a railroad to the Pacific Ocean is imperatively demanded by the interests of the whole country; that the Federal Government ought to render immediate and efficient aid in its construction; and that, as preliminary thereto, a daily overland mail should be promptly established.

17. Finally, having thus set forth our distinctive principles and views, we invite the co-operation of all citizens, however differing on other questions who substantially agree with us in their affirmance and support.

Supplementary Resolution. Resolved, That we deeply sympathize with those men who have been driven, some from their native States and others from the States of their adoption, and are now exiled from their homes on account of their opinions; and we hold the Democratic Party responsible for this gross violation of that clause of the Constitution which declares that the citizens of each State shall be entitled to all the privileges and immunities of citizens in the several States.

Printed and for sale at the Press and Tribune Office, Chicago. Available online at http://cprr.org/Museum/Ephemera/Republican_Platform_1860.html.

DOUGLAS CAMPAIGNS FOR THE HOMETOWN VOTE

Stephen A. Douglas was the only Chicagoan ever nominated by a major party for the office of president of the United States, until Barack Obama in 2008. Unfortunately for Douglas, the Democratic Party split along sectional lines and his chances of victory were greatly reduced. With characteristic vigor, Douglas took the unprecedented step of actively campaigning for the office by traveling the country, North and South, appealing directly to voters. In October he made a brief but firework-filled return to Chicago to rally his base of support. The Chicago

Tribune, *a strong supporter of Abraham Lincoln, mocked Douglas's dogged effort and revealed the paper's thinly veiled anti-Catholicism in their sarcastic references to his Irish American supporters.*

THE DOUGLAS WAKE.
Obsequies to the Departed.
GREAT FAILURES TO ARRIVE.
Immense Staying at Home.
WHO CAME FROM THE COUNTRY.
Who Marched in Procession.
STEPHEN'S LAST WORDS.
The Inevitable Negro Man.
MY GREAT PRINCIPLE.
The Torchlight Processions Last Night.
"DOUBLE, DOUBLE, TOIL AND TROUBLE."
Gems of the Evening.

From time immemorial it has been Ireland's cherished custom to "wake" their dead. They gather the more numerous in proportion to the prominence of the departed. The air is rent with ejaculations, and varied cries, expressive of emotion. Candles give their flickering light to the scene, nor is refreshment wanting, varying in kind and quantity like the illumination, in accordance with the means and lavish disposition of those most interested. Such an occasion as an Irish wake on a grand scale has just taken place here.

When the politically slaughtered Stephen comes home among his kindred, there is a beautiful fitness of things in giving him a royal wake, and to achieve this has employed the time and energies of the Squatteries of this city for some time past. They waked him yesterday and last night, and will not need to wake themselves to-day to the fact that the whole affair was an expensive sham, a failure; for they knew it all the while.

The Irish pitched into the wake with a will, they always do. They whooped, and howled, and carried flambeaus in the torchlight procession, and rode their stiff dray horses for hours yesterday and last night, and many of them will call upon the Committee to-day as per agreement for their "tin cints an hour," which was the special contract that drew many of them from their coal-heaving, and hod-carrying and lumber-piling on the occasion. . . .

How have the times changed (we do not now refer to the sale of the Chicago *Times*) since, in the highest possible feather, Stephen pronounced the oration and stood sponsor for "Young Tammany" in Garrett Block, when the Democracy of Chicago and Cook county were jolly very, and ran up bills for rent and outfit that were a prominent cause of the disruption that followed. Then Stephen was himself in good repute in his party, vaunted himself on his nationality, and in a very distressed condition of mind regretted that there were places south of Mason and Dixon's line where Republicans could not go with their doctrines.

Since that time the Democracy of Chicago and Cook County have been turned out to the shortest possible grass, and Stephen himself has become sectional, and with his "half loaf" nomination under one arm, and My Great Principle under the other, has been these weary months past in search of his mother. Now it was *"De profundis Clam-avi"* over Narragansett tautogs, and then among the gaping shellfish of Chesapeake; from the sea-side to the Green Mountains, and all along the slope of the Alleghanies; Stephen has journeyed far and wide, in the search. The wanderings of Telemachus were nothing to it. The beautiful fillial devotion embalmed in the "Exiles of Siberia" pales in comparison. And in the search Stephen took along his hand baggage of course, and aired My Great Principle at every station. . . .

The speech, his last words here before the people finally bury him, was his same old harangue, with few variations. The inevitable negro man, with his wooly head and high odor, was brought out and paraded before the audience and placed in a position fearfully impending, the result being a shower of ejaculations like following: "Ow, bedad, giv it to him!" "No, be jabers!" "Howly Vargin preserve us!" "Good for yeee, Steevin!" "Niver, by the howly Moses!" "Down with um!" these and others in the rich brogue, thickened with whiskey.

Then Stephen, like a travelling showman, put the African back into his box and took out the preachers. These he was severe upon, in his usual chaste style, for he decidedly opposes all pastoral interference with politics, save always the gentle offices of the Roman Catholic clergy in that direction. To this succeeded the pantomime of Union-saving, for the Union always plays Judy to Stephen's Punch, and she is always being very roughly handled and very much in danger, greatly to the horror and delight of his audiences. . . .

. . . Thus much of the speech, which lasted a little over an hour, and was decidedly the weakest, most vapid and most characteristically impudent ever delivered by Stephen in Chicago.

Chicago Tribune, October 6, 1860.

CHICAGO'S EMERGING URBAN CULTURE: A BASEBALL GAME

With two favorite sons as the main candidates contending for the presidency, Chicago in 1860 was obsessed with politics. The contest even spilled over into the emerging sport of baseball, then a leisure activity largely confined to middle-class men. The game was not a major spectator sport at this time, so the attendance of 1,200 fans reflects the particular interest in this contest as well as the potential of the sport to attract an audience. The Excelsior Base Ball Club was considered the city's best team.

THE POLITICAL BASE BALL MATCH—THE SCORE AND RESULT.

Yesterday afternoon was played on the grounds of Excelsior Base Ball Club, corner of West Lake and Ann street, the political ball match between the nine Lincoln and the nine Douglas men.

Some twelve hundred spectators were present. The following is the score:

Douglas.	Runs.
W. C. Hunt	4
R. D. Hughes	1
G. Simons	2
G. H. Kennedy	3
R. Davids	1
E. Simons	1
W. Lowe	0
F. H. Bostick	1
Chas. Burges	3
	16

Lincoln	Runs.
W. W. Kennedy	2
Jas. Malcom	1
G. C. Carpenter	1
A. Kennedy	1
L. Quick	1
Geo. Throop	2
J. J. Gillespie	2
G. O. Smith	1
Wm. Haughton	3
	14

No. balls passed E. Simons 6
No. balls passed J. J. Gillespie 5

John O'Neil—Umpire of Atlantic B.B. Club.

W. J. Maloom, H. C. Doty, Scorers.

Never mind, Lincoln boys, there's a victory in store where Douglas will make no "runs." He is a lame "short stop," and has been "caught out."

ELECTION DAY IN CHICAGO

Election day 1860 in Chicago was a ward committeeman's dream: warm and sunny, with heavy voter turnout in all precincts. Both Republicans and Democrats applied the old maxim of Chicago politics, "Vote early and often." When the votes were counted, Douglas clearly had won at least part of his battle: he had unified the Cook County Democratic Party behind him. He totaled 8,094 votes, while John C. Breckenridge, the candidate of the Southern Democrats, polled only 87 votes in the city. Unfortunately for Douglas, Lincoln and the Republicans were able to secure 10,697 Chicago votes. The "rail-splitter" won the city and the state of Illinois, and when about midnight word was received that Lincoln carried New York State, it was clear that he would be the next president. Jubilant Republicans took to the streets in an impromptu victory parade. At the head of the column the band played "Dixie."

THE DAY AFTER THE FIGHT.

SCENES IN THE CITY,
JUBILATIONS AFTER TRIUMPH
PROCESSION OF WIDE-AWAKES
Salutes, Bonfires and Fire Works.

The contest of Tuesday last, was carried to its close amid scenes of marked quiet, and as already before stated, nothing occurred to mar the peace and good order of the day. . . .

Our issue of yesterday morning gave returns sufficient to indicate the results of the election both local and general. It was only thereafter a question of majorities. When we went to press at 3 o'clock A.M., yesterday morning, hardly had the enthusiasm in our streets, and about the places of receiving election news, died away. Hundreds were abroad in the streets, and eagerly asking and exchanging the latest, unwilling to lose aught that was afloat, or to "go home till morning" if there was any good news yet to be received.

The enthusiasm kept over night, and gave its marked character to our city throughout the entire of yesterday. The practice of betting upon results, whatever may be said of it in the abstract, has come to bear too important a feature on such occasions to be overlooked in a reference to the same. . . .

Many thousand dollars changed hands since Tuesday. Hats sufficient to cover that hackneyed expression "A sea of heads," boots for an army of wearers, clothes, watches, and a wide range of articles of personal property, afloat on the result, have drifted securely into Republican hands, and very many of the class of wagers last referred to are among the spoils. No one anticipated such majorities, such a heavy surge as that with which the people have borne Honest Old Abe to the White House.

Yesterday, in weather, happily followed its predecessor, and was a clear, bright fall day throughout. From early in the morning until late at night the streets were thronged with Republicans, eager to hear the confirmation and swelling of the previous day's triumph. . . .

Last evening at seven o'clock a grand salute of 200 guns was fired from Randolph street bridge, near Market, by the Chicago Light Artillery. The Great Wigwam, where in May last the banner of the Republicans was first thrown to the breeze for 1860, was open and thronged by an exceedingly well-contended and jubilant assembly, largely made up of gentlemen accompanied by ladies.

While this was transpiring the Wide Awakes were out and forming on Michigan avenue. Some of the companies marched independently through our principal streets. . . . They then moved to the Lake Shore and joined in the torchlight procession which marched up Lake street to Dearborn, thence through Randolph to Market street.[22]

As they passed the intersection of Randolph and Clark streets, a brilliant flight of rockets and Roman-candles was let off from the roof of Evans' block, which was witnessed by large numbers of spectators in the crowded streets and the Court House Square. The streets, throughout the evening, in all sections of the city, were brilliant with bonfires. . . .

When the bonfires had burned low, and all the Roman Candles had fallen victims to internal inflamations, and the rockets were reduced to a like condition from similar causes, and all the Republicans were hoarse with shouting, and the Wide Awakes weary with their pageant, a not very late hour of the night saw silence and darkness brood over a thoroughly wearied city, all its citizens, irrespective of party, drawing satisfaction from the one common source that it was "all over at last," the major share, of course, the best pleased to know that "All's well that ends well.["] So ends the presidential election of 1860. Thus is peacefully inaugurated a change in our government, effected amid a vindictiveness of opposition unparalleled in our political annals. Peacefully, for not the most bitter Democrat in this city but laughs at the idea that the Southern States will not be able to "hang their own traitors," and then in a better sense hereafter than for years past, "keep step to the music of the Union."

Chicago Tribune, November 8, 1860.

THE PRESIDENT-ELECT VISITS CHICAGO

Lincoln made his last visit to Chicago two weeks after the election. For Chicagoans it was a chance to congratulate the man who for many was an old friend, as well as an opportunity to lobby the president-elect, who was in the midst of dividing the recently won political spoils of the national government. The meeting with vice

president–elect Hannibal Hamlin and Illinois Republican leaders played a role in
helping Lincoln flesh out his cabinet.

THE RECEPTION OF MR. LINCOLN AND MR. HAMLIN YESTERDAY.

The visit of the President and Vice President elect to this city, their first interview since their nomination, has made Chicago the centre of much interest during the past week. Yielding to the very general desire of our citizens to see the gallant standard bearers of Republicanism, yesterday morning was fixed upon for a reception at the parlors of the Tremont House between the hours of 10 and 12. The day was the most inclement of the season thus far, cold, snowing, and with general winter aspects abroad, yet the people were not at home.

From the hour earliest named, until noon, a constant stream of visitors poured in at the Lake street entrance of the Tremont House. The ladies, we were glad to see, had their full share in the representation, and the affair was an ovation throughout. For two hours and a half the line moved through the middle parlor on the Dearborn street front, where Mr. Lincoln stood and shook hands with each as they passed him. At his right stood Mrs. Lincoln, and next Mr. Hamlin. Everything moved off most pleasantly and creditably to all concerned. With his acquaintances, Mr. Lincoln exchanged a single word.

We were glad to notice that Mr. Lincoln seems in excellent health as does Mr. Hamlin, though the excitements and actual labor and pressure incident to the campaign, especially increased as the successful close drew near, must have been sufficient to test severely the strongest constitution.

Mr. Lincoln returns to Springfield, and Mr. Hamlin goes immediately east from this city.

Several interesting incidents are related of the reception. Mr. Lincoln being a very tall man, generally had to stoop some to reach the level of those who came to congratulate him, and saluting all, as he did, with both hands, the labor performed by the President elect much resembled the traditionary "man a-mowing." At least, it was severe. In the crowd were several short persons. It was refreshing to observe the pleasure experienced by Mr. Lincoln when he took a man by the hand somewhere nigh his own stature. One of these persons came after a long row of undersized ones. Mr. Lincoln raised his hands in well affected astonishment, and exclaimed: "You are up *some!*" This was accompanied by a look that created much merriment. *That* tall man, for once in his life, was duly appreciated.

In the crowd were a little boy, some four years of age, and his mother. The child was boiling over with enthusiasm, his cheeks glowed with pride, and he could not contain his feelings, so he cried out, "Hurray for Uncle Abe!" Mr.

Lincoln heard it, and the youthful Republican was treated to a "tossing up" toward the ceiling, which tickled him and the visitors hugely, and will be remembered through life by the boy.

Chicago Tribune, November 24, 1860.

LINCOLN'S APPEASEMENT OF THE SOUTH AND
THE FUGITIVE SLAVE LAW IN CHICAGO

*By the time Lincoln was inaugurated, the states of the Deep South had seceded and
formed the Confederate States of America. In an attempt to calm states of the Upper
South and demonstrate that the new Republican administration had every intention
of enforcing the existing constitution and laws of the United States, Lincoln ordered
rigorous enforcement of the Fugitive Slave Act of 1850. The administration, however,
did leak its intention to the "underground railroad" community in Chicago that
federal marshals would dragnet the city for escaped slaves. This set in motion a mass
flight from the city for Canada via the aboveground railroad.*

A Reign of Terror among the Colored People . . .

City Intelligence

. . . It is evidently the wisest course for them to pursue, as it is sheer folly for
them to remain, where they are in imminent danger of being returned to slavery.

Flight to Freedom

All day, yesterday, the vicinity of the Michigan Southern depot was a scene of
excitement and confusion. After the religious services at the Zoar Baptist Church
in the morning, which was densely attended, the leave taking commenced . . . the
fugitives and their friends, going from door to door, bidding each other good-bye
and mingling their congratulations and tears.—The colored clergymen of the city
were also among the number, and labored ardently in extending encouragement
and consolation to those about to depart. . . . In some instances, entire families were
going together, in which cases there seemed to be a general jubilation; in others a
few members, a wife leaving a husband, or a mother her children amid tears. . . .

. . . All the afternoon, drays, express wagons and other vehicles were busy
transporting trunks, bandboxes, valises and other various articles of household
furniture to the depot. The wants of the outer man had been attended to also,
and a goodly store of provisions, such as crackers, bread, beans, dried beef and

apples, were packed in, and a barrel of water in each car; for the fugitives were to be stowed away in the same cars with the freight, with plenty of fresh air, but no light, and in a crowded unwholesome state.

As the hour of departure . . . drew nigh, the streets adjacent to the depot and the immediate vicinity of the four cars . . . were thronged with an excited multitude of colored people of both sexes and all ages; large numbers of white people also gathered from motives of curiosity, and stood silent spectators of this rather unusual spectacle. The four cars were rapidly filled with the fugitives, numbering one hundred and six in all, and embracing men, women, youth and infants. In the rear car were two or three sick women, who were treated with the utmost tenderness. . . . The while business of the transportation was supervised by two or three colored men assisted by several white people. The minister of the neighborhood church where they had attended also went from car to car bidding them to be men when they got to Canada.

After all were aboard, . . . the immense crowd pressed up to the cars and commenced the last farewell. . . . Here and there was one in tears wringing the hands, but the majority were in the best of humor, and were congratulated by their friends lingering behind, that tomorrow they would be free. "Never mind," said one, "the good Lord will save us all in the coming troubles, and were now suffering a lot foreseen and prepared for. . . . Quite a number of children were among the crowd, who, ignorant of the cause of such a commotion, gave the rest constant trouble by getting into the wrong cars and climbing round and between the wheels. The larger proportion of the fugitives were stout, able bodied young men many of them well dressed and some of them almost white. . . . The elder ones evinced no levity but acted like those who had been hardened .

But all were finally stowed away, the bell of the engine sounded and the train started amid lusty cheers, many-voiced good-byes and the waving of hats and handkerchiefs as far as the eye could see. The fugitives heartily responded and the train vanished in the distance. . . .

About one thousand fugitives have arrived in this city since last fall, a large number of whom have left within the past few days.

Chicago Evening Journal, April 8, 1861.

"ONLY PATRIOTS—OR TRAITORS!":
STEPHEN DOUGLAS RALLIES CHICAGO FOR WAR

During the first year of the Civil War, Chicago was united behind President Lincoln, due in no small measure to the strong support he received from the man he defeated in the presidential race. Although small in stature, Douglas earned his name the "Little Giant" when he held Lincoln's hat at the latter's inauguration. Following the attack

on *Fort Sumter, Douglas supported Lincoln's call to arms. He returned to Illinois for
the expressed purpose of ensuring that there would be bipartisan support for the war.
Because of his action, the majority of the Democratic Party supported the call to arms,
and the so-called War Democrats were a key part of Lincoln's governing war coalition
throughout the difficult years ahead. The address abstracted below was originally
given to a joint session of the Illinois state legislature and then repeated when Douglas
returned to Chicago. These words were enthusiastically received in Chicago and were
influential throughout the North. It was the last speech of his long career. On May 2,
1861, he suddenly took ill and never recovered.*

MR. DOUGLAS' SPEECH

Fellow Citizens of Chicago:

I thank you for the kind terms in which you have been pleased to welcome me.
I thank the committee, I thank the citizens of Chicago, for this grand and imposing
reception. I beg you to believe that I will not do you nor myself the injustice to suppose for a moment that this ovation is intended as a mere personal homage to myself.
I rejoice to know that it is a forcible embodiment and expression of your devotion to
the constitution, the Union, and the flag of the country. [Cheers] I will not conceal
my gratification at the incontrovertible test which this vast assemblage presents, that
however differences of opinions on political topics and partisan questions may have
divided us, yet you all have a conviction that when the country would be in danger
my loyalty may be relied upon. That the present danger to this country is now imminent, no man can conceal. If war must come, if the bayonet must be used to maintain
the Constitution—I can say before God, my conscience is clean. I have struggled long
for a peaceful solution of the difficulty. I have not only tendered to these States what
was theirs of right, but I have gone to the extreme of magnanimity.

The return that we have received is War, armies marching upon our Capital,
obstructions and dangers to our navigation, letters of marquee to invite pirates
to prey upon our commerce, and a concerted movement to blot out the United
States of America from the map of the world. The question is are we to maintain
the government established by our fathers or allow it to be stricken down by those
who, when they can no longer govern, endeavor to destroy it.

What cause, what excuse do Disunionists give for breaking up the best Government on which the sun of heaven has ever shed its rays? They are dissatisfied with
the result of a presidential election. Did they never get beaten before? [Laughter.]
Are we to resort to the sword when we get beaten at that ballot box? . . . They
assume that the election of a particular candidate carries the presumption that
their rights are not safe in the Union. What evidence do they present of this? I

defy any man to show any act on which it is based. What act has been omitted to be done? I appeal to these assembled thousands that, so far as the constitutional rights of the Southern States are concerned—so far as the rights of slaveholders are concerned—no one act has been done, no one duty has been omitted to be done, under this administration, of which they can complain. . . .

If they say the Territorial Question, now for the first time, there is not an act of Congress prohibiting slavery anywhere. If it be the nonenforcement of the laws, the only complaint made has been, there has been rather too much energy and vigor employed in the enforcement of the fugitive slave law. . . . The election of Mr. Lincoln is a mere pretext. The present secession movement is the result of a tremendous, enormous conspiracy formed more than a year ago. [Cheers] . . . They use the slavery question as a means to accomplish their desired ends. They desired a northern man to be elected president by a sectional vote in order to consider that as evidence that the two sections could not live in peace, and so they might break up the Union.

But, this is no time for a detail of the causes. The conspiracy is now known. Armies have been raised. War is levied to accomplish it. There can be but two sides to the question. Every man must be for the United States or against it. There can be no neutrals in this war, only patriots and traitors.

Thank God Illinois is not divided on this question. [Cheers] I know they expect to present a united South against a divided North. They hoped in the Northern States party questions would bring civil war between Democrats and Republicans, when the South would step in with her cohorts, aid one party to conquer the other, and then make easy prey of the victors. . . .

We cannot close our eyes to the sad and solemn fact that war exists. The Government must be maintained, its enemies overthrown, and the more stupendous our preparations the less bloodshed and the shorter the struggle. But we must remember certain restraints on our actions, even in time of war. We are a Christian people, and the war must be prosecuted in a manner recognized by Christian nations.

We must not violate constitutional rights. The innocent must not suffer, nor women and children be victims. Savages must not be set loose. But while I sanction no war on the rights of others, I will implore my countrymen not to lay down their arms until our rights are recognized. [Cheers]

. . . It is a sad task to discuss questions so fearful as civil war, but sad as it is, bloody and disastrous as I expect it to be, I express it my conviction before God, that it is the duty of every American citizen to rally around the flag of his country.

I thank you again for this magnificent demonstration. By it you have shown you have laid aside party strife. Illinois has a proud position. United, firm, determined never to permit the Government to be destroyed. [Prolonged cheering]

Chicago Tribune, May 2, 1861.

TWO

The War Spirit

Chicagoans and the Call to Arms

$\mathcal{T}$HE FIRING BY Confederate forces on Fort Sumter electrified the people of Chicago, and across the Great Lakes region President Lincoln's call for volunteers to defend the Union was met with tremendous enthusiasm. The region was known at the time as "the Northwest," as if it were on the periphery of the nation. In the wake of the Civil War, the region would be more commonly known as the Midwest or the "heartland." The change in terminology was due to more than the development of the trans-Mississippi West during and after the Civil War. Rather, the war itself altered the nation's perception of the region and the region's understanding of its role in the nation. Prior to 1861 most of the great events of the national narrative had taken place in the East and were the accomplishment, with exceptions such as Andrew Jackson, of easterners. In the Civil War, the sons and daughters of the Midwest consciously and enthusiastically assumed a role in American history. By rescuing and completing the work of the revered "founding fathers," they made their region a "heartland" by placing it at the center of not only a restless country's expanding geography but also its history.

The American republic was saved from Southern secession by the remarkable response of the Midwest heartland to Lincoln's call to arms. Across the region, the majority of which was far removed from the seat of war, more than 12 percent of the population enlisted in the armed forces. In Illinois alone, 256,297 men served, more than 15,000 of whom were Chicagoans. In per capita terms, if Illinoisans went to war today in the same numbers as during the Civil War, 1.9 million men would be in uniform. Remarkably, this upwelling of martial enthusiasm came from a population with little experience in military affairs.[1]

The war had an immediate transformative impact on Chicago. "How the bustling, cheery life of Chicago became suddenly grave and serious," a businessman later recalled. "With what different eyes we saw everything about us. It was not the same sunshine that made the city so bright yesterday, and these were not the same faces of neighbors that then nodded so light-heartedly as they passed. The old flag had been fired upon, and that had wakened into stern determination the patriotism of every loyal heart."[2]

As with the popular rush to arms in so many other conflicts, the war spirit of Chicago in 1861 was a mixture of genuine patriotism and naïve, romantic notions of combat. Nothing epitomized this more than the life and death of the first Union officer to die in the war, a young Chicago law clerk by the name of Elmer Ellsworth. Frustrated in his desire to attend West Point, the young man nonetheless spent his time in prewar Chicago studying all things military. In April 1859, friends in a bedraggled militia company, the Chicago Cadets, offered him the captaincy of their unit. At the time, militia companies were generally little more than social clubs for young men. Ellsworth, however, had no interest in putting on a uniform simply to posture at public celebrations. The manner in which he overhauled the Cadets helped set in motion a wave of interest in volunteer companies across the North. Inspired by gaudy uniforms he had seen in illustrated newspaper stories about French light infantry, known as Zouaves, Ellsworth dressed his company in collarless blue jackets, baggy red pants, white leggings, a fez, and yards of gold trim. Just as striking was the style of drill he adopted, which was highly athletic with razor-sharp precision. Ellsworth built the morale of his men on Christian principles, with each member vowing to help a comrade struck by illness or unemployment, as well as forsaking games of chance, saloons, and brothels. Within a year the Zouave Cadets were the toast of Chicago and Illinois, and Ellsworth took his men on a twenty-city tour of the nation in which they successfully challenged any militia company that dared dispute their claim to the title "Champion Company of the United States and Canada."[3]

The Zouaves returned to Chicago as national celebrities. Songs were written in their honor, and they had drilled before President James Buchanan at the White House. Pictures of Ellsworth were hawked on street corners, and a contemporary recalled that "school-girls dreamed over the graceful wave of his curls." Ellsworth was the most celebrated American soldier of his generation, and he had never fought in a battle. His fame won him the honorary title of assistant adjunct general of Illinois and a place on Lincoln's staff when the Illinoisan went to Washington. Ellsworth was a symbol of the honor and glory that could be won by donning the uniform of a soldier. Ellsworth's death, which occurred a little over a month after the Fort Sumter attack, confirmed the image that warriors were noble and honorable. He was shot leading a federal advance into Virginia just after he had torn down a rebel flag. The news reduced Lincoln to tears. Ellsworth was waked at the White House, and his funeral was a state occasion, while newspapers quoted his last words, written to his mother the night before his death: "Whatever may happen, cherish the consolation that I was engaged in the performance of a sacred duty." The Ellsworth image of soldiering as noble, and patriotic death as honored, helped instill in the first wave of Chicago volunteers a romantic notion of war that endured through the first year of the conflict. The nearly four thousand Chicagoans who followed Ellsworth into Southern graves would learn to their cost that war had another face.[4]

Those grim realities were far from the minds of young men in the spring of 1861. Recruits flocked to the warehouses that served as temporary armories. Even before uniforms could be issued, the first Chicagoans were ordered to "the front." Illinois governor Richard Yates believed that the front was in Cairo, the dismal Ohio River town in his own state, which was farther south than Richmond, Virginia. Because the southern portion of Illinois had been settled mainly by Southerners and its commerce was tied to the slave states, there was considerable fear that the people there would support secession. In what was surely the worst example of the Chicago-downstate rivalry that would ever mark Illinois politics, Chicago outfitted an expedition of 595 men, 46 horses, and 4 pieces of artillery to "capture" Cairo. After occupying the city without a shot fired, the Chicagoans noticed that across the Mississippi in Missouri there was another potential rebel threat. This prompted James H. Stokes, who would later rise to the rank of general, to infiltrate a small group of volunteers who incognito entered St. Louis and under the very noses of armed rebel sympathizers took from the arsenal there 23,000 arms and 110,000 cartridges, not to mention a complete artillery battery. Cairo then went on to be the secure base from which Ulysses S. Grant waged his crucial campaign to crush the Deep South.[5]

During those first months of the war, there was tremendous competition among the citizenry to be admitted into regiments and for those regiments to be accepted into federal service. Even after the six Illinois regiments requested by Lincoln had been filled, thousands of young men flocked to Chicago, where twenty-four companies of would-be recruits continued to drill even though they were not accepted into service. This popular outpouring of patriotism reveals the deep commitment that ordinary Chicagoans had for the American Union, from the poorest immigrants to the sons of the elite. Irish Chicagoans thrilled by Stephen Douglas's call to arms formed the Irish Brigade (Twenty-Third Illinois Infantry). The Germans of the city formed a regiment (the Twenty-Fourth Illinois) under Frederick Hecker, a hero of the failed 1848 rebellion in their old country.[6] Less-numerous ethnic groups were not to be outdone, as Swedes, Norwegians, Jews, and Scots formed companies of infantry. While the Irish, to much derision, trained in a large brick structure that had formerly been a brewery, most of these troops relocated to the south of the city, where, near the resting place of Senator Douglas, they formed improvised camps of instruction. In prewar days, this had been a favorite area for picnics and summer beer gardens. Friends and relatives of the new soldiers flocked to visit their heroes at their improvised camps. They came with picnic hampers and officers' swords or regimental colors that were presented with great ceremony. If the war could have been won with growlers of beer or fried chicken drumsticks, the rebellion was all but doomed.[7]

PLAYING SOLDIER:
ELLSWORTH'S ZOUAVES BECOME NATIONAL CELEBRITIES

When the Civil War began, the most famous soldier in Chicago had never seen a battle. For many young Chicagoans, Elmer Ellsworth was a symbol of the fame, glory, and honor that could be won in uniform. Even his death, as the first officer killed in the conflict, obscured the misery and butchery that lay ahead. In the text below, one of Ellsworth's former soldiers recalls his rise and fall. Ellsworth's fame and example had a national impact.

ELLSWORTH'S ZOUAVES

Colonel Ephraim Elmer Ellsworth was born April 11, 1837, at Malta, Saratoga County, New York. . . . He received a good common school education, and at 18, in 1855, he came to Chicago. He was employed as a clerk in the office of A. F. Devereaux of Salem, Massachusetts, a solicitor of patents. Mr. Devereaux gave up his business shortly afterwards, and young Ellsworth commenced reading law, in the meantime earning a scanty support by what copying he could find to do in lawyers' offices.

He was a young man of fine appearance, of medium height, slim, but strong and compactly built, with black, curling hair, which he always wore rather long, and keen hazel eyes. He always had quite a martial turn, and among his early boyhood dreams was a West Point education and an army career. As he could not obtain a cadetship at West Point, his thoughts naturally turned to the militia, as it was then found in all cities of any size. He did not connect himself with any company, but turned his attention to physical culture in the gymnasium.

At this time he was exceedingly poor, and his struggle to maintain a respectable appearance and not go too hungry was severe, but he always considered that the privileges of a well-appointed gymnasium were more desirable than the luxury of a hotel or a fashionable boarding-house table. The fact that he could not afford the expense of a membership with any of the militia companies, perhaps, caused him to be critical of these organizations, as they then existed, and some memoranda of his plans for better and more effective militia organization are still preserved by an old friend in Chicago. They show that he had given the subject much careful thought, and was dreaming of the time when he might have enough influence to have these plans carried out for the good of the entire country.

DECIDES ON THE ZOUAVE TYPE.

The Crimean War in Europe was but just over, and tales of the efficiency and valor of the French Zouaves caused him to make comparison with the heavy infantry of the British, which was accoutered in the traditional close-fitting clothes,

FIGURE 8. E. Elmer Ellsworth, commander of the Chicago Zouave Cadets and the first officer killed in the Civil War. Courtesy of the Library of Congress.

high stocks, cumbersome belts, and heavy equipments. He saw the pictures in the illustrated papers of the Zouaves—loosely clad, with un-confined limbs, and in every respect in "light marching order"—scaling walls, swarming over parapets, nimble, active, and irresistible. How much better and effective than the old style. The Zouaves were small, but their rapid movements made them more than a match for greater numbers of tall, stately grenadiers of the old school. . . .

With a musket and a copy of Scott's and Hardee's tactics in his room he studied out improvements in the "Manual of Arms" as given in these authorities. He was always trying to shorten and quicken all movements, sometimes using Scott and sometimes Hardee, sometimes a combination of both, but always striving to get something more rapid and better than either. . . .

For several years there had existed in the city a military company of the old school . . . and they went into bankruptcy in April, 1859.

Ellsworth's great opportunity was at hand. With the assistance of some of the old members who had seen him fence . . . and "sling a musket" in his new "lightning drill," a new company was organized on the ruins of the old "National Guard Cadets" and called the United States Zouave Cadets, with Ellsworth Commandant. . . . Their new and startling uniforms, rapid movements, and brilliant and showy manual of arms and bayonet drill, captured the spectators, and their popularity as a company was assured.

At the National Agricultural Fair held in Chicago September 14, 15, and 16, 1859, the company drilled for a stand of colors and the national championship of militia. This drill was on September 15, 1859. They carried off the colors, but as only one company came in competition with them there was some complaint from militia companies in other cities at the award of the championship under the circumstances. This complaint and the Zouaves' method of meeting and answering it furnished the cause of all their future efforts, which led to the national fame of Ellsworth and his Zouaves.

Challenge to the Whole Country.
Following is the Gauntlet That Was Thrown Down:

"Chicago, Sept. 20, 1859.—The National Agricultural Society at their seventh annual fair awarded to the United States Zouave Cadets of Chicago a stand of champion colors, which any company of militia or of the regular army of the United States or Canada are welcome to if they can win them in a fair contest. For terms of drill, etc., apply to E. E. Ellsworth, Col/ Comdg. U.S. Zouave Cadets."

The company was much criticized by the press of the entire country for its audacity and presumption in issuing such a challenge to older and presumably better drilled companies. Regular army officers and officers of companies in old Eastern cities—and especially of New York—were particularly sneering in their

widely published remarks, and as for Southern cities, it was to them almost a declaration of war, and was answered in their usual fire-eating style.

. . . They proposed to start on a tour to all the principal cities of the country,
where they would meet and drill with any company that, for any reason, could not
come to Chicago in acceptance of the former terms and challenge.

"Further, if the colors are retained by us we shall claim for the City of Chicago
and the State of Illinois the honor of military championship of the United States
and Canada.". . .

The march east was one continued series of triumphs. The country was electrified by their wonderful drill. The press accounts of the day were most enthusiastic, and the militia—well, the militia companies of the cities through which
they passed would not drill with them, but most cordially acknowledged their
superiority and were loud in their praises. Such "alignments," "correct distances,"
"wheels," "perfect time," "musket slinging," "bayonet practice," "ground and
lofty tumbling," were "most wonderful.". . .

Philadelphia and Baltimore were captured, in drill room parlance, "in one time
and two motions." Washington was reached August 5th, and the cadets were invited to drill in the White House grounds before President Buchanan and a select
company of Washington notables.

At Pittsburg, August 8th. a drill was given and a beautiful and valuable sword
was presented to Colonel Ellsworth by Duquesne Grays. . . .

At Cincinnati generous hospitality was extended to the Zouaves, and drills
were given to admiring audiences.

And at St. Louis this was repeated.

All this and much more praises and compliments had been heralded through
the land in the newspapers of the day, and the "march of triumph of the Ellsworth
Zouaves" was the leading news item. . . .

The Company returned to Chicago on Tuesday, August 14th, 1860. They were
escorted by all the city military companies, a large torchlight procession of both
political parties, and a large body of citizens to the "Wigwam Building" on the
southeast corner of Lake and Market Streets, where Mr. Lincoln had been nominated for President of the United States. The immense building was crowded to
overflowing with enthusiastic admirers. After the reception ceremonies were
concluded they were escorted to the Briggs House, where a magnificent banquet was spread. . . .

Shortly after the triumphant home-coming of the Zouaves Colonel Ellsworth
went to Springfield, Illinois, and entered the law office of Lincoln and Herndon
as a student. He was quite effective as a campaign orator in Illinois during the
autumn of 1860. In February, 1861, he accompanied Mr. Lincoln to Washington
for his inauguration as President on March 4th. The president obtained for him

a commission as Lieutenant in the regular army and a detail for special duty in Washington. When Sumter was fired upon and the war began he was anxious to go at once into active service in the field, and to do this he resigned his commission as Lieutenant, went to New York City and obtained permission of the Chief of the Fire Department to recruit a regiment from among the firemen. He sent to Chicago for some of the men of his old Zouave Company, and they joined him at once. . . . They were mustered into service by General Irwin McDowell in the presence of President Lincoln in front of the Capitol May 7th. . . .

[After entering the city of Alexandria, Virginia,] Colonel Ellsworth, leaving Lieutenant-Colonel Noah F. Fernham in command, took from the right of Company A a squad of men and Sergeant Frank B. Marshall, and proceeded . . . to the Marshall House, to which his attention was called by seeing a large rebel flag flying from its top. . . . He ascended to the house top where he went to obtain a view of the surroundings. He secured the rebel flag, and in descending the stairs, which occupied three sides of a stairway hall, he heard a noise, immediately followed by a shot. Hastening down to ascertain the cause, he came around a turn in the stair just in time to receive the second charge of a double-barreled shotgun in the hands of James W. Jackson, the landlord. . . .

. . . When speculating on what "might have been" had he been spared to the army, . . . they believe that on the roll-call of great Captains, when this greatest of all wars closed, his name might have stood second to none.

Henry H. Miller, "Paper Read at a Meeting of the Survivors of the United States Zouave Cadets." Chicago History Museum.

WAR EXCITEMENT IN CHICAGO

Mary A. Livermore (1820–1905) was destined to play a major role in Civil War Chicago. She was a daughter of New England who became an abolitionist after a brief time working as a teacher on a Southern plantation. She came to Chicago as the wife of a Universalist minister and was the only female reporter to cover the nomination of Abraham Lincoln at the Republican Convention.

In Chicago, there was even more stir and excitement than I had seen elsewhere. Everybody was engrossed with the war news and the war preparations. The day was full of din and bustle, and the night was hardly more quiet. On the evening of the very day that Fort Sumter capitulated to the secessionists, an immense meeting of Chicago's citizens was held in the great republican Wigwam, where Abraham Lincoln had been nominated for the presidency and ten thousand men of all religious creeds and party affiliations came together to deliberate on the crisis of the hour. There was no talking for effect. All the speeches were short and to the point. The time for harangue was over; the time for action had come. Before the vast assemblage separated, Judge Manierre, one of the most eminent and popular men of the city, administered to this great body of people, the oath of loyalty to the government the multitude rose, and with uncovered heads and upraised right hands, repeated the words of the following other:

"I do solemnly swear, in the presence of Almighty God, that I will faithfully support the Constitution of the United States, and of the State of Illinois. So help me God."

Mary A. Livermore, *The Story of My Life; or, The Sunshine and Shadow of Seventy Years* (Hartford, CT: A. D. Worthington, 1897), 466–67.

HOW A BUSINESSMAN BECAME A SOLDIER

When the war began, Joseph Kirkland (1830–1894) was a Chicago businessman. After service as an officer in the Civil War, he became a successful novelist and historian. The following excerpt from his 1891 novel The Captain of Company K *uses the character of William Fargeon to relate how the author himself became caught up in the war spirit of 1861 and abandoned business for military service. Kirkland brings hindsight and humor to this recollection of the first days of the war.*

The vast plain auditorium of the Wigwam (where Lincoln had been nominated for the presidency less than a year before) was cloudy with dust and echoing with noise. . . .

Flags, music, speeches, thunders of applause—it seemed as if the Union must be almost saved already. Fargeon made the best speech of the evening. Wit, humor, invective, patriotism, poetry—all were at his command, and at every pause a fresh cloud of dust arose from the stamping and was blown abroad by the waving of hats and handkerchiefs.

On long tables in front of the platform were offered eleven subscription papers; ten for signatures of volunteers for companies A, B, C, D, E, F, G, H, I, and K, and one pledging money for expenses, care of soldiers' families; etc.

How the latter filled up sheet after sheet, and how the other ten—did not! When the meeting adjourned, one company, K had only eleven names on its paper. A committee was appointed to keep the Wigwam open and the papers accessible through the week. . . .

Will had one of his old wakeful nights. For the first time he began to appreciate what was the kind of feast to which he was inviting his fellow-citizens—what a wrench of heart and soul and body and mind it is for an ordinary man to say, "I will go to war. I will bid good-bye to all that I love, all my dear hopes of fortunes, my ease, my comfort, my safety of life and limb, and go forth to stand up before the armed enemy in battle.

Next morning he walked aboard, breasted the sweet spring sunlight—lovely, familiar, natural, unwarlike—and, with face pale and set, went straight to the Wigwam. The twelfth name on the list of Company K was:

William Fargeon &̶ ̶C̶o̶. [So used he was to signing the firm name that he did it unconsciously, and had to erase the closing part.]

What a buzz went up and down Lake street as the news spread! Company K had its 100 names before noon, and the regiment its 1,000 before night. The meeting which had been adjourned for a week had to be called for that very evening. The body of the hall was reserved for the enlisted men, the place of each company being designated by a little guidon. The ball was started and was gathering strength. The great building could not hold the spectators, and the welkin could scarce contain the cheers as those solid ranks of ten companies showed themselves in their respective places. After the band had played the "Star Spangled Banner," Mr. Penrose opened the meeting with prayer, as usual, and followed with a speech of high and fervid eloquence. He held his audience spell-bound while he spoke, and even for a minute of silence after he closed, and then came a storm of cheers, with waving of hats and handkerchiefs, that only ceased when he again arose and asked a hearing.

"This platform is short one man—its best man—the man but for whom we should not be here to-night. May I ask Mr. William Fargeon to—"

But what he wanted Will to do could only be guessed. The cheers were wilder and more persistent than ever, and cries of "Fargeon!" rent the air. At last Will arose and the tumult died down, only to break out again and again until it ceased from sheer exhaustion.

"Mr. Chairman, I am in the ranks, where I belong. I shall have to leave to some one else the work to be done outside of them."

As he resumed his seat he knew, by inward consciousness as well as by public demonstrations, that he had made the best speech of his life. Already it sounded terse and soldierly. Already he was a man of deeds, not words.

Joseph Kirkland, *The Captain of Company K* (Chicago: Dibble Publishing, 1891), 12–15.

CHICAGO GERMANS RESPOND

German Americans were the city's largest ethnic group. Here the Chicago-based Illinois Staats-Zeitung *expresses that community's reasons for supporting the Union war effort.*

THE UNION THE BATTLE FOR FREEDOM AND AMERICAN CITIZENS OF GERMAN DESCENT

We crossed the ocean and entered the Land of Promise, to live as human beings and free citizens on a free soil. The glorious banner of Stars and Stripes—not embroidered with pictures of wild animals, as are the standards of despots—attracted us mightily, for in it we saw the symbol of freedom and human rights, the shield of the oppressed of all nations, the sign of victory of a Revolution which eradicated the last vestige of monarchy from the New World, and which fanned a spark across the ocean that ignited such a wide-spread conflagration in Europe that the citadel of feudalism was completely ruined.

When we embarked on these shores, we set our feet upon the soil of a new home, a second fatherland; the last ties were severed, and we became free citizens of a great Republic. Many among us fought a severe fight for a material existence; many were bitterly disappointed when their immoderate hopes were not realized, when sanguinary expectations proved to be mere bubbles; but just as one finds a sweet kernel in a bitter shell, so they too found the foundations of liberty after many severe trials, struggles, and hardships; and although the building which was being erected thereon did not afford each one an equally comfortable shelter, and did not measure up to each one's conception of beauty and grandeur, the foundation was very good, since it permitted reconstruction, elevation, and expansion; and everyone who lived in that structure had the right and duty to assist in its erection.

That enormous building which rests on solid granite is the Union, founded on the sacred principles that "all men are created equal" and are entitled to equal rights. And we are cohabitants of this fine structure; we are citizens of the Union.

And we are indeed proud that we have just claims to the best name man can bear, and we demand every right to which that name entitles us. However, just as we demand our rights, and should not let anyone deprive us of them, so we should also be willing and prepared—and we are—to honestly and conscientiously perform the duties of citizens; just as we demand our inalienable rights, life, liberty, and the pursuit of happiness, be respected, basing our claims thereto on the sacred Declaration of Independence, so we should be ready at all times—and we are—to offer our money, our property, and even our life in the service of the Union, and to make any sacrifice for the preservation of the Republic; for we are its citizens.

Only lately, Americans of German descent were reminded of their duty, and we noted with a great deal of satisfaction and pleasure how gladly they responded to the call to arms. We were proud to see them leave their homes, wives, and children to fight against sedition and treason and to stake their lives to save the Constitution and the Union. The many German regiments hailing from all states, the German guards in the slave states, the eagerness and ability displayed by German soldiers in

FIGURE 9. Chicago volunteers training south of the city at Camp Douglas.
Courtesy of the Chicago History Museum.

battle, and the victorious stand of the German citizens of Missouri are irrefutable
evidence that our fellow citizens of German extraction know what they owe this
country and are meeting their obligations in a most gratifying manner.

May they always be loyal and never tire in the performance of their consecrated
work; and just as they quickly and eagerly rose in defense of their adopted country, so may they persevere and excel in battle. The greatest treasures of mankind,
the existence of the Union and the preservation of a haven of liberty open to all
who are oppressed, are at stake. We are convinced that our citizens of German
descent will take positions in the front ranks during this holy War, and will show
their English brothers how to appreciate and fight for liberty.

Illinois Staats-Zeitung, July 26, 1861.

A UNIVERSITY VOLUNTEER

*In 1861, John A. Page was a student at Northwestern University. His memoir reflects
the excitement of the war spirit through the eyes of a boy. Raised in a slave-owning
family in Delaware and educated in Europe, Page was nonetheless a Lincoln
supporter at the time of the secession crisis.*

The time had come to show your colors. Fort Sumter had been bombarded and
forced to surrender. We cast about to procure a flag to raise over the university building, but none could be found. Bunting could not be purchased; the loyal people
had exhausted the supply, so the girl students set their nimble fingers to work and

presented us one made from calico; and in the presence of the whole population of the surrounding country, we hauled it to the peak of the flagstaff and then and there raising our right hands swore to protect the honor of that flag with our lives.

It was a solemn, sad, and impressive scene: boys in their teens dedicating their young lives to their country. And well they kept their oaths; the village, the city, and the national cemeteries bear witness to their devotion to the Union. In every army of our land, east and west, the Northwestern students, the brawny lads of the West, shared with their countrymen the dangers of the battle field, the privations and hardships of the camp and the march. The prisons of the South and the lonely unknown grave claimed their quota of my companions.

The excitement became so intense that books were abandoned, many began to pack their trunks, all were waiting for something to turn up, when the news came that the President had called for 75,000 militia for three months' service. . . .

. . . Monday we marched to the morning train; there was standing room only, the cars being packed with country boys on the same mission as ourselves. Arriving in Chicago, we struck out for State Street, where, before the armory of the Ellsworth Zouaves, the crowd was so dense we could not get near it. We tried several other places where we heard they were enlisting men, but were too late. "No more men wanted," was placarded on the buildings, and the guard stationed so no one could enter.

The Military Battery of Chicago was an old organization. A number of us had friends in the command, and they had given us a tip and list of students they desired in the company; so we quit the crowd and went to their armory, where the same placard stared us in the face, "No more men wanted." But we found a number of the battery who quietly led us in the back way; they had kept places for us, but we must get [a] recommendation from some prominent person, as the clamor was so great outside to get into the battery they desired to fortify their refusal with our recommendations. These were easily procured. The complement of men being secured, the books were closed and the fact announced, from a second-story window, to the crowd below, who received it with a howl of disappointment.

We were informed, as they only had four guns (they were six-pounders), the old members would go to the front first, and as soon as they could get two more guns we would be notified. The citizens of Chicago presented the battery with horses, and we followed the fortunate ones to the depot to see them off for Cairo, where they had been ordered. Thousands of young men were clamoring to enlist, but the quota of Illinois had been filled; they, however, kept to work forming companies on their own account, drilling and preparing themselves for the future.

John A. Page, "A University Volunteer," in *Reminiscences of Chicago during the Civil War*, ed. Mabel McIlvaine (New York: Citadel Press, 1967), 82–85.

WHEATON COLLEGE STUDENTS DEBATE THE WAR

Daniel B. Holmes was a Wheaton College student when the war began. The school had a strong commitment to the antislavery movement. Belief in that cause propelled Daniel to enlist in 1861. His classmate, J. Franklin Ellis, elected to stay in school. In the two letters below, Daniel describes to his parents his initial experience in the army while his friend Ellis writes to explain to Daniel his reluctance to enlist. Daniel Holmes served in the Seventh Kansas Cavalry and was killed in 1862. Ellis enlisted in the 106th Illinois Infantry in the wake of Emancipation Proclamation; he was wounded but survived the war and became a minister.

Sept. 8, 1861

Dear Folks at Home,

I will confess right away I have acted contrary to instructions and have been mustered into service, perhaps this is but prelude to a tale of sorrow, misery, woe, and finally death. I don't know how that may be. I do know however I debated a couple of days, until the noncommissioned officers were elected and I have the honor of being a private.

Soldiering goes very well at present, we are quartered here at a hotel, drill more or less every day and I read a great deal.

I like marching and our military actions limited as they are, very much. Our Captain I like more and more every time I see him. If he gets transferred from our company I have the promise of also being transferred.

Hughes does not make a bad military officer.

All that is said about the temptations of camp life is not exaggerated.

Nowhere can a young man exert as powerful an influence for good or evil as in the army. We anticipate crossing Missouri this week as there are thousands of armed men along the H. & St. Joseph R.R., we apprehend a nervous time, though we will have a military escort, however we will trust God, and keep our powder dry.

My little library consists of the Bible, Shakespeare, Military Tactics and Napoleon and his Marshals. Our Company presents nearly every grade of character, though taken as a whole it is far above any company I have seen here. I went to church this morning or rather we were marched to church as a company. Heard an excellent discourse from a minister about 25 years of age. Heard an organ for the first time in my life.

I have had some experience keeping guard. We have a secession prisoner. I have stood guard over him a portion of three nights, have had no trouble with him. I have also had a little experience in being sick, just enough to see that our boys were as attentive and kind as they could be.

I can write no more now. Direct to Leavenworth.

Yours as ever Danny Holmes

~

November 10, 1861

Dear Schoolmate,

Your lengthy, large, logical letter came to hand a few days since. I was much pleased to hear from your patriotic, military honor.

I shall not attempt to reply to your arguments because I deem it unnecessary; not that the reasoning is fallacious or unworthy of notice, but that it is not applicable to me in my present circumstances. I look on the matter of enlisting in just this light exactly; that it is wholly an individual question which is to be decided by each one personally according to each one's convictions of duty. Let everyone weigh the subject considerably and candidly. Now, I have done this, and have concluded that I can effect more good by educating myself than by enlisting at present. I say emphatically that I shant strike a blow against secession unless I am permitted to strike it under the proclamation of unqualified emancipation to every creature, without boundaries, created in the image of God and animated by an immortal spark which the countless cycles of eternity cannot obliterate. You talk of establishing a permanent peace without abolishing slavery. Absolute absurdity! Not while God is the God of nations, and holds his throne in Heaven and governs in human affairs can that be done. You may be patriotic and go in for our country, setting the deliverance of God's outraged people out of the account. But let me tell you, every effort made to put down the rebellion will be made in vain, every drop of blood that flows will flow in vain unless our government comes boldly forth and takes its stand upon justice. It is all fatal folly to hesitate about the matter, to predict the evil consequences which seem likely to result from emancipation. In this case the way of duty is as plain as the course of the sun. God's eternal principles of justice are in this combat. If they are discarded by us then defeat is our lot. If we attempt to sustain them then will our arms be effectual. Fred. Douglass said that one with God is a majority. He might better have said that alone he is a majority. We shall find it so ere long at any rate.

I am fully as anxious that this government should do its duty as I am to do my own, because far more depends on its movements. In fact Lincoln must declare every man free before I can fight with either hope of success or approval of conscience. For patriotism is nothing, country is nothing, Constitution is nothing, if the case of those who have cried to the Lord and have been heard by him is set aside.

The boys are all well. I expect the girls are too.

I have engaged a school to teach this winter about four miles south of Wheaton. I wish you every safety and success.

In truth yours, J.F. Ellis

Daniel B. Holmes Papers, Manuscripts Collection, Chicago History Museum.

LETTER FROM THE "FRONT"

The earnest innocence of many volunteers is captured in this brief and perhaps apocryphal letter that was shared by one veteran soldier after the war with his comrades.

In the Face of the Enemy,

4 A.M., June 30, 1861.

My Dear Miss Smith—A few minutes ago, just before daylight, our pickets were attacked; the long-roll beat. We formed into lines of battle, and have advanced to the edge of a cornfield, across which we can distinctly hear the enemy making preparations to charge down upon us.

I remember my promise that in time of danger you should be in my mind; so on my cartridge-box, in the face of death, with my musket pointed toward the enemy, I am writing you these lines, and they may be my last on earth.

Yours, etc.

P.S.—Later. It was a *false alarm*. The pickets shot a mule.

Alfred T. Andreas, *Military Essays and Recollections: Papers Read Before the Commandry of the State of Illinois* (Chicago: A. C. McClung, 1894), 2:433.

CHICAGO CAPTURES CAIRO

Cairo, Illinois—located farther south than Richmond, Virginia, and inhabited by descendants of Southerners—stirred fears elsewhere in Illinois that it might side with the Confederacy. Its location near the junction of the Ohio and Mississippi Rivers had great potential strategic importance. Within days of the onset of hostilities, militia from Chicago were ordered to occupy the southern Illinois town. William Christian wrote this memoir long after the war and incorporated in it several documents from 1861.

Governor, Richard Yates,

As soon as enough of your troops are mustered into service, send a Brigadier General with four Regiments, at or near Grand Cairo,

Simon Cameron, Secretary of War.

On the same date the Governor sent a telegram to General R.K. Swift of Chicago, as follows:

"General Swift, As quick as possible have a strong force as you can raise, armed and equipped with ammunition and accouterments, and a company of Artillery, ready to march at a moment's warning. A messenger will start for Chicago to-night

Richard Yates,
Commander in Chief"

Acting on the above telegram recruiting offices were opened at various halls, Armories and vacant stores, in two days a battery of Artillery, and five companies of Infantry were ready for duty, and left Chicago on a train of cars for Cairo, Ill, on the evening of April 21ˢᵗ, 1861.

The telegram alluded to in the above, were only a few of those which passed between Springfield and Chicago, and the alacrity, and dispatch with which the orders were carried out is something wonderful to realize when we come to consider, that in realty there was no militia in Illinois, organized or equipped for such an undertaking, in fact the only use for militia in those days, were for 4ᵗʰ of July celebrations, and parades on public occasions. A few companies of Artillery were scattered throughout the State, but had probably never fired anything but a blank cartridge.

The nearest approach to a real soldier in Chicago, at that time, was the Ellsworth Zouaves, who under the command of gallant Col. Ellsworth had only recently returned from a tour of the eastern and southern states, where they had rested the laurels of victory, from all contesting Military companies and had won for themselves a renown, which had captivated the entire country.

It was probably owing to the fact, that two of the companies organized, on the call of the Governor were officered by members of this command, who were splendid drill masters, and also to the fact, that many of the recruits and participants in the Wide Awake companies, that marched and paraded in the Presidential campaign which elected Lincoln.

Lieut. Joseph R. Scott, Orderly Sergeant James R. Hayden, Press and James Guthrie, and a number of others of the Ellsworth Company, immediately started recruiting two companies, and drilling the recruits as fast as they enlisted, at the Ellsworth Armory, corner of Randolph and State streets. Capt. Fred Harding a veteran of the Mexican War, opened a recruiting office in a vacant store on the west side of Dearborn street, just north of Lake Street, two German companies were recruited at Turners Hall on the North Side. The Highland guards under Captain McArthur (Afterwards Major General) recruited at their Armory. . . . Capt. Smith's battery was recruited to full strength at their Armory all of which was accomplished in two days time.

A military officer was sent from Springfield Ill, and on Sunday morning, [April 21st] in a blustering cold north wind, all the commands were marched to General Swifts headquarters, 19 South Wells Street; where the infantry were supplied with guns, of many different patterns, and accoutrements, after an inspection the troops were sworn in a body into the state service.

In the evening each Company was marched to the Illinois Central depot, on the Lake Front between Lake and Randolph streets, where a train of twenty six cars, with two locomotives waiting for them. The sheds were soon filled with a crowd of citizens, fathers, mothers, wives and sweethearts, to bid God speed to the departing soldiers, many tears were shed and last injunctions given by fond mothers and fathers to departing sons. General Swift states in his report to the Adjutant General of the State that his command consisted of rank and file, of 595 persons, 46 horses for Artillery and 4 brass 6 pounder guns.

About 10 O'clock after fair wells had been said to relatives, and sweethearts, the soldiers climbed into the cars and the long train slowly, moved out of the depot, amidst the booming of cannon, the ringing of bells, and the blowing of whistles, the soldiers making themselves as comfortable as possible in the ordinary day coaches. The first important event was at Centralia where a halt was made. Gen. Swift was there informed that threats were being made to destroy the Big Muddy Creek bridge. The soldiers made a rush for the lunch stands, and anything eatable, to say nothing of drinkables. The train was again started, and arrived at Big Muddy Bridge about 5 O'clock in the afternoon. No armed force was visible, but it was deemed advisable to station a force there, for the protection of the bridge, and to prevent the interception of communications. Capt. Hayden's company of Col. Scott's Zouaves was detailed for the service. A section of Artillery was left with the detail. The command was without tents and were compelled to make their quarters in the adjoining timber as best they could. A change in the make up of the train was here made, as the force was supposed to be approaching the enemy's country as southern Illinois was known to have many Southern sympathizers. The Artillery on flat cars, was placed at the front of the train, and the Locomotives in the rear, the guns were manned and ready for action, and the muskets of the infantry were loaded, in this manner the train proceeded slowly on its way to Cairo, there it arrived about 11 O'clock P.M. on the 22nd day of April without encountering any opposition, a detail was made for the guard and picket duty, to prevent a surprise, the balance of the command remained in the cars until morning.

In the morning the men debarked from the cars, and were taken by companies to the Saint Charles Hotel for breakfast, where they were served as well, as any guest at the hotel, but there must have been some irregularities on the part of some of the soldiers, as the next meal was served in the basement and instead of crockery and silver spoons, the food was served on tin plates with pewter spoons, with boiled beef and bread instead of the regular hotel fare. As no tent had been furnished the command and soldiers were compelled to take up their quarters in some cattle sheds that had been used for Fair purposes, provisions were issued to squads of men and messes formed and good cooks were in demand. The levee protecting the city on the banks of the Ohio and Mississippi rivers formed a natural breast work on three sides. The Artillery was placed in position commanding the approaches of both rivers.

William Christian Memoir, May 29, 1911, Miscellaneous Pamphlets, Survivor's Association of the Cairo Expedition, Chicago History Museum.

THE "HAVELOCK" CRAZE AND MOBILIZATION OF THE "LADIES"

The excitement of the war spirit was caught by the young of both genders. While men and boys could volunteer to don the blue uniform, women's opportunities to contribute to the cause were much less obvious. Mary Livermore describes the early efforts to aid the war effort by what was then regarded as the "fair sex." It is estimated that between four hundred and one thousand women on both sides attempted to serve as soldiers during the Civil War.

Entirely unacquainted with the requirements of war and the needs of soldiers, it was inevitable that the first movements of women for army relief should be misdirected. They could not manifest more ignorance, however, nor blunder more absurdly, than did the government in its early attempts to build up an effective and disciplined army. Both learned by blundering.

It was summer; and the army was to move southward, to be exposed to the torrid heats of the season and climate. A newspaper reminiscence of the good service rendered British troops in India by General Havelock set the ball in motion. He had devised a white linen head-dress to be worn over the caps of his men, which defended them from sunstroke, and in his honor it was named the "Havelock." Our men must, of course, be equipped with this protection, and forthwith inexperienced women, and equally inexperienced men in the army, gave orders for the manufacture of Havelocks. What a furor there was over them! Women who could not attend the "sewing-meeting" where the "Havelocks" were being manufactured, ordered the work sent to their homes, and ran the sewing-machines day and night till the nondescript headgear was completed. "Havelocks" were turned out by thousands, of all patterns and sizes, and of every conceivable material.

In the early inexperience of that time, whenever regiments were in camp awaiting marching orders, it was the custom of many women to pay them visits, laden with indigestible dainties. These they furnished in such profusion, that the "boys" were rarely without the means of obtaining a "permit" to the hospital until they broke up camp. While the Havelock fever was at its height, the Nineteenth Illinois, commanded by Colonel Turchin, was mustered in, and was ordered to rendezvous at Camp Douglas. A detachment of the "cake and pie brigade," as the rollicking fellows called them, paid the regiment an early visit, and were received by the men who were not under drill, *en Havelock.* As the sturdy fellows emerged from their tents, all wearing "the white nightcaps," as they had irreverently christened the ugly head-dress, their appearance was so ludicrous that a shout went up from officers, soldiers, and lady visitors. They were worn in every imaginable fashion,—as nightcaps, turbans, sunbonnets, bandages, sunshades,—and the fate of the "Havelock" was sealed. No move time nor money was wasted in their useless manufacture.

En passant, I remember another occurrence of that afternoon when we visited the camp of the Nineteenth Illinois. I was watching companies that were drilling, a good deal amused at their awkwardness and their slow comprehension of the orders given them. One of the captains came to me, with an apology for intrusion, and begged to know if I noticed anything peculiar in the appearance of one of the men, whom he indicated. It was evident at a once that the "man" was a young woman in male attire, and I said so. "That is the rumor, and that is my suspicion," was his reply. The seeming soldier was called from the ranks and informed of the suspicions afloat, and asked the truth of them. There was a scene in an instant. Clutching the officer by the arm, and speaking in tones of passionate entreaty, she begged him not to expose her, but to allow her to retain her disguise. Her husband had enlisted in his company, she said, and it would kill her if he marched without her. "Let me go with you!" I heard her plead. "Oh, sir, let me go with you!" She was quietly conducted outside the camp, when I took her in charge. I wished to take her to my home; but she leaped suddenly from the carriage before we were half way from the camp, and in a moment was lost amid the crowds hastening home from their day's work.

That night she leaped into the Chicago river, but was rescued by a policeman, who took her to the Home of the Friendless. Here I found her, a few days later, when I made an official visit to the institution. She was extremely dejected, and could not be comforted. It was impossible to turn her from her purpose to follow her husband. "I have only my husband in all the world," she said, "and when he enlisted he promised that I should go with him; and that was why I put on his clothes and enlisted in the same regiment. And go with him I will, in spite of everybody." The regiment was ordered to Cairo, and the poor woman disappeared from the Home the same night. None of us doubted but she left to carry out her purpose. . . .

The number of women who actually bore arms and served in the ranks during the war was greater than is supposed. Sometimes they followed the army as nurses, and divided their services between the battle-field and hospital. I remember Annie Etheridge, of Michigan, who was with the Third Michigan in every battle in which it was engaged. When their three years' service was ended, the reenlisted veterans joined the Fifth Michigan, and Annie went with them. Through the whole four years of the war she was found in the field, often in the thickest of the fight, always inspiring the men to deeds of valor, always respected for her correctness of life. Soldiers and officers vied with one another in their devotion to her.

Bridget Devens, known as "Michigan Bridget," went to the field with the First Michigan Cavalry, in which her husband was a private, and served through the war. Sometimes when a soldier fell she took his place, fighting in his stead with unquailing courage. Sometimes she rallied retreating troops,—sometimes she brought off the wounded from the field—always fearless and daring, always doing good service as a soldier. Her love of army life continued after the war ended, and with her husband she joined a regiment of the regular army, stationed on the Plains.

Some one has stated the number of women soldiers known to the service as little less than four hundred. I cannot vouch for the correctness of this estimate, but I am convinced that a larger number of women disguised themselves and enlisted in the service, for one cause or other, than was dreamed of. Entrenched in secrecy, and regarded as men, they were sometimes revealed as women, by accident or casualty. Some startling histories of these military women were current in the gossip of army life; and extravagant and unreal as were many of the narrations, one always felt that they had a foundation in fact.

Mary A. Livermore, *My Story of the War* (Hartford, CT: A. D. Worthington, 1896), 112–14.

THREE

~

Ties between the Home Front and the Battlefield

*D*URING THE FIRST YEAR of the Civil War, there were close ties between Chicago and the young men the city had sent to defeat Southern secession. Most troops were sent to the western theater of operations, so the battlefront was fairly accessible via the Illinois Central Railroad.[1] A day's train ride could bring Chicagoans to the military hospitals and staging areas, while a further day via steamboat could take them to the front lines. For many the war was imagined as a novel, romantic adventure, and not just those in uniform sought out its glamour. The "boys" had also not been away from home very long and were fresh in the minds of friends, families, and neighbors. In the summer of 1861, when the largely Catholic Irish Brigade—the Twenty-Third Illinois Infantry—left Chicago for duty in Missouri, they were followed to the front by the Sisters of Charity, a small group of nuns who promised to tend to the men who fell ill or wounded. Other units were accompanied by ministers or medical professionals who unofficially offered their services for what was still expected to be a short war.[2]

The innocence and high emotion of that first year of the war is illustrated by the experience of Chicago's Irish Brigade. In July 1861 they were ordered to march into northern Missouri and occupy the river town of Lexington. The Irishmen's colonel, James A. Mulligan, assumed command of a total force of 2,780 men. Unfortunately, Lexington was directly in the path of a Confederate force of 28,000 men. Instead of allowing Mulligan to withdraw, General John C. Fremont hesitated, and the garrison at Lexington was surrounded by the rebels. For nine days the Irish Brigade held off repeated rebel assaults despite being short of both food and water. The fate of soldiers was major news in Chicago. A diarist wrote, "Mulligan and Lexington are on every tongue and according to all accounts he holds out gallantly. . . . The eyes of the whole country are on him."[3] Finally, with no hope of relief coming from Fremont, Mulligan surrendered his command. The soldiers were immediately paroled and within days were being slapped on the back in Chicago. Mulligan himself was held as a prisoner of war until November, when he was exchanged for a Confederate general. His return was treated as a state occasion. Mulligan's train was met in Joliet by the elites of Chicago politics and business, and after a triumphal parade, he was feted at a Tremont House banquet.

The sons of Erin, Chicago's most despised residents, had drawn first blood and even in defeat had emerged as heroes to the entire city.[4]

Chicagoans had to wait until the New Year before even the hint of victory greeted Union arms. Then on February 17 the city received word that General Ulysses S. Grant had led a large force of Illinois troops out of Cairo and captured the Confederate garrison at Fort Donelson. The victory bagged over twelve thousand prisoners and opened most of Tennessee (including the capital, Nashville) to Union occupation. Chicago went "wild with excitement." Not until the fall of Richmond would war news be greeted with such "frenzied" enthusiasm. Church bells rang and the streets thronged with celebrants. Students "added to the joyful confusion of the streets by shooting out of the schoolhouses like bombs from mortars with shrill and prolonged hurrahs leaping from their lips as they rushed through every part of the city."[5] But with word of victory also came news that on the wintry field of battle lay some three thousand wounded for which the army was incapable of caring. Doctors, ministers, and boxcars of hastily assembled supplies were rushed south from Chicago, reinforcing the bond between the city and its troops.

Although what Chicagoans reported seeing on the Fort Donelson battlefield had proved sobering, the massive carnage of the Battle of Shiloh in April 1862 was what finally transformed the city's view of combat and braced supporters for a longer and uglier war against the Confederacy. Shiloh was the bloodiest battle ever fought—up to that point—in North America. More men were killed and wounded at Shiloh than in all of the nation's previous wars combined. Out of sixty-five Union regiments involved in the battle, twenty-eight were from Illinois, many from Chicago. While it was a clear victory for the Union, there were no celebrations in the city. Numbed by the appalling losses and fearful for loved ones unaccounted for, the city sprang to action, guided by the experience gained from Fort Donelson. The city council voted $10,000 and the board of trade $3,000 for relief of the wounded. Trains were chartered and dispatched to the front with supplies and medical teams. At Cairo they were met by steamboats converted into floating hospitals that pushed up the dark rivers to the killing ground in Tennessee. On Shiloh's field they found "dead bodies stark and stiff" and thousands of wounded men "gashed and torn and scarred by every conceivable form of ghastly wounds" lying in the spring rain even days after the slaughter had ceased.[6]

The effectiveness of the response was in large part due to the U.S. Sanitary Commission, a voluntary civilian organization that gradually emerged to coordinate community support for the soldiers in the field. While technically supervised by a board of male commissioners, women anxious to participate in the work of the war constituted the backbone of the organization. For them the commission was an outlet for their talent and patriotic sentiments. By the time of Shiloh, branches of the commission had been organized in most of the North's leading cities. The Chicago branch was energized by activist women who had prewar experience in benevolence, operating asylums and the Home for the Friendless. Two Chicago mothers emerged as leading figures in the commission's work: Jane Hoge and Mary Livermore. They visited the military hospitals after Fort Donelson, but with large families in Chicago, they focused most of their work in the city, where they raised funds, organized donated goods, and coordinated the movement of medical supplies and volunteers for the front.[7]

While Chicago rushed aid to Shiloh, from the battlefield came a stream of tragic missives announcing the deaths of brothers, fathers, husbands, and sons. The caskets of some of these followed, and throughout April military funerals were a frequent sight in Chicago cemeteries. The grim toll stiffened the resolve of some but helped fracture the political unity that had followed Stephen Douglas's call to fight secession. Democrats in the city blamed military losses in the East on Republican bungling, Catholics who supported the war began to resent Protestant ministers' prominence in soldier relief efforts, and in local elections the Democrats won back the mayor's office in the spring polling.

Many Chicago soldiers responded to the horror of Shiloh with a more realistic approach to soldiering. The troops, one soldier reported, are "just as ready to do our duty as we were [before Shiloh], but to desire another hard battle, with the same chances of loss to our company, is quite a different thing." The images of "brave Ellsworth" and the 1861 illusions of honorable and glorious warfare had been swept away by the blood of friends and neighbors. With this realism came a harsher attitude toward the South and its "peculiar" institution. After seeing several of his comrades cut down by Confederate bullets, one Chicago artilleryman wrote, "My heart was filled with hatred and revenge against the enemy. . . . I could then hazard my life in any position to mow down their ranks with canister." Another soldier from the Chicago suburb of Elgin confessed to his wife, "If I had control when this army had marched through the Gulf states no landmarks would be left to show the boundaries of towns, counties, states." This harsher attitude was reflected in newspaper stories printed in pro-administration journals such as the *Chicago Tribune*. Rebels, it reported, had been found robbing Union graves and making "tools and utensils of their bones." The institution of slavery had hardened Southern hearts to any form of cruelty and had given the enemy the "malignant fury and foul lust of the savage."[8]

The soldiers and many on the Chicago home front together moved toward support of what historian Mark Grimsley has called "hard war." This was well illustrated by the actions of the Nineteenth Illinois Infantry just a month after Shiloh and the response of Chicago Unionists. The Nineteenth was composed of mainly Cook County men, including two companies that represented Elmer Ellsworth's Chicago Zouave Cadets. They were led by Colonel John B. Turchin, a Russian-born soldier trained at the Tsarist military academy, who had immigrated to Illinois in 1856. In May 1862, some of Turchin's troops occupied the town of Athens, Alabama. The people of the town welcomed the troops and professed to be loyal to "the old flag." When rebel cavalry counterattacked, however, they joined in helping to expel the Union troops. Turchin brought up reinforcements and again occupied the town. The Russian colonel then assembled the men of the Nineteenth Illinois and told them, "I shut my eyes for two hours." What happened next was an atrocity, as the angry soldiers tore the town apart. Property was broken or stolen, people were roughed up, and several African American servants were raped. A veteran of the campaign later remarked, "It was pitiful, but it was war."[9]

General Don Carlos Buell, who commanded the army, saw things differently and ordered Turchin tried before a court-martial. Although his fellow officers found Turchin guilty, Abraham Lincoln approved the Russian's promotion to the rank of brigadier general. Chicago Republicans immediately invited him home for a hero's welcome. There speakers lauded him as a man "who handled our enemies roughly" and whose promotion was a sign that "this kid glove business is played out." Turchin closed his address to great cheers when, like a Cossack warrior, he raised his sword over his head and said, "We have been talking about Union and Hurrahing the Union a great while. Let us now talk and hurrah for conquest."[10]

By the summer of 1862, the Civil War had developed its own violent momentum, and primal emotions often overcame what Lincoln had called the "better angels of our nature." Back in 1860 the men of the Ellsworth Zouaves had vowed to be Christian soldiers; after a year of war, they stood accused of war crimes. Yet even as the war became the focus of a growing partisan divide in the city, many soldiers and citizens of Chicago embraced the reality of a long, hard conflict. Southern treason in their view would have to be crushed and punished, and prewar conceptions of law and ethics had to bend to the needs of the moment.

CHICAGO TROOPS LOSE THEIR FIRST BATTLE

The Chicago Tribune *reports on the emotional anguish but dignity of Colonel Mulligan's surrender of the Irish Brigade.*

THE SIEGE OF LEXINGTON
THE SURRENDER OF COL. MULLIGAN.
PARTICULARS OF THE FIGHT. . . .

On Wednesday the 17th, an evil from the first apprehended fell upon Col. Mulligan's command. They were cut off from the river and their water gave out. Fortunately a heavy rain, at intervals, came greatly to their relief. But to show how severe the straits of the men, the fact may be stated of instances occurring where soldiers held their blankets spread out until thoroughly wet, and then wrung them into their camp dishes, carefully saving the priceless fluid thus obtained. Rations also began to grow short. The fighting at this time, from the 16th to the 21st, knew little cessation. The nights were brilliant moonlight, and all night long the roar of the guns continued, with an occasional sharp sortie and skirmish without the works. .

From the first but one spirit pervaded our troops, and that was no thought or word of surrender, except among some of the Home Guards [Missouri militia], who had done the least share of the work and the fighting. The cavalry behaved nobly, and could the full details be written up, some of their sharp, brave charges on the enemy's guns would shine with any battle exploits on record.

Gen. Price sent Col. Mulligan a summons to surrender, to which the gallant commander sent a refusal, saying, "If you want us you must take us." But the defection and disheartenment of the Home Guards intensified daily, and on Friday the 21st, while Col. Mulligan was giving his attention to some matters in another portion of the camp, the white flag was raised at his own instance by Major Becker of the Home Guards, from the portion of the entrenchment assigned to him.

Capt. Simpson, of the Earl Rifles, called Col. Mulligan's attention to Maj. Becker's action instantly, and the Jackson Guard, Capt. McDermott, of Detroit, were sent to take down that flag, which was done. The heaviest part of the fight of the day followed in a charge upon the nearest battery of the enemy, the Illinois Cavalry suffering severely.

The Home Guards then left the outer work and retreated within the line of the inner entrenchments, about the college building, refusing to fight longer, and here again raised the white flag, this time from the centre of the fortifications, when the fire of the enemy slackened and ceased. Under this state of affairs, Col. Mulligan, calling his officers into council, decided to capitulate, and Capt. McDermott went out to the enemy's lines, with a handkerchief tied to a ramrod, and a parley took place. . . .

. . . The boys of the Brigade many of them wept to leave behind their colors, . each Company in the Brigade having its own standard presented to it by their friends. At the surrender the muster rolls of the Companies were taken to Gen. Price's headquarters, the list of officers made out, and these ordered to report themselves as prisoners of war.   The scenes at the capitulation were extraordinary. Col. Mulligan shed tears. The men threw themselves upon the ground, raved and stormed in well nigh frenzy, demanding to be led out again and "finish the thing." In Col. Marshall's Cavalry Regiment, the feeling was equally great. Much havoc had already been done. . . . Numbers of the privates actually shot their horses on the spot, unwilling that their companions in the campaign should now fall into the enemy's hands. . . .

Col. Mulligan's praise is in every man's mouth, and the men say that Gen. Price praised his defense in warm terms. . . .

Chicago Tribune, September 25, 1861.

RETURN OF THE IRISH BRIGADE

The Irish Brigade was given a hero's welcome upon its return to Chicago after the release from rebel hands.

Five companies of the Irish Brigade, lately mustered out of service, returned to this city last evening, arriving at half past six *via* the Chicago and St. Louis Railroad. An immense crowd of friends and curious spectators assembled about the depot and thronged the adjacent streets. As the train approached the depot, a universal welcome burst forth from thousands of lusty throats for the gallant heroes of Lexington. As they disembarked, an attempt was made to form them into companies, but impatient of delay, the men burst from the ranks, and singly and in squads, left with their friends for home. Scattered remnants were formed and headed by music, and escorted by Capt. Slaughters's company from the Yates' Phalanx, marched to their temporary quarters at the Wigwam, after partaking of a generous collation provided for them. The "boys" spent the night right merrily, and many a cheerless home was lighted up anew with joy. Although mustered out, they were all anxious to enlist again under Col. Mulligan.

Chicago Tribune, October 11, 1861.

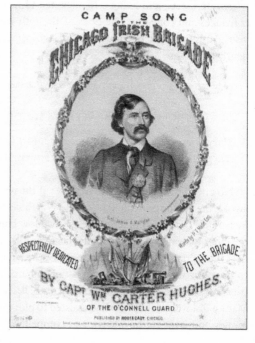

FIGURE 10. Following their gallant stand at Lexington, Missouri colonel James Mulligan and the Chicago Irish Brigade were toasted and celebrated in song. Courtesy of the Library of Congress.

DWIGHT L. MOODY EVANGELIZES CHICAGO TROOPS

One of the most notable individuals in Civil War–era Chicago was a young evangelical minister named Dwight L. Moody. His propensity to accost strangers on the street with the question, "Do you know Jesus?" led some to dub him "crazy Moody." Moody's work with the YMCA in Chicago and his efforts to minister to Chicagoans in the army helped the young minister perfect the approach that would after the war make him one of the leading figures in American Evangelical history. The following account of a visit with the troops was recorded in the Nineteenth Illinois Infantry's regimental newspaper. The Nineteenth was composed of many men who been part of Elmer Ellsworth's Zouave Cadets.

A WELCOME VISIT

D. L. Moody, the active missionary of the Young Men's Christian Association of Chicago, having been invited by the chaplain of the 19th to visit our regiment, arrived at Lebanon Junction on Wednesday evening last, since which time he has labored unceasingly both day and night in distributing books, papers, tracts, hymn books, &c. Many of the boys have signed the temperance pledge and commenced to lead a different life. The secret of Mr. Moody, both here among the soldiers and at home is that he makes a personal application of the gospel truths to those whom he meets, and living a life devoted to his master, his advice and example convinces and converts. The boys of the 19th will long remember Mr. Moody's visit. All regret that his duties in Chicago prevent him from remaining permanently among us.

Zouave Gazette (regimental newspaper of the Nineteenth Illinois Infantry), October 30, 1861.

CHICAGO CELEBRATES ITS SOLDIERS' FIRST VICTORY

Mary Livermore's account of the victory at Fort Donelson, in which Chicago's own sons participated, reveals the close bonds between the battlefield and the home front.

No one of the later or larger victories of the war, not even the fall of Richmond, awoke the enthusiastic delight of the Northwest like the fall of Fort Donelson. Bells rang; cannon thundered the general joy; bands perambulated the streets of the cities, playing the national airs, deafening cheers often drowning their music; flags were flung out from almost every house, and where there was any reluctance to give this manifestation of loyal delight, from sympathy with secession, the overjoyed people took possession and compelled the display of the national colors. Many a disloyal wretch who had assisted to plot the rebellion, and had contributed money and arms to the enemy, was compelled to enter his house under the flag of the stars and stripes, which he had been forced to purchase. Men rushed from their stores, offices, counting-rooms, shops, and work-benches, to congratulate one another. They met on the streets and threw their hats in air, embraced one another, wept, and shouted.

The public schools of Chicago had each purchased a flag by joint subscription, and a flagstaff had been planted on the roof of every one of the handsome brick schoolhouses for just such occasions as this. So the boys ran up their flags amid immense cheering, and, under the direction of the teachers, the day was given up to patriotic dissipation. National songs were sung, patriotic scraps of speeches found in the reading-books were recited, and the location and importance of Fort Donelson were explained to the young people. When the hour of dismissal came, they added to the joyful confusion of the streets by shooting out of the schoolhouses like bombs from mortars, with shrill and prolonged hurrahs leaping from their lips as they rushed through every part of the city. Night came, and the people crowded the churches to return thanks to God. Meetings were held to raise funds for the relief of the wounded. The streets blazed with bonfires, and the glare of the flames was like that of a great conflagration. Nor did the rejoicings cease until physical exhaustion compelled an end of them.

With the news of the victory the telegraph flashed the terrible needs of the wounded men. During the first day of the fight a cold, heavy rain fell ceaselessly, converting the roads into rivers of mud, through which the troops painfully toiled. During the night the rain changed to sleet and snow, and the wind blew in fierce, wintry gusts, the weather became intensely cold, and the thermometer dropped to zero. Our brave fellows were mostly young, and not yet inured to the hardships of war. With the improvidence of inexperience, they had thrown away their blankets on the march, and had only the insufficient rations they had brought in their haversacks, of which they had been very careless. They had no tents; were obliged to bivouac in line of battle, lying on their arms; and as the rebel pickets were out in strong force, no fires could be kindled, as their position would be revealed. . . .

There was a great lack of hospital clothing, and one of the largest halls of Chicago was loaned to the women for its manufacture. To this hall they flocked in such numbers, that it was necessary to apportion the days of the week to the various districts of the city, so as to accommodate all the willing workers. Every sewing-machine office in the city put its rooms, machines and operators to the same service, to the entire suspension of its own business. Never was clothing manufactured more rapidly; for the machines were run into the small hours of the morning, and there was no slacking of effort while the urgent demand lasted. It was the same all over the West. The facts of the desperate battle, the severe exposure of the wounded, the incomplete preparations for their removal and care, the great destitution of surgeons, instruments, supplies, of everything that was needed,—as these became known to the people, their patriotic generosity was stimulated to fever heat.

Mary A. Livermore, *My Story of the War* (Hartford, CT: A. D. Worthington, 1896), 177–82.

THE SHOCK OF SHILOH:
A CHICAGO ARTILLERYMAN'S ACCOUNT OF THE BATTLE

Heavy casualties at Shiloh struck many Chicago homes. Seldom did newspapers report the carnage of battle in anything approaching realistic terms. An exception was the Tribune's publication of a battlefield letter from James Milner, a young Chicago artilleryman, to his father.

I thank God that I am still preserved, and I am still permitted to communicate with my friends at home with my own right hand. We have at last had our wish for a hard battle gratified and never again do I expect to hear the same wish from the lips of our men. We are just as ready now to do our duty as we were, but to desire another hard battle, with the same chances of loss to our company, is quite a different thing. You will lean the story of the battle from the newspapers, so I will only inform you of what I saw, heard, and felt during those two terrible days.

The Sabbath dawned upon us clear and warm. At the watering call I took a team of extra horses, of which I have charge . . . to a meadow to let them feed on some new grass. While there I heard what sounded like skirmish firing and thought it best to hurry towards camp. [After moving up to the battle line Milner's unit was flanked by advancing Confederate troops.] Now we began to realize the horrors of war. . . . In this action we suffered. Ed Russell, a young man whom you have seen behind the counter of Smith's bank, as gentlemanly a man as we had in the battery, had his bowels torn out by a solid shot. He lived but a half an hour. His last words were as he lay on his face, 'I die like a man.' And good man Farnham, a Christian man, my tentmate for six months . . . was shot through above the heart. . . . Flannigan a merry hearted Irishman and the intimate friend of Ed Russell, was shot through the mouth. [At this point, the infantry fighting in front of the battery broke and ran. Their flight took them across the battery's field of fire.] We yelled at them to keep away from our fire, but they didn't hear. I ran forward and waved my hat, but to no purpose, and I went back to my post and fired through them. [The battery's own retreat nearly cost them their howitzer as the men struggled to harness the panicked horses.] We saved the howitzer, having eight men wounded in the performance. . . . I now knew we were beaten and in full retreat. I stopped, and with the aid of some infantry, helped one of our guns out of a mud-hole, and walked on till we came to a road jammed with wagons: I felt then I had never witnessed so painful a sight as a disorganized army. Here I found Billy Williams . . . riding in a baggage wagon. He said to me in a pitiable tone, 'Jimmy, won't you come take care of me, I am shot through?' I had to refuse. This was truly painful. I helped him down and put him into an ambulance. [In the wagon, Milner discovered another wounded comrade, Jerry Paddock.] I got into the ambulance and examined Paddock's wound, I found that he was shot through the liver, and that there was no blood coming through the wound, I made my mind he was bleeding internally, he was very frail, and I thought he must die. I put his handkerchief over his wound and went back to my gun. My heart was filled with hatred and revenge against the enemy. . . . I could not restrain my tears and felt that I would hazard my life in any position to mow down their ranks with canister. After this I had a feeling of utmost indifference as to my fate. [The Chicagoans joined Union troops who formed final line of defense near the bank of the Tennessee River and as night fell held off the rebel army.] It now began to rain and were subjected to the discomfort of a wet night in the open air. . . . A weary night dragged by slowly. With the light of day the battle was renewed. We had recovered nearly all the lost ground of the day before. The fire opened fierce from the start, and we did not wait long for orders to

FIGURE 11. Memorial to the men of the Chicago Light Artillery, Rosehill Cemetery, Chicago. Photograph by the author.

the front. Our position was near the center, and we commenced shelling with the
four guns we were still able to man. [Twice General William Tecumseh Sherman
personally directed the battery forward to stem a Confederate counterattack.]
General Sherman again rode up and ordered us to a new front. 'Come on,' he
said, 'I'll lead you,' and he did. We limbered up, mounted our seats . . . and we
galloped forward through a fierce storm of shell and bullets. 'Well up to the front,'
said Lt. Wood, and we took up position in advance of the infantry and poured in
a rapid fire of shell. General Sherman who (as Gen. Wallace says is perfectly crazy
on the subject of artillery) told a Louisiana officer in the presence of one of our
men, it was the grandest thing he ever saw done by artillery. . . . It was the liveliest
engagement of all, for the time it lasted, and I really enjoyed it. . . . We were tired
out. The rain was falling, and I for one felt more dispirited here than at any other
time." [Rebel troops were in full retreat and the battle was all but over.] I have gone
into these tedious details to show you exactly what war is. I have since rode over
the whole battlefield, but will spare you the horrid and disgusting details of the
thousands of suffering wounded, and mangled corpses I saw.

Chicago Tribune, April 18, 1862.

"SOURCE OF REBEL BARBARITY"

*In the wake of Shiloh, the city's Republican newspapers responded by taking a
harsher attitude toward the South. Chicago readers began to be treated to stories
that demonized their former countrymen and laid a foundation for a harsher
prosecution of the war.*

SOURCE OF REBEL BARBARITY

The feeling of the world is shocked by the cruelties and atrocities practiced by
the Confederates in this war. And yet no person should be surprised who has read
the history of slavery in other lands, or has much knowledge of human nature. No
man can hold his fellow man in chains, without at the same time riveting fetters on
his own highest powers and best impulses. . . .

There is much said of Christianizing the African by slavery, but not enough
spoken of barbarizing the American by the same peculiar institution. . . .

To poison wells and springs; to betray your enemy by the foulest treachery
and the most lying professions of truth and friendship; to refuse prisoners food
and drink, clothing, fire and shelter; to neglect the wounded, and delight in their
pains and agony; to leave the dead unburied, mutilate their remains, and feed an
unglutted hate and revenge in making tools and utensils of their bones; these all
are the customs and practices of barbarians. The tribes of negroes who have not
yet left their native Africa still practice them in their wars; and we do not know of

an atrocity or cruelty which the black savages are said to perpetrate that cannot find its match in those which disgrace the rebels in this war.

Chicago Tribune, April 11, 1862.

A WAR OF EXTERMINATION:
CHICAGO TROOPS AND THE SACK OF ATHENS, ALABAMA

In May 1862 an incident occurred that underscored the harsh way many of Chicago's civilians and soldiers had begun to view the people of the Confederate states. On May 1, 1862, rebel cavalry with some aid from the townspeople of Athens, Alabama, drove the Union garrison from the recently captured town. Because the people of the town had previously proclaimed themselves Unionists, the men of the Northern army felt that the civilian population had acted with deceit. After the recapture of the town by the Union, Colonel John B. Turchin gathered the men of the Nineteenth Illinois around him and proclaimed, "I shut my eyes for two hours," giving the troops license to sack the town. Vandalism, rape, and robbery were among the outrages reported in the wake of the atrocity. Ironically, the Nineteenth Illinois had been composed of many former YMCA members who only a year before had vowed to remain "Christian soldiers." The commander of the Army of the Cumberland, General Don Carlos Buell, was criticized by many Northern newspapers as being too concerned with reconciling Southern civilians and not pursuing the enemy vigorously.

OFFICIAL FINDINGS OF THE TURCHIN COURT-MARTIAL, AS PUBLISHED BY GENERAL BUELL, ON AUGUST 6, 1862:

"[He] allow[ed] his command to disperse and in his presence or with his knowledge and that of his officers to plunder and pillage the inhabitants. . . . [T]hey . . . attempted an indecent outrage on [a] servant girl . . . destroyed a stock of . . . fine Bibles and Testaments, which were torn, defaced, and kicked about the floor and trampled underfoot. . . . A part of the brigade went to the plantation . . . and quartered in the negro huts for weeks, debauching the females. . . .

Mrs. Hollingsworth's house was entered and plundered. . . . The alarm and excitement occasioned a miscarriage and subsequently her death.

Several soldiers . . . committed rape on the person of a colored girl. . . .

The court finds the accused [guilty as charged] . . . and does therefore sentence . . . Colonel J.B. Turchin . . . to be dismissed from the service of the United States. . . .

It is a fact of sufficient notoriety that similar disorders . . . have marked the course of Colonel Turchin's command wherever it has gone.

U.S. War Department, *Official Records: War of the Rebellion*, series 1, vol. 16, 273, 274, 275, 277, http://ehistory.osu. edu/osu/sources/recordView.cfm?page=273&dir=023 (accessed May 2014).

Instead of dismissing Turchin from the service with a dishonorable discharge, the Lincoln administration, supported by a growing wave of public opinion that the war needed to be prosecuted more vigorously, promoted him to the rank of brigadier general, and he was welcomed back to Chicago for a hero's triumph. Before a packed house of overheated Republicans, Turchin was cheered as a man "who handled our enemies roughly." What follows is an excerpt from Turchin's brief address.

I have studied secession and secessionists in Missouri, Kentucky, Tennessee, and Alabama, and I tell you it is no use to fight against them unless we use every means in our power. They are too powerful to be fought otherwise.

Who are these guerillas? They are citizens who pretend to be peaceful, but who are plotting treason all the time. They are all the time looking out for a straggling Yankee. As soon as he finds one, he gets two neighbors, they take their shot guns, go out and catch him. They look out for pickets and shoot them. You know how they murdered Gen. McCook.[11] That is what I call a war of extermination. We must do the same, and until we use all men, slaves included, we cannot put them down. [Applause]

What I have done is not much; but what I could do, were I allowed, might amount to something. My friends I must close. We have been talking about the Union and hurrahing for the Union a great while. Let us now talk and hurrah for conquest. [Applause]

Chicago Tribune, August 20, 1862.

LETTERS FROM THE HOME FRONT

In 1861 Mary C. Hall settled in Joliet, Illinois, a suburb of Chicago. Hall was an unmarried woman originally from Vermont who worked as a housekeeper to an uncle, as well as for several boarders. These excerpts from her letters to an unnamed friend convey an unquestioned devotion to the Union cause and provide an intimate account of a woman on the home front—concerned about the fate of friends and family in the army and trying to balance her daily chores with the special demands of wartime.

Joliet, Ill. Jan. 30th 1863.

My dear Friend,

. . . Housekeeping brings its cares, and because I have a small family the people think I must have time for <u>every thing</u>, and festivals, S.A. [Soldier Aid]

Societies, donation visits, they come in, just as I think I am to have a quiet time for writing letters. . . .

Truly,
Mary C. Hall

~

Like other civilians, Hall eagerly listened to returning soldiers tell of their exploits on the battlefield and found comfort in her faith when war news was grim.

Joliet Sat Evening June 6th 1863.

My dear Friend

  . . . Several of our citizens and Doctors have gone down to Vicksburgh to care for our wounded. The first Reg. that went from here the 20th Ill numbers now 134 men. They have been in ten battles and have never retreated or been beaten. Two of the wounded . . . returned last night. They give thrilling accounts of the assaults upon the enemy's fortifications. They say that for three weeks all of Grant's baggage consisted in his riding whip. Judge Norton has just returned from there. He reports that Grant could take the city any day but it would be at immense sacrifice of life and he prefers the slow process. Our reverses at the Rappahannock sicken me. Has God forsaken us, or is He only trimming the lamp that it may burn more brightly? . . .

Mary C. Hall

~

Below, Mary expresses her anxiety and disbelief over the fate of her good friend and possible sweetheart George Rouse when word reached her that he was captured. She coped by immersing herself in dinner parties for wounded soldiers home from the 100th Illinois and hosting an event for seventy-nine guests.

Monday Morning Jan. 20th 1864

My dear Friend

  . . . Last Saturday I rec'd a note from Dr. Woodruff from Chattanooga saying that two weeks since, Mr. Rouse was ordered to Knoxville in command of the Convalescent Corps and the equipage, etc. belonging to the 100th (that having gone on a forced march) and when about fifty miles from Chattanooga the train was attacked by Guerillas and Mr. Rouse with others was captured, and nothing has been heard of them since. For some unaccountable reason

I do not believe that he was captured—though I cannot help feeling very anxious. There is no mail communication yet opened from Knoxville to Chattanooga, and the fact that I do not hear from is no surety that anything wrong has happened to him.

Five wounded soldiers belonging to the 100th were allowed furloughs to come home and spend the Holidays, and each family has vied the other in showing them kindness and attentions—and the result has been a succession of gayety [*sic*] unknown to Joliet by even the oldest inhabitants. Dinners and tea parties and six large other parties within three weeks was awful to endure. I could not escape my fate, and so one day sent out 89 invitations and the next evening 78 of the invited guests appeared. Of course I had much to do to prepare but I had splendid luck with everything. My Salads and Jellies were pronounced faultless. The table looked beautifully, every article on it was prepared by my hands and you can imagine the care I experienced until the last guest had departed. As soon as the storm was over and the trains made connections, the soldiers, also Dr. Woodruff departed and every thing has collapsed and we are in a state of quietus. It seems good to get to bed before morning and have a quiet day. It nearly made me sick, but now I feel as well as ever. . . . I am going to tell you about D. [illegible]. It all seems so queer in the retrospect to me that I suspect it will seem still stranger to you who do not know him. Very soon after he came from Richmond, we had a talk. I told him everything concerning the suspension of correspondence between Rouse and myself last summer, answered all his questions truthfully, in short, sat coolly in the rocking chair by the grate knitting work in hand, and turned myself inside out. The interview was a long one, and finally Henry said, "Molly, I would not give you up to anybody but George; he is my best friend and is worthy of you, and as neither of you have ever deceived me I keep firm my faith in you, and you may rely upon me as your best friend henceforth and forever." Afterward we went along, frankly and unembarrassed, and he was my escort to and from parties, when Uncle could not go, treating with the most respectful brotherly manner. . . .

Affectionately, Mary

~

Mary's friend George Rouse was not captured but joined General Sherman's march to Atlanta. Her letter expresses an eerie premonition that he might not survive the campaign, but she had invested so much of herself in support of the Union cause that she was prepared to accept what fate had in store for her. Her volunteer war work kept her busy and feeling useful.

Monday Morning May 16th 1864

My dear Friend,

. . . Mr. Rouse left Chattanooga with the Army of the Cumberland May
4th. He has been promoted to Division Gen: Staff as Inspector General of the
Division. His trunk came Saturday as Sherman has ordered that Officers shall
only carry a certain number of pounds, all extras are sent to the rear. The
rest of the officers stored their baggage in Nashville. I cannot see why Mr.
Rouse should send his way back here unless he had a strong presentiment that
he never should need it more. I am very anxious to hear of the result of the
skirmish at Dalton. They anticipate a dreadful battle at Atlanta and I can hardly
wait for the arrival of the morning papers. It seems to me that our successes
in La. will dishearten the Rebs in Georgia, so that they will not offer much
resistance to Sherman's Army. I have arrived at that state where I can pray for
victory to our Cause as if it must be won by the sacrifice of <u>my all</u>. It has been
a great struggle and now I feel comparatively calm and resigned to whatever
may at any moment come to me. We are working every day for the soldiers in
our Society and it's almost time for me to go. . . .

Yours Affectionately,
Mary

⁓

*Here Mary summarizes a longer account of Sherman's March to Atlanta with the
type of details eagerly devoured by one far removed from the battlefront.*

Monday Morning, Scott St. Joliet
May 30th 1864

My dear Friend,

. . . When I got home, I found a letter from Dr. Woodruff of twenty pages,
being a journal of the incidents of their march from Chattanooga to Resaca.
It was finished at Kingston, where they rested a day and washed—the first
opportunity for three weeks. The march has been tedious—the mountains so
slippery, that at one point they crawled ½ a mile upon their hands and knees,
leaving the horses to be taken around by men detailed for the purpose. They
started with an army of 140,000 with Atlanta as the goal of their march. I rec'd
two or three lines from Mr. Rouse dated "Buzzard's Roost". His duties are
very arduous. . . . He is in the 2nd Brig. (Wagner's) 2nd Div (Newton's) and 4th
Army Corps (Howards). Thomas is only Corps Commander while Sherman

has command of the whole. They have confidence in him, but expect an awful
contest at Atlanta. The expected to arrive there yesterday, and probably while
I am writing the battle is raging. May God give them victory. While Sherman
allows no paper correspondents with his army unless they carry a musket, he is
very desirous that the men under his command shall receive and send this mail.
Henry says when the subsistence train comes up and they halt for fresh rations,
then I ought to see the boys scamper for the mail. Those who stand by and don't
get a letter are the laggards in the next day's march. My next door neighbors have
lost a son recently in La. He was with Butler. He was a splendid young man and
only spoke once after he fell and only to say—dead! dead!

The Father is in Chattanooga employed by the government, and the mother
is alone with her grief. She seems resigned and for the sake of the cause to which
he was sacrificed, she seems almost glad that she had him to give.

Oh! The wailing ones over our land! That is the price of our victories. . . .

Yours Affectionately,

Mary C. Hall

~

*This letter provides a detailed account of how women supported the war effort and
makes clear the central role of Chicago's Sanitary Commission in directing and
gathering the resources supplied by women like Mary Hall.*

Aug. 1st 1864

My dear Friend,

. . . Your question in regard to what is most needed by the soldiers, I hardly know
what to say. Every week we receive orders from Chicago. Sometimes it is shirts that
they want. Again drawers towels and napkins. After the battle of Kennesaw—It
was shirts—open on the shoulder and side, and drawers. Last week it was fruit and
vegetables. We are sewing all the time, on shirts, towels, napkins sheets & drawers.
And if anything in particular is needed we drop them and take that up. We have dried
and canned currants, made wine, canned pie plant, gooseberries and small fruit. That
they must have. Last Friday I canned myself a bushel of currants, putting a pound of
sugar to five of currants. The Chicago Sanitary provide us with the cans. I rec'd a note
from Dr. Woodruff yesterday, in which he says "Molly save everything in the shape
of pickles, onions, cucumbers, cabbage, for the army must have them." In April we
pickled 4 barrels of sliced and pared potatoes, putting spices horseradish and a few
onions between each layer—scalded the vinegar and poured over it. That was sent to
the Reg. by express, the cost of transportation being alone sixty dollars. They reported
it as being excellent. It was the only thing in shape of pickles that we could get at that

time and they were suffering while at Athens for it. My impression is that nothing comes amiss. Though dried fruit are better than canned because they are easier transported, and now that the armies are so far away this is a great item—Hospital clothing they must have. We had a Strawberry festival, (which nearly killed me) the net profit of which was $300.00. This has been paid nearly all to poor soldier's families, of which many are in our midst, which without our help must suffer for food. The army has not been paid for four months—and Sat.—a child came begging at the door, and I asked her where she lived and it was only the next street—she said her mother was sick and had not any thing to eat. I put on my hat took an umbrella and followed the little thing to learn the truth of her statement. I found a respectable looking woman, sick in bed, three children and not one crumb of anything in the house. She was too proud to beg, her husband in the army, and she had borne it until starvation was before her. I supplied their present needs—sent Dr. Mc___ to her, and reported her case to the Pres. of the Aid Society, who will supply her with all necessaries.

We continue all ways to raise money—a pic-nic is on the lake now—we hire the cars, and then have the profits of the excursion. . . .

Since writing the above the [illegible] boy had brought me a letter from Mr. Rouse—two miles from Atlanta. He says they are tired and sluggish and impatient for the capture of Atlanta, for then they expect to have a few days rest. His brother only 17 years old is a prisoner in Libby was captured in La.

It is the most desponding letter I have ever rec'd from him. He thinks he will have an opportunity of serving his full time of enlistment, and another term before the close of the war, "but as I firmly believe that I am working in the noblest cause that mortal ever died for I do not shrink from the consequences. You do not know how often I wish you were near me, where I could talk to you, so many things I want to say that I cannot find time to put upon paper. With you, I feel the need of sustaining grace, but I am not unhappy. I feel cheerful, and really enjoy my day."

~

In the below letter Mary received the news that she had dreaded regarding her friend George Rouse. She took comfort that his last words were of her.

Joliet, Illinois Aug. 18th 1864

My dear Friend,

My letter of Aug. 6th addressed to you had hardly left my hands when a telegram came giving the intelligence that my dearest friend had passed away. He never rallied after the amputation, but gradually grew weaker and weaker and

fell asleep on the night of the fifth day. His sufferings were very great until the
last day when he was able for the first time to retain any nourishment. He was
conscious to the last moment. His good friend Deacon Williams was with him
and two hours before he died, he said to him, "George you are going fast—you
cannot live longer than morning." He answered "do you really think so Dea?"
then added "I am ready—God has been very merciful to spare me so long and
I trust for Christ's sake he will save me at last"—he then asked Lt. Williams to
unite with him in prayer, he did so, afterward he sunk fast—a few moments
before he died, he roused up and said "I want to speak to you of Mary. She has
been a very very dear friend, so kind, so good, so noble, may God bless her"—
These were his last words upon earth, and are to me of untold comfort.

I cannot speak to you of my grief. It is overwhelming and sometimes I think
we shall not be long separated.

I do not want to throw away my life and I trust that the Holy Comforter will
give me strength to enable me to take up the burden of life where George laid
it down, and walk on alone, helpful and trustful, cheerful to do the daily duties
imposed upon me, and looking forward to a "new country ever a heavenly
[country]." The consciousness that he was a Christian has made me bear the
awful suspense of the last few months and now, I think of him as at rest, no
more weary marches, the goal reached, the victory sure.

If he must die away from home there is much to comfort in his death. No
aggravating circumstance attending it. Col. Buell kindly relieved Lt. Williams
from other duty and he and Henry were with him constantly—until the last day
a demonstration was made in the line of battle so that Henry was away when he
died. . . .

I have written incoherently but you will pardon—write me often, and never
give up praying for the noble soldiers.

Affectionately,

Mary

~

*Here Mary relates her continued war work as victory was near at hand. She was
especially jubilant at the Sanitary Commission's new method of collecting funds
through subscriptions rather than "begging."*

Joliet, Illinois March 4th 1865

My dear Friend,

With an inexpressible feeling of relief do I appear to you this afternoon,
for I have just taken the last stitch in a piece of worsted work designed for the

[Northwest Sanitary] Fair. It is an Ottoman-cover worked in double stitch on canvass—Persian pattern, in imitation of the elegant Persian carpets and I think very handsome. I commenced it with the New Year and have given to it six weeks of steady close work, using nine ounces of worsted. . . .

I have given up going East this Summer. I had hoped to accompany you on one begging expedition for the Sanitary over your town, for by your letters I judge the majority are not in favor of its operations.

For the last eighteen months I have called upon one of my wealthy neighbors soliciting his name to the monthly subscription paper. Until last month, I have not received a cent from him, <u>then</u> he handed me ten dollars and said with a choked voice, "When you want more come to me." . . .

This year I am collector, and every month I call upon the subscribers and when they see me and the book, they know what is wanted and it is much pleasanter than the old way of <u>begging</u>. Sometimes I find a man who "is sick of the war" and "the soldiers don't get nothing" "the surgeons eat it all up." etc. I punish him by giving his name a peculiar scratch, and letting him alone. I write this that you may try it, if you are troubled to raise funds. I do not think you ought to feel that you are doing nothing in these times—if you do all you can in the place God has put you, is it not enough?

Mary C. Hall Letters, Chicago History Museum.

FOUR

Confined Confederates

Camp Douglas and Chicago

$\mathcal{M}$ORE CONFEDERATE SOLDIERS are buried in Chicago than on any Civil War battlefield. More rebels died in the Lake Michigan city than at Antietam, where the war saw its bloodiest single day, and nearly as many as were killed in the three days of desperate fighting at Gettysburg. In one of the largest mass graves in North America, more than four thousand prisoners of war are buried on the South Side of Chicago. Today manicured grass grows over the mound into which their remains were heaped and a bronze statue atop a marble column adds dignity to the site, but Beaux-Arts memorials cannot obscure the tragic fact that those men died away from the guns in a rich and prosperous city under the "care" of their fellow countrymen. The Camp Douglas prisoner of war camp is one of the best examples of how after a year of frustration, the war to preserve the Union became a hard, ugly conflict. It is also an illustration of the bond between the home front and the battlefield. When Chicago soldiers wrote of making the rebel civilians feel the sting of war, Northern civilians became hardened to the sufferings of rebel prisoners.[1]

Chicago was no more prepared to be a major holding center for prisoners of war than it had been to be a recruiting center for federal troops. In February 1862, when rumors circulated that many of the twelve thousand rebels captured by Grant at Fort Donelson would be coming to Chicago, newspapers scoffed at the idea as "absurd." After all, there were no facilities for housing and guarding prisoners in Chicago, save for the already well-stocked city jail. What journalists failed to realize, however, was that nowhere in the United States was prepared to handle the massive number of men Grant had captured during his Tennessee campaign. Federal officials reasoned that Chicago, located at the terminus of a rail line that reached nearly to the seat of war, was more suited than most places to improvise a temporary prison.[2]

"Temporary" was the key word in federal thinking about Camp Douglas. Initially a couple of months was thought to be the likely time necessary to hold the rebels. Early in the war, captured soldiers were either quickly paroled, as in the case of Chicago's Irish Brigade taken after the siege of Lexington, or exchanged based on informal agreements between local commanders. Therefore, the first prisoners to arrive in Chicago were moved into barracks and stables built on a sandy lakefront lot south of the city. The facilities there had been hastily knocked together on land that had belonged to the late Stephen Douglas to temporarily house Union recruits who were being mustered into federal service. Hence the makeshift facility was named Camp Douglas. The site was not favorable either from a sanitary point of view or with an eye for winter quarters. It was poorly drained and subject to icy blasts off of the lake. Considerable investment would have been necessary to remedy both defects, but any thought of this was dismissed because officials thought both training camps and prisoner of war facilities would be needed for only a short time. Most of the nearly 40,000 Union recruits who passed through the camp of instruction stayed only a few weeks: nonetheless, 42 died of disease. Conditions would become much worse when 4,400 Confederates were forced to stay in the camp for several months.[3]

Ironically, among the first Union troops to serve as guards at Camp Douglas were the men of the Irish Brigade. James A. Mulligan, their colonel, served as commandant of the prisoner of war camp from February to June 1862. Having himself been a prisoner of the rebels, Mulligan tried to improve the camp's drainage, sanitation, and barracks, only to be repeatedly stymied by higher authorities, particularly Lieutenant Colonel William Hoffman, who headed the Commissary General of Prisoners. Conditions at the camp deteriorated markedly in April, when the prison population doubled with rebels taken at Shiloh and Island No. 10. Many prisoners suffered from dysentery, and several hundred eventually died. Throughout this time, the Union army offered immediate release to rebels who would swear allegiance to the United States and join federal forces. The Irish Brigade was particularly successful at getting Southern immigrants from the Emerald Isle to join their ranks. For many of these "galvanized" Yankees, exchanging gray for blue seemed the best way to get out of Camp Douglas alive.[4]

By August 1862, most of the rebel prisoners left alive were freed from Camp Douglas through a formal prisoner exchange between the contending armies. The wretched camp was empty for only a few weeks, however, before it received a new shipment of inmates. Because of one of the quirks of the prisoner exchange program, these men were Union soldiers captured at Harpers Ferry by General Thomas "Stonewall" Jackson during the Antietam campaign. Jackson released the men on their "honor" that they would not participate in the war until they were officially notified that they had been exchanged. Nearly nine thousand of these dispirited men were then sent by the government to Camp Douglas, where they were expected to wallow in the same mud, filth, and germs that had exacted a heavy toll on the rebel prisoners. The men resented being confined in the camp and reacted by tearing down fences and burning several of the leaky barracks. Eventually a regiment of Illinois troops had to be assigned the duty of guarding them.[5]

The Union men were finally liberated from the limbo of parole in December and January. They cleared out just in time for more Confederates to be confined in the camp after the Battle of Stones River. These men captured on winter battlefields and unprepared for a Northern climate suffered grievously. The situation grew worse when smallpox broke out among them, and within three weeks 260 men had died and another 400 were hospitalized. "At this rate," a Union officer complained, "we shall have our responsibilities all underground before the last of spring." Every day a wagon left the camp with a cargo of pine coffins. For $1.50 per body, an undertaker was paid to take the unfortunates to the city cemetery for internment. Ironically, the place they were buried is today known as Lincoln Park. After the war, the city discovered that the undertaker had carelessly carried out his duties, and the shallow graves became a health hazard. The bodies had to be disinterred and taken to a new cemetery, where they rest today in a mass grave.[6]

The most troublesome prisoners to ever be held at Camp Douglas were the Kentucky horsemen of General John Hunt Morgan. Twenty-five hundred of them were captured in July 1863 after a daring raid across southern Indiana and Ohio. These troops were experienced with unconventional warfare and were determined to break out of confinement. They climbed over fences with makeshift ladders, they crawled through sewage pipes, they bribed guards, and they dug innumerable tunnels. If they were caught, they were sent to a special dark dungeon, and there too they dug a tunnel and effected an escape. Their ingenuity prompted tighter security measures and increasingly harsh disciplinary measures. These measures included rigorous enforcement of the camp "deadline," cruel physical punishments for petty offenses, and daily roll call assemblies held outdoors in all weather. In postwar memoirs, former prisoners complained bitterly over these harassments. In addition, the camp's sanitation system was gradually improved, and the barracks were elevated in order to reveal escape tunnels.[7]

More than the hijinks of Morgan's Raiders were behind the growing severity of camp administration. The "hard war" measures that Union troops were inflicting on rebel property in the South were mirrored at Northern prison camps. The conflict coarsened social values as it wore on, and the deaths of thousands of Northern boys helped form a callus over prewar moral scruples. Widely reported abuse of Union captives in the South resulted in formal calls to retaliate against Confederate soldiers in Northern camps. Whereas early in the war Chicagoans had held rallies to aid the rebel prisoners and brought them clothing and Bibles, in 1864 the Chicago Board of Trade actually petitioned President Lincoln to cut Camp Douglas rations: "We are aware our petition savors of cruelty," they wrote, but the time had come for "retaliatory measures." Confined Confederates also suffered more because their stay in Camp Douglas lasted longer. In April 1864, the prisoner exchange system completely broke down over the rebels' refusal to treat former slaves serving in the Union army as military personnel. The POWs then faced the prospect of staying in the camp for the duration of the war.[8]

The dreary months passed slowly for the prisoners. In summer, they played baseball, horseshoes, or marbles outside. Card games were a staple throughout the year. Although Bibles were abundant, only a handful of other books circulated in the camp. A couple of literary inmates edited for a time an unofficial newspaper, *Prisoner Vidette*, a handwritten series of brief articles that were passed around camp from prisoner to prisoner. The first issue, for example, announced a concert by "Morgan's Nightingales," a glee club. Many prisoners had pocketknives, and they put these to good use carving pipes, which for a time found a market among city residents. Others whittled musical instruments from bones or boards, including a fiddle, a clarinet, and a fife. Nonetheless, prisoners had a strong desire to be away from the camp, "free and in the field." As individual escape became more difficult, the most determined prisoners formed a secret society, which eventually claimed over a thousand members, who were pledged to coordinating a mass escape. Hopes for this desperate measure ran high when they were actually able to open communication with Confederate secret agents in Chicago and acquire a small cache of arms. In the end, however, these hopes were also frustrated, and freedom came only after Appomattox.[9]

Camp Douglas was an awful example of the blunt brutality of Civil War America. The tragic death toll among the prisoners led to the camp being condemned as "eighty acres of hell" and "the deadliest prison in American history" and frequently being referred to as the Northern Andersonville.[10] The best available estimate would put the camp death toll in three and a half years of operation at 4,454 or 17 percent of the total number of men incarcerated in the camp. Such a grim total, however, pales when compared to what occurred in Andersonville, Georgia, where in little more than a year and half 13,000 Union soldiers died. At Andersonville and also Virginia's Belle Isle, prisoners were not even given barracks but were forced to live in tents and earth dugouts. Prisoners did suffer badly in Chicago, and some of the suffering was intentional. A large percentage of the camp deaths, however, resulted from exposure to unfamiliar Northern, urban conditions. A full 20.5 percent of the Camp Douglas death toll was from smallpox, a disease fought with vaccinations in the North but much less so in the South. Dysentery and typhoid among prisoners were exacerbated by Chicago's fouled drinking water supply, which was both notorious and injurious to its native population. It may seem strange that thousands of prisoners died adjacent to one of the most prosperous cities in the United States; in fact, that very proximity helped make the camp so deadly.[11]

"AN ABSURD RUMOR"

When the Union army made plans to send rebel prisoners of war captured by
General Grant's army at Fort Donelson to Chicago, the city's reaction was one of
disbelief. The Tribune *made it clear that Chicago was completely unprepared to*
handle this war duty.

An Absurd Rumor—The rumor was prevalent upon the streets yesterday that orders
had been received to put Camp Douglas in readiness for the accommodation of
five thousand rebel prisoners. This is decidedly *the* joke of the season. The idea
of keeping five thousand prisoners in a camp, where the strongest guard couldn't
keep in a drunken corporal, is rich. The whole population would have to mount
guard and Chicago would find herself in possession of an elephant of the largest
description. If the authorities will give Chicago permission to hang the whole
batch as soon as they arrive, let them come.

Chicago Tribune, February 14, 1862.

REBELS ARRIVE IN CHICAGO

Within days of the shock of hearing Chicago would host rebel POWs, plans were
issued that Union troops housed at Camp Douglas were to vacate the training camp
to make room for the captured Confederates. Chicago's excellent rail and water
routes brought rebel prisoners of war to the city by late February 1862. Chicagoans
flocked to the camp to get a view of the "enemy"; many flattered themselves that
some of the rebels appeared willing to defect to the North.

The Confederate Prisoners.
Arrival in the City.
Incidents of the Route, &c., &c. . . . .
On the Road.

The Southern soldiers arriving here on Thursday night came by two routes,
a portion over the Illinois Central road from Cairo, and the remainder by river
to St. Louis, and thence to Chicago by the St. Louis, Alton & Chicago road.
They left Fort Donelson on Sunday night by boat. When first taken in charge
by detachments of the Fifty-second Illinois regiment, Col. Sweeney,—specially
detailed for escort duty—some among the furious made a show of resistance,
having the impression that our forces wanted to impose upon them, but when
informed that they were to be well treated, they changed their course and became quite fraternal. . . .

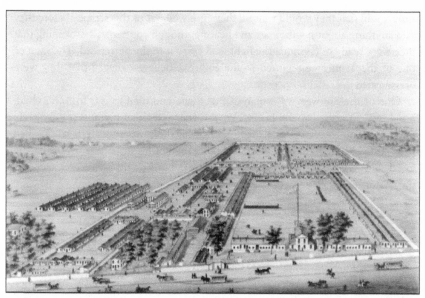

FIGURE 12. Camp Douglas. From *Harper's Weekly*, April 5, 1860.

... Everything passed quietly with the prisoners along the entire route from St. Louis to Chicago, and at only one point were they insulted or abused. This was at a station where they met a detachment of Eastern cavalry, a number of whom being intoxicated, assailed the train with bricks and stones, breaking the car windows and injuring their inmates. They also chased the cars for some distance after they had started, seemingly determined to wreak their vengeance upon the helpless prisoners. The names of the regiment should be published, and the perpetrators of the act punished as they so richly deserve.

The Arrival in Chicago.

This train arrived in the city on Thursday night, and the prisoners were at once taken in charge by a detachment of police and their original escort, and marched to Camp Douglas, where temporary quarters had been assigned them. Camp Douglas was at an early hour besieged by thousands of citizens, anxious to obtain a sight of secessionists. ...

Incidents, &c., &c.

... The Tennessee men whom we met invariably said that they had had enough of fighting, and if they could be liberated would at once settle down to a quiet life. Many expressed a wish to settle in Illinois. The Mississippians, when interrogated, simply said that they would wait till they "got well out of this scrape" before they said anything about it—their air and bearing, though courteous, betokening that they were ready to continue the fight, and carry it to the better end. The men of one of the Tennessee regiments—the 49th, we believe—alleged that they were pressed into the rebel service. . . .

One of the captives, a German of fine form, and used to war from his childhood, sought out a captain in Col. Voss' Cavalry Regiment almost immediately upon entering the camp, and made known his desire to enlist. He said he had been compelled to fight with Floyd and other men of his stripe, against the flag he loved, and now he wanted to make amends by fighting on his own account against the traitors and their serpent colors.

Chicago Tribune, February 22, 1862.

~

By early March, it was apparent to Chicagoans that Camp Douglas was ill-equipped to handle the large number of prisoners it was charged to care for, as poor sanitation led to sickness among the men.

SANITARY CONDITION OF CAMP DOUGLAS

The sickness and mortality among the prisoners at the camp is increasing rather than diminishing, notwithstanding the efforts of the surgeons to prevent it. A large barn in the camp has been comfortably fitted up, and yet there is not hospital room enough. There are now about three hundred and twenty-five prisoners in the hospitals, beside a large number in their quarters. Fifty new cots and bedding to correspond were added to the hospital stores yesterday. Quite a number of sick are discharged each day, but this is more than made up by the new patients.

Chicago Tribune, March 5, 1862.

THE LIMBO OF PAROLE: NEW YORK AND
VERMONT TROOPS ENDURE A SEASON IN CAMP DOUGLAS

The first group of Confederate prisoners vacated Camp Douglas when they were exchanged for Union prisoners. In the fall of 1862, Union troops captured by Stonewall Jackson at Harpers Ferry were sent to Camp Douglas for their paroles to be finalized. According to the terms of their parole, they could not serve any military function until they were formally exchanged. Therefore, they were held at Camp Douglas as virtual prisoners of their own army. The squalid conditions of the camp led these indignant Union troops to mutiny against their delayed liberation.

Chicago was reached at 9 o'clock in the evening. It was very dark, and the men were about worn out. As soon as the train stopped, the conductor ordered every man to leave the cars immediately. As we were strangers in that part of the world, the majority of us concluded to camp in a field close by until morning. In an hour or two it began to rain, and by midnight it poured down in torrents. We were drenched to the skin, and upon consultation, we resolved to separate into squads and go in search of shelter. Seven of us started off together, but made wretched slow progress through the mud and thick darkness.

At last, we saw a light flickering from the window of a small shanty, and we made for it. The stoop of the shanty was reached, and one of the party knocked loudly at the door; and in a moment a bolt was pulled back, the door opened, and Bridget stood before us, while Pat lay drunk upon the floor. The following amusing conversation then took place, while we were soaking in the rain.

Soldier. "Mrs., can we stay in your barn overnight? We are wet to the skin."

Bridget. "Och! yes, of course ye can, and may the Lord have mercy on yee s."

Husband. "H-o-o-l-d your tongue, Biddy. By the powers of Saint Patrick, I'll kill every mother's son of yee's if ye dont be after gettin out o this, ye murderin spalpeens."

Bridget. "Be aisey my darlint, the boys must have some shelter. Soldiers go in the barn and lie until mornin, an meself I'l take care o Pat."

Husband. "Bad luck to yee s."

Soldier. "Good night, Ma m. We re much obliged to you for your kindness, but that old reprobate on the floor there needs tanning."

The party went into the barn, but as it leaked badly, and there was no floor in it, we shivered until morning, and did not close our eyes in sleep. In the morning all hands wrung out their wet clothes, and warmed themselves by Biddy s fire. We gave her postage stamps (common currency then) for milk and bread, and then left, thanking the good old lady for her kindness.

Almost all of the regiments were quartered in Camp Douglas. But the 115th, 39th 1st. N.Y. (Garibaldi Guards), and the 9th Vermont, occupied horse stalls, in the Illinois state fair-grounds. From four to sixteen men were placed in each stall. The camp was named "Tyler," in honor of our Brigadier, but it ought to have been named "starvation," in honor of Chicago rations.

Owing to the damp quarters, poor rations, and little care, almost all of the regiment were more or less sick by the first of November, and large numbers soon died. The hospitals were crowded to overflowing; and none of the poor sick soldiers were carried from the wretched horse stalls, until death was close at hand. Each company had from twenty to forty sick with the fever. The dead house was always full, and the dead cart constantly moving. Six weeks saw at least forty of the regiment placed beneath the sod.

By the 20th of November everything began to look hard at Camp Douglas. The troops were badly treated, and half starved. Rations were furnished by contract, at 10 cents per day.

The bacon was alive with maggots, the bread hard, sour, and black, and the sugar the color of Sand.

At last, almost all of the men refused to do guard duty, or take a gun in their hands; and those who were better disposed were overawed by the majority. At one time, the 115th regiment alone, did not refuse to take guns; and during all the trouble and excitement, they remained firm for the right. Although threatened by the other troops, they never refused to do duty, and even assisted in putting down mutiny in the other regiments. A heavy detachment that undertook to preserve the peace and perform guard duty at Camp Douglas, were pelted with clubs, brickbats, and stones, but held their ground until ordered away. Scenes of riot and arson were of frequent occurrence, and a regiment's barracks were burned up nearly every night.

The soldiers blocked up the road with lumber, so that the steam fire engines from the city could not reach the flames. All this took place at Camp Douglas, half a mile from the stalls occupied by the 115th. The "N. Y. refused to take guns, declaring that their paroles would not allow it. But the General commanding thought differently, and determined to bring the mutiny to a speedy close. For that purpose, the 115th were ordered to prepare to form line. . . . The General addressed them in the meantime, telling them that unless they submitted, he would have the last man of them shot, and place all of the officers in irons. The men concluded to accept the terms; so they declared themselves ready to take guns.

Soldiers from the regular army were finally sent to Camp Douglas to do guard duty, and they received orders to shoot any man who attempted to cross any of the beats without a proper pass. Some of the soldiers did attempt to pass, contrary to orders, and one or two of them were shot. This incensed the soldiers so much, that they threw stones and clubs at the Regulars, and hooted at each one showing himself. Things went on from bad to worse until November 20th, when orders came for the Harpers Ferry troops to report at Washington.

We bade good bye to Chicago with few regrets. Farewell "paradise of mud," "City of stairs, rats, and lager beer saloons." Good bye shivering fevers, wretched horse stalls, and rotten bacon, Farewell !

To a few kind and noble-hearted young ladies of Chicago, we all owe thanks while we live, and may heaven bless them, is our prayer.

James H. Clark, *The Iron-Hearted Regiment: An Account of the 115th New York* (1865), 36–41.

ESCAPE FROM CAMP DOUGLAS

Escape from Camp Douglas was possible through bribery. Below is an account of one of General Morgan's Kentucky cavalry men who successfully paid an enterprising Union guard for his clandestine release.

RUNNING THE BLOCKADE.
BY GEN. BENNETT H. YOUNG, LOUISVILLE, KY.

On the 26th of July, 1863, while riding with Gen. John H. Morgan on the Ohio raid, I was made a prisoner of war. The long march of one thousand miles from Burkesville, Ky., to Salineville, Ohio, running through twenty-six days, had been a tremendous strain on the physical endurance of General Morgan's troops. When captured I was first carried to the Ohio penitentiary and left there a short while, then sent to Camp Chase and thence to Camp Douglas, Chicago, Ill., whence I escaped in January, 1864. . . .

The Federal sentinel whom I had bribed by paying a hundred dollars to allow me to climb the fence at Camp Douglas had also been induced by the money of other Kentucky boys to grant them the same privilege. Cash was plentiful with Morgan's men. They had postal communications with outside friends, and this accommodating "bluecoat" had driven a thriving business in trading with those restive raiders. It was said about the prison at that time that he had made about eight thousand dollars while engaged in the brokerage escape business. As the evidence of his trade began to accumulate, and as he really had enough to take care of him, certainly during the war, he wisely concluded to emigrate to Canada, where he could meet the Kentucky gentlemen whom he had obliged by permitting them to scale the walls of Camp Douglas.

General Bennett H. Young, "Running the Blockade," *Confederate Veteran* 24 (September 1916): 392.

~

Those who could not bribe their way out of Camp Douglas dug tunnels. A few prisoners managed to elude the camp authorities, but before more could follow them, their burrowings were discovered.

ESCAPE OF REBELS FROM CAMP DOUGLAS

On the night of the 22nd inst. twelve rebel prisoners made their escape from White Oak prison in Camp Douglas, and have not yet been re-taken. They were confined in the second story of the prison, in the next room to a guard, and made use of the same holes in the floor above and below that the rebels escaped through during Col. DeLand's stay at the Camp. Their manner of concealing their work was most ingenious. While part of them were at work filing off nail-heads so that the floor might be raised, the others sang loudly, rattled chains, and otherwise engaged the attention of the guard, in such a manner that not the slightest suspicion of their proceedings ever entered the minds of those over them. Reaching the ground they burrowed their way in a zig-zag direction under the fence, depositing

FIGURE 13. Rebel prisoners at Camp Douglas. Prison barracks in the background. Courtesy of the Chicago History Museum.

the dirt in an old sink, of the existence of which Col. Strong was ignorant. They commenced to prepare for their escape nearly six weeks ago. At the time of their leaving twenty-five of the rebs were in the prison, and why only twelve chose to escape is a mystery.

The day before the escape of these prisoners, two rebels were discovered digging a tunnel under the new barracks just erected in the southeast portion of the grounds. Of course they were put into the prison. A lucky change it was for them, as they were among the missing the next morning.

Chicago Tribune, March 25, 1864.

GALVANIZED YANKEES

By the fall of 1863, the Chicago Tribune was still claiming that Camp Douglas was a model prison camp and Colonel Charles V. Deland was an exemplary commandant. Hope still ran high that many POWs could be rehabilitated into Union men.

THE CITY.
MATTERS AT CAMP DOUGLAS.

During the past few days, Col. DeLand, Post Commandant, has been quite briskly engaged in manufacturing Union citizens out of rebel sympathizers, under

Gen. Burnside's Order No. 141, published a few days ago. Under this order, the persons named below have taken the oath and been permitted to have interviews with their relatives imprisoned in Camp Douglas. . . . When we remember in every case the interview is required to be held in the presence of the Colonel commanding, the annoyance would seem almost insufferable, yet he seems to endure it with commendable fortitude, and mingles current business with the tears of mothers, wives and sisters. . . . Col. DeLand invariably leaves a good impression on the minds of the visitors generally, for while he is firm and unyielding in the performance of his duty, he is humane, and gives evidence of a kind heart and obliging disposition—the statement of the Copperhead organ to the contrary, notwithstanding. He serves all in turn, and uses no favoritism. The same rules apply in the prison discipline, which loses a large share of its rigidity by being tempered with an evident interest in the health and comfort of his charge. Whatever ignorant, vicious, and disappointed disloyal parties may say, to the contrary, Camp Douglas is a model prison, and Col. DeLand has proven himself competent to the task of keeping it so. . . .

Doubtless there are many who take the oath in good faith, and have no hesitancy in doing so, while others . . . wear it as lightly as a garment, and consider themselves divested thereof, upon leaving the camp, if their overheard after communications to the friends are indicative of their true sentiments. There are a few who persistently hold out, and utterly decline to take the oath, but are anxious to communicate with their friends inside, independent of the constituted military rules and regulations. Attempts are made daily, in one way or another, to send letters, knives, pistols, clothing, &c., direct to the prisoners.

Chicago Tribune, September 22, 1863.

~

Rebel prisoners of war continued to escape imprisonment by joining Union forces.

"REBELS FOR THE NAVY"

Five hundred rebel prisoners, forming a portion of those taken by Sherman's army, arrived at Camp Douglas on Saturday night on their way to Boston and Portland, where they enter the United States Navy, for which service they have been recruited by Acting Master Harty. These men complete a total of 1,600 rebels enlisted by Capt. Harty for the navy since January last.

Chicago Tribune, June 13, 1864.

~

Years after the war, Sir Henry Morton Stanley, the famous correspondent who much later found David Livingston in Africa, recounted his time spent in Camp Douglas as a POW. Here he describes the fetid conditions and human misery in the camp. After several weeks in Camp Douglas, Stanley became one of the "Galvanized Yankees" and joined the Union army to get out of the camp.

Our prison-pen was a square and spacious enclosure, like a bleak cattle-yard, walled high with planking, on the top of which, at every sixty yards or so, were sentry-boxes. About fifty feet from its base, and running parallel with it, was a line of lime-wash. That was the 'deadline,' and any prisoner who crossed it was liable to be shot.

One end of the enclosure contained the offices of the authorities. Colonel James A. Milligan [*sic*], one of the Irish Brigade (killed at Winchester, July 24th, 1864) commanded the camp. Mr. Shipman, a citizen of Chicago, acted as chief commissary. At the other end, at quite three hundred yards distance, were the buildings allotted to the prisoners, huge, barn-like structures of planking, each about two hundred and fifty feet by forty, and capable of accommodating between two hundred and three hundred men. There may have been about twenty of these structures, about thirty feet apart, and standing in two rows; and I estimated that there were enough prisoners within it to have formed a strong brigade—say about three thousand men—when we arrived. I remember, by the regimental badges which they wore on their caps and hats, that they belonged to the three arms of the service, and that almost every Southern State was represented. They were clad in home-made butternut and grey.

To whatever it was due, the appearance of the prisoners startled me. The Southerners' uniforms were never pretty, but when rotten, and ragged, and swarming with vermin, they heightened the disreputability of their wearers; and, if anything was needed to increase our dejection after taking sweeping glances at the arid mud-soil of the great yard, the butternut and grey clothes, the sight of ash-colored faces, and of the sickly and emaciated condition of our unhappy friends, were well calculated to do so.

We were led to one of the great wooden barns, where we found a six-foot wide platform on each side, raised about four feet above the flooring. These platforms formed continuous bunks for about sixty men, allowing thirty inches to each man. On the floor, two more rows of men could be accommodated. Several bales of hay were brought, out of which we helped ourselves for bedding. Blankets were also distributed, one to each man. . . .

Mr. Shipman soon after visited us, and, after inspection, suggested that we should form ourselves into companies, and elect officers for drawing rations and superintending of quarters. I was elected captain of the right-hand platform and berths below it. Blank books were served out to each captain, and I took the names of my company, which numbered over one hundred. By showing my book at the commissariat, and bringing a detail with me, rations of soft bread, fresh beef, coffee, tea, potatoes, and salt, were handed to me by the gross, which I had afterwards to distribute to the chiefs of messes. . . .

Within a week, our new draft commenced to succumb under the maleficent influences of our surroundings. Our buildings swarmed with vermin, the dust-sweepings were alive with them. The men began to suffer from bilious disorders; dysentery and typhus began to rage. Day after day my company steadily diminished; and every morning I had to see them carried in their blankets to the hospital, whence none ever returned. . . .

The latrines were all at the rear of our plank barracks, and each time imperious nature compelled us to resort to them, we lost a little of that respect and consideration we owed our fellow-creatures. For on the way thither, we saw crowds of sick men, who had fallen, prostrate from weakness, and given themselves wholly to despair; and, while they crawled or wallowed in their filth, they cursed and blasphemed as often as they groaned. In the edge of the gaping ditches, which provoked the gorge to look at, there were many of the sick people, who, unable to leave, rested there for hours, and made their condition hopeless by breathing the stenchful atmosphere. Exhumed corpses could not have presented anything more hideous than dozens of these dead-and-alive men, who, oblivious to the weather, hung over the latrines, or lay extended along the open sewer, with only a few gasps intervening between them and death. Such as were not too far gone prayed for death, saying, 'Good God, let me die! Let me go, O Lord!' and one insanely damned his vitals and his constitution, because his agonies were so protracted. No self-respecting being could return from their vicinity without feeling bewildered by the infinite suffering, his existence degraded, and religion and sentiment blasted.

Yet, indoors, what did we see? Over two hundred unwashed, unkempt, uncombed men, in the dismalest [*sic*] attitudes, occupied in relieving themselves from hosts of vermin, or sunk in gloomy introspection, staring blankly, with heads between their knees, at nothing; weighed down by a surfeit of misery, internal pains furrowing their faces, breathing in a fine cloud of human scurf, and dust of offensive hay, dead to everything but the flitting fancies of the hopeless!

Henry M. Stanley, "Prisoner of War," in *The Autobiography of Sir Henry Morton Stanley* (Boston: Riverside Press, 1909), 210–12.

THE MISERY OF CAMP DOUGLAS

The best account of the prisoner experience at Camp Douglas came from the pen of William D. Huff, a rebel private in the Thirteenth Louisiana Infantry who was captured during the Battle of Chickamauga and after fourteen days arrived at

Camp Douglas. Huff kept a diary of his time in the camp. He illustrated the diary
with clever sketches of life in confinement. Selected entries from the diary follow.

Oct. 4ᵗʰ, 1863

Arrived at Camp Douglas. The day was very cold and we were kept standing in the
open square for about 4 hours. Had had nothing to eat for 2 days. Were put in barrax.
They are long low buildings partitioned off into rooms with a stove in each and are as
comfortable as could be expected for a prison. In the rear of each barrax is a building
intended for a kitchen but there was so many prisoners when we arrived the most of
the kitchens had to be used for barrax. Camp Douglas contains 30 or 40 acres, is level
and sandy, about 2 miles from Chicago and ½ mile from the lake. It has barrax on
every side leaving the center cut by a double row of barrax in squares. Wood is scarce
and supplied every day by carts. Water is supplied by hydrants of which there are
scarcely enough. Often a Yank comes and makes the Rebs wait until he has drawn his
water and then we can get ours. We are guarded by the Michigan Sharp Shooters and
sharp shooters they are too, for they practice often on some of us and shoot in the
barrax if lights are not out punctually at 9 o'clock. No intercourse is allowed between
the guards and the guarded. . . . An old fellow comes around every two or 3 days with
a wagon and gives a small quantity of tobacco for the offal and old meat boans.

Oct. 24

Snow in pure fle[e]cy heralds come the silent and cold messengers of king winter
announcing to us his freezing majesties intention to remain untill spring. . . .
While in Dixie the golden sunshine of Indian summer is guilding the hills and
the soft breeze is filled with the odor of new mown hay, we are chilly and shivering beneath Jack Frost's icy breath. . . .

Nov. 11

The barrax occupied by the Yankees caught fire today and a large portion of
them were destroyed. We were all ordered to our quarters. The fire created quite
an excitement among both Federals and Prisoners. The Evening paper contained
the following report of the fire: "Camp Douglas is on fire and the prisoners
escaping." No such good luck happened. One of the features of Camp Douglas
is the brokers who deal in almost everything. They buy and sell Confed money,
green back and sutler tickets and the sutler store is crowded from morning till
night. Gambling of every description is carried to perfection here. . . .

Jany. 1st, 1864

Every Confederate prisoner will remember this day. I'm going to head Qrs. to
report I had my nose, years and chin frozen this morning. Frost was on the rafters

and planks of the roof and some places icles of 2 inches hung down. This was caused by the breath congealing and freezing to the roof. It was all we could do not only to keep warm but to keep from freezing. The guards even were frozen on the fence and had to be relieved every half hour. Brig. Gen. Orme was put in command on the 6th in place of Col. C.V. Deland....At intervals of about a month a load of hay is brought to supply the place of mattresses. A scene than takes place that would beggar description. . . . The wagon drives in but before it is in the centre of the square the rebs fall out and with the cry "hay" they charge and stop it where it is met. The driver is nowhere. One fellow gets an arm full and starts to his barrax but before he gets clear of the crowd his armful is reduced to a mear handful. Three or four more interprising than the rest climb to the top of the load. By this time the driver, armed with whip and pitch fork, gets through the crowd and some he pushes off. One fellow requires a menace with the fork before he will lieve. The driver now commences to throw off the hay when a score of hands raises to catch their lot as it falls. . . . Tobacco is getting to be an article of importance to us who are lovers of the wead and it is seldom we can get enough to make a comfortable smoke. The weather is more changeable here that I have seen it anywhere.

Feb. 27th

Last night several prisoners attempted to scale the fence. One was shot and it is said he will die. Weather is dismal and gloomy, rain keeps us within doors. . . .

March 4th

Today five months ago I landed here and I see no chance of exchange. Yet indeed I have every reason to believe that I will spend five months more under blue coat rule. I drew some comic pictures of the convalescents to day which made the Old dry Doctor laugh. Winter is not gone yet for it is snowing strong and swift. . . .

April

Comes in wet and cold this morning. Had to get out to roll call at sun rise and stand for an hour or more. It is bad enough to stand that long but when we have to stand for 2, 3, or even 4 hours it is almost beyond all human endurance and this is the case if any one of the men is missing. It is hard indeed to keep 4 or 5,000 men freezing because one or two is missing but we have to stand untill the missing one is found. . . . Many of the prisoners have escaped lately by tuneling but that is about "played out" now for they are raising all the barrax 4 feet above the ground. . . .

April 7th

I am in hospital again but can scarcely tell what I am doing. My head is as big as a sugar hogshead. . . .

April 13th, 1864

My Birthday. What a difference between today and this day 3 years ago. I can scarcely believe it is possible that I am the same person. . . .

June

Summer is coming and we have given up all hopes of exchange. John Morgan is in Kentucky again. Camps have been put up all around the fence and are kept burning all night that the guards may see a prisoner before he gets to the fence and can fire at him. It is rather dificult to escape but now and then some fellow is lucky enough to do so. Several of my old companion have gone to another barrax and my only way of passing time is with my pencil and guitar but it is heard to get strings so I use my pencil more than my Music. . . . Engraving is almost played out so it is rather dificult to keep in tobacco. They have taken our cooking vessels from us and instituted kitchens and shortened our rations giving us nothing but pork and bread and not quite enough of that. I do not mean fresh pork. Oh! No but salt pickled pork, old and fat and not water enough to wash it down. It is rather tough living but we have to stand it. I think if the comishoner were here for a weak they would agree on an exchange.

July 4th

The stars and stripes are hoisted over every penicle [pinnacle] and building in Chicago. The great Yankee Nation is burning and imense amounts of powder today, rockets, roman candles and cannon fill the air with sulphurous gas by their constant explosions. They are making a great noise not to hurt any one. But the greater their general loss and the more noise any how for they wish to make every one believe and even try to cheat themselves into the belief that they are always victorious. Sic transit Yankee decorum. . . .

August 9th

My friend and mess mate John D. Murtah was shot in attempting to escape from here. The ball penetrated the hip making its exit at the groin. I do not think the wound is dangerous. . . . They have taken all of our bottles, jars, crocks, etc., etc. away from us. All boxes, barrels and even shelves have been taken from us so we have no place to put our bread or to lay our clothes or any thing else. We have to hang up every thing. Plates, knives, forks, spoons, bread, every thing must be hung on a nail for not the smallest shelf is allowed. . . .

August 24th

I am sick today and can't go to roll call. The flux is on me again. Weather very hot. . . .

August 29

Most dead. If I don't get medicine soon I will die. Dr. Cook says he will send me to hospital if possible.

August 30th

Still no help. I am so weak I can scarcely sit propped up to write. My mess and sleeping mate Allyn is the best man in the world to me. Oh! If I could get to Dixie, sweet Old Dixie again. . . .

Sept. 22nd

Was sent again to general Hospital. Put in Ward C. It is now one year the day before yesterday (20th) since I was captured. Yes, one year on times dial but it has left <u>all</u> the <u>traces</u> and <u>marks</u> of <u>ten years</u> on my countenance and constitution. Only to think of the many changes that have taken place and friends parted forever since the begining of the fiscal year ending Sept. 20th, 1864. Oh if some great hand could seize the pen and give a catalogue of each sorrow broken heart. The floods of my tears and heart broken sighs that have been torn from their source by the last 12 months of this strougle of parents and child, the one for mastery and the other for Liberty and independence. What a volume it would be, second to none in marvels but that Great Book given by Him to guide us to light and happiness. Such is War. . . .

October 29

In barrax 9 the rebs killed and ate the Sutlers dog. Food is <u>very scarse</u> and men have fainted for want of it. In cold days it is nothing uncommon to see men fall down from weakness. I am still sick and weak but it is all Allyn and myself can do to act gentlemanly about our <u>little</u> piece of Beef and bread. Most of the prisoners eat all at the time of drawing and go without untill the next day. It is horrid to live as we do and no one can form an idea of our miseries except those who have endured them. Many catch and eat rats when they can. In fact, if this continues untill mid-winter I do not see how we are to live. Old men are dying very fast and small pox is prevelent killing from 2 to 11 a day. The light step and merry faces of <u>last</u> winter are gone. No music or dancing or singing. All move slow and as if to a funeral. Their sunken eyes speak of hunger. . . .

CHRISTMAST

Christmast came in mild for this place. It was freezing of course but not as heard as it has been for some time past. We did not get bread today intell it was almost dark so our Christmast dinner was meat and water. What a diference between

Christmast 64 and the same in 60. Vast indeed is the diference and eaqualy vast is the diference in the same persons who met in 60. Where now is the party of that gay night. Alas those that are not in the grave are scattered "to the 4 quarters, etc." Such are the heard decrees of fate and all thats left of former times is the indelible lines of memory which show all as it was that the miseries of the present may be felt more keenly and it is only when dreaming or thinking of the past that I catch a glimpse of what I formerly was or enjoyed. . . .

January 25th

Today they made a search for money among the prisoners and they found a quantity of gold among the new ones that came in a short time ago. From the old ones they get but little for they are too sharp and have not been trained here for nothing. . . . It is so intensely cold that we had roll call in the barrax. Many are making applications for the oath [of allegiance to the United States] to get rid of their sufferings. . . .

April 1, 1865

There has been rumors of heavy fiting around Richmond but we cannot believe any thing we hear. . . .

April 6

Rumors that Lee will surrender. 100 guns fired today which makes me believe R. is gone sure enough. It is a gloomy day for us. . . .

April 13

My Birth Day and me still in prison and clouds of adversity gathering around my country.

April 15

Today every thing is a stir for it is stated that Lincoln is assassinated. I believe it for the Yanks assert it and their actions prove it. They are mad today and are doing all sorts of things to the boys, kicking them, beating them and several are in the dungeon for saying they are glad of it. . . . I am almost afraid to say anything about it for they are too much enraged. . . .

May 2nd

This morning they sent word that 500 men could go on exchange. I maneuvered to get my name on the list and succeeded.

May 3rd

Today signed parole exchange. Have been searched and put in exch. barrax to lieve tomorrow morning. Have my rations and every thing ready to leave. My heart is lighter than it has been for 20 months.

William D. Huff Civil War Prison Diary, Manuscripts, Research Center, Chicago History Museum, Chicago, IL.

CHICAGO URGES HARSHER TREATMENT OF REBEL PRISONERS

One of the reasons Huff's treatment at Camp Douglas became more onerous in the last months of the war was that news of the awful conditions suffered by Union prisoners in Confederate hands became known to Northern civilians and soldiers. Here the Chicago Board of Trade presses President Lincoln to make abuse of rebel prisoners a matter of national policy. Lincoln, however, merely assured the Chicago businessmen that he had complained of the problem to General Robert E. Lee.[12]

Chicago, October 20, 1864

His Excellency ABRAHAM LINCOLN,
President of the United States:

The undersigned members of the Board of Trade of the city of Chicago, having been informed from authentic sources that a large number of Federal soldiers are languishing in Southern prisons, especially at Andersonville, Ga., destitute of shelter from rain and from the burning rays of the sun, without sufficient clothing to cover their nakedness; and that they are famished with hunger that would gladly be appeased by the flesh of horses or mules, and are consequently dying in untold numbers, pray you to effect an honorable exchange of prisoners without delay, or to retaliate by subjecting rebel prisoners to the same treatment in all respects.

We are aware that this, our petition, savors of cruelty, and no earthly consideration could induce us to inaugurate the measure were it not for that the sufferings of our brothers in the field, who have gone forth to battle for the life of the Government with the assurance of all possible protection and care, appeals to us in a manner with induces us to urge retaliatory measures as a matter of necessity.

We claim not to be excelled in loyalty by any portion of the country and pledge ourselves for the prosecution of the war until the complete restoration of the Union is accomplished, asking no more and urging you to submit to nothing less than that such measures as rebels mete to loyal soldiers shall be measured to them again, whether in the prison or on the battlefield.

They fire upon our pickets, we retaliate; they meet us in open field and engage in wholesale slaughter, and we retaliate; they take our soldiers prisoners and submit them to such treatment as is sure to engender disease, starvation, death; but the prisoners taken by us are clothed, fed, and as comfortably cared for as our own men, and when an exchange of prisoners is made we give them soldiers hale and hearty, ready to again enter the field and give us battle, but receive in return men pale and emaciated, fit only for the hospital. We deem it due to them, especially to those now in Southern prisons, to protest against this unequal warfare.

If consideration and kindly treatment of prisoners could waken in our enemies a sufficient sense of humanity to lead to a reciprocity of treatment these abuses would have been corrected long ago.

It is not too much to say that nothing in the conduct of the war presents so great an obstacle to those who would otherwise volunteer, and nothing will cause the drafted soldier to take such reluctant steps to the field so much as the dread of the horrors of Southern prisons.

The object of this petition is not to give you information upon what we know you lament as well as we, but to give you an idea of public opinion formed upon a stern necessity.

This petition was presented to the full board at their session on this day and was unanimously adopted by them.

With high consideration, sir, your obedient servants,

John L. Hancock, President

Jno. F. Beatty, Secretary

United States War Department, *Official Records of the War of the Rebellion,* series 2, vol. 7, part 1 (Washington, DC: Government Printing Office, 1899), 1014–15.

THE NORTHWEST CONSPIRACY

As the tide of the war began to turn against the South with rebel military defeats after Gettysburg in 1863, Confederates and their Northern sympathizers hatched a plan to instigate an insurrection in the Northwest. The Sons of Liberty, as this secret group of so-called copperheads called themselves, planned to liberate rebel POWs and seize weapons from federal arsenals to overthrow the governments of Ohio, Indiana, Illinois, and Missouri. They hoped they could form an alliance with the Confederacy and force the dismembered North to surrender. This far-fetched plan and cold feet among some of the conspirators (along with their discovery) defused the conspiracy before it had a chance to be implemented.

THE DANGER TO CHICAGO.

A shiver of genuine horror passed over Chicago yesterday. Thousands of citizens who awoke to the peril hanging over their property and their heads in the form a of stupendous foray upon the city from Camp Douglas, led by rebel officers in disguise and rebel guerillas without disguise, and concocted by home copperheads, whose houses had been converted into rebel arsenals, were appalled as though an earthquake had opened at their feet. Hundreds of Democrats who had before deemed our warning of the impending danger an election roorback,[13] [sic] avowed their intention to vote, and if need be fight, to-day for the Union ticket. Who can picture the horrors to follow the letting loose of nine thousand rebel prisoners upon a sleeping city, all unconscious of the coming avalanche! With arms and ammunition stored at convenient locations, with confederates distributed here and there, ready for the signal of conflagration, the horrors of the scene could scarcely be parallel in savage history. One hour of such a catastrophe would destroy the creation of a quarter of a century of civilized life, and expose the homes of nearly two hundred thousand to every conceivable form of desecration.

No man sees the danger to his country so plainly as when brought to his own door. Very many of our citizens, of both political parties, have read of the doings of these miscreants elsewhere with utter incredulity. They have believed it impossible for the heart of man to conceive the project of a midnight raid upon a peaceful city, far from the seat of war, by ruffians

Recently plotting in its midst and preparing the implements for murder and conflagration under its own roofs. They think differently now. The blood curdles in their veins as they look into the pit upon which, for a week past, they have been treading. The view they have had of the beast at their own firesides is sufficient for all purposes of conviction. They have seen with their own eyes what the Northern allies of rebellion are capable of. They have had a glimpse of the reality which awaits them if these sympathizers with treason can once clutch the reins of government. They have learned a new lesson in the saving virtues at law and order. The majesty of the Constitution of the United States, and the beauty of its flag, have never appeared in such living light, as when the bayonets of Colonel Sweet surrounded the villains who were just ready to turn Chicago into a temporary hell.

Chicago Tribune, November 8, 1864.

～

R. T. Bean, one of the Confederate POWs, later explained how the rebels in Camp Douglas planned a massive breakout at the time of the 1864 presidential election.

Much has been written about the "great conspiracy" to release the Rebels confined in the nation's Northern prison. It was perhaps talked about less than any other move as originated with a view to consummation. The oath was administered to me by a Mr. Waller, who, I thought, was Texan. We went under my barracks, and, with my hand grasping a Bible, I repeated after him the most terrible, blood curdling oath ever concocted for the brain of man. Every word seemed branded upon my mind with letters of fire, and for four weeks afterwards I hardly knew who or what I was. As yet today I can recall but few of its striking features. If anyone had it entire, it should be published for the benefit of our politicians who wish to insert strong, emphatic planks in their platforms. Mr. Thomas S. Logwood, now of Chicago, says about two thousand took this oath in Camp Douglas, but my recollection is that the number was fifteen hundred, just enough to supply the eleven thousand prisoners with company officers (the general and regimental officers were on the outside). A Northern writer had said that the destruction of Chicago was the first thing to be done after getting out. There is no truth in this statement whatever. We were to take or destroy munitions of war, but private property was not to be touched. Had we not gone through Indiana and Ohio with the fairest records ever left by an invading army? We were not members of the 15th Army Corps, nor had we ever "marched through Georgia." I have seen it stated that the outbreak had actually been started and that we were fired on by the guards. Wrong again. A park of artillery was massed within two hundred yards of the prison, and it was ready for action at all times, but never used. Their guns I often saw. . . .

We could not have gone South on the railroads in Illinois, and were too weak and debilitated to walk.

R. T. Bean, "Seventeen Months in Camp Douglas," *Confederate Veteran* 22 (June 1914): 311.

FIVE

The Politics of War

$\mathcal{H}$IGHLY PARTISAN RHETORIC has always been a hallmark of the rough-and-tumble American democratic process, and the issues that led to the Civil War and the subsequent events of that conflict witnessed highly charged political battles that would put present-day partisanship to shame. The *Chicago Tribune*, owned by Joseph Medill, was an ardent supporter of Lincoln beginning with the Republican Convention of 1860. Medill was further heartened by Lincoln's emergence in 1862 as a champion of slave emancipation. From the vantage point of human rights, history, hindsight, the saving of the Union, and the end of slavery put the *Tribune* on the right side of history. However, for those who were caught in the immediacy of the debate or were asked to pay history's high price, the legacy for future generations of the right or wrong of war policy was less than clear. Republican Party political and military tactics often violated cherished values of the republic, such as freedom of speech, freedom of the press, the right to habeas corpus, and freedom from government compulsion to perform military service. For immigrants in particular, the latter brought back unhappy associations with the autocratic militaristic states many had fled, as did the Republican Party's sometimes strident assertion of Anglo-Protestant values.[1]

The cultural and religious divisions in Chicago that had been laid bare by 1862 were exacerbated in the succeeding years of the war by increasing class tension. Resentments grew as it became clear that some safe behind the battle lines economically benefitted from the wartime economy while others faced the horrors of battle and even paid the ultimate price with their lives. War weariness prompted some to seek a peaceful compromise to end the war—even if that meant letting the Southern states leave the Union. The racist rhetoric and policies of the Democratic Party in the decades leading up to the Civil War preconditioned its adherents to accept the justice of a war to save the Union but not one that advanced racial equality. Chicago Republicans, like their counterparts across the North, convinced that theirs was a "heavenly cause," branded their opponents as enemies of the nation rather than as rivals in the political arena. Democrats who did not fuse into a coalition with the Lincoln administration were termed "copperheads," after the poisonous snake that would strike from the grass where it lay concealed.[2]

The issue of emancipation more than any other shattered the bipartisan unity that Stephen Douglas had forged in his 1861 "patriots or traitors" speech to Chicago. For many Democrats, federal action against slavery threatened "the Union as it was" and any hope of a negotiated end to the sectional conflict. At the same time, many men and women engaged in putting down the rebellion sought a means to both punish traitors and crush the rebellion. For them, striking at the root of Southern society—its slave system—seemed a moral and military necessity. Chicago's soldiers and civilians were divided over the issue.

Initially, Wilbur F. Storey, owner and editor of the *Chicago Times*, was inspired by Stephen Douglas's warning that there were only "patriots—or traitors" and tried to support Lincoln's cause to save the Union. Defeat at Bull Run in 1861 and inaction in the West discouraged and angered many in Lincoln's Republican Party. The abolitionist minority in the party began to build support to change the war from one intended only to save the Union to one that would also end slavery. This agitation drove many former Douglas Democrats into opposition to the war. The Emancipation Proclamation, announced in preliminary form in September 1862, proved a turning point. In its wake, Storey and the *Chicago Times* never said a good word about Lincoln, and Chicago became increasingly divided over support for his leadership of the war effort.[3]

Storey was a brilliant journalist, a forerunner to the colorful and aggressive newspaper tycoons of the late nineteenth century, and a founder of the "no-holds-barred" school of journalism that would later be made famous in Chicago. Storey, however, was no friend to African Americans. To him emancipation was a death sentence for the white race in America and Lincoln had "nothing but nigger on the brain." He scornfully referred to Lincoln as "foolish, lank, nerveless, almost brainless," "an old joker," and "Czar Abraham." Lincoln's administration was a "piratical crew" and the country was a "hopeless wreck"—and that was when the war was going fairly well. When the Army of the Potomac was repulsed at Fredericksburg on the eve of the Emancipation Proclamation becoming the law, Storey's *Times* lamented "the most stupendous homicide of modern times," which left Lincoln's hands "dripping with gore."[4]

The Emancipation Proclamation came at a time in the war when the Union army clearly needed more men than could be obtained simply by a call for volunteers. While Chicago was not subjected to a draft until later in the war, many parts of the Midwest first faced conscription in 1862. To administration opponents, the draft together with the periodic suspension of the right of habeas corpus and emancipation made the war seem like a fight to give rights to the black man and take them away from the white. After a succession of Republican political successes in Chicago and in Illinois, the Democrats reversed their fortunes in the fall of 1862 by winning not only the state legislature but also the Chicago City Council and mayor's office. Storey's *Times* became the official organ of city hall, while in disgust Lincoln's supporters in the business community refused to allow the sale of the newspaper at the Board of Trade, railroad stations, and even the Young Men's Christian Association reading rooms.

Storey was the journalistic champion of Chicago Democrats opposed to emancipation. By the summer of 1862, he was locked in a bitter partisan war of words with Joseph Medill's *Chicago Tribune* and to a lesser extent the moderate Republican *Chicago Daily Journal*. Storey relished pushing back against the *Tribune's* version of events, and he questioned the integrity and competence of Republican politicos high or low, not excluding the president. For its part, Medill's *Tribune* prodded Lincoln to strike against slavery. Because the inner civil war in Chicago was fueled by culture and class as well as war politics, it permeated most public issues from the number of polling places in Bridgeport to which party controlled judgeships to who ran the school board to the racial composition of the students in the classroom.[5]

Bitter partisan wrangling in the North invited military interference in the political arena on the part of General Ambrose E. Burnside. After his mishandling of the Battle of Fredericksburg in late 1862, Burnside was transferred to the Department of the Ohio. Unable to tolerate any criticism of the war effort, Burnside issued his controversial General Order Number 38 criminalizing any form of war opposition. He first used this order against former Ohio congressman and candidate for Ohio governor Clement Vallandigham, who championed the copperhead peace movement; Burnside had him arrested and tried, despite his civilian status, in a military court. The *Chicago Times* claimed that Vallandigham was a champion of "free speech and peace," and the *Times* called this action a "funeral of civil liberty." Thin-skinned Burnside then turned his attention to the *Times* when it called him the "Butcher of Fredericksburg," and he ordered its shutdown. Chicago Republicans were thrilled by this action. Democrats took to the streets, their ranks fortified with burly Irish dockhands; they rallied in the courthouse square to protest this usurpation of constitutional rights and threatened to burn down Joseph Medill's brand new *Tribune* building. Storey filed an injunction in the U.S. Circuit Court, and Judge Thomas Drummond issued a restraining order against Burnside's action until its legality was determined.[6]

Fearful of a full-scale riot, moderates on both sides, such as Democratic mayor Francis Sherman and Republican senator Lyman Trumbull, recognized that this breach of civil liberties did nothing but exacerbate civic divisions. Although Lincoln did not appreciate the *Times* diatribes against his administration, he agreed that Burnside had overstepped his authority and asked him to repeal the order. A potentially explosive partisan battle in Chicago that threatened to infect the entire North was thus defused. Wilbur Storey, whose newspaper was already highly regarded as a source of up-to-date war news, could now rightly pose to a national audience as a martyr to the cause of endangered democratic freedoms.[7]

The prospect of a draft also divided Chicagoans. In 1862 as the war dragged on and enlistments declined, Congress passed the Militia Act. It empowered the Lincoln administration to call upon state militias and set state quotas. If a state failed to meet its obligations, the federal government was empowered to activate state regulations to conscript men for service. The fact that the draft law allowed wealthy individuals to avoid service by paying a three-hundred-dollar commutation fee heightened class tensions. Later this rule was changed, but the well-heeled were still able to avoid service by providing a substitute to serve in their stead. The threat of a draft was often enough to motivate many to join the military, as they would not get enlistment bonuses if they were forced to join. The bonus system offered positive inducements to patriot service. Although the State of Illinois did not offer a bonus, the City of Chicago and most of the city's wards did offer cash incentives, which amounted to several hundred dollars—a tidy sum when working men earned a dollar a day for hard physical labor. The bonus led to the emergence of a new wartime occupation: the bounty jumper. Chicago became the Midwest center for men who enlisted to collect a bonus and then immediately deserted. Unlike many other midwestern states, Illinois was able to meet its quotas through volunteers until late 1864.[8]

The draft increased class tensions in Chicago. Historian Lorien Foote has documented that draftees or bonus men (those who enlisted for the cash incentive) were often from the lower classes and were disparaged by soldiers of a more established background who had enlisted in 1861 or 1862. They were subjected to harsher discipline, as they were seen as lacking in self-restraint and prone to disorder. Bounty jumpers in particular were disparaged as the worst example of an urban sporting or criminal class. These notions shaped the way Chicago newspapers described resistance to the draft and shaped postwar class conflict.[9]

However, heavy pressure to meet these quotas compelled local authorities to record the names of potential recruits. As enrollment officers made their rounds in Chicago neighborhoods, some met stiff resistance, especially in the poor, working-class and mostly Irish districts. Antidraft violence in Chicago never approached the horror of the New York City riots of July 1863. This may have been partly because a larger percentage of working people in Chicago were property owners with a stake in their communities. Also, Chicagoans fearful of the draft were smart enough to show their displeasure by attacking the enrollment process and not waiting to have their names pulled out in an actual draft lottery. The most obvious and easy way to do this was to simply lie about one's identity. This might be done in combination with another frequent tactic: physical intimidation of government agents.

Bridgeport was home to the most serious riot over the draft in Chicago. In one incident, between three hundred and four hundred Irish men, women, and children violently repelled enrollment officers' attempts to record the names of men eligible for the draft. After the Bridgeport riot, the *Tribune* took the Irish to task for their resistance to the draft, accusing them of disloyalty to the Union and an unwillingness to follow due process of law. While the Republican organ acknowledged that many Irish had already shown valor on the battlefield and had died for freedom, it argued that Irish resistance to the draft blighted the reputation of the entire Irish community and made them undeserving of the freedoms the Union provided them.[10]

The concerted opposition to draft enrollment in Irish Chicago may have convinced Republican leaders, including Joseph Medill, that actual forced conscription might result in violence similar to what occurred in New York. On the eve of Chicago's first draft, Medill traveled to Washington to ask for a reduced quota for Cook County. The president gave him a verbal dressing-down for his "cowardice," and Lincoln reminded him of the *Tribune*'s call for war and emancipation. Lincoln turned a "black and frowning face" to Medill and said, "You and your *Tribune* have more influence than any other paper in the Northwest. . . . Go home and send us those men."[11]

Many men tried to avoid the draft by fleeing their districts. Chicago was a popular way station for "skedaddlers" from elsewhere in the Midwest who intended to catch a ship to Canada. Secretary of War Edwin Stanton issued an order that no citizen eligible for the draft was allowed to leave his county, his state, or the country without a pass. Federal provost marshals patrolled the docks and rail terminals, and Chicago policemen were given five dollars for every draft dodger they captured, which made them happy to cooperate with the imposition of martial law. The Provost Marshall's Office also did a nice business working with informers willing to turn in a fellow worker or lodger in return for a stack of greenbacks.[12]

The draft crisis empowered Chicago peace Democrats to invite the Democratic National Convention to the city in 1864. Chicago, therefore, became the center of the Democratic challenge to Lincoln and the Republican war effort. Their platform debate ranged from "peace at any price" to suing for peace while pursuing war. Democrats settled on General George B. McClellan as the most viable candidate to unseat Lincoln in the November elections. McClellan essentially supported the Union war effort; unfortunately for him, the majority of the delegates at Chicago did not. Led by Wilbur Storey and Clement Vallandigham, the Chicago convention famously branded the war effort a "failure" and called for negotiations with the Confederacy even though that course would likely lead to the end of the Union. This platform enthused Cyrus McCormick, the Virginia-born manufacturer, and he was nominated a "peace candidate" for the House of Representatives.[13]

This type of political division and obvious war weariness encouraged the Confederacy to send secret agents to Chicago led by Captain Thomas Henry Hines of Kentucky. Hines offered thousands of dollars of covert Confederate funding to peace candidates. The rebel secret service also hatched what would become known as the Northwest Conspiracy—an attempt to liberate rebel POWs, destabilize the Midwest, and persuade peace Democrats that the Union was dead. However, in the end there was not enough combustible political sentiment in Chicago for Hines and his men to spark an open revolt. Hines did make a desperate, last attempt on Election Day in November 1864 to liberate prisoners at Camp Douglas. The plot was uncovered and foiled, but panicked civic leaders arrested more than 150 people, most of whom were only guilty of Democratic sympathies. Eight rebel agents were brought before a military commission in Cincinnati. Two defendants were sentenced to prison, and only one, an English adventurer named George T. St. Leger Grenfell, was sentenced to hanging (after the war, his sentence was commuted to a life of hard labor).[14]

This "fire in the rear" was extinguished in Chicago as Union victories in the autumn of 1864 at Atlanta and the Shenandoah Valley, along with the capture of Mobile, kept Lincoln in the White House that November and brought the Confederacy to near collapse.

FEAR OF DISLOYALTY

Julian S. Rumsey served as the Republican mayor of Chicago from 1861 to 1862. His ardent support for the Union led him to believe that anyone not for Lincoln and the Republican position on the Union and war was a spy or traitor. In August he issued an ordinance requiring all citizens who had not taken an oath of allegiance to the United States to leave Chicago.

ORDINANCE CONCERNING DISLOYAL CITIZENS

Passed, August 27, 1861 . . .
Julian S. Rumsey, Mayor

Gentlemen of the Common Council:
I have good reason to believe that there are in this City many persons whose sympathies are entirely with the so called new confederacy of the South. That, in short, there [are] secessionists and spies among us, furnishing all the information in their power to the enemies of this Union; and feeling that this, a representative City of the North-West, should take an active part in the great contest now being waged for the perpetuation of the Government, I recommend the passage of the following ordinance: (Signed Julian S. Rumsey, Mayor)

An Ordinance Concerning Disloyal Citizens

1st Be it ordained by the Common Council of the City of Chicago:

That any citizen of the United States who is now or may hereafter become an inhabitant of this City, who is not ready to take the oath of allegiance to the government of the United States be and is hereby requested to leave the City immediately, and the "Citizens Union Defense Committee" be requested to investigate and ascertain with regard to the views of any suspected individual, and request, that they shall take such oath, and in case of refusal, to publish the names of such persons in the daily newspapers of the City, and report the same to this Council at its first meeting after such fact is ascertained.

2nd That said Committee be requested to make the necessary arrangements for the administration of such oaths with some qualified officer so that there shall be no expense incurred by the person so required to prove his loyalty.

Ordinance Concerning Disloyal Citizens, August 27, 1861, Julian S. Rumsey, Mayor, Common Council Proceedings, Illinois Regional Archives Depository, Northeastern Illinois University.

~

The Republican press viewed the visits of Chicagoans to Camp Douglas to talk with and assist Confederate prisoners in a highly partisan manner. The Tribune castigated men and women who visited prisoners as "sesech," claiming they engaged in disloyal conversations.

A TIMELY ORDER—VISITORS TO BE EXCLUDED FROM CAMP DOUGLAS THE CHANGE OF TONE IN THE REBEL PRISONERS

The game of a few active secessionists, whose presence we are sorry to remark in the city, has at last played out, so far as their regular visitations and consultations with the rebel prisoners now confined at Camp Douglas is concerned. It is high time. It may prove hard for the male and female Secesh; we cannot call them women and men, for by their conduct they have forfeited all claims to these honorable appellations—who for some time past have been daily hatching plots of treason there, and by their conversations have been siding and abetting the cause of the Jeff Davis Confederacy. But all loyal citizens will cheerfully comply with the following orders, which was made known to Col. Mulligan on Saturday.

Chicago Tribune, March 10, 1862.

ACCUSATIONS OF PRISONER MISTREATMENT

The Tribune *reacted defensively to criticism of mistreatment of prisoners at Camp Douglas from other Northern newspapers, labeling all critics as copperheads.*

SYMPATHY FOR THE CHICAGO REBEL PRISONERS.

CONTRIBUTIONS FROM NORTHERN COPPERHEADS.
Excitement at the Corn Exchange, Philadelphia.

The false statement made by the Chicago *Times*, a few days since, respecting the destitution and suffering among the rebel prisoners, has excited the sympathy of a peculiar class, known as "secession sympathizers" in the Eastern cities where the facts are not known. It is not a part of the Union creed to allow even rebels to freeze or starve to death, or to suffer from the want of any articles they can supply. While it is right and proper that contributions should be made to these prisoners, we protest against their being made under the impression that they are improperly treated at Camp Douglas, or that they are "treated like cattle." The prisoners and their surgeons admit that the authorities at Camp Douglas have done everything in their power to render the prisoners comfortable, and most of them are now more comfortably situated than they have been for many months past, on the rations and under the treatment of the Confederate army.

We have been among the Confederates and know whereof we speak. We have seen them in the service, their camps and their conditions. The Confederate camps at Donelson, Shiloh, and Island No. 10 contained an assortment of rations which a Union dog wouldn't have touched. Compared with those, the rations they now have are sumptuous feasts, and the same obtains with clothing. We therefore protest and the rebels themselves protest against the statement that they are suffering from neglect. The Northern Copperheads have no excuse for their sympathy on this score.

Chicago Tribune, February 13, 1863.

COPPERHEADS AND CITY POLITICS

In 1862 Mayor Francis C. Sherman, a brick manufacturer and owner of the Sherman House, who served the city from 1862 to 1865, made an unsuccessful bid to unseat Republican congressman Isaac Arnold. However, in the statewide elections, Democrats took control of the state legislature and were able to appoint William Richardson, a Douglas Democrat, as senator, and eight of thirteen Democrats won congressional seats. In Chicago's local elections, however, prowar Union candidates defeated Democratic challengers. The Tribune *described the Republican win as a victory against treason. The election also pitted Chicago's German and Irish communities against each other. The Democratic vote was expected to be buoyed by the presence of the Ninetieth Illinois Infantry, the Irish Legion, which was assigned to nearby Camp Douglas. The Republicans countered this at the last minute by ensuring that the Eighty-Second Illinois Infantry, a largely Chicago German unit known as the "Hecker regiment," was cycled through Chicago on the way from the training camp to the front, so that these troops could participate in the election.*

THE ELECTION.
HOVE IN SHERMAN
HOVE OUT.
Mr. Arnold's Majority in the City
Over 400; in the County
Nearly 2,000.
CLEAN SWEEP OF THE UNION WAR TICKET.
Treason Rebuked in Chicago.
VOX POPULI, VOX DEI.

The election yesterday passed off very quietly, thanks to the excellent public arrangements, without which much rioting and fighting must have occurred. In the Seventh and Tenth Wards several attempts were made by the unterrified Democracy to get up a fight, but the prompt action of the police prevented. In the Fourth Ward . . . a speck of war occurred. Two men, an Irishman and a German, got into an affray, and were promptly arrested by the police. At that instant a squad of the Irish Legion rushed at the police to rescue the prisoners. The police drew their revolvers, but still the soldiers pressed on, and would undoubtedly have accomplished their object, had not their officers kept them back at the point of the sword.

About three o'clock in the afternoon, the gallant Hecker regiment arrived and proceeded to their various wards to vote. Again the Democracy were rampant although the Irish Legion had voted without any interference. They were subjected to every kind of insult. At the Seventh Ward polls a crowd of Irish drew knives and threatened that the Heckers should not vote except over their dead bodies. The idle threat was unheeded by the company . . . and they marched up in solid phalanx and deposited their votes, every man being challenged. The valor of the crowd oozed out as they advanced and they sullenly retired. In the Third Ward and in other wards their votes were ruled out although they were legal voters. The Irish Legion were allowed to vote as they pleased. At the Third Ward polls, Democratic votes were deposited by boys not twenty years of age, as can be testified to by the enrolling officer. Remonstrances were made by citizens, but the inspectors paid no heed to them. The most outrageous acts of illegal voting were perpetrated by the

Democracy. Whole droves were illegal voters imported into many of the Wards, and to such a degree was this carried in the Tenth Ward, that the Democratic inspectors openly reproved the leaders who brought them there. One entire company of the Legion was marched to the polls and their votes rejected.

But in spite of the desperate efforts of the bogus Democracy the cause of the Union was triumphant, gloriously triumphant.

Chicago Tribune, November 11, 1862.

∽

The Democratic Chicago Times *attributed these losses to voter fraud.*

The democracy would have carried the city handsomely but for one of the most shameless and scandalous frauds that has ever been perpetrated at an election. What is called the Hecker Regiment arrived here at about 2 o'clock P.M. from Springfield, ostensibly on their way to Washington, having been brought this round-about route, at a large cost to the government, for the use to which they were put.

Chicago Times, November 6, 1862.

∽

The Tribune *affirmed its position that the Union could be saved only through military might and that the troops could be sustained only by Republican electoral success. Any other policy or course of action was treason.*

NO-PARTY HUMBUG.

An evening paper of loud "Conservative" pretensions, insists that a "no-party ticket shall be nominated by the loyal citizens of Chicago." The idea of combating the Copperhead organization with a "no party" ticket is simply preposterous, and will cause disgust and lead to inevitable defeat. The unconditional Union men must organize and act together as a party, to oppose and defeat the Copperhead party. A "party" simply means a political organization. And it is necessary for true and reliable Union men, to bond themselves together in a political organization, to . . . beat the disloyal, who are united together in the Copperhead party. The no-party scheme is managed and advocated by a set of political eunuchs, and if the campaign is left to their management, the Copperheads who are positive, ultra men, disloyal and devilish, in their aims, but nevertheless, earnest, bold, and "unterrified," will ride rough-shod over them, and rout them with all the ease and certainty with which a pack of wolves tear and devour a flock of sheep.

Rebel armies can only be resisted successfully by Union armies. A regiment of armed rebels must be opposed by a regiment of armed loyalists. When the Copperhead allies of the rebels resort to the ballot-box, they must be met at the ballot-box. When they employ the machinery of a compact, well-drilled political organization, they must be met by the machinery of the opposing party.

Chicago Tribune, March 5, 1863.

~

In April 1863, Francis Sherman was reelected mayor. Thirteen Democrats and ten Unionists were elected alderman, giving Democrats control of the council twenty to twelve.[15] The Journal, *a Republican organ, warned its readers against this "copperhead."*

The election of "Hove In" Sherman, the candidate of the *Chicago Times* as Mayor of Chicago, tomorrow, would be gratifying to every rebel, and every rebel sympathizer in the country who should hear of it and who had heard of his vetoing the patriotic Union resolutions of the Chicago Common Council.

Chicago Journal, March 20, 1863.

~

While Francis Sherman rejoiced in the Democratic victory in Chicago, he was shaken by the public stance his son took in siding with the Republicans. Frank Sherman was the colonel of the Eighty-Eighth Illinois Infantry, and he believed that the leaders of the Democratic Party in Illinois, especially the Chicago Times, *abetted secession by opposing Lincoln's abolition and conscription policies. In February, Frank published in the* Tribune *a strongly worded call for a nonpartisan pursuit of victory over the South. Here he privately presses Mayor Sherman to break with the* Times *and the peace Democrats.*

April 3, 1863

Dear Father,

I see that politics runs high with you yet. I hope you are not so wedded to any party that you will allow it to carry you beyond patriotism and the love of country. Excuse me for writing thus, but it does seem to me, Father, that there is neither democracy nor patriotism in the acknowledged organ of the so-called Democratic party, the *Times*. I do not believe that you endorse the sayings and doings of this filthy sheet, which is heaping dust upon the self-sacrificing soldier who has left his home and all that he holds dear for love of country to face the perils of the field and camp.

Suppose you differ with the present administration as to many of its measures and blunders in the conduct of the war, as to the enforcement of the laws and bringing back a portion of the refractory subjects who have been misled by the sophisms urged upon them by designing men who wished nothing more than their personal aggrandizement and to gratify an inordinate ambition to rule or ruin, what then? Must a great principle be perverted by demagogues; must we be bound by chains of steel to the chariot of party, and forget that we have a country without which we as the people who have for the last eighty years been working out the great problem "Is man capable of self-government" must come to naught, anarchy, chaos?

The question now is shall this principle become active and diffuse happiness for all to come and those who come after us, or shall it be buried in the ruins of demagoguism and party strife. . . . Cast aside, I implore you, Father, all considerations of party until this infamous war is closed and peace once more sits enthroned in our once-happy land. Cast not a straw in the way of the wheels of state which are now creaking under the heavy burden put upon them, and by your position and influence show the world that you can rise superior to party when the stake is played for is our country. God bless her, my country, the United States of America, first or last, right or wrong, still my country. . . . Great responsibility rests upon the men of influence and substance at home, and it becomes them to take the side of patriotism and of this country in this her hour of trial. Be warned! No terms must be offered to treason but absolute submission to the offended laws. It must, it cannot be otherwise; the laws must be avenged or we become a second Mexico—all that we hold dear gone, vanished, without morals, law, or stability—the laughing stock of the world, knocked about like a shuttlecock at the caprice of every adventurer who may for the time gain the ascendancy by means of advantageous circumstances which he may be smart enough to seize upon. Father, there should be one party at the present time and its platform should be death to traitors wherever found, and the last man and cent that can be raised or found to prosecute this war, to maintain the birthright that we inherited from the glorious fathers of the revolution.

I know that you are true and patriotic, a firm supporter of our country and desire nothing more than the triumph of the Union cause. You want peace; so do I, but not dishonorable peace. That can never be. I claim to be as good a Democrat as I ever was. That does not interfere with my support of the government under which I was born and whose protecting arm has ever been ready to shield me, one of her sons, from wrong. Shall I shrink now that she needs me? Shall I forget the many blessings she has showered upon me and mine? No, never! Then rally around the old flag, see it not trailed in the dust and all will be well. Amen.

These thoughts have been suggested to me by your letter and the accounts of party strife now going on at home for power, the loaves and fishes, and the impediment thrown in the way to stop the return of absentees and deserters who have received the bounty of their country and sworn to protect her, by those who call themselves 'Democrats.' You and I, Father belong to no such party as that. The true democracy should rise en masse and trample out such scoundrels.

I am well and so is Ellen. We both join in sending love to you all. I have no news to write but what you have heard. We are laying in camp here doing the usual routine of duty with an occasional skirmish. Again, love to all, and believe me as ever your loving son, Frank.

Francis T. Sherman Papers, 1862–65, Manuscripts Department, Research Center, Chicago History Museum, Chicago, IL.

REACTIONS TO THE EMANCIPATION PROCLAMATION

Richard Puffer, a private from the Chicago suburb of Palatine, served in the Eighth Illinois Infantry. At the time the Emancipation Proclamation was issued, his regiment was encamped in rain-soaked Memphis, Tennessee. Like many Democrats he saw Lincoln's action as an ill-timed radical move.

Camp of the 8th Illinois Infantry
Memphis, Tenn. Feb. 12th '63

Dear Sister,

We have been here expecting to go down river every day since we came but time passes & no transports appear, meantime the soldiers spend their time to amuse themselves. Some (& they are not a very small class) go to the city & get drunk & spend their money (if they happen to have any) free, others plod about camp in the mud & curse Abe Lincoln, Jeff Davis & everybody connected with the war. There is not a little outspoken treason in the army. I believe that there are many officers high in command that will form any movement to overthrow the government & the sooner the volcano breaks forth & spends its force, the sooner we shall have peace & quiet. I would be sorry indeed to see the prairies of Ill. become the theater of war. But I can see but one way to avoid it & that is for the Administration to throw off that radical influence which has ruled it for the last 8 months. I am sure the army will not sustain it & we all know that the great central states pronounced against it last fall. Then where are they to look for support. The last act, or one of the last acts of Congress & that was the negro Soldier bill was in my opinion the last nail in their coffin only one thing will save them, that is an unparallel success of our arms & we have no right to expect that at present. It is impossible to move in the present state of the weather. I believe it impossible for the administration to carry out the proclamation & other radical measures & Therefore I oppose them. I do not care how quick this war is brought to a close. I have slept on the soft side of a board in the mud & every other place that was lousy & dirty. I have drunk out of a goose pond, horse tracks for the last 18 months all for the poor nigger & I have yet to see the first one that I think has been benefited by it, not the first thing has been done for their future welfare, but they are left to shift for themselves, if they stay here they will be made slaves of or worse, if the go North the same prejudice meets them there. But you know I am no orator nor especially a paper so I will drop the subject. . . . But I must close, give my regards to all inquiring friends & accept this from your absent Brother,

                                                                              Dick

              Do not share this.

Richard Puffer Collection, Research Center, Chicago History Museum.

~

The largely German American Eighty-Second Illinois Infantry had a significant proportion of its men from Chicago, including a company raised by the Jewish community, one composed of Scandinavians, and many sons of the 1848 Revolution veterans. Their reaction to the Emancipation Proclamation reflected their commitment to liberal politics.

Lt. Col. Salomon, Headquarters 82nd Regt. Ill. Vols, Camp near Stafford C.H., Va., to Richard Yates—Feb 4, 1863

~

At a meeting of the Officers of the 82nd Regt. Ills. Vols. held this day, Lieut. Col. Edward S. Salomon was chosen chairman and Adjutant Eugene F. Weigel secretary, and the following resolutions were offered, and unanimously adopted.

~

In consideration of the critical position of our country at present and of the intrigues of miserable politicians and partisans, who while the true and loyal citizens of our state, with the sacrifice of blood and life, endeavor to destroy the enemies of our most sacred rights, aid and abet these enemies, at home, by means of treasonable, and our state degrading resolutions, be it resolved:

1. That we, the German soldiers and citizens of the state of Illinois, who have declared themselves willing to sacrifice all for the preservation of the Union, have heard with the greatest indignation of the miserable treachery of the men, who dare to call themselves our representatives.

2. That we endorse with pleasure the emancipation proclamation of our President, and are at any moment ready to execute it with arms in hand.

3. That we regard our Governor Richard Yates, as one of the noblest, truest and most high minded patriots of the United States, and that we refute the infamous attacks and slanders, which have been made upon him by secesh-sympathizing members of the legislature of Illinois, as low and mean in the highest degree, and that we regret that we are no longer at Camp Butler, to have an opportunity of liberating the halls of our capitol, from this detestable scum.

FIGURE 14. Officers of the Eighty-Second Illinois Infantry. The unit was largely made of German Americans with companies of Scandinavians as well as one of Polish and German Jews. The regiment's leaders, Frederick Hecker and later Edward Salomon, were strong supporters of the Emancipation Proclamation. Courtesy of the Chicago History Museum.

4. That we condemn the majority-report of the house committee on federal relations most decidedly, and that we consider the authors and all those, who voted in favor of this report as rebels and traitors, who deserve to be hung by the side of Jeff. Davis and consorts.

5. That we, contrary to this report, consider the minority report of the same committee, as the noble expression of the sentiments of true patriots, and acknowledge and esteem the same as such with all our heart, and that we are convinced that the same will be endorsed by every soldier of the state of Illinois.

6. That we hope and wish that this rebellion may soon be suppressed, but only by force of arms, and that then the traitors in the north as well as the leaders of the rebellion in the south, may not evade their just punishment.

7. That these resolutions be published in the 'Illinois-StaatsZeitung' and the 'Chicago Tribune', [p. 3] and copies thereof be sent to the Governor of Illinois and to our representatives in Congress, as well as to our Colonel Frederic Hecker, who, unfortunately, was prevented by disease, from participating in this demonstration.

⌒

The above resolutions were read to the Regiment at Dress Parade & unanimously adopted.

Richard Yates, Family Papers, 1789-1936, Box 11, Folder 1, Abraham Lincoln Presidential Library. Springfield, IL.

⌒

The Democratic Chicago Times, *which had tried to coax Lincoln into taking a "conservative" position on the question of emancipation, despaired over the preliminary proclamation and challenged abolitionists to prove the military efficacy of the policy.*

The President has at last weakly yielded to the "pressure" upon him about which he has so bitterly complained, and issued his proclamation of negro emancipation!

It is not yet a month since he announced his purpose to "save the Union in the shortest way under the Constitution." Now he announces his purpose to save it by overriding the Constitution.

For he has no Constitutional power to issue this proclamation of emancipation—none whatsoever. The Constitution forbids it by its spirit from beginning to end. And the President has no power to deviate from the Constitution—none whatsoever. He is himself the creature of the Constitution.

Nobody need argue with us that, he has the power under military law. Military law does not destroy the fundamental civil law. In war, as in peace, the Constitution is "the supreme law of the land."

The government, then, by the act of the President, is in rebellion, and the war is reduced to a contest for subjugation. It has assumed the character that abolitionism has designed from the outset that it should assume. When the war shall be finished, whether the South shall be subjugated or not, the character of the government will have to be determined, if indeed the military power shall not have already determined it.

The President himself has furnished some of the most unanswerable arguments against the expediency of such a proclamation, and this even so late as at the interview the other day with the committee of religious lunatics from this city. . . . We trust it [the Proclamation] will shorten the war. It is the instrumentality by which abolitionism has undertaken that the war should be closed in thirty days at the farthest. Indeed, we have been told that under it the President would be able to stamp armies out of the earth. Let them stamp at once, for we are anxious to see the flaming giants of abolitionism throwing themselves into the fight and throwing the rebellion into dismay, as promised. We are anxious to behold the stupendous and magnificent results which were to flow, like a mighty stream, from the proclamation. Surely we are not to be utterly and totally deceived as to the results.

Chicago Times, September 24, 1862.

THE DRAFT COMES TO CHICAGO

In an attempt to avoid being listed for a draft, many men tried to escape to Canada. This, however, was in violation of Secretary Stanton's order that no man was allowed to leave his city or state of residence without a military pass. The Chicago Tribune fully supported the Militia Act and restrictions on citizens' rights, thus adding to the political tensions of the city. Many of those named were Irish, but not all, illustrating a more pervasive resistance to policies of conscription.

Chicago Under Martial Law
No More Running Away.
Arrest of Fugitives.
They Must Stay at Home.

Chicago is at last under martial law and the exodus of cowards and sneaks is henceforth to be stopped. Every man hereafter must stand by his post, will he nill he [*sic*]. For nearly a week our city has presented the disgraceful spectacle of full-grown, able-bodied men slinking off for Canada like whipped curs by rail and lake, with no apparent method of stopping them. The prompt and stern action of the War Department, however, has put a period to the Hegira, and all those timid individuals who have been packing their trunks and gathering together their stray funds for a few weeks residence in Her Majesty's dominion, might as well unpack and reinvest their money here for they have got to stay at home by the mandate of those whom it will be well to obey. The Government speaks now and lays its strong hand upon every man and says "Stop! I want you," and it will be a most excellent thing to stop moreover, for the Government is not to be trifled with. Undoubtedly many timid individuals will have to undergo a most terrible scare when the draft comes. Many sudden invalids may stand in danger of getting chronic. Many loving and strongly domesticated individuals will have to forego the pleasure of seeing their aunts and grandmothers who live in Detroit, Buffalo and Lockport. But then it can't be helped. We feel for them in their extremity, but can find no balm of consolation for them. They might as well take the dose gracefully, if it is bitter. They have the profound sympathy, and will undoubtedly secure the protection of the community which is always extended to the naturally timid.

The first application of martial law was made by Superintendent Bradley last evening, who made a descent upon the eastern bound trains about the hour of starting, and captured a squad of fugitives, who were bound mainly for Detroit. They were all taken to the police office and examined. The following is a list of them with the amount of money found upon them, etc. Those marked with a star were discharged all right.

Patrick Maloney. . . . . $ 9.45
Patrick Reardon 17.00
Patrick Delaney 18.00
John Barnett. 40.00
*Frank Mitchell 9.50
*Gustavus A. Morton. 25.46
A.S. La Due 00.00
James Morrill 7.50
*Geo. Menelaus 18.75
Thomas Boling 45.60
*S. Heath 19.83
*Edward Hornby 28.13
*F.W. Berry 25.50
William Kippen 25.00
Bernard Morrill 00.00
William Long 11.50

William Daley. 197.68
Daniel Doran 66.50
*Edw. D. Chapin 23.17
*Henry D. Dunbar 278.62
James Connelly 28.85

From the above, it will be seen that the individuals had provided themselves with just funds enough to last until after the draft. Those who are not starred in the above list are in confinement. C.P. Bradley is acting Provost Marshal until one shall be appointed. Hereafter no one can leave the city for the East without a pass. All of the roads and boats will be strictly watched, and parties are already stationed at points outside the city where connections could in any wise be made. . . .

P.S.—We are informed that several individuals who slipped away by boat yesterday, will probably arrive soon by the U.S. steamer *Michigan*, which is patiently waiting for them.

Chicago Tribune, August 9, 1862.

~

THE CANADIAN EMIGRATION.
The Emigrants in Trouble.
BAD EFFECTS OF A SUDDEN DRAFT.

Not content with the warning afforded by the arrest of the score or more of individuals of all nationalities going to see their Canadian uncles and aunts on Friday night another batch attempted to run the blockade on Saturday morning. *They* were a sharp set. *They* were not to be caught. Oh! no! They took their satchels and went to Hyde Park to meet the Eastern bound train. Uncle Sam was there before them, however, in the shape of a posse of police who kindly relieved the emigrants of their satchels, and treated them to a free ride to the Court House—nineteen in number, coming partly from the Michigan Central and partly from the Michigan Southern railroads.

The excuses rendered were funny in the extreme. One individual remarked that he was "just going to see his aunt, sure." Another had just heard of the lamentable illness of his grandfather, who lived in Chatham, C.W. [Canada West—modern Ontario]. A small, weazen-faced [*sic*] man . . . was going to bring his wife home. Another had just heard of the birth of an heir, and another was going for his health. A strict examination was made into the circumstances of each case, resulting as follows:

Benj. F. Blair, from Des Moines, bound for Detroit, discharged.

Wm. W. Leslie, from Clinton, Iowa, bound for Detroit, gone to Camp Douglas.

Robert Leslie, from Clinton, Iowa, bound for Detroit, gone to Camp Douglas.

Robert Tobin, from St. Louis, bound for Detroit, gone to Camp Douglas.

Edward Barnes, from Oquawks, bound for Lafayette, discharged.

Daniel Donovan, from St. Louis, bound for Detroit, gone to Camp Douglas.

Michael Sullivan, from St. Louis, bound for Canada, discharged.

Michael Young, from St. Louis, bound for Detroit, gone to Camp Douglas.

Andrew Begoe, from St. Clair, Ills., bound for New York, discharged.

Bernard Comiskey, from Blue Diggings, Wis., bound for Detroit, gone to Camp Douglas.

Christopher Duff, from Blue Diggings, Wis., bound for Detroit, gone to Camp Douglas.

Robert Taggart, from Chicago, bound for Ireland, gone to Camp Douglas.

John Crawford, from Colorado, bound for England, gone to Camp Douglas.

Godfrey Lather, from Marquette, bound for Michigan City, discharged.

Frank Wheeler, from Ormond, Wis., bound for Canada, discharged.

John Wheeler, from Ormond, Wis., bound for Canada, discharged.

Henry Christopher, from Stevens' Point, bound for Quebec, discharged.

In addition to the above, those arrested on Friday night, who were not discharged, were sent to Camp Douglas.

Marshal Bradley was busy all day Saturday in the pursuance of his new duties, and granted no less than three hundred passes to persons desirous of leaving the city.

Sunday night, on the departure of the trains for the East, the cowards were on hand as usual. The police arrested a score or more, and gave them quarters in the Armory. Among them were two Israelites who, during the day had applied to Marshal Bradley for passes, and were refused. They will make excellent soldiers.

Chicago Tribune, August 11, 1862.

~

*Lucrative bounties paid by states and municipalities provided an important induce-
ment to enlistment in the Union army and helped many communities avoid a draft.
During the war, several new trades emerged related to the enlistment process. Some
men acted as enlistment brokers. They would provide volunteers to communities in
desperate need of meeting their quotas, while assuring young men that they would
secure the highest possible bounty. Bounty jumpers were men who would enlist to
collect an enlistment bonus but quickly desert the army and hide in a large city like
Chicago, before enlisting again for another bonus. Here a loyal citizen informs on
men who tried to induce him to join them in a bounty-jumping scheme.*

State of Illinois⎫
Cook County ⎭ Personally appeared before me a Justice of the Peace of said
County Joseph L. Heim and being first duly sworn upon his oath says as follows:
I am an engineer employed as fireman in Munn and Scott's Chicago and North
Western Elevator in the City of Chicago. I know George Bloomingdale. I first saw
him at the Elevator about five months since, he came there to get employment.
I have seen him there frequently since that time. On Friday last the 20th instant at
the same place, he made a proposition to me to go into the Bounty jumping business, he said it would take two to do the business and he would act as Broker and
I could act as Recruit as he had a crippled hand and could not pass as a Recruit,
he said we could go where they paid the highest Bounty, if we could not do it in
Chicago we would go to the State of New York or any other place, he said I could
get seven hundred and fifty to eight hundred dollars Bounty and pay the money
to him pretending to send it to my folks, that I probably could get a furlough
for a day or two after the enlistment and then we could both go together to a
strange place where were not known, he said there would be no trouble in getting
a furlough, he would furnish Citizen's clothes and a false whiskers so that I would
not be known, he said he would bring a man around on Monday who is in that
business, he accordingly came there on Monday in Company with another man,
we then had further conversation on the subject, Bloomingdale said he thought
he could pass himself at Lieutenant Horr's Recruiting Office as Lieutenant Horr
was not very particular, in that case we were both to be enlisted and the man that
came with him would play Broker, that man said the Navy Recruiting office would
be open on Wednesday and he would see if he could get us in there, he said he
understood the business, he enlisted four men in Louisville and got a large Bounty
and he then got them off.
Joseph L. Heim
Sworn and Subscribed before me on this 25th day of January A.D. 1865,
J.S. Milliken, Justice of the Peace.

District One Provost Marshall—General Bureau Records, Letters Received, 1863–65, National Archives, Great
Lakes Region, RG 110, Box 15.

~

It was the task of the Provost Marshal's Office to both conduct the draft and arrest deserters, draft dodgers, and bounty jumpers. Captain William James, provost marshal in Chicago, received a heavy correspondence from colleagues across the Midwest who required his help in arresting bounty jumpers who sought to hide out in Chicago. Federal draft law had a strong class bias that was deeply resented by many working people. A wealthy man selected for the draft could avoid military service by paying for another man to serve as his "substitute." The cost of a substitute was often more than a workingman's yearly wages. Brokers acted to procure substitutes, and bounty jumpers often served as substitutes only to quickly desert. In this Wanted notice, note the large number of tattoos reported on the suspects. These markings indicated that the men were from a rough social background, in this case sailors.

Provost Marshal's Office   Marengo, Dec. 13th 1864
2d District Illinois

$30 Reward

The above reward will be paid to any person who will arrest and deliver to these Head Quarters or to the nearest Provost Marshal, either of the following named Deserters or $60 for both who were Enlisted at this Office and deserted on the evening of the 9th inst. at Chicago en route to Springfield, Ills. Viz

James Kelly—Substitute for Alexander Strong
John Kelly—Substitute for Joseph Talbott

Description

James Kelly—age 22—Eyes Black—Hair Dk—Complexion Dark—Height 5ft 5 ½. Born in Ireland. Occupation—Sailor—"Crucifixion on right arm, Eagle and Star on left" marked in indelible ink—measurement of Chest Inspiration 33, Expiration 30 inches.

John Kelly—Age 28—Eyes Hazel—Hair Black—Complexion Dark. Height 5 ft. 9. Born in Ireland. Occupation Sailor. "Anchor on right foot. Star on the left—man smoking on left leg—Ship and Eagle on the back—United States and the ship *Constitution* on the back between the Shoulders. Bracelets on the wrists and other marks." Measurements of Chest: Inspiration 37 Expiration 34 inches.

They are hard cases and, evidently old Bounty Jumpers. If arrested please give information at this office.

I am Respectfully Your Obdt Servt.
A.B. Toon, Capt. & Prov Mar
2ᵈ Dist. Ill.

District One Provost Marshall—General Bureau Records, Letters Received, 1863–65, National Archives, Great Lakes Region, RG 110, Box 15.

~

Penetrating the largely immigrant Bridgeport community to tally the names of
potential draftees was a maddening experience for an enrolling officer. The memory
of residents often failed when they were asked the names of neighbors, relatives—
even their own names! The threat of arrest usually was enough to restore their
cognitive ability, however.

TROUBLES OF AN ENROLLING OFFICER

The enrolling officer for this district is well known in this community as a peaceful, well disposed gentleman, by profession a lawyer. . . . In the pursuance of his duties he visited Bridgeport to ascertain how many of the inhabitants of that classic region were subject to the draft, an inquisition which was received with great disfavor by all the natives, especially Mrs. Mulrooney, who keeps a grocery, which means a tenement wherein cabbage, dudheens [tobacco pipes] and whisky are dispensed and boarders without number are elegantly entertained. The widow Mulrooney is a little bustling woman who entertains the highest opinions of her success in dodging the tax-gatherer and other such curious persons bent on obtaining either money or information. Our enrolling officer, nothing daunted by the forbidding aspect of things, boldly entered the grocery, and asked the Mulrooney if she kept boarders. Mulrooney at once made up her mind that she had a tax-gatherer or something of that sort to deal with and retorted by asking him if he intended to insult a lone woman. As nothing was further from his intentions, he expressed himself to that effect and explained that he was the enrolling officer and that his duties required him to ascertain the names of all able-bodied men. The widow wanted to know if he was not paid for finding out the names, and if so, why he came to her for them. This was an *argumentum ad hominem* which was a poser. He wisely made no attempt to answer, but pressed his questions. Then the widow Mulrooney became oblivious. She couldn't remember the names of her boarders, and was mysteriously uncertain about their numbers. So rapidly did her memory fail her, that she soon forgot whether she had any boarders, and kept on forgetting at a rate which was rapidly tending towards a mental chaos. The officer himself began to have doubts about the existence of Mrs. Mulrooney and her boarders, and almost questioned his own identity. Such a remarkable case of mnemonical failure has rarely, if ever, occurred. The cure, however, was as speedy and thorough as the disease. Our officer, despairing of relieving the widow's memory by the ordinary methods, instantaneously restored it by taking the widow into custody. Then her memory returned unto her. She knew the number of her boarders, when they came, how long they were going to stay, their names, what they had in their trunks, how their scores stood, the names of their uncles and aunts for a dozen generations back—in fact, everything which it was proper for her to remember in order to satisfy the inquiries of the enrolling officer. We give the widow Mulrooney as a sample of a large class where the officer had an equally interesting time in ascertaining what the law requires.

The indifference or unwillingness to impart information, is not confined to the Mulrooneys alone, by any means. People in higher walks, proprietors of manufactories, and business houses, have refused to furnish the names of employees. . . . The proprietor only furnished them when he found that his own personal liberty was involved.

Chicago Tribune, October 1, 1862.

~

By December 1862, Chicago's enrollment lists numbered 23,151 men eligible for service.

NUMBER OF MEN IN CHICAGO LIABLE TO DRAFT.—By official authority it is stated that the enrollment books give the whole number of men in Chicago liable for the draft as 23,151, and place the number of enlisted from the city at 2,445. In the different Wards the number of those upon whom the draft would be operative is set down as follows: 1st Ward, 2,774; 2nd 2,498; 3rd 2,113; 4th 1,259; 5th 2,147; 6th 3,161; 7th 3,317; 8th 1,527; 9th 1,208; 10th 3,157.

Chicago Tribune, December 1, 1862.

~

Some residents went to desperate lengths to avoid losing a loved one and breadwinner to the draft. Here an Irishwoman went so far as to brandish a butcher knife to fend off enrolling officers. Note the charged ethnic and gendered language deployed by the Tribune.

THE CONSCRIPTION ACT.

A WOMAN ARRESTED FOR RESISTING AN ENROLLING OFFICER.
She is Examined Before U.S. Commissioner Hoyne,
and Held to Bail in $1,000 for Trial.

We have already alluded in these columns to the progress of the enrollment, and to the fact that in the Democratic wards of the city, every avenue of information has been denied to the enrolling officers by those of the Copperhead stripe— the Republicans willingly furnishing their names and such other particulars as were desired. In their resistance to the Conscription Act, the Copperheads have not contented themselves with denying information, but, urged on by the teachings of the Chicago *Times*, have openly threatened the lives of the enrolling officers. Not desirous, however, of assuming the responsibility of a violation of the laws themselves, they have urged on the women to resistance, imagining that the female was too sacred for the law to touch, and that in an onslaught of Amazons, enrolling officers would precipitately flee, and never venture again within their jurisdiction in quest of information which might lead to the necessity of their peaceable husbands fighting for their country.

One of the results of Copperhead doctrines, teachings and intentions manifested itself yesterday morning, in the examination of Mrs. Ellen McCafferty, before United States Commissioner, P. A. Hoyne, on a charge of resisting an enrolling officer in the discharge of his sworn duty. The accused was, as her name indicates, a native of the Emerald Isle, but for a number of years past resident in this city. She is the wife of Patrick McCafferty, night watchman for C. H. McCormick & Co., and is a young and rather handsome woman.

It appears from the evidence adduced on the investigation, that three or four days ago, Joel Lull, Enrolling Officer under the Conscription Act, for the Seventh Ward, in the course of his duty called at the house where the McCaffertys live, on the corner of Polk and Halsted streets, and not finding the man at home, sought from the wife the facts he desired, to make his record complete. Instead of answering the very reasonable inquiries of the polite official, Mrs. McCafferty seized a bootjack and threatened to brain Mr. Lull on the spot, if he did not "clear himself out of the house." The officer, not desiring any trouble, left, intending to call again, when he hoped to find the man at home. Accordingly, on Thursday he again went to the house, and Mrs. McCafferty was again alone; but this time Mr. Lull had an able assistant in the person of Policeman Thomas Cummings, and both together they advanced toward the Amazon. Mrs. McCafferty was ready for them, and in a moment made her appearance, armed with a large butcher knife with a blade something over a foot in length, which she brandished wildly in the air, declaring that, if the "infernal Abolishioners" did not leave her house, she would give them "a grave on her own door-step." She was positive she could whip both, and at least was willing to try. "At any rate, they could not put down her man's name for to be drafted." Again the attacking forces retired, and under the advice of Provost Marshal [William] James proceeded to Commissioner Hoyne, and, filing the necessary affidavit, procured a warrant for the woman's arrest. . . .

The Commissioner, after hearing the testimony, decided to hold Mrs. McCafferty to bail in $1,000, to answer any indictment that may hereafter be found against her in the United States Court. The utter folly of attempting to resist an official of the Government must be obvious to every one. The Provost Marshal is determined to carry out his instructions to the letter, and will do it regardless of consequences.

How much better, then, for all persons to submit quietly, and patiently await the result. The enrollment will be carried on, despite all opposition, and a ready acquiescence and submission to the laws of the land will prove in the end much more satisfactory than any opposition which can be inaugurated.

Chicago Tribune, June 13, 1863.

~

The Tribune's *coverage of draft resistance in the Bridgeport neighborhood strongly reflected the political and cultural bias of its editors, who mixed their strong support for the Union cause with an unsympathetic view of the Chicago Irish. The following account was certainly correct in its description of the poor neighborhood's unsavory reputation, but it also shows no understanding of the struggles members of this community had faced in their lives and the price they were being asked to pay to live in a country in which they had only just arrived.*

RIOT IN THE THIRD WARD.

Enrolling Officers Stoned and Injured.

ONE OF THE OFFICERS NOT EXPECTED TO RECOVER.

A large portion of the Third Ward, especially upon Fourth Avenue, south of Twelfth street, and in the locality thereabout known as "The Patch," is inhabited by a lawless, reckless class of the community, embracing the very lowest, most ignorant, depraved and besotted rabble that can be found in the city. Fights, rows, and even murders are not infrequent among them, and after nightfall, it is unsafe for any person to pass through the locality unless armed to the teeth. The natives of this neighborhood are all Copperheads. They read the Chicago *Times*, and they pursue its teachings to the letter.

It is among this class of people that Mr. A. H. Carter, a most estimable citizen, formerly Steward of the City Hospital, and Mr. J. H. Bailey, both enrolling officers, have been attempting to obtain the names of residents in accordance with the Conscription Act. Every obstacle has been thrown in their way, and threats and even violence have been resorted to for the intimidation of the officers. Finding that they were determined to prosecute their duties, in spite of all opposition, they positively refused to give their names, and the officers were obliged to have recourse to the law. They accordingly made affidavit before United States Commissioner Hoyne, yesterday, and a warrant was issued for the arrest of two men, living on Fourth avenue, near Liberty street, who had refused to give their names. Armed with the process, the two enrolling officers, in company with Officer Hart and Deputy U. S. Marshal Webb, started for the locality above mentioned. On the way, Officer Hart arrested a man named Eugene Sullivan, who had refused to give his name, and, without any difficulty or resistance, brought him before the Commissioner. He gave bail in the sum of $1,000, for a hearing, and was released.

In the meantime the other officers kept on their way until they reached the corner of Fourth Avenue and Liberty street. Deputy Marshall Webb went into a shanty near the Rock Island machine shops and arrested the two men, handing them over to the enrolling officers. The men at first offered no resistance, but at the same time seemed unwilling to go and used a number of opprobrious epithets. They had proceeded but a short distance, however, when the prisoners openly refused to go any further. Force was used to compel them, when almost instantaneously a mob of three or four hundred infuriated Irish—men, women and children—gathered together, and howling like demons, commenced an onslaught upon the officers with bricks, stones, bottles and every missile they could find. The attack was so terrible that the officers were obliged to release their prisoners in order to save their own lives. Deputy Webb escaped unhurt. Officer Bailey was struck by a stone in the face, inflicting an ugly but not serious wound, and also had one of his thumbs badly hurt. Officer Carter was struck in the head by a brick, and felled senseless to the ground. Some of the workmen in the machine shop near by rescued him from the mob, and he was taken, still senseless, to Hitchcock's drug store, where an examination was made by physicians. His skull is fractured badly, and at the present writing the physicians think he cannot recover.

With the absence of the enrolling officers, the disturbance quieted. Provost Marshal [William] James, as soon as he heard of the disturbance, visited the ground in person and made thorough inquiries, but could find nothing which afforded any clue to the perpetrators of the outrage. But the Provost Marshal and Government officials will not remain content until they have ferreted out the offenders.

It would be idle, now that the affair has happened, to show how it might have been prevented. The mob have openly set at defiance the law, and the first result of that defiance is the probable murder of one of our best citizens—a most estimable man in every respect. This is to be attributed solely to the teachings of the Chicago *Times*, and to nothing else. That vile, treasonable sheet has urged on these men to violence, and the riot of yesterday is to be charged to it; and if Mr. Carter dies, to it also belongs the responsibility of his death.

Chicago Tribune, June 26, 1863.

~

After the Bridgeport riot, the Tribune *lectured the Irish on the price of freedom.*

A WORD WITH IRISHMEN.

There is but one class of people in this city who refuse to give their names to the enrolling officers—the Irish. They exhibit less loyalty than any other nationality. The enrolling officers have no trouble with the Americans, the Germans, the Scandinavians, the Scotch, English, French or Hollanders, all of whom answer the questions in relation to their ages and names truthfully and promptly. But the Irish throw all sorts of obstacles in the way. Many of them dodge and hide from the marshals, and when found they give false names and try to deceive the officer or mulishly refuse to answer. In some instances they threaten personal violence. Frequently they beat or otherwise maltreat those who give their names in to the officers. And in one case they collected a mob and assaulted the officers, nearly murdering them.

It was only the other day they were the loud champions of law, and fierce in their denunciations of "arbitrary proceedings." "Let the law take its course, let the law be obeyed," they shouted. But this was when they were helping to shield a traitor, who was laboring to sap and undermine his country. But when the enrolling officers came round to procure the names of those capable of doing military service in defence of their country, they are swift to violate the law and trample it under foot.

Why do the Irish behave so badly? No class of people are more largely debtors to our free institutions. They sought our shores to enjoy free government and to escape from British tyranny. No class of people are fonder of voting or holding office, or sharing the good things that Freedom scatters among her votaries. Why, then, should they hesitate to defend the Government and the institutions which have conferred upon them so many blessings? Their conduct is basely ungrateful, and the stigma they are fixing upon themselves will take many a year to obliterate. A class of people that will not cheerfully fight in defense of free government are unworthy of its enjoyment. Now is the time that tests men's patriotism. The man that will not stand by his country in the hour of peril has no right to expect benefits from that country when the storm abates and the danger is past.

If the Irish intend to resist the draft and refuse to fight for the Union, what right have they to vote or hold office? If they will not help defend the country why do they remain in it? The Republic wants none but loyal citizens and willing defenders. The disloyal, whether foreign or native born, are not welcome. The Irish should make up their minds to obey the laws, and contribute their equitable share to the National defence, as do the Americans, the Germans and other nationalities, or cease to exercise the high privilege of citizens. If they would be citizens, they have duties to perform which they must not shirk or refuse to fulfill. . . . The Irish are not a privileged class who may enjoy all the benefits but need not bear any of the burdens. They are no better than Americans or Germans, or Scandinavians or other classes of citizens. And they have no right to avoid the enrollment, or escape the draft by mob violence, deceit or dodging.

. . . Many Irish give in their names without objection. It is a fraud on them for others of their countrymen to dodge the enrollment. The behavior of the Irish is not in consequence of any inherent cowardice or hatred of freedom, for they are a fighting, pugnacious race, and passionately fond of the enjoyment of the largest liberty compatible with the public safety. But it must be the baneful result of the treasonable teachings and influence of Copperhead leaders who poison them with lies, and fill them with prejudice against the beneficent Government that fosters and protects them. The Copperhead demagogues want to keep them out of the army for the double purpose of depriving the Republic of defenders and using them to elect friends of rebels to office—to prevent them from fighting the rebels, and to keep them at home to help open a fire-in-the-rear on the soldiers in the field. And this is the ignoble role the Copperhead demagogues would make the Irish play in the present terrible crisis!

Chicago Tribune, July 2, 1863.

THE SUPPRESSION OF THE *TIMES*

Frederick Cook was a reporter for the Chicago Times who later worked in the same capacity for the Tribune. He left a relatively unbiased account of one of the most divisive events of Civil War–era Chicago—the closing of the leading Democratic newspaper in the Midwest by federal troops.

One of the most exciting events in the annals of Chicago was the suppression of the Times on June 2, 1863, by military edict. General Ambrose E. Burnside, chiefly distinguished for a magnificent pair of side-whiskers, had command of the department that included Chicago, with its headquarters at Cincinnati; thence, on June 2, 1863, there issued a mandate, excluding the New York World from the mails within his military jurisdiction, and an order to General Benjamin Sweet, commander at Camp Douglas, to take charge of the Times office and prevent any further issues of that notorious "copperhead" sheet.

THE EDITOR NOT DISPLEASED

To call this order a blunder is the mildest characterization that can be applied to it. The unthinking mass of Republicans hailed it with delight, and gave it stout support. But the more sober-minded leaders of the party fully appreciated its

FIGURE 15. Wilbur Storey, editor of the *Chicago Times*. From Frederick Cook, *Bygone Days in Chicago*. (Chicago: A. C. McClurg, 1910). 332.

menace not only to civil liberty, but to law and order. Perhaps the one personally least concerned in this crisis was the owner and editor of the *Times*, Wilbur F. Storey. It required no prophet to predict that the order would not stand; and in the meantime it gave the paper a country-wide notoriety, while the act served only to give color to the often reiterated charge (that for which the paper was suppressed), namely, that "the war, as waged by military satraps of the administration, was a subversion of the Constitution and the people's rights under the law."

To the Copperhead leaders the order came as a godsend. Through an irresponsible military zealot they had at one bound been fixed in the saddle, booted and spurred, with the hated "abolition" enemy divided, distracted, and on the run. Let it be remembered that Chicago was in fact a Democratic city; that it had a Democratic Mayor and Council; and that the *Times* was the municipality's official organ.

Danger of Rebellion

The order was in effect a declaration of martial law. Only by a military force could it be carried out and maintained, for the entire civil machinery, including the United States court, was opposed to it. Another step, and the city, the State, and wide areas beyond might be in the throes of a civil war within a civil war. As soon as the news of what was to happen spread among the people, the strain between the opposing sides became threateningly tense, and with "Copperheadism" most resolutely to the fore; while on every side one heard the threat, which grew with each hour, "If the *Times* is not allowed to publish, there will be no *Tribune*.

As soon as the news of the intended suppression reached the *Times* office, every department received a rush order, and the press (this was before the days of stereotyping, and the duplication of "forms") was set in motion at the earliest possible hour; while the issue as fast as printed was bundled out of the building into safe quarters for distribution. A horseman was sent to Camp Douglas, with orders to speed to the office as soon as a detachment of the garrison was seen to leave the camp. He arrived shortly after two o'clock with the report that the "Lincoln hirelings" had started; and within an hour a file of soldiers broke into the office and formally took possession. . . .

A Mass Meeting

All through the day great crowds were gathered about the Randolph Street entrance of the publication office; and by evening the thoroughfare from State Street to Dearborn Street was a solid pack of humanity. Meantime the city had been flooded with handbills calling upon the people to resent this military interference with the freedom of the press, and making announcement that a mass meeting in protest of the order would be held in the evening. When the time for this meeting came, and a thousand oft-repeated cries of "Storey," "Storey" had met with no response, the crowd spontaneously moved two blocks west to the Square, where by eight o'clock an estimated crowd of twenty thousand people was gathered, which was to the full the city's total voting population.

The situation certainly called for serious, deliberate, and concerted action on the part of all law-and-order-loving citizens. While the rank and file of the opposing currents stood face to face in sullen, menacing opposition, the conservative leaders of both sides were in council to avert threatening trouble. At a mob demonstration the Copperhead faction would undoubtedly have had a numerous advantage, besides having the partisan police on its side. . . .

Another Meeting Asks the Rescinding of the Order

While the mass meeting was in progress outside, another was taking place in one of the court rooms. Judge Van H. Higgins was at this time a stockholder in the *Tribune*, and its property was in danger. Largely through his efforts prominent men from both sides had been brought together, and Mayor Sherman was called to the chair. . . .

. . . the following preamble and resolution were adopted:

"*Whereas*, In the opinion of this meeting of citizens of all parties,, the peace of this city and State, if not also the general welfare of the country, are likely to be promoted by the suspension or rescinding of the recent order of General Burnside for the suppression of *The Chicago Times*: therefore

"*Resolved*, That upon the ground of expediency alone, such of our citizens as concur in this opinion, without regard to party, are hereby recommended to unite in a petition to the President, respectfully asking the suspension or rescinding of the order."

The Resolution Forwarded to the President

. . . The resolutions were at once forwarded to the President, with an additional telegram signed jointly by Senator Trumbull and Congressman Arnold, praying him to give the voice of the meeting immediate and serious consideration. . . .

Colonel Jennison Protects the "Tribune" Office

How serious the menace to the *Tribune* was regarded may be judged from the fact that the correspondent of the New York *Herald* closed his dispatch for the night, "At this hour the *Tribune* still stands." None were more alive to the danger threatening their property than the owners of this resolute war paper. According to reports the old Clark Street rookery opposite the Sherman House, and within sound of the clamor of the great assemblage, had been transformed into an arsenal, with Colonel [Charles R.] Jennison, of "Jayhawking" notoriety, in command. This whilom lieutenant of "Ossawattamie" Brown, during the trying "Bloody Kansas" days, was endowed by the mass of Republicans with an almost superhuman prowess; and at the same time was a veritable red rag to the Copperhead bull. He was togged in quite the present cowboy fashion; and whenever seen on the street was followed by a crowd of gapping admirers. . . .

A Meeting in Support of Suppression

The Democrats having had their inning, there was a gathering in force of Republicans of the following evening, their obvious object being to call to account those members of the party who had memorialized the President to undo the work of Burnside. When Senator Trumball undertook to address the meeting he found the crowd in a very ugly mood. He was frequently interrupted, again and again charged with consorting with "traitors," with aiding and abetting the enemy, while over and over again there were cries, "We want Jennison," "Jennison is the man for us." . . .

On the following day, June 4, General Burnside announced that the President had rescinded both the *World* and *Times* military order. The result was that the circulation of the *Times* was largely increased.

Frederick Francis Cook, *Bygone Days in Chicago: Recollections of the "Garden City of the Sixties"* (Chicago: A. C. McClurg, 1910), 51–58.

THE PRESIDENT AT GETTYSBURG

The editor of the Chicago Times, *Wilbur F. Storey, was a bitter opponent of emancipation and African American equality. In this editorial reply to Abraham Lincoln's famous Gettysburg Address, Storey challenges Lincoln's opening reference to the Declaration of Independence. Republicans had long used the opening words of the Declaration to attack the institution of slavery, while Democrats pointed to the Constitution's veiled wording concerning slavery as proof that the founders accepted slavery as just.*

It is not supposed by any one, we believe, that Mr. Lincoln is possessed of much polish in manners or conversation. His adherents, however, claim for him an average amount of common sense, and more than an ordinarily kind and generous heart. We have failed to distinguish his pre-eminence in the latter, and apprehend the former to be somewhat mythical, but imagine that his deficiencies herein being less palpable than in other qualities constituting a statesman. . . . These qualities are unfailing guides to appropriateness of speech and action in missing with the world, however slight may have been the opportunities afforded their possessor for becoming acquainted with the usages of society.

The introduction of Dawdleism[16] in a funeral sermon is an innovation upon established conventionalities, which, a year or two ago, would have been regarded with scorn by all who thought custom should, to a greater or less extent, be consulted in determining social and public proprieties. And the custom which forbids its introduction is founded on the propriety which grows out of the fitness of things, and is not therefore merely arbitrary, or confined to special localities, but has suggested to all nations the exclusion of political partisanship in funeral discourses. Common sense, then, should have taught Mr. Lincoln that its intrusion upon such an occasion was an offensive exhibition of boorishness and vulgarity. An Indian in eulogizing the memories of warriors who had fallen in battle would avoid allusion to differences in the tribe which had no connection with the prevailing circumstances, and which he knew would excite unnecessarily the bitter prejudices of his hearers, Is Mr. Lincoln less refined than a savage?

But aside from the ignorant rudeness manifest in the President's exhibition of Dawdleism at Gettysburg, and which was an insult at least to the memories of a part of the dead, whom he was there professedly to honor, in its misstatement of the cause for which they died, it was a perversion of history so flagrant that the most extended charity cannot regard it as otherwise than willful. That, if we do him injustice, our readers may make the needed correction, we append a portion of his eulogy on the dead at Gettysburg:

"Four score and ten [sic] years ago our fathers brought forth upon this continent a nation consecrated [sic] to liberty and dedicated to the proposition that all men are created equal. [Cheers.] Now we are engaged in a great civil war, testing whether that nation or any other [sic] nation so consecrated [sic] and so dedicated can long endure."

As a refutation of this statement, we copy certain clauses in the Federal constitution: "Representatives and direct taxes shall be apportioned among the several States which may be included in this Union, according to their respective numbers, which shall be determined by adding to the whole number of *free* persons, including those bound to service for a term of years, and excluding Indians not taxed, three-fifths of *all other persons*."

~

"The migration or importation of such persons as any of the States now existing shall think proper to admit shall not be prohibited by the Congress prior to the year 1808, but a tax or duty may be imposed on such importation, not exceeding ten dollars for each person."

~

"No amendment to the constitution, made prior to 1808, shall affect the preceding clause."

~

"No person held to service or labor in one State under the laws thereof, escaping into another, shall, in consequence of any law or regulation therein, be discharged from such service or labor, but shall be delivered up on claim of the party to whom such service or labor may be due."

Do these provisions in the constitution dedicate the nation to "the proposition that all men are created equal"? Mr. Lincoln occupies his present position by virtue of this constitution, and is sworn to the maintenance and enforcement of these provisions. It was to uphold this constitution, and the Union created by it, that our officers and soldiers gave their lives at Gettysburg. How dared he, then, standing on their graves, misstate the cause for which they died, and libel the statesmen who founded the government? They were men possessing too much self-respect to declare that negroes were their equals, or were entitled to equal privileges.

Chicago Times, November 23, 1863.

The anti-Lincoln tone of the Chicago Times *became even stronger as the war progressed. On December 8, 1863, Lincoln took a first step toward Reconstruction of the divided nation by issuing a presidential proclamation offering amnesty to Confederates in Union-occupied territory, provided they took an oath that they would "abide by and faithfully support" the Emancipation Proclamation. Wilbur Storey and the* Chicago Times *bitterly denounced the offer as un-American and actually encouraged rebel military resistance.*

Perhaps the South should consent to these terms. If she does, the degradation they suffer will not be half as severe as should be inflicted upon a people who could accept that degradation. If she does, she is not fit to be in the Union upon any terms of equality with the other States, or to exercise any political privileges of any name or nature. If she does, her people should be compelled to change situations with the slaves, and governed only by this government's lash. No true American could propose such degradation to fellow citizens and the fact that they have been made is proof that their author is either insane with fanaticism, or a traitor who glories in his country's shame. If the Confederates are not dogs, they will free, arm, and marshal their slaves for the conflict, by offering still greater bribes than are offered by the Abolitionists, before they will think of submission to the President's terms.

Chicago Times, December 23, 1863.

~

In the wake of the suppression of the Chicago Times, *editor Wilbur Storey found himself subjected to personal physical attacks. One former employee, with some exaggeration, recalled that "every loyal citizen believed that he ha[d] a God-given right to attack" the editor. For Storey the attacks and the suppression were part of a pattern of violence by Republicans that would justify a violent response by Democrats. This editorial was widely reprinted in the South, and it presaged the armed organizations that would emerge during the 1864 general election.*

It is not improper, in this connection, to add, that when the Times shall cease to be printed, by reason of partisan mob violence, it is the purpose of the Democracy of Chicago that no other paper shall be printed in the city, and we have [not] the slightest doubt, that this purpose shall be executed. And it is not improper in this connection, to further add, that we fear it will be a sorry day for the peace of the city when the Times shall be serious interfered with by mob violence. We say this not in the way of threat but simply to state a fact that will be as obvious to others as to us if others choose to put themselves in the channel of current information. Elsewhere Abolition mobs seem to have an unobstructed saturnalia. They will not have this in Chicago. . . . The outrages by roving soldiers, just now so general, are of course by the consent and encouragement, tacit or otherwise, of the officers of the soldiers, and they are too, the legitimate consequence of the teachings numerous Abolition generals, politicians, and almost without exception, the Abolition press. They can be stopped in a day if the Administration at Washington chose to stop them. They are not stopped, and no intention is apparent of stopping them. Every consideration of right, justice, and law justifies the Democracy in falling back upon the power of their own strong arms for self-protection, self-defense, and punishment of the aggressors. . . . It is now for the Administration at Washington and the Abolition press and politicians all over the country to determine how much blood shall be spilled and how much property shall be destroyed in the maintenance by the Democracy of their stern resolutions to preserve, enjoy, and freely exercise their personal and political rights.

Chicago Times, reprinted in the *Memphis Daily Appeal,* April 1, 1864.

THE COPPERHEAD CONVENTION

The ill-advised shutdown of the Times *by the blundering General Burnside made the newspaper's editor, Wilbur F. Storey, a national martyr for the cause of free speech and gave antiwar Democrats a valid complaint with which to rally opposition to the Lincoln administration. The Democratic National Convention that was held*

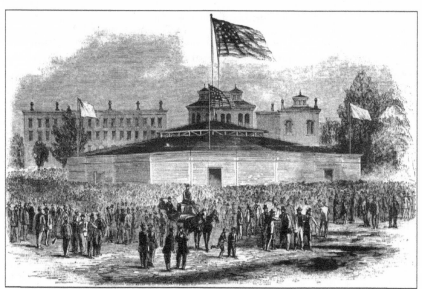

FIGURE 16. The temporary convention hall erected in Lake Front Park for the 1864 Democratic Convention. From *Harper's Weekly*, September 3, 1864.

in Chicago the following summer was a gathering of the most vociferous critics of President Lincoln and the war. The Chicago Platform agreed to by the Democrats at the convention declared the war a "failure" and called for peace with the South.

In the deliberations of the Convention, which took place in a huge auditorium specially erected for the occasion at the southern end of the lake front, restraint of speech was for obvious reasons deemed advisable; but outside, at impromptu gathers about the leading hotels, most of the speakers (when addressing what can be characterized only as howling mobs) lashed themselves into paroxysms of denunciation of everything in any manner tending to give encouragement or effective support to the war.

Great Excitement During the Convention

. . . The shibboleth of the hour was "Peace at any price"; and when the one side charged that such an attitude was treason to the nation, the other retorted that coercion was treason to the Constitution. In the Republican press this political submergence of the city was usually spoken of as a Rebel invasion; and when in addition to so much that was disquieting, the air was filled with rumors of plots for the release of the 10,000 or more "Johnny Rebs" in durance at Camp Douglas, it is within bounds to say that the substantial classes were in a state of mind bordering on panic. . . .

Sample of the Speeches

Of the utterances of the speakers who harangued the great mass from different improvised rostrums—the principal ones being the east and south balconies of the Sherman House—the following extracts from the *Times* reports are fair samples:

Hon. John J. Van Allen—"We do not want a candidate with the smell of war on his garments. The great Democratic party should have resisted the war from the beginning."

...

Hon. S.S. Cox, of Ohio (later of New York)—"Abraham Lincoln has deluged the country with blood, created a debt of four thousand million dollars, and sacrificed two millions of human lives. At the November election we will damn him with eternal infamy. Even Jefferson Davis is no greater enemy of the Constitution."

...

Hon. W.W. O'Brien, of Peoria—"We want to try Lincoln as Charles I. of England was tried, and if found guilty will cry out the law."

...

Stambaugh, of Ohio—"If I am called upon to elect between the freedom of the nigger and disunion and separation, I shall choose the latter. You might search hell over and find none worse than Abraham Lincoln."

...

G.C. Sanderson—"It is time this infernal war should stop. Have we not all been bound hand and foot to the abolition car that is rolling over our necks like the wheels of another Juggernaut? If the Southern Confederacy by any possibility be subjugated by this abolition administration, the next thing they will turn their bayonets on the free men of the North, and trample you in the dust."

...

Hon. and Rev. Henry Clay Dean, of Iowa—"The American people are ruled by felons. With all his vast armies Lincoln has failed! *failed!* FAILED! FAILED! And still the monster usurper wants more victims for his slaughter pens.

Frederick Cook, *Bygone Days in Chicago: Recollections of the "Garden City" of the Sixties* (Chicago: A. C. McClurg, 1910), 77–89.

THE NORTHWEST CONSPIRACY AND THE ELECTION OF 1864

Buckner S. Morris migrated to Chicago from Georgia and Kentucky in the city's founding years and was elected mayor in 1838. During the 1850s, Morris was a Know-Nothing. During the war, Morris became an outspoken critic of the Union effort. This led the Tribune to label him a copperhead. In 1864 he was arrested and incarcerated for nine months for allegedly participating in the Northwest Conspiracy. A military court, however, exonerated him of treasonous activity. Morris returned to the city a broke and broken man with a sullied reputation.[17] *The Tribune's reporting on former mayor Morris's political bid to head Cook County reflects its highly partisan views of political opponents.*

THE KNOW NOTHING COPPERHEAD TICKET.

The copperhead ticket for Cook County is headed by Buck Morris. There is a peculiar fitness in this selection. He is a representative man, a living embodiment of copperhead principles. He is the pet of the secesh concern, and reflects its sentiments to perfection. His house, his heart, his purse, are always open to secessionists and rebels. Every secessionist from the South, who visits Chicago for the purpose of aiding rebel prisoners to escape from Camp Douglas regards him as a friend and ally.

Never since the rebels made war on the Union has Buck Morris felt or expressed a loyal sentiment. His sympathies have been wholly with Confederates. If he ever prays, it is for their success and the downfall of the Abolition Union, as he calls the Government of the United States. . . . While the Know Nothing party existed, he was its recognized leader in Illinois. In 1856, he ran as the Know Nothing candidate for Governor against Col. [Richard] Bissell, who was the Republican candidate. He clung to the Know Nothings until the organization was dead and buried; after which he joined the Breckenridge wing of the Democracy, but never recanted his nativistic principles. At heart he is as bitter a Know Nothing now as he ever was. But that will be no objection to him in the eyes of the Catholic Irish. Most of the active leaders of their party are old Know Nothings. The copperheads could nominate no candidate to head their ticket who would be more acceptable to the Irish than an ultra pro-slavery Know Nothing, and it was to please them and the Editor of the secesh *Times* that he was nominated.

Chicago Tribune, November 2, 1863.

~

When the Lincoln administration ordered three thousand troops to garrison Camp Douglas during the Democratic Convention in Chicago in August 1864, many of

Lincoln's Democratic opponents believed that he intended to interfere with their
selection of a Democratic challenger in the November elections. The Order of the
Sons of Liberty was a secret society founded in February 1864 to protect free elections
and a free press and promote peace. It was led by Clement L. Vallandigham, former
congressman of Ohio. Storey of the Chicago Times warned Democrats that "when
personal liberty in this country can only be protected by the intervention of secret
organizations, it may as well be surrendered altogether."[18] The organization was
filled with incompetent extremists who welcomed Confederate financial support and
also showed interest in a conspiratorial plan to use escaped rebel POWs to defend a
peace Democrat platform and candidates. John B. Castleman and Thomas H. Hines
were the two Confederate officers in charge of the effort to free the Camp Douglas
prisoners and to disrupt the Union war effort in Illinois.

THE NORTHWESTERN CONSPIRACY. . . .

A number of Confederate prisoners had escaped from confinement in the
Northwest, and many of those coming from Camp Douglas made their way into
Canada. To these the Commissioners were willing to supply means to return
to the Confederate States—and they were urged to lose no time in returning to
their regiments—except in July and August, when the colony was kept for service
against the prisons from which they had escaped. . . .

It will be observed that in August the garrison was largely increased at Chicago,
and three thousand troops were placed on duty. This led to an apprehension that
the administration intended to interfere with the meeting of the Democratic Convention on the 29th of August, and this fact was used to stimulate the prejudice
throughout the West and justify the assembling of a large body of men, outspoken in their determination to resist the possible outrage. There was thus furnished
sufficient excuse for the county commanders of the Order of the Sons of Liberty
to mobilize the members of their organization on the plea that they should attend the convention, and ought to resist any attempt to interrupt its deliberations.
Mr. Vallandigham's representatives were furnished means for transportation, and
had ample time to make proper distribution and explain to the more faithful and
courageous county commanders why the rank and file should come to Chicago
and resist any further attempt on the liberties of the citizens. These representatives were further urged to make provision for keeping reasonably in hand the
delegations from the various counties; but it must be confessed that events fully
justified the belief that some of the principal agents employed were lacking either
in fidelity or courage, or in both.

In Canada there were less than one hundred Confederate soldiers, and to the
discretion of some of these it was not altogether safe to trust the success of the

enterprise. Sixty men were chosen for service at Chicago. Many of these men had escaped from prison under circumstances which illustrated their daring and fertility of resource. . . .

The difficulty of providing for and properly controlling the suddenly liberated prisoners, in the event the attempt to effect their release should be successful, had been fully considered, and a programme which, it was believed, would meet it had been matured. The undertaking was certainly an arduous one in this respect, as well as hazardous in its first details. . . .

On the 27th and 28th of August the Confederates detailed for this important service proceeded to Chicago, traveling in small parties and assuming the appearance and conduct of men attracted there by the political interest of the occasion. They stopped at places designated in advance, the greater part of them having been instructed to go to the Richmond House.

. . . We believed our plans perfectly feasible, though ultimate success necessarily depended on the response made by the "Sons of Liberty" to our first movement. The whole enterprise had been thoroughly discussed and considered by the officers of that organization. Men commended to us by Mr. Vallandigham had been entrusted with the necessary funds for perfecting the county organizations; arms had been purchased in the North by the aid of our professed friends in New York; alliances offensive and defensive had been made with peace organizations, and though we were not misled by the sanguine promises of our friends, we were confident that with any sort of co-operation on their part success was reasonably possible. During the excitement that always attends a great political convention, . . . we felt that we would be freer to act unobserved, and that we could move with promptness and effect upon Camp Douglas. With nearly five thousand prisoners there, and over seven thousand at Springfield, joined by the dissatisfied elements in Chicago and through Illinois, we believed that at once we would have a formidable force, which might be the nucleus for much more important movements. Everything was arranged for prompt action, and for the concentration and the organization of all these bodies. It was, as we felt, the first step that was the most difficult and the most serious. Success was only possible by prompt and concerted action during the convention. The Confederates were ready. The men chosen for this work were no mere adventurers; they had enlisted in an enterprise where they knew success was doubtful, and that failure meant probable death. . . .

The National Democratic Convention met at Chicago, August 29th. It was the expectation of Confederate officers, as it was the hope of the members of the Sons of Liberty, that the convention would be controlled by "peace" men; that its platform would declare for peace measures, and that the nominee would in his own person represent the opposition in the North to any further prosecution of the war.

... Though our confidence in the zeal of the members of the Sons of Liberty had measurably weakened, we believed that we would, at Chicago, secure the co-operation of numbers sufficient to justify an attack on the prisons, and our plans had been made accordingly. Arms were ready, and information had been conveyed to the prisoners of war of our intention. Chicago was thronged with people from all sections of the country, and among this vast crowd were many of the county officers of the secret organization on whom we relied for assistance. . . .

It was essential to the success of any undertaking for us to know definitely what armed forces the representatives of Mr. Vallandigham could provide. For this a meeting of the officers of the organization was held at the rooms of Hines and Castleman at the Richmond House the night before the convention, August 28, 1864.

It soon developed that the men employed for gathering the members of the order had not faithfully performed their duties, and that the preparation for immediate and open hostility to the administration had destroyed the confidence or dissipated the courage of some of the men whose leadership was necessary. . . . From reports made at this meeting it did not appear that the notice to move county organizations had been properly given, or that sufficient preparation had been made, and it was evident that even the men who had come to Chicago were not kept in hand so as to be promptly available in organization. It was shown that such counties as were represented had their forces scattered generally over the city, intermingled with a vast multitude of strangers. Thus, while a large number of the order were present, they were not present in controllable shape, and were therefore not useful as a military body.

From whatever cause this state of things existed, it did exist, and it was deemed necessary to adjourn the conference to the evening of the 29th of August, to give the officers present time to look up their forces and report back what number each could absolutely control at a few hours' notice. The evening of the 29th of August came, but on the part of the timid timidity became more apparent, and those who were resolute could not show the strength needed to give confident hope of success. The reinforcement sent by the administration to strengthen the Chicago garrison had been vastly exaggerated, and seven thousand men was the number rumor brought to the ear of the Sons of Liberty. Care had been taken to keep informed as to what troops came to Camp Douglas, but the statement made by Hines and Castleman, to the effect that only three thousand were present, did not counteract the effect produced by the rumor that the Federal forces there numbered more than double that number.

Inside the prison some organization had been effected. Information had been conveyed to prudent prisoners that aid from outside would come, and they were watchful for the attack without as a signal for resistance within. The small force, composed even of the Confederates present, could have secured the release of the prisoners, because any assault from the outside would have led to a simultaneous one on the part of the prisoners, and the escape of most of them would have been certain. Their control, however, was necessary for their protection, and this could not be secured except by such a force as would overwhelm the garrison and promptly organize the prisoners. It would have been an unkindness to the prisoners themselves, and of no use whatever merely to release the Confederates at Camp Douglas, under circumstances which would have resulted in their subsequent recapture and punishment. When, therefore, a count was taken of the number of the Sons of Liberty on whom we could rely, it seemed worse than folly to attempt to use them. There were not enough to justify any movement which would commit the Northwestern people to open resistance, and not even enough to secure the release and control the organization of the prisoners at Camp Douglas as the nucleus of an army which would give possible relief to the Confederacy. . . .

With this state of things existing, it could not be safe or wise for the Confederates to linger in Chicago after the disappearance of the great throng which had assembled; it was necessary, therefore, to look beyond Chicago for a field of action.

Thomas H. Hines and John B. Castleman, "The Northwest Conspiracy," *Southern Bivouac*, n.s., 2 (June 1886–March 1887): 442, 572–74.

~

In November 1864, rebel agents returned to Chicago with the intent to join with the Sons of Liberty in the city and free the Camp Douglas prisoners on the eve of the presidential election. Ernest Duvergier de Hauranne was a witness to the collapse of their plans. The son of a prominent French family, de Hauranne was in Chicago to observe American democracy at work. What he saw instead was the last gasp of Civil War partisan passions pathetically played out in the streets of Chicago.

November 7, 1864

This morning on awakening the city learned with amazement that it had just escaped a terrible calamity. A vast conspiracy had been exposed, a plot organized by the Democrats and the Rebels that was to have been carried out tomorrow. According to the posters outside the offices of Republican newspapers, there was a plan to free the ten thousand prisoners-of-war at Camp Douglas and to furnish them with arms for looting and burning the city. The crime was engineered by the "Sons of Liberty" and the conspirators have accomplices in Chicago. Two or three colonels, a captain and a judge . . . and a number of city employees and militia officers have been clapped into prison. Sixty guerrillas sent from the South were captured while they were awaiting the signal. The authorities have seized two wagons loaded with arms and munitions of war. All this…is proclaimed by the laconic, mystifying and seemingly panic stricken posters around which people crowd together as if in a state of shock. At the office of the *Evening Journal* the goggle-eyed crowd can see formidable samples of the arsenal with which the ten thousand Rebel prisoners were to have been equipped: one large horse pistol, one army revolver, one small pocket pistol in its case, a little powder flask and a box of cartridges the size of a watch. The conspirators' entire armament could be packed in a candy-box.

I almost forgot to mention the most terrifying weapon of all, the one most certain to spread panic—a large, rusty knife that looks like the stub of a broken cavalry saber—"found . . . under the shirt of a man who answered, when questioned as to the knife's purpose: 'It's to cut the abolitionists' throats!'" You see what kind of stage effects are used to arouse the indignation of the most enlightened people in the world! The Republicans pretend to be filled with righteous indignation; the Democrats, taken by surprise or at least pretending to be, claim that they are the victims of an atrocious hoax. They say the whole thing is just a crude trick, a pretext for intimidating arrests and threatening troop movements; the accused are called spies and accomplices of the authorities, and the alleged guerrillas are said to be hirelings of the police. Thereupon a new poster appears and the Republican papers run new articles giving more details of the conspiracy; they tell how the guerrillas got drunk in a tavern and how, when the "wiskey" [*sic*] had loosened their tongues, the Republic was saved. This whole story is unconvincing, and I can see in this business only monstrous fraud. The Democrats would certainly like to match it with a similar piece of trickery borrowed from Barnum's bag of tricks, but as the opposition party, with the governor, the city government, the army and the police against them, they are reduced to playing the martyr's role: they complain, they accuse, they reproach; but their position is a sorry and unenviable one because the mob always sides with those who furnish them the best entertainment. . . .

November 9, 1864

President Lincoln has been elected by a large majority. Since yesterday it has been evident that the Republicans would carry Chicago. . . . All night long, people have been crowding into the newspaper offices and even into the lobby of my hotel, avidly reading the hourly dispatches brought from the telegraph company and posted up in big letters on the walls. The Democratic papers, which yesterday were spouting fire and flames, have a hang-dog look this morning and try to console themselves for their defeat by emphasizing local victories.

. . . This turbulent democracy, which had seemed on the point of tearing itself to pieces, spontaneously felt the need to impose self-discipline and to invest the choice of a new government with gravity and order. . . .

November 10, 1864

This morning I went to Camp Douglas. . . . Since the scare of November 7, and for several days afterward, visitors' passes have been refused to all outsiders, so I was not able to see the prisoners themselves in their quarters; but I have seen with my own eyes the proof of the fantastic plot which I outlined to you the other day with so little belief in it. Major W.*, who commands the camp, has shown me the loaded rifles, the cases full of loaded revolvers, the supplies of cartridges, powder and detonating caps that were seized in a hotel near the camp gate. The weapons are of such a nature as to leave no doubt concerning the use to which they were to have been put, and the abundance of the supplies, the haste with which they seem to have been prepared, the innocent appearance of the trunks that held them—all this convinced me that the Republicans have invented nothing but the theatrical touches and the ridiculous details that have only had the effect of casting doubt on the real truth. . . .

Camp Douglas serves as a prison for ten thousand Confederates guarded only by a single regiment of ill or convalescent soldiers. The Major himself, a young man of twenty-five, crippled for life, hobbles about on his crutch with an agility that is painful to watch. The only physical defense is a frail wooden fence with a guards' platform running around the top. Sentinels are posted here and there, but it could easily be breached by one or two blows of an axe. It is understandable that sixty resolute men could plan on gaining access at night to the prisoners' quarters, arming them and then setting them free to loot the city.

* misidentified

Ernest Duvergier de Hauranne, *A Frenchman in Lincoln's America*, transl. and ed. Ralph Bowen, 2 vols. (Chicago: R. R. Donnelley and Sons, Lakeside Press, 1975), 2:17–24.

REPUBLICANS TRY TO RESIST THE DRAFT

The reelection of Abraham Lincoln in November 1864 all but doomed the Confederacy. In an effort to maintain pressure on the battered rebel armies, the reelected president called for a final draft. Even strong supporters of the administration such as Joseph Medill dreaded enforcing this call, and he headed a delegation of leading Chicago Republicans to personally appeal to Lincoln for a reduction in their draft quota. Ever the politician, Lincoln patiently heard Medill out and led him to the War Department to hear from the military men, but when the Chicagoans persisted in requesting special favors for their city, Lincoln lost his temper. In 1895 Medill related the incident in an interview with the journalist Ida Tarbell.

" . . . The argument went on for some time, and finally was referred to Lincoln, who had been sitting silently listening. I shall never forget how he suddenly lifted his head and turned on us a black and frowning face.

"'Gentlemen,' he said in a voice full of bitterness, 'after Boston, Chicago has been the chief instrument in bringing this war on the country. The Northwest has opposed the South as the New England has opposed the South. It is you who are largely responsible for making blood flow as it has. You called for war until we had it. You called for Emancipation, and I have given it to you. Whatever you have asked you have had. Now you come here begging to be let off from the call for men which I have made to carry out the war you have demanded. You ought to be ashamed of yourselves. I have a right to expect better things of you. Go home, and raise your 6,000 extra men. And you, Medill, you are acting like a coward. You and your *Tribune* have had more influence than any paper in the Northwest in making this war. You can influence great masses, and yet you cry to be spared at a moment when your cause is suffering. Go home and send us those men.'

"I couldn't say anything. It was the first time I ever was whipped, and I didn't have an answer. We all got up and went out, and when the door closed, one of my colleagues said: 'Well, gentlemen, the old man is right. We ought to be ashamed of ourselves. Let us never say anything about this, but go home and raise the men.' And we did—6,000 men—making 28,000 in the war from a city of 156,000. But there might have been crape on every door almost in Chicago, for every family had lost a son or husband. I lost two brothers. It was hard for the mothers."

Ida M. Tarbell, *The Life of Abraham Lincoln,* 4 vols. (New York: Harper and Brothers, 1909), 2:149.

SIX

The Business and Politics of War

$\mathcal{T}$HE OUTBREAK OF CIVIL war in America dealt a body blow to the economy of Chicago. The Illinois and Michigan Canal and the Illinois Central Railroad were key transportation arteries that linked Chicago commerce to the Southern states of the Mississippi Valley. With the firing on Fort Sumter, that commerce in sugar, pork, grain, and manufactured goods ground to an immediate halt. Former trading partners donned gray uniforms and crowed that with Chicago cut off from the Gulf of Mexico, "grass would grow" in the streets of the city. For a time it looked as if they were right. Secession kicked off a banking crisis in Chicago. By the end of 1861, 89 of 110 banks in Illinois had failed. Most of these institutions had relied on stock from Southern states as their security, and secession was followed by a repudiation of those bonds by Confederate debtors. This set off a panic among legitimate depositors. When banks failed, millions of dollars were lost across the Midwest by workers and business owners alike who were left holding the worthless currency issued by these banks. Bank riots occurred in Milwaukee, but Chicago remained peaceful. Nonetheless, by New Year's Day in 1862, less than $150,000 remained on deposit in the entire city.[1]

The havoc of the banking crisis, however, masked the makings of a rapid economic recovery for Chicago. Merchants and manufacturers found themselves swamped with orders for military equipment. For leather goods makers, for example, 1861 proved a boom year. By June, Turner and Sidway, the city's largest saddle and harness maker, had executed $100,000 in army contracts. After outfitting the cavalry with saddles, blankets, and reins, the city also provided the necessary mounts. In 1861 alone, 8,332 horses were sold to the army in Chicago. By war's end the annual trade in horseflesh would double. Shoe making and ready-made clothing were two prewar businesses that could barely make headway against established eastern competitors. Suddenly both trades were lavished with military orders, and by 1863 their volume had increased tenfold. As the greatest port on the Great Lakes, Chicago had many ship chandlers. Their trade burgeoned as acres of canvas were transformed into regiments of tents. Chicago did not play a major role in the production of weapons of war, although the city lobbied mightily in April 1861 to be selected by the government as the site of a new federal armory, designed to supply rifles and cannon for the western armies. The selection of Rock Island, Illinois, on the Mississippi was a bitter blow to the city's industrial aspirations.[2]

The war did, however, trigger the industrialization of Chicago by building upon the city's existing economic strengths. When war broke out, Chicago was already the leading rail hub in America. In 1862, with Southern legislators no longer present to object, Lincoln pushed through Congress a bill to build a Pacific railroad along the central route. It was a decision that would guarantee Chicago the lion's share of the trade of the Far West. More important to the events of the war, however, was Stephen Douglas's gift to Chicago, the Illinois Central Railroad. Its right-of-way was a direct line from the city to General U. S. Grant's supply base on the Ohio River, and as he, and later General William T. Sherman, advanced deeper into the Confederacy, rails and rolling stock made in Chicago kept their troops in beef, pork, and hardtack. The car shops of Chicago clanged with activity night and day. Two major rolling mills were built along the Chicago River during the war to keep up with the demand for iron rails. By 1865 the North Chicago Rolling Mill had perfected the manufacture of the first long-lasting steel rails in America. This was the beginning of the great concentration of steel making on Chicago's South Side and in northern Indiana, the heart of what in the next century would be critical to winning the world wars.[3]

Military trains leaving Chicago were loaded with barrels of beef and pork. When the war began, Chicago was already the beef-packing center for the nation. By April 1862, the city had stolen from Cincinnati the title "Porkopolis," for all of the pigs slaughtered and packed. It was able to do this because of the vast rail network that put Chicago in easy reach of all midwestern producers. By 1864 the number of packing houses had nearly doubled, and there were so many herds of beeves and pigs being driven through the city that they clogged the streets and in one tragic incident collapsed a Chicago River bridge, plunging pedestrians and animals into the dark, polluted waters. That year the Chicago Pork Packers Association saw the necessity of centralizing and rationalizing their operations. The result in 1865 was the famous Union Stockyards, which for nearly one hundred years secured Chicago's claim as "hog-butcher to the world" and made it the ultimate destination of "per-near" every cowboy-driven herd on the Chisholm Trail. With Chicago already the nation's center for grain distribution, the war years laid the foundation for the city to emerge as a center for the food by-products industry and to play a role in the creation of the financial commodity markets.[4]

The Civil War made another important contribution to the industrialization of Chicago by helping to stabilize its financial foundation. The virtually unregulated financial system of antebellum America invited any scoundrel to open a bank and issue his own paper currency. Backed by little more than a good printer, much of this currency was worthless. It was hard for consumers to know what banks were sound and which currencies had real value. The Lincoln administration demonstrated how financial regulation could enhance economic growth and business prosperity when it sponsored a series of banking reforms that gradually squeezed trashy paper money out of circulation. New "national" banks were chartered to issue currency backed by the United States. Faith in these bills was faith in the future of the nation. The First National Bank of Chicago opened in July 1863, and Chicagoans enthusiastically embraced the cause and the security it represented. By the end of the war, there were thirteen new national banks in the city with combined deposits approaching $30 million. This was the capital cornerstone needed for industrialization. When the decade of the 1860s drew to a close, this pool of local capital had joined with eastern monies to enable the number of factories operating in the city to triple since the outbreak of the war.

Ironically, amid the wartime industrial surge, Chicago's most prominent manufacturer did not thrive. Cyrus Hall McCormick, owner of the nation's largest agricultural equipment factory, was a Virginian by birth, and at a time when the Union most needed labor-saving devices the company's production declined and what the factory did produce, McCormick focused on marketing in Europe. McCormick was a staunch Democrat and a bitter enemy of the Republican Party and even Stephen Douglas, because he felt they were too antagonistic toward the South. Once war came, McCormick played an important role funding political opposition to Lincoln and the Union war effort. His most effective move was his June 1861 decision to sell the *Chicago Times* newspaper to Wilbur F. Storey.[5]

A marked change in Chicago workplaces at this time was the growing presence of women. At military equipment and garment manufacturers, women made up between 10 and 15 percent of the workforce. Labor-saving devices such as the sewing machine and Chicago's growing population played an even larger role in overcoming the loss of male workers to military enlistment. It would be wrong, however, to assume that women played the type of role in Civil War production that they would play in the 1940s. While some working-class women found work in war-stimulated businesses, the daughters of the middle class had their greatest impact on the prosecution of the Civil War through their pioneering involvement with the U.S. Sanitary Commission.[6]

In the winter of 1862, like the Union war effort itself, the Sanitary Commission and its volunteers were in crisis. The discouragement and doubt that afflicted the whole Northern people in the wake of the defeat of the Army of the Potomac before Richmond and later at the Battle of Second Bull Run, and worse still at Fredericksburg, drained the last drops of the optimistic "war spirit" of 1861. Worse still for the Sanitary Commission, there were widespread reports that money and supplies donated for the troops did not make it to the men in need but instead either rotted in storehouses or was sold by the unscrupulous for personal profit. These charges led to a reorganization of the commission, spearheaded by its Women's Council. Chicago leaders Jane Hoge and Mary Livermore journeyed to Washington, DC, where they participated in a national meeting that reorganized the commission. Under the new plan, Chicago would serve as the central distribution center for all supplies gathered in the states of the "Northwest." This added tremendously to the work of the women of Chicago, but they were more than up to the task.[7]

The new system received its first test in February 1863 when Jane Hoge on a visit to General Grant's army outside Vicksburg discovered that scurvy was sapping the army's strength. When she sent a dispatch back to the city stating, "Rush forward anti-scorbutics for General Grant's Army," the commission was able to marshal the efforts of patriotic men and women throughout the region. Soon the Chicago office was forwarding cabbages, pickles, onions, and over 60,000 pounds of dried fruit. The Chicago office also created in the city a "Soldiers' Rest" where troops in transit could receive a bed and a meal, while for men who were invalids or too ill to travel an old hotel was transformed into the "Soldiers' Home." Unfortunately, the cost of these endeavors once more threw the finances of the Northwest Sanitary Commission into crisis.

Determined to address the problem, Jane Hoge and Mary Livermore attended the meeting of the commission's male directors. The men responded "languidly" to the woman's proposal to hold a fund-raising fair, however, and they "laughed incredulously" when Livermore estimated that she would be able to raise $25,000.[8] With the sound of that laughter ringing in their ears, the two women set about building regional support for their fair. In September 1863 they brought to the city more than three hundred women representing local soldier aid societies and won their wholehearted cooperation. The goal was to assemble a massive amount of donated items for sale, and so that "all classes" might be represented, they accepted donations of items valued for as little as a few pennies, as well as items worth thousands of dollars. As goods began to flood into the city, Livermore rented out every major assembly hall in the city. When this was not enough, she had a new exhibition building constructed with lumber and cash donated to the fair. The Northwest Sanitary Fair became a rallying point for men and women of the midwestern home front, an opportunity in the face of a growing copperhead movement to express their support for the war effort.

The fair opened on October 27, 1863, with a massive parade. Thousands of visitors flocked to the city to take in the spectacle. The fair was arranged in buildings around the courthouse square. Inside were acres of donated goods from foods to farm equipment, from clothing to pianos, and everything in between. Abraham Lincoln supported the effort by donating for auction the original signed copy of the Emancipation Proclamation. The fair also boasted a museum of war artifacts, an art gallery, a theater, and a food court. What the ladies of the Sanitary

Commission had created was a forerunner of the modern shopping mall. After two weeks of great excitement, the fair closed and Livermore and Hoge met with the much-chastened men of the Sanitary Commission, to whom they delivered a check for the staggering sum of $86,000. More important than the immediate injection of needed cash, the fair had made a major contribution to the overall war effort. It bolstered support among a war-weary population, it cemented the working relationship between Chicago and many midwestern relief organizations, it provided a model for other cities to follow (eventually every major city in the North followed Chicago's lead, and these fairs raised a combined $4.4 million), and it gave confidence to Northern women that they could excel at managing complex enterprises and that they deserved both an equal opportunity and equal rights. The great sanitary fairs in Chicago (there would be a second, even larger fair in the spring of 1865) were an example of the way the Northern population was able to exploit modern marketing techniques to sustain the Union cause.[9]

Music was another popular culture vehicle produced in Chicago that rallied people to the cause. George Frederick Root found the city to be a perfect place for him to develop his musical abilities. He was especially enchanted by the unpretentiousness of this new frontier city, and its access to nationwide transportation allowed his music publishing house, Root and Cady, to distribute its products throughout the country. Root's ambition was to make music relevant to the life of every American. To do this he helped organize music conventions to be held in every major American city and traveling educational programs to promote the teaching and learning of music.[10]

Through his travels, Root developed an appreciation for open frontier society. He wrote, "People from different social grades in the older settled places of the East meet here on a level. Social distinctions are in nobody's way, for there are none." This experience became formative to his music. He appreciated the experiences and opinions of ordinary people and their emotional connections with music and sought to incorporate that aesthetic into his music, searching for "the people's song." In 1859 Root settled in Chicago and joined his brother, Ebenezer Towner Root, and Chauncey Marvin Cady in their music business of Root and Cady. The firm sold musical instruments, sheet music, and books. When the Civil War started, the company could barely keep up with the demand for band instruments. The heady days of the Civil War led George to write music that stirred not only people's patriotism but also the full range of their emotional experiences with war.[11]

During the course of the war, many of the most famous and effective Union songs were written and published in Chicago, from "Just Before the Battle, Mother" to "Tramp, Tramp, Tramp, the Boys Are Marching" to "The Vacant Chair" to "Marching through Georgia." The man behind this remarkable output was George Frederick Root. In July 1862 he was asked to write a song for a monster war rally

designed to build support for President Lincoln's call for more troops. The resulting song, "The Battle Cry of Freedom," set the courthouse square crowd on fire,
and in a few short weeks the tune had blazed its way across the North. "The
effect was little short of miraculous," a soldier recalled. "It put as much spirit and
cheer in the army as a victory." Soon fourteen separate printing presses across the
country were producing the song. Root later estimated that he sold "between five
hundred and seven hundred thousand" copies of the sheet music to a Northern
public of only 20 million people. It was, in per capita terms, one of the best-selling
songs in American history.[12]

Root's popular war songs were as needed on the home front as they were by the
soldiers. By the summer of 1862, the prewar religious, ethnic, and racial divisions
in Chicago had bubbled to the surface. For the white working class, longstanding
fears of economic competition with Southern blacks had been awakened by pro-
emancipation agitation, and the draft opened up the possibility of forced military
service. Economic difficulties heightened these anxieties. While business boomed
in Civil War Chicago, workers faced a much more difficult time because of the
rapid rise in prices for food, clothing, and housing. By 1863 the cost of clothing for
Chicago workers had increased 100 percent, rent had risen 66 percent, and the cost
of the butcher's or baker's bill had doubled. The fact that workers' wages in Chicago were higher than in many eastern cities did nothing to calm the concerns of
men who saw their buying power erode. The result was frequent and unpredict-
able strikes. Ironworkers, printers, brick makers, coppersmiths, shoemakers, and
garment workers all struck for cost-of-living raises. During the last two years of
the Civil War, nineteen new labor unions were created in Chicago. A minor panic
ensued in the army quartermaster's office when Chicago railroad workers walked
off the job in the summer of 1864. With inflation rampant throughout the war,
even successful job actions were only a temporary relief. Many of the new unions
attempted to secure political influence by siding with the Democratic Party in the
1864 election. Concern over the draft and the party's traditional appeal to immigrants pushed some activists in that direction. However, when the *Chicago Times,*
the voice of local Democrats, attempted to break the printers' union and the local
party nominated tight-fisted industrialist Cyrus Hall McCormick for Congress,
workers became disgusted with party politics.

A turning point for the Chicago working class was reached in late 1864. The
reelection of Abraham Lincoln to the White House to some extent eliminated
the divisive issues of emancipation and slavery from the political arena. Previously
these issues had divided the Irish from the Germans and native-born Americans.
Faced with the common challenge of inflation and the growing industrialization
of labor, white workers began to coalesce as a class-conscious political force. A
sign of this new unity was the creation in 1864 of the General Trades Assembly,

which brought together all of the building trades in the city. Also created was a new weekly newspaper, the *Workingman's Advocate*, designed to be the voice of "the producing classes of the Northwest."

In the first three years of the war, Chicago had greatly prospered. The majority of its citizens had rallied to the cause of saving the Union. With energy and imagination, Chicagoans had by the fall of 1864 largely managed the challenges of war, but they had an uneasy feeling that they were on a tiger's back, and they had no idea how or when they could get off.

BANKING: CRISIS AND RECOVERY

Chicago's first financial experience with the coming of war was a collapse of many of its banks. As a frontier city and state, Chicago and Illinois, respectively, were chronically short on gold and silver specie—the preferred means of exchange by the national business community. Anxious to encourage investment and economic growth, Illinois had few capital requirements for state-chartered banks and no way of monitoring the soundness of the currencies they issued. When rebel merchants refused to make good on their debts to Northern businessmen and the value of Southern securities plummeted, Chicago bankers found that no one wanted wildcat currency. Their only recourse was to devalue the bills. Out of 110 banks in Illinois, 89 failed. Chicago lost $12 million, holding only $147,073 at the end of 1861. In 1863 Congress authorized national banks, guaranteeing the soundness of currency issued. The Chicago Board of Trade played a leading role in ensuring the exclusive acceptance of federal notes.

THIRTY-TWO ILLINOIS BANKS THROWN OUT.

The crisis with the Illinois Banking system has come at last. The Chicago bankers have been carrying it for as long as they could, and in order to save themselves, and our mercantile and business community, they have felt themselves forced to throw out the bills of thirty-two Illinois Banks. The warnings which the TRIBUNE has so frequently given, we are sorry to see are now fully realized. When, in spite of our remonstrances, the system expanded and millions of currency, based upon the stocks of Southern States, were thrust into the pockets of the people, we seconded the efforts of our bankers to sustain it as long as possible, hoping that stocks would rise, and that our State would be able gradually to get rid of this currency cancer which, by the high rates of exchange it produced, was eating out the very life-blood of our prosperity. The course marked out by our bankers would probably have been successful had not somebody sent circulars all over the country discrediting most, if not all, of the banks that are now thrown out. The circular was headed "Stand from Under," and parties were warned not to take them. The consequence was that for several days the bills of these banks have been coming in in packages, and the mixed currency sent out from the city has been sorted and the bills of these same banks returned. In a few days more our bankers and businessmen would have held several millions of this currency. To reduce it, therefore, to its real value, was the only resource left them.

Chicago bankers have been waiting patiently for State bonds to rise, but they have obstinately refused to do so. The course they have been obliged to pursue involves greater loss to them than to their customers. Every bank in the city has a large amount of this rejected money on hand, ranging from a thousand dollars in the small brokers' offices, to hundreds of thousands of dollars in the larger banks.

Chicago Tribune, April 1, 1861.

~

WHAT "WILD-CAT" BANKING HAS COST THE CITY AND THE STATE

Now that disaster, widespread and appalling, has fallen upon our people, from the extent to which reckless adventures and penniless sharpers have taken advantage of the defects in our General Banking Law, it is well to estimate carefully our losses in order that we may learn wisdom from experience and the more certainly guard against such an immense drain upon our resources in the future. On November last, the total amount of the circulation of the Banks of Illinois was, in round numbers, twelve millions and a half dollars. For this enormous issue of bank bills the people of Illinois had paid dollar for dollar wheat, corn, beef, pork and other products, and it was to them, for the time being, so much solid capital accumulated by their industry and economy, and but for this wicked war which rank treason had brought upon the country, it would still have been available for all the purposes of legitimate commerce

The experience of the last two months has sealed the fate of our present banking system. Possibly a few banks may make good their securities, but they can at best only maintain a sickly and unprofitable existence. The loss, therefore, upon retiring our currency may as well be borne first as last. . . . Illinois must lose FIVE MILLIONS OF DOLLARS from the currency mongers who fastened the infamous system upon us. A few short months have swept this immense amount of capital out of existence, and our people must eat the bread of carefulness for years before they can make up for what has been lost.

Our city must bear much more than her share of this immense sacrifice. We have taken some pains to learn how much of this currency was in the hands of our banks and business men at the time it "went under," and the amount the city is likely to loose from this base "promise to pay" in the "lawful coin of the realm." The Marine Banks alone had in March last about $2,500,000 of deposits, nearly all of which was in Illinois currency. To say that five millions were in the city would not be an over estimate. Forty per cent loss on this would be TWO MILLIONS OF DOLLARS . . . the amount is just about equal to the entire banking capital of the city. It is equivalent to wiping out every bank in Chicago. . . . It need hardly be added that a most serious calamity has fallen upon us. To sink the entire available banking capital of the city in three month's time, must have a most depressing effect upon her entire business interests.

Chicago Tribune, June 24, 1861.

~

THE CURRENCY

The evils under which we are suffering are brought upon us in a great measure by the traitors of the South. As they are inseparable to the rebellion, and the wisest could not have foreseen them, we should bear them with becoming patience. Who could have believed a year ago that Tennessee, Virginia and Missouri, with the madness of the suicide, would have plunged headlong into rebellion and war? By so doing they have brought the absolute destruction of millions of values upon us; but their condition is infinitely worse than ours. We have lost our money; they have lost infinitely more money; and their self-respect and the respect of the world are also gone. In a year's time we can retrieve all we have lost; it will be the work of a whole generation for them to recover even a part of what their reckless folly and wickedness have cost them.

We see no reason, therefore, for alarm much less for despondency and gloomy forebodings. The West has an ample supply of grain and provisions, and the eastern seaboard and Europe must have them. It a very few weeks our customers will be obliged to tender us coin, or its equivalent, and, having an abundance for ourselves, we are in a position to wait patiently till hunger forces open the channels of business. Having food and raiment, of the first a superabundance, and of the latter enough, we can afford, each man exercising forbearance toward his debtors, and endeavoring to deal justly with his creditors, to wait the moving of the waters.

Chicago Tribune, May 20, 1861.

~

By the summer of 1861, Chicagoans began to see how wartime opportunities might pull them out of their economic collapse. Eastern manufactures could not meet the entire demand, and the Chicago Board of Trade guaranteed coin exchange for business transacted with them, easing the city's reputation for shaky financing and guaranteeing Chicago's grain market. Chicagoans also realized the potential for supplying the army with foodstuffs and equipment.

ILLINOIS AND THE WAR.

. . . Letters have been received in this city from the highest eastern commercial sources, manifesting the greatest gratification at the actions of the Board of Trade of Chicago, which reduced values to a coin basis and has simplified the transactions in our markets and placed Illinois for the first time in her history, in a position to avail herself of the extraordinary advantages with which nature has blessed our State. . . . The experience of all time demonstrates that in all countries engaged in war, the tendencies of the price of food is upward. . . .

. . . It is evident that Illinois will command the market, and that the application of capital to the soil will, in the next few years, leave a great impression upon our State.

Chicago Tribune, June 1, 1861.

~

THE NORTHWEST AND THE WAR.

The effect the war will have upon the resources of the Northwest is a question which, as might be expected, receives careful discussion in business circles here. In the manufacture of all articles necessary for the clothing and the equipment of the army, the New England and the Middle States will be mainly benefited. . . . The government will unquestionably find it advantageous to purchase largely from some of our dealers and manufacturers, but the supplies which relate to the subsistence of the army must come directly or indirectly from the Northwest. Our producers of wheat, corn, beef, pork, &c., must supply the army mainly throughout the war, be it long or short. The derangement caused by the collapse of our Illinois currency, and the stagnation in the channels of trade everywhere, following the bombardment of Fort Sumter, and the certainty of war, depressed the prices of our principal staples, and cast a gloom over business and financial circles. But it is becoming apparent that this cannot last.

Chicago Tribune, July 21, 1861.

THE SINEWS OF WAR

Within two weeks after the firing on Fort Sumter, the War Department turned to Chicago Lead Works for bullets. Chicagoans were happy to deliver them to

Southerners. This marked the beginning of Chicago's economic turnaround after the currency collapse and demonstrated the potential of Chicago's serving as a supplier to the wartime government.

LEADED MATTER

On Friday last three car loads of lead for bullets was sent from this city on an order from the War Department, and made at the Chicago Lead Works. . . . There is plenty more of that staple in Illinois, which we shall be happy to send down for the pills . . . the traitors so sorely need. May "every bullet have its billet" for the cure of secession.

Chicago Tribune, May 1, 1861.

∽

Eliphalet Wickes (E. W.) Blatchford was the owner of lead works in Chicago and St. Louis. Prior to the war most of his business focused on the manufacture of lead water pipes. This letter from the frantic first weeks of the war indicates the chaos caused by the rush of men into the ranks and the sudden influx of military contracts. The cloak and dagger tactics referenced in the letter were typical of Chicago railroad detective Alan J. Pinkerton, who used the war to make a national reputation and detective business for himself.

Chicago April 23, 1861

My Dear Own Mary,

I had intended to write to you last evening but upon my return home about 8 found that Aleck Moore from the store had sent 3 times for me desiring me to come to the Armory on my coming home. . . .The works are running steadily on government order. It will be completed tomorrow. The letters, fact of which I sent you copies Sunday PM, I did not tell you at the time because I could not, were forwarded to Washington, by a bearer of dispatches to President Lincoln. It was arranged through Mr. Judd and Mr. Pinkerton, the famous police officer. His man had the letters stitched into the collar of his coat, the buckram having been previously removed.

On Monday I received at special commission from the State to furnish them at Springfield 10,000 lbs of one ounce balls and 2000 the size for their army pistols. The latter I despaired of doing, but tried to accomplish the former, not until yesterday morning did I receive word I could have them from St. Louis. Today the order is countermanded for their deliver at Springfield, and they are ordered to us here, and I am ordered to fill with canister for the artillery service. I have already filled 1400 with slugs and had to take such canisters etc. as they finished with. For these I have from the Quarter-Master General a carte-blanche to get them up as I can, and I intend they should be beautifully done. I shall not commence them till Friday.

Of course all this makes my factory a busy place. . . . I enclose a letter from Father. It has the true ring of '76.

And now I must say goodnight to my own dear Mary. I wish you were here for me to say this to. Kiss little Paul. . . .

Ever tenderly your own Husband,

Eliphalet

E. W. and Mary Blatchford Papers, Box 1, Folder 5, Special Collections, Newberry Library, Chicago, IL.

~

Chicago already had a base for manufacturing essential military supplies for the army, ranging from leather and canvas making to brass and iron works that made the city ripe for government contracts.

ARMY CONTRACTS—Messrs. Turner & Sidway, Saddlers and Harness Makers…have executed army contracts to the amount of over $100,000 already. . . . Among these they have turned out 10,000 knapsacks, 18,000 haversacks, 10,000 enameled water-proof camp blankets, 12,000 cartridge boxes and fixtures, 500 cavalry equipments.

Chicago Tribune, June 21, 1861.

~

CAMP EQUIPAGE.

The present war, while it has stimulated the industrial resources of the country in every direction, has also served to develop in our own midst, the resources of an establishment always prominent, and now second to few establishments of the kind in the United States. We refer to Gilbert, Hubbard & Co. . . .

Since the outbreak of the war, this firm have enlarged their establishment and directed their attention to the manufacture of tents, flags, regimental colors, and other concomitants of the camp. Their immense warehouse . . . is a vast hive, buzzing with the hum of industry. . . . [A] hundred sewing machines driven by steam and presided over by as many girls, fill the room with deafening clatter. . . .

The excellence of their work is attested by the daily receipts of orders from every part of the West. Government is fast learning the fact that it is poor economy to ship articles of camp equipage from the East to the West, when they can be manufactured at such low rates in Chicago.

Chicago Tribune, November 18, 1861.

~

BRASS AND IRON WORK.

. . . The present war, stimulating industry in its every branch, has satisfactorily demonstrated the fact that Chicago already, with its limited manufacturing resources, can successfully compete with the East in this direction. New interests are in process of formation, and our old houses are enlarging their foundries and workshops and increasing their facilities, and . . . everything indicates the successful establishment of manufactures which shall enlarge our census lists, give labor to the unemployed, enrich our finances, and give Chicago a fresh impetus towards a healthy and substantial business condition.

Chicago Tribune, November 23, 1861.

~

SUCCESS OF WESTERN IRON WORKS.

The increase of railroads in the West, the hard service required of the iron by our immense freight trains, and the fact that the rails manufactured at Ward's Mills at Chicago and Wyandotte are superior to any others, have greatly increased the demand for the products of both these establishments, which are now worked to their utmost capacity.

The Chicago Rolling Mills now employ two hundred hands, have ten furnaces in operation, consuming sixty tons of coal per day, turning out about fifty tons of railroad iron in the same time, which is more than ever made before.

Chicago Tribune, June 14, 1862.

~

War as a Utilizer.
New Branch of Manufactures.
The Military Equipment Business of Chicago.
Details of the Business.
Over a Million Dollars Expended in Chicago.

The manufacture of military accoutrements in this city is a branch of industry recent in its inauguration, and though strictly the offspring of a necessity, has developed to a magnitude and indicated resources and excellencies which point to a permanent character and wide-spread patronage.

As we witness to-day the departure of regiment after regiment, well armed, thoroughly equipped and excellently uniformed, it recalls recollections of the earlier days of the war, when our troops left us, unprovided in any of these respects. . . .

The necessity of furnishing so large a body of troops with the habiliments of war, and the impossibility of obtaining needed equipments from former sources of supply, compelled the establishment of manufactories in our midst, which have supplied cavalry and infantry equipments in immense quantities, and amounting in value to over *one million dollars*. . . .

Quality of the Goods.

The quality of the goods manufactured here, particularly in the line of cavalry equipments, has been pronounced by competent judges, decidedly above the average. A lot was manufactured by the house of Condict, Wooley & Co., furnished to Farnsworth's Cavalry Regiment, and taken to the Potomac, where the work was brought into comparison with that manufactured in the best Eastern manufactories, and for excellence of stock, superiority of workmanship, and adaptability to the peculiarities of the service, was pronounced unequalled. . .

. . . During the height of the manufacturing season, three hundred and fifty men were employed, and the force was worked night and day. . . .

Gustave Leverenz, 57 West Randolph Street.

This gentleman, who is one of our oldest and best known German citizens, was one of the earliest in the field, and contracted largely with the Union Defence Committee. He has confined his attention principally to the manufacture of Infantry equipments, although he has made a large number of baggage wagon harnesses, and 500 sets of Cavalry equipments. His sales to the Government for military purposes exceed $50,000. . . .

Ward & King.

These gentlemen have furnished their manufactures to the Government, the Union Defense Committee and the State of Ohio. . . . The total value of sales for military purposes was $10,000. Twenty men were employed, to whom was paid in wages a total of $2,500, or a weekly average of $18. The stock used was bought in Chicago.

D. Horton, 80 Randolph Street.

This gentleman has made 4,500 complete Infantry accoutrements, 2,000 of which were for the Union Defence Committee, and the balance for the United

States Quartermaster's Department at St. Louis. . . . Total of sales of military accoutrements, about $15,000 (estimated); workmen employed, twenty.

Turner & Sidway, No. 208 Randolph

. . . This firm have for the last three years, and previous to the rebellion, been engaged in the general saddlery jobbing trade, making all articles in their line upon their own premises. . . . In May, 1861, they abandoned their legitimate business and entered exclusively upon the manufacture of military equipments. . . . Since that time they have manufactured and sold 12,260 full sets of cavalry equipment. . . .

The greatest number of employees during this season was 461, the average number 400; amount paid for wages for 1861 $60,522.85. Of employees, from fifteen to fifty at different times have been females, who in consequence of the war, and the stagnation of general business, have been thrown out of employment. They prepare work for the sewing machines and operate them, and do much of the labor heretofore performed by men. . . .

Summary. . . .

The aggregate of these contracts we have no means of determining. . . . It may safely be set at $150,000. Assuming this estimate to be correct, the aggregate of manufactures of military accoutrements—Infantry and Cavalry, in this city, during the year 1861, and to date, amounts to **$1,155,000.**

Chicago Tribune, January 30, 1862.

∼

CHICAGO BREAD.

The Chicago Mechanical Bakery has furnished a million and a half of pounds of bread for the army in Kentucky. Kendall's bakery has also sent to that department upwards of a million pounds, and has shipped seven hundred and fifty tons direct to Washington. Our soldiers ought certainly to be well bred boys after such a distribution.

Chicago Tribune, February 5, 1862.

∼

THE U.S. QUARTERMASTER'S DEPARTMENT.
ITS OPERATIONS AND RESULTS.
New Methods of Contract Making.
$900,000 Distributed in Chicago. . . .

. . . It is a matter of the utmost importance that the people should know how the Government is represented in *its* supplies to our troops, and this leads us to the United States Quartermaster's office, its employees, its operations, and its results. Here are the avenues of fraud and speculation; here is the locality where immense sums of money change hands; here is where the contracts are made for supplying our troops with the equipments and necessities of war, and yet so quietly and unostentatiously is this immense business transacted that one is scarcely aware such an institution exists in our midst as a Governmental supply office, or such an officer as a Quartermaster.

The Quartermaster's Department was established in this city last summer [and is currently under the charge of Captain J. A. Porter]. . . .

One can hardly appreciate the immense business of this Department who has not visited it and made it a study. Associated with Capt. Eddy, stationed at Springfield, he has the supplying and equipping of all the regiments in Illinois, Wisconsin, Iowa and Minnesota, and yesterday was busily engaged in filling a requisition for miscellaneous supplies for Leavenworth, Kansas, embracing almost every conceivable article needed in camp, from a portable saw mill on wheels to tenpenny nails. From sixty to one hundred letters daily must be answered; telegraphic dispatches from Washington and all points in the West are in constant reception and demand prompt responses; callers innumerable from privates wanting back pay and corporals wanting passes, to Colonels wanting equipments for their regiments, speculators wanting contracts, and some people wanting nothing, pour in and out the doors in a steady stream. . . .

Every want of the regiment is here supplied. The Paymaster's funds pass through his hands. The contracts for subsistence must be made by him before the Commissary furnishes it. All articles of camp and garrison equipage, uniforms, horses, forage, saws, axes, camp kettles, mess pans, knives and forks, tents, tools, saw mills, lumber, nails, fuel, boots and shoes—everything, in fact, required for the field, the camp and the garrison, must be furnished by the Quartermaster, upon requisition. For this purpose, a warehouse has been established in Robbins' Block, corner of Wells and South Water streets, and is at present stocked with over $300,000 worth of these articles.

The immensity of the business may be inferred from the fact that during the past three months Capt. Potter has disbursed between *eight and nine hundred thousand dollars*. During the past month alone, he has supplied in the vicinity of 8,000 overcoats, 34,000 bushels of oats, 1,000 tons of hay, and over 2,000 cords of wood. At present he is filling a requisition for $15,000 worth of saws, axes, and other hardware, for Leavenworth, and will at once enter upon the complete fitting out of three regiments at Camp Douglas, in readiness for instant marching. *All of this money has been expended in Chicago*, thus enriching our own citizens, and stimulating the trade and manufactures of the city.

Capt. Potter is eminently a business man, and brings to his department the application of the ordinary common sense rules which obtain in individual business transactions. He hypothecates nothing, and only purchases when his store is out. In his negotiations he has never reached the maximum fixed by Government, but taking advantage of competition makes his contracts at reasonable figures, thus giving Government the benefit of a healthy economy which must absolutely startle it out of its propriety, especially in these days of fraud, villainy and knavery. The nineteen cent ration contract was immediately thrust aside by Capt. Potter, and equally good rations are furnished at 12 9-10 cents; a similar reduction was made in forage, and the horses are boarded at the city stable prices; horse contracts have been reduced to figures ranging between $85 and $100, instead of the old $110 system which usually enriched outsiders to the tune of $40 or more per horse. In this manner thousands of dollars are saved for the Government.

Chicago Tribune, January 8, 1862.

∽

HORSES WANTED

Messrs. Gage & Mix advertise that they will purchase 2,000 cavalry horses. From the very commencement of the war, Illinois horses have ranked as A No. 1, in comparison with any from any other section, and the 8th Illinois cavalry (supplied with horses from the firm) was the best equipped of any regiment that had ever been put in the field. . . . for the class they want, liberal prices will be paid at the Government corral on State street.

Chicago Tribune, September 24, 1863.

BECOMING PORKOPOLIS

Before 1861 Chicago already processed more beef than any other city in the nation. The Civil War made Chicago the "Hog Butcher of the World," a title previously held by Cincinnati. However, "Porkopolis," as Cincinnati dubbed itself, was situated on the Ohio River and cut off from Southern suppliers. Nor could it match Chicago's geographic superiority in water and rail transportation. Illinois and Iowa farmers solidified Chicago's dominance when they began to send their corn-fed livestock to the secure market of Chicago rather than St. Louis. Between 1860 and 1864, the number of meat packers in Chicago grew from thirty to fifty-eight pioneering large-scale, mass-production processes that culminated in the opening of the Union Stockyards on Christmas Day 1865. The following documents illustrate the excitement in the city as its citizens watched this industry grow.

CHICAGO PROVISION TRADE.

Pork and Beef Packing for 1861–62.

The Beef and Pork-packing season in Chicago for 1861–62 is now closed, and the result exceeds the highest anticipations of the trade. We have long held the position of being the greatest Beef-packing market in the world; but even the most sanguine of our citizens did not dream of taking from Cincinnati the title of Porkopolis, at least for ten years to come. But the facts show that while Cincinnati this last season has packed 483,000 hogs, there have been packed in Chicago by regularly established packers no less than 514,118 hogs, besides 55,212 beeves. . . .

This result is a mark of progress not to be lightly passed over by our citizens, or by those who design making Chicago their future scene of operations.

Chicago Tribune, April 10, 1862.

~

HOGS BY THE MILE

. . . To the packer and dealer, the fact that up to last Saturday night 1,056,110 hogs and 52,617 cattle have been received here. . . .

Let us put these hogs nose to tail, and stretch them out in this manner, and then we may get an idea of the business. . . . The procession of grunters would be a trifle over 1,200 miles in length. . . .

Chicago Tribune, February 3, 1863.

~

UNION STOCK YARD AND TRANSIT COMPANY.

Advantages Accruing from Its Establishment. . . .

Following the universal law of mutual gravitation, a law equally dominant in the physical, moral, and commercial worlds, the men whose interests largely depend on stock, have started a movement to combine and centralize the operations of dealers, by the establishment of a Union Stock Yard and Transit Co. The bill for the incorporation of the company has already been introduced into the Senate of our State. . . . The list of corporations is altogether made up of our most generous and enterprising businessmen.

The need for such an institution has long been felt. We have now four yards in operation—the Pittsburgh & Fort Wayne, Michigan Southern, Cottage Grove and Sherman's. The rule has been, and now is, that all the cattle and hogs are sometimes at one yard and all the operations at another. Quotations have often been "wild" and peculiar facilities have been offered to "sundown brokers," and others who aimed to make a special profit between the stock raiser and the slaughterer; the difference in the price, of course, always coming out of the pocket of the consumer. With the Union Yard in operation we shall have a much larger and better market for stock, a place where the dealers on each side can meet each other, and ascertaining current rates by direct comparison of views, can transact their business and go home. The dealer will not be so often put to the expense of keeping his stock overnight, nor will the middle man be able to bring his peculiar talents into play. The arrangement will be better to the seller, the buyer and the public, to say nothing of the improvement in the condition of the stock, which will be much better provided for in one yard than where several minor ones are devoted to its reception.

The location, too, will secure many advantages. It will be in the South Division of the city, at a point common to the three eastern roads, and easily accessible from all others, tracks from which will be laid to connect. The position is the best that could be selected, no other point being equally accessible to stockmen and buyers.

Chicago Tribune, January 1, 1865.

∽

CHICAGO THE GREATEST BEEF AND PORK PACKING POINT IN THE WORLD.

. . . [T]he number of hogs packed in the city during the season amounts to 750,147, against 904,759 during the season of 1863–4. The number of Beeves packed foots up 92,459 head, against 70,086 last season. . . .

As it is, Chicago still maintains her supremacy as the *largest pork packing point in the United States and in the world.* For the fourth consecutive season Cincinnati has to succumb to her youthful competitor, and as the great western prairies are opened up by railroads and settled by an industrious population, "Porkopolis" will find herself further distanced each succeeding year.

Chicago Tribune, January 30, 1865.

Money generated by supplying the war effort stimulated retail businesses and construction as Chicago laid a foundation for its future emergence as the "emporium of the world."

AN ENCOURAGING TOKEN

The war is bad enough and brings its burden of woes to every door, but there are abundant proofs that all the woes of evil that are shared by less favored (and more guilty) communities South, have not been realized in Chicago. Grass is not growing in our streets, trade has not left its channel dry. There are buyers yet, and stocks over which shoppers hangle lovingly. . . . The dry goods establishment of P. Palmer & Co., is ten years old.... The fruits of its ten years of trade are shown in what is now presents to the eye of the visitor. The exterior of goodly marble stock of five stories high. . . . The interior at business hours is the grand arcade of our lady shoppers.

Chicago Tribune, March 28, 1862.

~

A NEW ELEVATOR.

Another new grain warehouse has been commenced upon the South Branch of the Chicago River, and is in rapid progress of erection, for the Chicago, Burlington & Quincy Railroad. This building will be 251 feet long, eighty-four feet wide, with a clear depth of bin for grain of fifty feet, and is intended to be, in all respects a model building for the purpose of storing and handling grain. There will be used in the construction of this building, 2,600 piles, 500 cords of stone, 850,000 bricks, 2,000,000 feet of timber and lumber, and fifty-five tons of iron fastenings. The storage capacity of the house will be 750,000 bushels, the grain being received from cars running directly into the building, on two tracks of eight cars each. There will be twelve elevators, each carrying 110 bushels per minute. The scales for weighing the grain will be Fairbanks' best 500 bushel scale, and will be twelve in number. The machinery for the building is manufactured in Chicago, embracing all the improvements that have been suggested by experience, and will have, in addition, some things entirely new. The engine will be a condensing "beam engine," of thirty-six inch cylinder and thirty-six inch stroke, manufactured expressly for this building.

Chicago Tribune, July 22, 1862.

~

COTTON PACKING AND SORGHUM REFINING IN CHICAGO

When the present rebellion was inaugurated, and all communication cut off, a portion of the people of the North feared lest the two important staples of cotton and sugar might be almost entirely excluded from the market, that we had always been dependent upon the South for those articles, and as a matter of course we always were to be. There were those who thought differently, and set about making the effort to produce these staple articles upon Northern soil. . . .

Mr. R.W. Bender, on the 1st of January put in operation the "West Side Sorghum Refinery." . . .This establishment has a capacity for refining twenty barrels of syrup or molasses per day, an average of over two barrels per hour—employing eight hands.

. . . Cotton growing in Southern Illinois has proved so successful that Messers. Rappley & Sheldon . . . have erected a Cotton press. . . . The bales of Illinois cotton, in quality and size compare favorably with those from the Southern States.

Chicago Tribune, January 29, 1863.

~

THE CITY. . . .

Status of Chicago. . . .

Amid all these trials, bereavements, excitements and progresses, Chicago has been a prominent actor; and also a large sufferer, yet rather individual than collective. Indeed she may be accepted as an epitome of the nation itself, taking an extreme of time as well as of magnitude: the experience of Chicago during the past three years will not unfairly indicate that of the nation during as many centuries. She has grown and increased mightily both in spite and in consequence of the war, and the nation itself will rise a giant refreshed from its struggle with the evil.

Chicago Tribune, January 1, 1864.

~

WHOLESALE DRY GOODS.

Old Friend under a New Name—The Firm of Farwell, Field & Co.

The wonderful growth of Chicago and her vast commercial influence is in no respect exhibited more forcibly than in the development of the Dry Goods business. .... Hence while by virtue of her position, Chicago forms the key to the Great West, and the enterprise of her merchants gathers its exhaustless products for the sustenance of the East and of Europe, she is also the depot whence are sent out all over that tributary region the material with which to clothe the great army of producers. Dry goods houses were located here in 1831. .... The trade has kept pace in its development, with that of other departments of commercial activity, and the Dry Goods merchants of Chicago now supply at wholesale the retailers of the whole Northwestern country.

Chicago Tribune, February 3, 1864.

~

BUILDING IN CHICAGO.

Building in Chicago is being prosecuted this year with unwonted rapidity. Ours is a city which from its first inception has always grown at a tremendous pace. But it is now growing faster than ever. Each new increment but gives additional stimulus to extension, and our yearly growth is now counted by thousands of dwellings and tens of thousands of inhabitants.

Our present activity in building is wonderful especially in view of the difficulties which forbid extension in other places on account of the war. High prices of material, and scarcity of labor seem to influence but little the sum total of achievement. On every corner, and in the middle of almost every block we see buildings in progress. The thoroughfares are blocked with bricks and scaffolding, torn up sidewalks warn the pedestrian to go some other way, wagons filled with material wend their way slowly along the road and at times completely choke out the buggy or hack. Artisans swarm on the walls and joists, making their ringing blows heard far above the usual street din, and at the noon meal scores of their wives may be seen clustering around the piles of lumber or brick, each with her little dinner pot or pail for the refreshment of the bread winner of the household. Wages are so high that other classes of men are almost tempted to envy the man who gains his livelihood by a building trade. Contract prices are so high as to seem out of reach, yet contractors have their hands full, and refuse offers daily. It is the height of prosperity.

Chicago Tribune, July 21, 1864.

~

Albert D. Richardson was a Tribune *correspondent who wrote his memoirs when the war concluded. His observations of Chicago during those years reflect the city's bustling prosperity as well as its safe distance from the conflicts of war.*

. . . Despite Rebel predictions, grass did not grow in the streets of Chicago. In sooth, it wore neither an Arcadian nor a funereal aspect. Palatial buildings were everywhere rising; sixty railway trains arrived and departed daily; hotels were crowded with guests; and the voice of the artisan was heard in the land. Michigan Avenue, the finest drive in America, skirting the lake shore for a mile and a half, was crowded every evening with swift vehicles, and its sidewalks thronged with leisurely pedestrians. It afforded scope to one of the two leading characteristics of Chicago residents, which are, holding the ribbons and leaving out the latch-string.

I did not hear a single cry of "Bread or Blood!" As the city had over two million bushels of corn in store, and had received eighteen million bushels of grain during the previous six months, starvation was hardly imminent. War or peace, currency or no currency, breadstuffs will find a market. Corn, not cotton, is king; the great Northwest, instead of Dixie Land, wields the sceptre of imperial power.

Albert D. Richardson, *The Secret Service: The Field, the Dungeon, and the Escape* (Hartford, CT: American Publishing, 1865), 157.

THE PUSH FOR EMANCIPATION

On September 7, 1862, a public meeting "of Christians of all denominations" was held in Chicago to push for the immediate adoption of national emancipation. After so resolving, the meeting's participants nominated two Chicago ministers, William W. Patton and John Dempster, to travel to Washington, DC, to press the case upon President Lincoln. Unbeknownst to the ministers, Lincoln had already drafted a preliminary Emancipation Proclamation, but he had been advised by his cabinet to await a Union victory before issuing it. Lincoln was under great pressure as he met with the Chicagoans. Union forces had recently been defeated in the Peninsula Campaign, had been routed at the Second Battle of Bull Run, and were at the moment of the meeting attempting to contend with rebel invasions of Maryland and Kentucky. Lincoln used the interview to test his arguments and gauge public sentiment for emancipation in the North. The text below is the Chicago ministers' account of their dialogue with Lincoln, beginning with Lincoln's reply to the resolutions of Chicago Christians.

"What *good* would a proclamation of emancipation from me do, especially as we are now situated? I do not want to issue a document that the whole world will see must necessarily be inoperative, like the Pope's bull against the comet! . . .

". . . Understand, I raise no objections against it on legal or constitutional grounds; for, as commander-in-chief of the army and navy, in time of war, I suppose I have a right to take any measure which may best subdue the enemy. Nor do I urge objections of a moral nature, in view of possible consequences of insurrection and massacre at the South. I view the matter as a practical war measure, to be decided upon according to the advantages or disadvantages it may offer to the suppression of the rebellion."

Thus invited, your delegation very willingly made reply to the following effect; it being understood that a portion of the remarks were intermingled by the way of conversation with those of the President just given. . . .

We observed, further, that we freely admitted the probability, and even the certainty, that God would reveal the path of duty to the President as well as to others, provided he sought to learn it in the appointed way; but, as according to his own remark, Providence wrought by means and not miraculously, it might be, God would use the suggestions and arguments of other minds to secure that result. We felt the deepest personal interest in the matter as of national concern, and would fain aid the thoughts of our President by communicating the convictions of the Christian community from which we came, with the ground upon which they were based. . . .

That to proclaim emancipation would secure the sympathy of Europe and the whole civilized world, which now saw no other reason for the strife than national pride and ambition, an unwillingness to abridge our domain and power. No other step would be so potent to prevent foreign intervention.

Furthermore, it would send a thrill through the entire North, firing every patriotic heart, giving the people a glorious principle for which to suffer and to fight, and assuring them that the work was to be so thoroughly done as to leave our country free forever from danger and disgrace in this quarter. . . .

The President rejoined from time to time in about these terms:

> "I admit that slavery is the root of the rebellion, or at least its *sine qua non*. The ambition of politicians may have instigated them to act, but they would have been impotent without slavery as their instrument. I will also concede that emancipation would help us in Europe, and convince them that we are incited by something more than ambition. I grant further that it would help *somewhat* at the North, though not so much, I fear, as you and those you represent imagine. Still, some additional strength would be added in that way to the war. And then unquestionably it would weaken the rebels by drawing off their laborers, which is of great importance. . . .

We answered that, being fresh from the people, we were naturally more hopeful than himself as to the necessity and probable effect of such a proclamation. The value of constitutional government is indeed a grand idea for which to contend; but the people know that *nothing else has put constitutional government in danger but slavery*; that the toleration of that aristocratic and despotic element among our free institutions was the inconsistency that had nearly wrought our ruin and caused free government to appear a failure before the world, and therefore the people demand emancipation to preserve and perpetuate constitutional government. Our idea would thus be found to go deeper than this, and to be armed with corresponding power. ("Yes," interrupted Mr. Lincoln, "that is the true ground of our difficulties.") That a proclamation of general emancipation, "giving Liberty and Union" as the national watch-word, would rouse the people and rally them to his support beyond any thing yet witnessed—appealing alike to conscience, sentiment, and hope. He must remember, too, that present manifestations are no index of what would then take place. If the leader will but utter a trumpet call the nation will respond with patriotic ardor. No one can tell the power of the right word from the right man to develop the latent fire and enthusiasm of the masses. ("I know it," exclaimed Mr. Lincoln.) That good sense must of course be exercised in drilling, arming, and using black as well as white troops to make them efficient; and that in a scarcity of arms it was at least worthy of inquiry whether it were not wise to place a portion of them in the hands of those nearest to the seat of the rebellion and able to strike the deadliest blow. . . .

In bringing our interview to a close, after an hour of earnest and frank discussion, of which the foregoing is a specimen, Mr. Lincoln remarked: "Do not misunderstand me, because I have mentioned these objections. They indicate the difficulties that have thus far prevented my action in some such way as you desire. I have not decided against a proclamation of liberty to the slaves, but hold the matter under advisement. And I can assure you that the subject is on my mind, by day and night, more than any other. Whatever shall appear to be God's will I will do. I trust that, in the freedom with which I have canvassed your views, I have not in any respect injured your feelings."

◦

Four days after this meeting, Union forces turned back Robert E. Lee's army at Antietam, and in the wake of that victory Lincoln issued the preliminary Emancipation Proclamation.

Document of September 15, 1862, in *The Collected Works of Abraham Lincoln*, ed. Roy P. Basler (New Brunswick, NJ: Rutgers University Press, 1953), 5:419–25.

CHICAGO ON A RAMPAGE

The rivalry between New York City and what that town's journalists would later refer to as "the Second City" seems to have begun during the Civil War as Chicago rose in economic power, which translated into political power.

CHICAGO ON THE RAMPAGE.

We have ever held the young City of Chicago in fair esteem as a representative of Western enterprise and prosperity. Its natural position at the extreme southern point of Lake Michigan, made it the gateway of a large commerce seeking water transportation to the East, and its bifurcated little river could not have been planned better by art to accommodate the trade that the young city was destined to control. . . .

But in the year 1860 aforesaid, the National Republican Committee selected Chicago as the place at which their National Convention should be held. . . From having been the most busy, business-like and admirable, if not modest city in the country, Chicago, since that Convention, has become one of the most blatant, crazy, and arrogant political communities that we ever read of. It has acted since 1860 as if it had not only created ABRAHAM LINCOLN from the dust of the earth, but had made him President; and would unmake him, and make others in his stead; and so continue ordering men and things for this poor Republic *ad infinitum*, according to the will and pleasure of the said City of Chicago.

We can hardly remember a week since the present Administration came into office, when the newspaper press of Chicago was not badgering it for want of sense or backbone—not a month has passed without bringing a delegation to Washington to "look after things" and instruct the President. . . .

. . . Chicago surpasses Boston in conceit and self-idolatry, and, refusing to be only the "hub," arrogates the importance of the axle-tree of creation. It is time to put down the breaks on this too ambitious town. It is going too fast. . . . A pause, a season of reflection and a little ice-water to the head, will do all classes in Chicago a vast amount of good.

New York Times, June 14, 1863.

THE NORTHWEST SANITARY FAIR, 1863

In October 1863, the first of the great fairs that were organized to raise money for the soldiers was held in Chicago under the leadership of Jane Hoge and Mary A. Livermore. The fairs were important opportunities to rally a war-weary home front, and they played a major role in sustaining ties between home and the men in the increasingly more distant armies of the Union. Sanitary Commission work, either at the front as nurses or at home through fairs and soldier aid societies, also played a key role in laying a foundation for the post–Civil War women's movement. Pioneer feminists such as Mary Livermore used the executive experience won through commission work to work to change "the laws made by men for women."

FIGURE 17. A portrait gallery of the leading women of the woman suffrage movement, all of whom were against slavery and supported the Union war effort. Chicago's Mary Rice Livermore was among the most important women in the nation. She helped to create the first sanitary fair to aid the Union war effort. The pictured women are *(from the top and from right to left)* Lucretia Mott, Elizabeth Cady Stanton, Mary Livermore, Lydia Maria Child, Susan B. Anthony, Grace Greenwood, and in the middle Anna Dickinson. Courtesy of the Library of Congress.

This first Sanitary fair, it must be remembered, was an experiment, and was preeminently an enterprise of women, receiving no assistance from men in its early beginnings. The city of Chicago regarded it with indifference, and the gentlemen members of the Commission barely tolerated it. The first did not understand it, and the latter were doubtful of its success. The great fairs that followed this were the work of men as well as of women, from their very incipiency—but this fair was the work of women. Another circular was now issued, and this enumerated and classified the articles that were desired. It was a new experience to the Northwest, and advice and plans were necessary in every step taken.

In every principal town of the Northwest "fair meetings" were held, which resulted in handsome pledges that were more than fulfilled. Towns and cities were canvassed for donations to the "Bazar" and "Dining Saloon." The whole Northwest was ransacked for articles, curious, unique, *bizarre*, or noteworthy, to add to the attractions of the "Curiosity Shop." Homes beautified with works of art, paintings, or statuary, were temporarily plundered of them for the "Art Gallery," and all who possessed artistic, dramatic, decorative or musical talent were pressed into the service of the "Evening Entertainments." Executive women were chosen in every state, who freighted the mails with rousing appeals from their pens, or with suggestions born of their experience, frequently visiting different sections to conduct meetings in the interest of the great and noble enterprise. . . .

A temporary hall was erected . . . for the reception of the heavy and bulky machinery contributed. . . . Mrs. Hoge and myself sought a builder. A gift of lumber had been made for this use; and we desired to contract with him for the erection of the hall. The plan was drawn, the bargain made, the contract written, and we both signed it.

"Who underwrites for you? "asked the builder.

"What?" we inquired in concert. . . .

". . . You are married women; and, by the laws of Illinois, your names are good for nothing, unless your husbands write their names after yours on the contract."

"Let us pay you then in advance," we said. "We have money of our own earning, and are able to settle your bill on the spot. . . ."

"The money of your earning belongs to your husbands, by the law. The wife's earnings are the property of the husband in this state. Until your husbands give their written consent to your spending your earnings, I cannot give you the promise you ask. The law must be respected."

Here was a revelation. We two women were able to enlist the whole Northwest in a great philanthropic, money-making enterprise in the teeth of great opposition, and had the executive ability to carry it forward to a successful termination. We had money of our own in bank, twice as much as was necessary to pay the builder. But by the laws of the state in which we lived, our individual names were not worth the paper on which they were written. Our earnings were not ours, but belonged to our husbands. Later in the conversation, we learned that we had no legal ownership in our minor children, whom we had won, in anguish, in the valley of death. They too were the property of our husbands.

We learned much of the laws made by men for women, in that conversation with an illiterate builder. It opened a new world to us. We thought rapidly, and felt intensely. I registered a vow that when the war was over I would take up a new work—the work of making law and justice synonymous for women. I have kept my vow religiously. . . .

An inaugural procession on the opening day of the fair was proposed, and the proposal crystallized into a glorious fact. The whole city was now interested. The opening day of the fair arrived. The courts adjourned; the post-office was closed; the public schools received a vacation; the banks were unopened; the Board of Trade remitted its sessions. Business of all kinds, whether in offices, courts, stores, shops, or manufactories, was suspended. All the varied machinery of the great city stood still for one day, that it might fitly honor the wounded soldiers' fair. Could a more eloquent tribute be paid our brave men, pining in far-off hospitals, who had jeopardized life and limb in the nation's cause? . . . "I always knew," said one old man at our elbow in the crowd, while we were watching the procession, "that the heart of the people was right; they did not know their danger for a long while; now they have found it out, and this is what they say about it." . . .

The inaugural ceremonies being over, we will follow the multitude to Bryan Hall, transferred for the nonce into a bazar, rivalling those of the Orient in bewildering beauty. A semi-circle of double booths followed the curve of the gallery, and another semi-circle was arranged against the wall, a broad aisle being left between for a promenade. In the centre of the hall, under the dome, a large octagonal pagoda was erected, two stories high; the lower floor occupied by fair saleswomen and brilliant wares, while in the gallery, overhead, the band discoursed sweet music through the afternoon and. evening. . . . The national flag was festooned, and clustered in all appropriate places. It floated overhead, it depended from arches, it entwined columns. . . . If the goods and wares exhibited for sale were as astonishing in profusion as in variety, there was no lack of purchasers. From eight o'clock in the morning until ten at night, and sometimes until a later hour, the six halls of the fair were densely packed with eager and interested crowds. . . . Arrangements had been made with the railroads to run excursion trains, at low prices, each day, from different parts of the country. This brought daily new crowds of large-hearted, whole-souled country people, who brought with them a fresh gush of national feeling and glowing patriotism, and before whose unselfishness and devotion to. country, the disloyalty of the city shrank back abashed. . . .

It was decided to give a grand dinner on the closing day of the fair to all the soldiers in Camp Douglas, the convalescents in the Marine and City Hospitals, and the Soldiers' Home. About eight hundred in all were present. . . . To those whose feebleness detained them in the hospitals, boxes of tempting and delicate viands were sent,—such as the surgeons endorsed,—and committees of ladies accompanied them, and served them to the invalids, sometimes in bed. They even spent the larger part of the day in the hospitals, a veritable gala day. Now followed a scene. Two hundred young gentlemen from the business circles of the city, had proposed a dinner to the ladies of the dining-hall, and as the boys went out, these gentlemen came in. The girl waiters doffed their white aprons and caps, and the gentlemen begged them to retire to Upper Bryan Hall, while the tables were reset with the help of servants, and the dinner prepared. After an hour or two of waiting, the ladies were escorted to the dining-hall. The gentlemen had attired themselves grotesquely in the uniform of white aprons and caps, which they regarded as the serving-gear of the fair. The motley condition of the tables gave evidence of the handiwork of unskilled men, and not of servants. It was evident they were in for a frolic.

Who that partook of that dinner will ever forget it? Happy she who did not receive a baptism of oyster soup or coffee, as the gentlemen waiters ran hither and thither like demented men, colliding with each other, to the great damage of tureens and coffee urns, and the immense bespattering of the fair ones waited upon. . . . Shout after shout of laughter pealed from the merry girls at the contretemps of their servitors. Now and then came a little shriek at a smash of crockery or the upsetting of a coffee cup. Faster and faster ran round the awkward waiters, until, at last, the masculine attendants, whose caps had fallen on their necks, and whose aprons had got twisted hind-side-before, gave up in utter despair. They declared themselves "completely tuckered out," and begged the ladies to help themselves to anything they liked, or could find.

In the evening, not satisfied with the fun of the afternoon, the young people, aided by carpenters, cleared away the booths, working like Titans, and wound up the fair with a vigorous dance, that closed, as the clock struck eleven. At the same time, the German ladies of the fair gave a grand ball at Metropolitan Hall, which was largely attended, and pecuniarily was a great success.

And so ended the Northwestern Fair, whose net receipts were nearly eighty thousand dollars, with unsold articles, of sterling value, slowly disposed of afterwards, to make the sum total nearly a hundred thousand. Other fairs followed in quick succession— in Cleveland, Boston, Pittsburg, St. Louis, and finally in New York and Philadelphia. But none of them were characterized by the enthusiasm, originality, earnestness, and contagious patriotism that glorified this, and made it forever memorable.

Mary A. Livermore, *My Story of the War* (Hartford, CT: A. D. Worthington, 1888), 409–16.

WOMEN IN THE WORKPLACE

Work with the Sanitary Commission or soldier aid societies were not the only outlets for female labor opened by the war. As the conflict intensified and more men were swept into the army and navy, new employment opportunities opened up for women. In the areas of garment production and retail sales, women's entry into these fields during the war made them important areas of female employment for the next century.

EMPLOYMENT OF FEMALE LABOR

The peculiar, and most praiseworthy, characteristic of some of our establishments is the employment of females in every branch of business for which they are at all qualified. There are so few avenues open to female labor, and so few means by which women can earn an honest livelihood, that whoever opens a new pursuit, and gives them suitable employment at remunerative wages, should be looked upon as a public benefactor. The importance of this matter will henceforward compel the attention of the American people as it never has before. War is upon us with all its evils; and by no means the least of these is the consequent preponderance of females throughout the country. Under the most favorable circumstances possible, this leads to poverty, destitution and crime; and "social evils" innumerable spring from such
- unnatural conditions of things. But the evils will be greatly augmented in American life. A vast majority of women, deprived of their natural protectors by war have been accustomed to many of the refinements and luxuries of life. Almost none of them have ever depended on their own exertions for a living. Thrown on the world to support themselves, their course must be ever downward, till female labor is in greater demand and better requited. We look upon this inception as the dawning of a better day for women and hope the time is not far distant when the lighter commercial pursuits of life will be wholly entrusted to their hands.

Salaries Paid Saleswomen.

The salaries paid saleswomen depends on the character and capacity of the person. Very few are of much service until they have undergone a sort of apprenticeship. Of those now in one store, two are paid $8, seventeen others are $7; and one gets only $5 per week. The salaries of two others we failed to get, but it exceeds the average of those given, judging from their responsible positions.

Number and Salaries of Workwomen.

In the Cloak manufactory about 100 women are employed the year round, at salaries ranging from $4.50 to $6.50 per week. Girls that run the machines are usually paid $5 per week. The forewoman and two assistants are paid $10 each per week. The saleswomen in the lower rooms have generally been selected from the workroom; and this possible promotion and increase of pay have been strong incentive to good conduct.

With one exception, all dry goods establishments that tried the experiment of employing saleswomen continue them yet. All employers speak in high terms of the uniform tact and integrity of the women employed, and of the advantage of the system. "May it be perpetual" must be the sincere desire of every disinterested and thinking person. Its pecuniary advantages are sufficient to recommend it alone; but grander considerations than these should determine our conduct on questions such as these.

Chicago Times, February 3, 1864.

RISE IN THE COST OF LIVING

The prosperity that war brought came at the cost of a general inflation in prices. Rising costs curbed the profits of producers as they faced growing supply bills, while laborers found that their fixed wages no longer secured prewar buying power. For the first two years of the war, however, politics, race, ethnicity, and gender divided workers and frustrated any attempts at a united response to wage or working condition issues.

We have been paying a little more each month for so long, that to many of us it seems scarcely the increment should be so great. Take coffee for instance: in 1861-62 burnt coffee an excellent article, could be purchased for between 20 and 28 cents per pound. Now the same is sold for between 65 and 75 cents a pound. Here is an advance of nearly 30 percent. Sugar which was then worth from 8 to 12 cents, is now worth 25 to 38 cents. Butter which then sold for 10 to 12 cents, is now worth from 40 to 50 cents. Soap has increased in value from 6 to 16 cents per pound, beef from 7 to 20 cents per pound, and other articles in proportion. . . .

The worst of this is that the burden falls unequally. Certain classes of men are better paid for their services—comparatively speaking—than before the commencement of the war, while very many others receive but little more, if any, than three years ago. Teachers, police officers, men on yearly salaries, and all whose pay is fixed . . . or whose work of finger or brain is not in good demand, have suffered, while the pay of many has constantly increased. The laborer is now able to command a higher salary than a teacher or a clerk. . . . Thus it is. Times of great excitement always develop inequalities rapidly. Thousands have built up for themselves magnificant fortunes by speculating substantial sums since the commencement of the war; tens of thousands have suffered in proportion. There is no help for this. An inordinate gain is never made but at the expense of others, and in this sense what makes one rich aids to make many poor.

Chicago Tribune, July 20, 1864.

CHICAGO WORKERS UNITE!

The continued rise in the cost of living during the Civil War led to wildcat strikes by workers struggling to keep up with the price of necessities. In April 1864, the press reported that labor conflicts between "the employers and the employed are more frequently read of than those more bloody essays between defenders and attackers of the Union." The busy railroads and the car shops that kept their rolling stock moving were important sources of labor activism.

ANOTHER STRIKE BY RAILROAD EMPLOYES [SIC]

On Tuesday about sixty of the employes in the Car Works of the G. & C.U.R.R. Co. [Galena & Chicago Union Railroad], in this city, threw up their situations, representing, in their demand for an increase of wages, that they are receiving only $1.65 per day, while the same class of workmen in the car shops of the Illinois Central, Chicago & Rock Island and Chicago & Northwestern Railroads receive $2.23 per day for the same service. Superintendent Talcott replies to their demand that the same wages are paid in the Galena shops as for the same service in other shops in the city. Thus the matter stands at present.

Chicago Tribune, February 11, 1864.

~

The Galena and Chicago Union Railroad's unwillingness to yield to organized workers led to further trouble with its engineers. The Brotherhood of Locomotive Engineers had succeeded in winning wage increases from all of the Chicago railroads but the Galena and Chicago. When the Brotherhood tried to force them into line, the railroad successfully struck back by importing engineers from other railroads. Public support for the Brotherhood's strike was weak because of widespread understanding that the railroads were vital to the Union war effort. The engineers were an elite among workers, yet like the railroad owners they cast the conflict in the gendered language of manhood, revealing that the "free labor ideology" of the prewar years was in flux.

Office of the Galena and Chicago Union Railroad Company,
Chicago May 2, 1864

To—— Esq.;

Dear Sir: The subjoined resolutions were adopted by the Board of Directors of this company on the twentieth ult., and the following copy thereof is respectfully presented:

Resolved, that the management of railroads is vested in the Board of Directors, who are elected by the stockholders, to manage and control the interests and business of such corporations, and are by them held responsible for the proper discharge of their duties. Any and all combinations of any number of class of employees attempting, or threatening to usurp a portion of this control, endangers the value of all property invested in railroads.

Resolved, that we fully recognize the principle that the rights of employees should never be violated; that if by improper treatment, inadequate or insufficient wages, or uncertainty of payment of the same, they are injuriously affected, the right belongs to them to seek individually, more satisfactory terms elsewhere; but no railway management can recognize as a right, any dictation as to the wages they shall pay, the rules or regulations they adopt, or whom they shall or shall not employ; and societies used to prevent free action of either party in these particulars, if unchecked, would not only destroy all value in railroad property, but would strike a destructive blow to the commercial and agricultural prosperity of the entire country.

Resolved, that in the enhanced expenses of living, we recognize the propriety of increasing wages, and approve of the action inaugurated by the executive officers of this road, to take effect the beginning of this year, for such a judicious increase as would be both fair and equitable, as between the stockholders we represent, and the men we employ; and that we remember with dissatisfaction, the advantages taken by the engineers at the close of the past year when this was being considered and at a time when such large property interests were imperiled by the storm, for the presentation of a demand discourteously expressed, for an increase of pay to all, whether merited or not; and, further, we approve of the circular issued, to take effect March 1, 1864, both as an indication that the executive officers of the road under this board were disposed to assume, and vindicate that control properly belonging to those who own the road, and as showing a disposition on their part to so equalize and regulate the labor and its remuneration, that a few over-bearing and over-officious engineers could no longer claim the highest pay for the least work, to the disadvantage of those who were ready and willing to perform their duty. . . .

Resolved, that while it may be possible for organizations to be formed, whose purposes shall be "to elevate the standing of engineers as such, and their character as men," they are always in danger of being controlled by designing men for their own sinister purposes, and of being brought into collision with a proper management of railroads, thus jeopardizing the interests of both parties, as has been developed by the organization known as "The Brotherhood of the Footboard," and we recommend to all engineers who have any character, as men, to unite with the managers of the railroads in discountenancing and discontinuing this combination, which has benefited none, but threatened to be a fertile source of injury to all.

Resolved, that we hereby tender our thanks to the managers of railroad center in Chicago for their assistance and co-operation., and for their prompt rejection of impracticable terms of dictation, and also to managers of roads in Eastern states, for their aid in supplying us with engineers worthy of their positions. In our opinion a great and lasting benefit has been effected not to our road alone, but to all other railroads wherever located, and to the vast interests of the whole country dependent on railroads for prosperity. . . .

Very respectfully your ob'dt serv't,

W.M.L. Secretary

Fincher's Trade Review, June 4, 1864, reprinted in American Bureau of Industrial Research, *A Documentary History of American Industrial Society,* vol. 9, *The Labor Movement* (Cleveland: Arthur Clark, 1910), 106–7.

~

The event that impelled Chicago workers to set aside their cultural and ethnic differences was a strike by typesetters at the Chicago Times. *The ever-irascible editor of the paper, Wilbur Storey, sought to break the printers' union, Chicago's oldest union, by employing women workers. When the union men complained, he used his paper to attack them as being against the rights of working women. Storey won the battle but started a war as workers from scores of unions in the city united and published their own newspaper, the* Workingman's Advocate.

A STRIKE AT THE TIMES UNITES WORKERS

Mr. Storey had a special dislike for printers, and regarded them as vermin. A difference came up with the union printers who at one time held possession of the office, and in which he was compelled to yield. The union secured control of the composing-room, and thereafter the noted hard breathing through his clenched teeth—indicative of rage—was heard as he strode about the building.

That he should be successfully defied by a printer was the deadliest of insults. For at least two months his exhibition of anger was constant, and then he suddenly became changed; his expression of wrath softened, disappeared, and was succeeded by something in the nature of a smile.

The union men, who keenly watched him as he came into the composing-room every night to supervise the "make-up," saw this transformation and were happy. They knew that the hissing breath boded evil, and, when there appeared a suggestion of a grim smile on his face, it was concluded that he had become reconciled to the inevitable, and that henceforth the union would be a fixture in the establishment of the Times.

For a month or so the union was elated, and word was sent all over the country that the Times had finally become a union newspaper.

One evening the printers strolled into the composing-room and were immeasurably stumped at a spectacle which presented a young lady, "stick" in hand, in front of every "case," and picking up type with the swift exactness of a veteran. It was a coup d'état which, in an hour, resulted in the throwing-out of the union and the installation of the female compositors.

It was when the union men saw these women busy at the cases that there dawned on them the meaning of the half-smile which had lately illumined Storey's face. They were overwhelmingly routed, and the Times was once more a "rat" office.

So soon as the union had obtained possession Storey had devised a scheme for revenge. A secluded place was secured, and, with entire secrecy, women were selected and taught type-setting, the effort requiring some months. As a checkmate to the union, the move was a complete success, but in all other respects it was a total failure.

Women do not seem to have the endurance necessary for all-night work—at least, such was the case with those employed by the Times. They were inclined to too much gossip; they lacked in mechanical exactness, and were often absent from indisposition. As they fell out of the ranks, their places were taken by masculine non-union printers. In time, both the feminine and the union printers were excluded.

Storey's extraordinary firmness in his fight against the union is shown by the fact that, although the members of that body succeeded several times in getting possession of the works, they never gained a permanent foothold. There were repeated strikes, during which Storey took off his coat and worked at the case, assisted by such employees of the literary department as understood type-setting, and such "rat" printers as could be picked up, and brought out as much of a paper as he could until non-union printers from other cities could be obtained to fill the cases.

Franc B. Wilkie, *Personal Reminiscences of Thirty-Five Years in Journalism* (Chicago: F. J. Schultz, 1891), 154–56.

~

The Times *and* Tribune *became allies in the fight against the growing workers' movement, and they tried to use wartime political issues to divide workers. Here the labor newspaper* Workingman's Advocate *tries to warn unions to avoid that trap.*

Following the publication of the resolutions adopted at the Labor Mass Meeting, adopted last Saturday night, the Times says the meeting adjourned after giving three cheers for [George] McClellan [Democratic candidate for president]. This is a malicious lie, and a willful distortion of the facts. It is true, after the meeting had been adjourned, some individual, (either thoughtlessly, or for the purpose of giving the newspapers some slight pretext for denouncing it as a political gathering) called for three cheers for McClellan—which elicited but a weak response. Immediately from another quarter came a call for three cheers for Lincoln, which met with no better success, and the crowd dispersed, both Republicans and Democrats, satisfied that they were acting in a common cause, regardless of each other's political views. The attempt of the daily papers to create discord in the ranks of the laboring masses by raising false cries such as this regarding politics will not avail. The people are opening their eyes to their own importance, and regardless alike of the fawning praises, or lying abuses partisan newspapers, will pursue as straight-forward and determined course in all matters affecting their dearest interests as laboring men, preferring to act with their political parties only when such parties, both in theory and practice, through their organs and otherwise, recognize their just rights as workingmen.

Workingman's Advocate (Chicago), September 17, 1864.

POPULAR CULTURE PRODUCTION AND CHICAGO: WAR MUSIC

Civically sponsored war rallies played an important role in maintaining support for the war and boosting enlistment for the army. Music was a vital tool utilized to sustain public support of the Union war effort. Chicago musicians, particularly George Frederick Root, helped to build a vibrant patriotic popular culture that influenced the bulk of the Northern population.

～

In common with my neighbors I felt strongly the gravity of the situation, and while waiting to see what would be done, wrote the first song of the war. It was entitled "The first gun is fired, may God protect the right." Then at every event, and in all the circumstances that followed, where I thought a song would be welcome, I wrote one. And here I found my fourteen years of extemporizing melodies on the blackboard, before classes that could be kept in order only by prompt and rapid movements, a great advantage. Such work as I could do at all I could do quickly. There was no waiting for a melody. . . .

I heard of President Lincoln's second call for troops one afternoon while reclining on a lounge in my brother's house. Immediately a song started in my mind, words and music together:

"Yes, we'll rally round the flag, boys, we'll rally once again,
Shouting the battle-cry of freedom!"

I thought it out that afternoon, and wrote it the next morning at the store. The ink was hardly dry when the Lumbard brothers—the great singers of the war—came in for something to sing at a war meeting that was to be holden [sic] immediately in the court-house square just opposite. They went through the new song once, and then hastened to the steps of the court-house, followed by a crowd that had gathered while the practice was going on. Then Jule's magnificent voice gave out the song, and Frank's trumpet tones led the refrain—

"The Union forever, hurrah, boys, hurrah!"

and at the fourth verse a thousand voices were joining in the chorus. From there the song went into the army, and the testimony in regard to its use in the camp and on the march, and even on the field of battle, from soldiers and officers, up to generals, and even to the good President himself, made me thankful that if I could not shoulder a musket in defense of my country I could serve her in this way. . . .

. . . [W]hen anything happened that could be voiced in a song, or when the heart of the Nation was moved by particular circumstances or conditions caused by the war, I wrote what I thought would then express the emotions of the soldiers or the people. Picturing the condition and thoughts of the soldier on the eve of an engagement, I wrote "Just before the battle, mother" and "Within the sound of the enemy's guns." When our brave Colonel Mulligan fell, his last words were "Lay me down and save the flag." The day after the news of that event reached us, the song bearing that title was issued. It was much sung at that time in remembrance of that distinguished and lamented officer. I tried to help the enlistments by "Come, brothers, all, 'tis Columbia's call," and to hit the copperhead element of the North by "Stand up for Uncle Sam, boys." I voiced the feelings of the people in regard to the treatment of prisoners by "Starved in prison," and gave a more hopeful view in "Tramp, tramp, tramp, the boys are marching." "O, come you from the battle-field?" and "Brother, tell me of the battle" represented the anxiety of those who had fathers or sons or brothers in the army, and "The Vacant Chair" the mourning for the lost one. One of the thrilling scenes of the war is described in "Who'll Save the Left?" and the grief of the Nation at the death of President Lincoln by "Farewell, father, friend and guardian." This is only a partial list of the songs that I wrote during the war. Only a few had an extended use and popularity, but none was entirely useless.

One day early in the war a quiet and rather solemn-looking young man, poorly clad, was sent up to my room from the store with a song for me to examine. I looked at it and then at him in astonishment. It was "Kingdom Coming,"—elegant in manuscript, full of bright, good sense and comical situations in its "darkey" dialect . . . the melody decidedly good and taking, and the whole exactly suited to the times. "Did you write this—words and music?" I asked. A gentle "Yes" was the answer. "What is your business, if I may inquire?" "I am a printer." "Would you rather write music than set type?" "Yes." "Well, if this is a specimen of what you can do, I think you may give up the printing business." He liked that idea very much, and an arrangement with us was soon made. He needed some musical help that I could give him, and we needed just such songs as he could write. The connection, which continued some years, proved very profitable both to him and to us. This was Henry C. Work, whose principal songs while he was with us were "Kingdom Coming," "Babylon is Fallen," "Wake, Nicodemus," "Ring the Bell, Watchman," "Song of a Thousand Years," "Marching Thro' Georgia" and "Come Home, Father."

Mr. Work was a slow, pains-taking writer, being from one to three weeks upon a song; but when the work was done it was like a piece of fine mosaic, especially in the fitting of words to music. His "Marching Thro' Georgia" is more played and sung at the present time than any other song of the war. This is not only on account of the intrinsic merit of its words and music, but because it is *retrospective*. Other war songs, "The Battle-cry of Freedom" for example, were for exciting patriotic feeling on *going in* to the war or battle; "Marching Thro' Georgia" is a glorious remembrance on coming triumphantly out, and so has been more appropriate to soldiers' and other gatherings ever since. . . .

The growth of our business after the war commenced was something remarkable. The name of Root & Cady went all over the land on our war songs, and on our little musical monthly, *The Song Messenger of the Northwest*. Those among the people and in the army who liked our publications seemed to turn to us for everything they wanted in our line when it was possible. We kept everything in the way of musical merchandise from pianos and organs to jew's harps, and all the music of the day in book or sheet form. My brother attended to the business detail in all the departments, Mr. Cady to the finances and general management, and I to the publications. . . .

. . . We published a New Year's extra [of *The Song Messenger*] in those days which we sent broadcast . . . from the North and West as far South as we could. . . . I used to write a song for this extra. . . . December was now approaching. . . . One day my brother said, "We must have that song or we can not get the paper into the hands of the people by New Year's Day; go write it now while it is on your mind." In two hours I brought him the song. We tried it over and he said, "I must confess I don't think much of it, but it may do." I was inclined to agree with him about the music, but after all was a little disappointed, because I had grown quite warm and interested in writing the words. They were on a subject that was then very near the hearts of the loyal people of the North. The song was "Tramp, tramp, tramp, the boys are marching." . . .

When the war began no one thought it would last long—a year was the outside limit in most minds, but in the second year the magnitude of the undertaking began to appear. So many young men of the North were in the army that I made no more attempts to hold the Normal [Root's music classes] until the war was over.

George Frederick Root, *The Story of a Musical Life: An Autobiography by Geo. F. Root* (Cincinnati: John Church, 1891), 132–41.

∼

"NATIONAL ANTHEMS"

It is noticeable that the present war, although it has caused the issuance of thousands of songs, from all sorts of singers, it has given birth to none, or at least but few, really genuine national anthems—anthems which will become incorporated into the volume of our history, and go down to posterity as thrilling tuneful reminders of the days when a great nation's life was imperilled, and its fate trembled in the balance. . . .

Have we such an anthem? It seems to us we approximate very nearly to it in the "Battle Cry of Freedom," the universally known lyric from the pen of George F. Root, esq. While in the method and merit of its composition it may not aspire to an anthem, most certainly as a song of the war it is destined to live and become part and parcel of its record. It was dashed off upon the eve of a war meeting and caught its spirit, when the composer and every other loyal man was all aglow with patriotic zeal. To-day it is sung in the camps at Vicksburg, at Murfeesboro, and among the Palmettos. On that fatal day at Vicksburg, when the Iowa troops were hurled back from the belching batteries, bleeding and almost decimated, they broke out in strange unison with roar and clash—"Yes, we'll rally round the flag, boys!" When the solemn starry nights close their curtains around the camps of the gallant Rosecrans, the ringing strains commencing in one tent spread to the next and to the next, from tent to tent, from camp to camp, mile upon mile, until the whole army sounds the grand battle shout. When the great squadron shook its sails to the breeze at Fortress Monroe, and dropped southward for the hot beds of treason, the last sounds that caught the ears of the watchers on shore were the strains of the "Battle Cry of Freedom." In the camp and by the fireside, the soldier who has been sent and the friends who sent him, alike sing the stirring lyric. . . . While we may congratulate the composer, we may also congratulate ourselves, that Chicago has contributed so fine a lyric to the war literature and music of the country.

Chicago Tribune, December 25, 1863.

∼

Root's first song, "The First Gun Is Fired!" was written on April 14, 1861, within days of the firing on Fort Sumter. It was first performed on April 18 in the courthouse square for nearly twenty thousand patriotic Chicagoans. Root and Cady passed out the sheet music so the crowd could accompany the well-known Lumbard Brothers. It became one of the war's more popular songs.

"THE FIRST GUN IS FIRED!"

The first gun is fired!
May God protect the right!
Let the freeborn sons of the North arise
In power's avenging might;
Shall the glorious Union our fathers made
By ruthless hands be sunder'd?
And we of freedom's sacred right
By trait'rous foes be plunder'd?

Chorus

Arise! Arise! Arise!
And gird ye for the fight,
And let our watchword ever be,
"May God protect the right!"

The first gun is fired!
Its echoes thrill the land,
And the bounding hearts of the patriot throng,
Now firmly take their stand;
We will bow no more to the tyrant few,
Who scorn our long forebearing,
But with Columbia's stars and stripes,
We'll quench their trait'rous daring,

Chorus

The first gun is fired!
Oh, heed the signal well,
And the thunder tone as it rolls along
Shall sound oppression's knell,
For the arm of freedom is mighty still,
But strength shall fail us never,
The strength we'll give to our righteous cause
And our glorious land forever

Chorus

~

Root's memory may have failed him in his recollections of when the following song was first performed. The Tribune *reported that it was sung for a board of trade war meeting on July 25, 1862, two days earlier than Root reported. The newspaper noted that on that day it was performed by "a well trained chorus of voices, J.G. Lumbard sustaining the solo and the band furnishing the accompaniment." Nonetheless, Chicagoans embraced the song and ended any meeting during the war with a rousing rendition of the song. The song became so popular throughout the country that fourteen printing presses could barely meet the demand. One report called it the "Northern Marseilles." The song was also adopted for Lincoln's reelection in 1864.*

BATTLE CRY OF FREEDOM

Oh, yes we'll rally 'round the flag, boys, we'll rally once again,
Shouting the battle cry of freedom,
We will rally from the hillside, we'll gather from the plain,
Shouting the battle cry of freedom!

(Chorus:)
The Union forever! Hurrah, boys, hurrah!
Down with the traitor, up with the star;
While we rally 'round the flag, boys, rally once again,
Shouting the battle cry of freedom!

We are springing to the call of our brothers gone before,
Shouting the battle cry of freedom!
And we'll fill our vacant ranks with a million freemen more,
Shouting the battle cry of freedom!

(Chorus)

We will welcome to our numbers the loyal, true, and brave,
Shouting the battle cry of freedom!
And although they may be poor, not a man shall be a slave,
Shouting the battle cry of freedom!

(Chorus)

So we're springing to the call from the East and from the West,
Shouting the battle cry of freedom!
And we'll hurl the rebel crew from the land we love the best,
Shouting the battle cry of freedom!

(Chorus)

FIGURE 18. George Frederick Root, the North's leading writer of patriotic music. He wrote "Battle Cry of Freedom" for a Chicago war rally. From Frederick Cook, *Bygone Days in Chicago*, 1910.

Root wrote this song that follows in 1864 in an attempt to enter the thoughts and sentiments of a Union prisoner of war trying to encourage hope in his comrades.

TRAMP, TRAMP, TRAMP, THE BOYS ARE MARCHING

In the prison cell I sit, thinking, mother, dear, of you,
And our bright and happy home so far away,
And the tears, they fill my eyes 'spite of all that I can do,
Tho' I try to cheer my comrades and be gay.

Chorus:
Tramp! Tramp! Tramp!
The boys are marching;
Cheer up, comrades, they will come.
And beneath the starry flag
We shall breathe the air again
Of the free land in our own beloved home.

In the battle front we stood, when their fiercest charge they made,
And they swept us off a hundred men or more,
But before we reached their lines, they were beaten back dismayed,
And we heard the cry of vict'ry o'er and o'er.

Chorus

So within the prison cell we are waiting for the day,
That shall come to open wide the iron door.
And the hollow eye grows bright, and the poor heart almost gay,
As we think of seeing home and friends once more.

Chorus

~

*Henry C. Work wrote the song "Marching through Georgia" for Root and Cady in
1865 to commemorate General William T. Sherman's march in late 1864. It became
the favorite musical accompaniment at postwar soldiers' reunions.*

MARCHING THROUGH GEORGIA

Bring the good old bugle, boys, we'll sing another song;
Sing it with a spirit that will start the world along,
Sing it as we used to sing it, 50,000 strong,
While we were marching through Georgia.

Chorus
Hurrah! Hurrah! We bring the jubilee!
Hurrah! Hurrah! The flag that makes you free!
So we sang the chorus from Atlanta to the sea,
While we were marching through Georgia.

How the darkeys shouted when they heard the joyful sound!
How the turkeys gobbled which our commissary found!
How the sweet potatoes even started from the ground,
While we were marching through Georgia.

Yes and there were Union men who wept with joyful tears,
When they saw the honored flag they had not seen for years;
Hardly could they be restrained from breaking forth in cheers,
While we were marching through Georgia.

"Sherman's dashing Yankee boys will never reach the coast!"
So the saucy rebels said and 'twas a handsome boast;
Had they not forgot, alas! to reckon with the host,
While we were marching through Georgia.

So we made a thoroughfare for Freedom and her train,
Sixty miles in latitude, three hundred to the main;
Treason fled before us, for resistance was in vain,
While we were marching through Georgia

PORK FOR PORKOPOLIS

While Chicago businessmen grew rich on government contracts, the city fathers labored to access federal funds to improve the municipal infrastructure. The pet scheme of the war years was to have the old Illinois and Michigan Canal widened and deepened as a "national defense" measure. Chicago wanted the waterway improved to reverse the flow of the Chicago River—then filled with sewer runoff—to keep it from polluting the Lake Michigan drinking water supply. Congress, however, turned a cold shoulder to Chicago's appeal and a new waterway. In 1863, Chicago began construction of a tunnel that reached two miles out into the lake to secure unpolluted water, but that was only a temporary solution. Eventually the city funded a new waterway, the Sanitary and Ship Canal, which opened in 1900. In this document, Mayor Francis Sherman makes his case for the new canal as a war measure.

SHIP CANAL AND ARMORY.

The propriety of enlarging the canal connecting the Illinois and the Chicago Rivers, so as to admit the passage of ships and large steamers, is now engaging the attention of Congress. The entire feasibility of this project, at a very small expense, has long been settled. Its incalculable advantages both for commerce, and the national defense, must be apparent to the most careless observer. Uniting the vast trade of the lakes with the trade of the Mississippi and Gulf of Mexico, equally vast, it will also furnish a sure and safe channel, by which gunboats and floating batteries may be moved from Lake Michigan for the defense of the Gulf Coast, and from the Gulf and the rivers of the interior for the defense of the northern frontier. It is believed that Congress will at this session make appropriations for this object, as well as for a national armory and ship yard, somewhere on Lake Michigan. Should they do so, the effect upon the growth and prosperity of Chicago will surpass the expectations of the most sanguine.

Inaugural Address of Mayor Francis Sherman, May 5, 1862, in *Proceedings of the Common Council*, 1862, 2–5, Chicago Public Library.

SEVEN

~

The War in the Wards

*I*N THE FAST-GROWING, rapidly industrializing city of Chicago, the Civil War was about more than the North-South sectional conflict. While soldiers fought on battlefields and politicians wrangled in the city council and legislature, another war was fought in the streets, neighborhoods, and workplaces of Chicago. The Civil War was an important milestone in the development of the city's web of ethnic, religious, and racial communities. While the ranks of elite and middle-class society, business owners, and professionals were dominated by Yankee transplants from New England and New York, the working class of Chicago was largely made up of immigrants whose strong backs actually dug the city's foundation and who contested for ownership of the bustling frontier town. For Anglo-Americans arriving from the East, the city seemed wide open with opportunity. "The *camaraderie*, or 'hail fellow well met' feeling," a newcomer from New England recalled, "is one of its most striking features. People from different social grades in the older settled places of the East meet here on a level. Social distinctions are in nobody's way, for there are none, and the best man wins."[1] Immigrants from across the sea, with accents or brogues, and especially those from the South with darker skin, often experienced a different city. During the Civil War, Irish, Germans, African Americans, and native-born workers jostled uneasily with each other and with the Yankee elites for a place in a society in which it was possible to imagine that the old rules and restraints might be transformed by a revolutionary conflict.

Chicago's Irish community was at the center of the city's inner civil war. It was an immigrant community that emerged between 1836 and 1848 when diggers were needed to excavate the Illinois and Michigan Canal. The newcomers congregated in a place originally dubbed Hardscrabble just southwest of the city. Later graced with the name Bridgeport, because it was the canal's northern terminus and the head of navigation on the South Branch of the Chicago River, Hardscrabble was a name that better described the difficult life of the poorly paid and often laid-off canal construction workers. By the early 1840s, the Irish constituted 10 percent of the city's population. As the canal neared its completion, famine raged in Ireland, sending the destitute fleeing. Many eventually made their way to Chicago. By 1850, the Irish-born numbered 6,096 or 20 percent of the city's population, and within a decade the Irish-born population rose to 19,889. This figure excludes the children born in America of Irish parents. Bridgeport swelled with Irish residents, and a new Celtic settlement sprang up along the North Branch of the Chicago River. It became known as Kilgubbin, after a town in County Cork, Ireland, where three large estates evicted their tenants during the 1840s. Even worse than Bridgeport, it was a place of wretched shanties, riotous street life, and high crime.[2]

The Irish came to Chicago a damaged, downtrodden people reeling from generations of British conquest, dispossession, and religious and civil rights discrimination. The exploitative neocolonial economic system that sent raw exports to support Britain's industrialization left little capital in Ireland to develop its own industry. An American slave traveling with his master through Ireland in the 1830s commented that the physical deprivation of the Irish peasant was worse than anything he had seen slaves suffer in the American South. Irish tenants were beaten into bowing and scraping before the Anglo-Irish Protestant landowners. The final embittering experience for Irish emigrants to America was the Great Famine of 1846–49. While it is well known that the famine was triggered by a potato blight, destroying the main subsistence crop of the Irish peasant, "famine" is a misnomer. A more accurate term would be the "Great Hunger," as there was plenty of food in the country. Under British policy, however, other successful food crops were exported while the Irish starved. As many hollow-eyed Irish emigrants boarded ships to take them to America, they watched other vessels sail toward England heavily laden with food they had grown themselves—an embittering experience that fueled Irish nationalism.[3]

When they arrived in Chicago, most Irish immigrants had only the shirt or dress on their back, and they were fit only for unskilled work. They had few cultural resources from which to draw strength, save the Catholic Church. Their hardscrabble existence often strained family life and led them to drink and crime. In Chicago, Anglo-Protestant elites decried their presence, while the Democratic Party embraced Irish immigrants' zeal for political engagement in their new home.

The *Chicago Tribune* was the print pulpit from which native-born Americans attacked Irish religious and political behavior. Its publisher, Joseph Medill, was the son of Ulster Presbyterians, ancient enemies of Irish Catholicism. Throughout the 1850s and 1860s, Medill routinely identified Irish Catholics with crime, poverty, and corrupt politics and regarded their identification with Irish nationalism and hopes for an Ireland independent of "enlightened" British rule as antiprogressive and contrary to the interests of the United States. To Medill, his editor, Horace White, and the emerging Republican Party, America was a place to cast off Old World ways and attitudes and adopt the sober, hard-working habits of a forward-looking, free-labor society. American Protestants doubted that Catholics could be loyal to the United States when their religious and spiritual allegiance was to a foreigner in

Vatican City. They mocked the Irish as being beguiled by the bosses of the Roman Church and the Democratic Party—blind to arguments based on independent, rational thought. Medill's editorial pen reflected these historical influences.[4]

Faced with this reception, the Irish closed ranks. They clung to and defended their faith, which had sustained them through hundreds of years of persecution in Ireland, and they turned to their parishes to generate a nurturing and supportive community. They embraced the vicious antiblack rhetoric the Democratic Party used to attack antislavery activism. For many Irish, embracing American racial prejudice came easily as a way to boost their own self-esteem. When they lifted their heel, it came down on the city's most vulnerable denizens—African Americans. By striking a blow at the city's small but growing African American population, the Irish both protected unskilled labor jobs and lashed out at Protestant antislavery elites.

Medill's *Tribune* regarded German immigrants in Chicago quite differently than the Irish. If the Irish were a plague to be endured, the Germans were models of the promise of free labor in the land of opportunity. Most Germans came to America with "social capital"—education, economic resources, skilled labor, and a rich cultural heritage in music, literature, and philosophy. Most Germans left their homeland to maintain and improve their lot in life. They had been prosperous farmers, tradesmen, craftsmen, and business owners who faced a decline in their standard of living because of overpopulation and the growth of industrial production. A booming, frontier town like Chicago offered these immigrants fresh opportunities. In 1843 Chicago had 816 residents counted as born in Germany or Norway. By 1860 the German-born population had swelled to 22,230. Most Germans settled on the Near North Side of the city and transformed the "Nord Seite" into a prosperous area of the city. Many of its inhabitants were artisans, shopkeepers, and laborers. Some Germans with less social capital sought employment in the Bridgeport area among the unskilled city workforce.

Some Germans were also exiles of the failed Revolution of 1848, which sought to create a unified, modern, constitutional German state. The conservative, aristocratic old guard managed to put down these upstarts and banished them from their states and principalities. Americans generally viewed these failed revolutionaries as having the same modern, liberal political principles as themselves. Many were also "Free Thinkers" who believed that ideas and opinions should be based on logic, reason, and science. While some American Protestants worried that this system of thought might border on atheism, it was still consistent with basic modern American values. These political values made central European immigrants seem civic minded. Protestant America in general respected and valued the fraternal and cultural (if not the trade union) organizations the Germans created in America.[5]

Chicago's German Americans were not viewed as a monolithic religious block like the Irish. They were split primarily between Catholics and Lutherans, with some Jews and adherents to other Protestant sects. German Catholics did suffer anti-Catholic diatribes. However, Germans primarily were attacked by nativists for clinging to their language as well as their Sunday enjoyment of beer gardens with music and dancing for the whole family. For a time, Chicago Irish and Germans were drawn into political alliance by the rise of the Know-Nothing Party in the city. The famous Lager Beer Riots brought to a head an attempt by nativists to restrict saloons and beer gardens. However, after the immigrants stopped the nativist surge, the Irish and German communities quickly grew apart. By 1858 Lincoln's clear repudiation of nativism, embrace of free labor, and articulate attack on slavery had attracted German voters to the Illinois Republican Party. The Irish remained loyal to the Democratic Party and its laissez-faire approach to cultural practice, accepting Catholicism as well as Southern slavery.[6]

During these boom years, Chicago also attracted other Europeans. By 1860, 1,313 Norwegians, 816 Swedes, and 150 Danes had come to work in the city's mills, factories, and railroad yards and created a Scandinavian community along the North Branch of the Chicago River. Other small numbers of immigrants, such as the French, Poles, Hungarians, Bohemians, Italians, and Dutch, made the city home.[7]

At the center of the cultural conflict in Civil War Chicago was the city's African American population. Officially, it consisted of only 955 free persons in 1860, although the unofficial and fugitive population was likely considerably larger. The largest concentration of African Americans was along the South Branch of the Chicago River, near to work on the teaming docks of the lumber district and in uncomfortably close proximity to the Irish stronghold of Bridgeport. Their spiritual heart was Quinn Chapel, which began as a small prayer group in 1844 at Canal and Lake Streets. After the passage of the Fugitive Slave Act in 1850, blacks in Chicago organized their own unofficial police organization to protect them from slave catchers.

During the 1850s, Chicago abolitionists used the city's water and rail network and access to Canada to make it a critical junction along the Underground Railroad. However, while most Illinoisans rejected slavery, few were sympathetic to blacks and their quest for freedom and equality. Illinois's Constitution of 1848 granted the suffrage only to white males who had established citizenship. Article XIV directed the General Assembly to prohibit black migration to the state. The infamous Black Codes prohibited blacks and mulattos from marrying whites, engaging in contracts, voting, and attending school with whites. Anyone encouraging black migration to Illinois for work faced stiff penalties. African Americans in the state and city were thereby left in legal limbo. Free blacks had no legal status, and if they lacked papers to prove their status, they could find themselves victims of slave catchers under the Fugitive Slave Act of 1850. John Jones, a free black merchant tailor, and H. Ford Douglas were the city's leading black abolitionists. They aided the underground movement of slaves to freedom and fought against prejudice. Nonetheless, members of Chicago's small abolitionist community, whether black or white, were seen by many people as troublemakers who fueled sectional animosity. Joseph Medill's *Chicago Tribune* flew in the face of this sentiment. The newspaper frequently profiled the African American experience and in many ways served as the city's conscience. Like many other liberal Protestants, Medill saw slavery as the root of America's domestic problems and African Americans as people deserving of equality before the law.[8]

The Confederate attack on Fort Sumter and Stephen Douglas's call for Democrats to defend the Union initially ensured that across Chicago's divided cultural landscape came a determined desire to support the government. In 1861 the Twenty-Third Illinois Infantry, the so-called Irish Brigade, won glory in the early battles in Missouri. A second Irish regiment, the Ninetieth Illinois Infantry, known as "the Irish Legion," was formed a year later. German Americans led the way in creating two regiments, the Twenty-Fourth Illinois Infantry and the Eighty-Second Illinois, each of which had a large number of Chicagoans. African American expressions of patriotism were ignored until 1863 when John Jones led recruiting for the famed Fifty-Fourth Massachusetts, which despite its name included numerous black Illinoians and men from other states anxious to strike a blow against slavery. Many white Chicagoans who enlisted to fight for "the Union as it was" were less enthusiastic about the prospect of emancipation, and that political issue divided the working people of Chicago.

Not until after the 1864 election (if not the end of the Civil War) did the "Negro issue," religion, and ethnic pride cease to divide working people in Chicago. As the conflict ended, the "people's" struggle for an eight-hour workday and collective bargaining rights was only beginning. Chattel slavery had been crushed, and the white working people of Chicago cast aside their cultural differences to end what they increasingly called "wage slavery."

CHICAGO'S IMMIGRANT POPULATION

As the Illinois Constitutional Convention met to consider its antiblack constitution in the spring of 1862, Democrat Francis C. Sherman, a bricklayer in his youth before becoming a wealthy hotel owner, was elected mayor of the city. In his inaugural address, Sherman alluded to the Lager Beer Riot and his sympathies for working-class recreation. Sherman also expressed the Democratic contention that radicals were to blame for the war but that the Lincoln administration was leading the country effectively through the crisis. Only months later when the Democratic general George B. McClellan was removed from army command and talk of emancipation was circulated, however, Sherman (like many other Chicago conservatives) turned against Lincoln.

Gentlemen of the Common Council:

In assuming the honorable office of Mayor of the city, I deem it proper to express to my fellow citizens my deep sense of the confidence they have reposed in me. I hope to justify that confidence by the faithful performance of my official duties. While I may not bring to the task the ability and intelligence which some of my predecessors have displayed, I may safely promise to practice myself, and to require from those under my control, the homely virtues of prudence, punctuality, industry and perseverance.

This is not a fit occasion for a detailed statement upon city affairs. I shall therefore confine myself to some general observations. [Sherman goes on to discuss issues related to public works, police, city finances, education, fire department, etc. In discussing the enforcement of vagrancy and liquor laws he noted the following.] It is a matter of pride with me that I am personally familiar with the habits and interests of the laboring classes, and I will take particular care that ordinances passed for their protection, and for the suppression of the antagonistic class of disorderly characters, shall be duly enforced. Care should be taken at the same time that innocent amusements indulged in at proper hours, and with due regard to the comfort of others, should not be interfered with . . .

THE REBELLION.

It will not be improper for me to refer to a subject of momentous interest to every citizen and lover of his country. The differences of opinion and feeling which for fifteen years have been growing up between a portion of the people of the slave-holding States and a large and controlling portion of the people of the free-labor States, have at last culminated in a civil war, which has startled the world by its magnitude. Conservative men, North and South, have long foreseen it, and have endeavored to avert it, by withdrawing from Congress the discussion of these exciting questions, which are of little practical importance under our form of government, yet lay at the foundation of these differences. Although their efforts have proved unavailing, the wisdom of their counsels is now acknowledged, and will be always hereafter recognized in the government of this country. For this civil war the national government, being clearly in the right, maintaining the constitution which all are bound to obey, has met with the earnest and united support and the most devoted sacrifices of the people, without regard to party. Fortunately for the country, and for the cause of free government throughout the world, the Administration of Mr. Lincoln has proved itself patriotic, conservative and able. Our arms have already been covered with many glorious victories, and the day seems near at hand, when rebellion and disloyalty shall be driven from the land, and peace, fraternity and prosperity again restored. In accomplishing this result, the wishes and efforts of all except the factionists and visionary fanatics will concur, and the future history of the country, illustrating a sound and conservative policy, will probably be unmarked by internal disorder or insurrection.

THE CONDITION OF CHICAGO.

In conclusion, allow me to congratulate you, that notwithstanding the general disturbance of financial and business relations, the enterprise, capital, and resources of Chicago have secured us to a great extent from the misfortunes that have befallen other cities. Our trade and manufactories are increasing with wonderful rapidity, real estates is saleable at improving prices, new buildings are projected and being built in great numbers, and with proper attention to our interests, we may hope before many years to take the front rank among the great cities of this continent.

Francis Cornwall Sherman, "Inaugural Address of Mayor Francis C. Sherman, May 5, 1862," Chicago Public Library, Municipal Reference Collection, online at "Mayor Francis Sherman Inaugural Address, 1862," in Chicago History, Chicago Public Library, http://www.chipublib.org/mayor-francis-cornwall-sherman-inaugural -address-1862.

NOT ALL CHICAGOANS PROSPER

These statistics for the Cook County Poor House provide a stark contrast of the economic misfortunes of its immigrant population and highlight the prominence of the Irish as the most troubled population.

The Cook County Poor House.—The number of inmates in the County Poor House at present is 229. Of these sixty-six are Irish, five English, forty-seven Germans, ten Swedes, three Norwegians, two Bohemians, twenty-four French, There are forty-two insane persons, twenty-two of whom are females. There have been seven deaths and four births during the quarter ending June 1st.

Chicago Tribune, June 4, 1862.

IRISH VERSUS AFRICAN AMERICANS

Chicago's first race riot occurred in July 1862. At the time, Chicago Evangelicals were vigorously lobbying Lincoln to issue an emancipation order. Mass recruiting rallies were also being held in the city to meet the government's call for more troops without resorting to a draft. The disturbance began when an Irish omnibus driver, Richard Kelly, refused to allow an African American, W. E. Walker, to ride on his horse-drawn omnibus. When Walker refused to leave the vehicle, Kelly subsequently beat him. Soldiers from a Chicago German regiment intervened and saved Walker from further violence. They escorted him to another bus stop and ensured that Walker was eventually able to secure a ride. Unfortunately, the crowd attracted by the affray spread out through the central city, attacking African American men. Kelly was eventually brought up on assault charges. The testimony from that trial details how the riot started. The entire incident reflected Chicago's working-class tensions between Irish and African Americans as well as the view that white abolitionists were the real cause of racial strife.

THE OMNIBUS RIOT.

Testimony in the Case.
The Jury Unable to Agree.

The omnibus riot case, at the corner of Clark and Randolph streets, on Monday, in which W. E. Walker, a colored man, was ejected from an omnibus and brutally assaulted by the driver, Richard E. Kelly, came up yesterday for a hearing before Justice De Wolf, at the Recorders' Court Room. Chancellor L. Jenks appeared for the negro, and a long array of counsel . . . for the defence. The defendant insisted upon a jury of twelve. As it would be difficult to select twelve men in the city who had not expressed an opinion, or were not prejudiced, after considerable discussion by counsel, it was agreed to limit the number to eight. . . .

Mr. Jenks, in his opening argument to the jury, narrated the facts in the case as he should prove them, without indulging in any unnecessary buncombe. . . .

Mr. Asay launched out with a flaming diatribe. The statements of the prosecutor were all false. He (Asay) was a Republican, and always voted the ticket when there were honorable men's names on it. His client [Kelly] was a peaceful man, deserving of particular commendation. He had come to Chicago to seek bread for his little ones. Some men under these circumstances would have stolen, but he preferred to be an honest man. On Monday the prosecutor entered the omnibus smoking. He was requested to get out, but refused, and a tussle ensued. In protecting the negro the Sheriff was trying to force the negro down the throats of people. Such conduct was impolitic at this time. The whole thing was a plan of politicians to get up a hubbub in Chicago.

The counsel then proceeded with the hackneyed strain of Abolitionists. The Abolitionists were guilty of getting up the riot. The Abolitionists were inciting on the negro. The Abolitionists were the guilty parties. The prosecutor was backed up by wealthy Abolitionists, who were bad, reckless men, and so on. . . .

The Testimony for the Prosecution

Capt. G.P. Osler, sworn—I reside in Chicago; am in the towing business; was present on the occasion of the trouble on Clark street; stood but a few steps from the coach...the prosecutor sat in the rear, on the opposite side; the driver came in, stepped on the other side and told the negro to get out; he said, "I won't carry any damned niggers in my 'bus;" the negro refused to move, and defendant drew off as if to hit him; he begged him not to strike; defendant said, "Get out!" to which the negro replied, "No, I won't;" defendant next fumbled at his pocket as if he was after a weapon, then pushed him off his seat; saw something which looked like a butt of a pistol; he didn't take it out, however, but drew off and struck the negro under the left eye; they then clinched and then tumbled together in the bottom of the coach the negro on the top, until a policeman or officer came along and separated them...*the negro was not smoking, I swear he was not; didn't hear the negro say any improper or profane language*; he said, "don't strike me;" . . . The first language used by the defendant was, "Get out of here you damned nigger; I don't carry niggers." [other witnessed confirmed this testimony] . . .

Testimony for the Defense

B. M. Warner, sworn— . . . was coming down on the cars; first saw negro in the omnibus with a cigar in his mouth; don't know as it was plaintiff.

Mary McDonald,—I was in the omnibus Monday morning; saw the colored man on the sidewalk with another colored man with a cigar in his mouth.

Cross-examined—Can't say I saw the colored man have a cigar in his mouth while on the bus; . . . driver said he would not carry a nigger in his bus.

James G. Abbott, sworn—Am Superintendant of omnibuses; it is against our rules to smoke on an omnibus.

The testimony of the plaintiff was offered in evidence, but objected to on the ground that a negro is not allowed to testify in our courts. Overruled.

Mr. E. Walker, sworn—Have resided in Chicago eight years; never saw the defendant till Monday . . .

Question—Were you smoking on the 'bus? . . .

Answer—I had no cigar in my mouth or in my hand.

Mrs. McDonald, recalled—The nigger did have a cigar on the sidewalk, but I can't swear I saw him smoking it in the 'bus.

Chicago Tribune, July 17, 1862.

ECONOMIC COMPETITION BETWEEN THE IRISH AND BLACKS

Chicago in the 1860s was one of the busiest ports in the world. Miles of docks along the South Branch of the Chicago River were the site of lumberyards and a magnet

FIGURE 19. The Chicago River docks were a key engine of the regional economy and a place of economic struggle between Irish, Bohemian, and African American workers. Courtesy of the Library of Congress.

for young men with strong backs seeking work as longshoremen. Irish and African American working-class competition for work and wages is clearly illustrated by incidents on Chicago's docks. When only a few ships needed to be unloaded, schooner captains could hire gangs of workers, who milled about the docks looking for work for a mere $10 to $15 for the job. However, when many heavily laden ships needed to be relieved of their burden, lumbershovers could command over $50 to complete the work. In this account, Irish workers had successfully negotiated with a schooner captain to unload his ship for $45. While the deal was being finalized, a group of African Americans undercut the Irish bid, agreeing to do the job for $13. The violence that resulted was an all-too-common occurrence on the docks during the Civil War.

A RIOT AMONG LABORERS.

On Saturday, a riot occurred upon Twelfth street, which at one time threatened most serious consequences, but finally, by the prompt action of the police, was quelled before much damage was done. It seems that a gang of laborers applied to the captain of the schooner *Meridian*, lying at her dock in the river near Twelfth street, to unload her cargo, offering to do it for $75. The usual price for such service was $15, and they finally agreed to do it for $45. Pending the settlement, a squad of negroes came along and took the job for $13, the captain offering the other crowd another job. The crowd, however, became indignant and immediately set upon the negroes, when a general riot ensued. The officers who were promptly sent for quelled the riot. After their departure, however, it broke out again with renewed violence. The officers returned, took possession of the vessel, and threatened to shoot any person who came on board. Another posse arrived, under Capt. Nelson, and by vigorous measures against stopped the riot by the arresting of eight of the ringleaders, who will have their examination Monday.

Chicago Tribune, August 11, 1862.

~

ANOTHER MOB.

There were reports current upon the street yesterday that a mob of Irishmen was raising to drive off a few negroes engaged in unloading a schooner. A man brought the information to Police Headquarters, but Mr. Turtle refused to interfere.

Chicago Tribune, July 15, 1864.

~

RIOT.

Yesterday afternoon there was quite a speck of a riot at the wood yard of H. W. Hoyt on River street, near Rush street bridge. Being in great want of laborers, Mr. Hoyt had obtained the services of a couple of colored men to aid in piling wood in his yard. A little after noon he was waited upon by a number of Irishmen and ordered to dismiss the colored workers. He refused to do so, and was then told that they should not be permitted to work upon any consideration, and threatened with great violence if they were not at once dismissed. Mr. Hoyt was resolute, and soon a large crowd of infuriated Paddies gathered, and after freely abusing Mr. Hoyt, commenced an assault upon the negroes, who were roughly handled. The assistance of the police was called for, and officers O'Donnell and Rogers were sent to restore order. They succeeded in dispersing the crowd and arresting two of the rioters named Williams and Pat Kernan, who were taken before Justice Miller, and held to bail in the sum of $500 each.

Chicago Tribune, July 30, 1864.

~

The Chicago Tribune *blasted the Irish for their belief that black laborers were an economic and social threat to them. The editorial writers certainly had logic on their side when they pointed out that there was plenty of work for everyone in the city. The Irish experience as illustrated above, however, provided them with enough evidence that demonstrated that the increased competition of unskilled labor suppressed wages, and the paper's exhortations fell on deaf ears.*

MOBBING NEGROS.

How Irish Men Oppose Their own Interests—What "Degrades Labor"—
How to Elevate It—Who Ought to be Abolitionists.

A day or two ago a mob of four or five hundred Irish shoremen made an assault
on a party of a dozen negro laborers working on a lumber dock, compelled them
to flee for their lives. The blacks had committed no offense whatever, except wanting to support themselves by honest labor. For this they were mobbed. The secesh
concern [*Chicago Times*] states the case thus:

> Yesterday morning a gang of about a dozen negroes were employed on
> the lumber dock of C. Mears & Co., at the foot of Kinzie street, near the
> lighthouse. They, of course, took the places of white laborers who needed
> employment. A number of the shoremen and other laborers waited upon
> Mr. Mears [Republican lumberman Charles Mears] during the day, and re-
> quested him to discharge the negroes, as it was degrading to them to see
> blacks working upon an equality with themselves, and more so, while their
> brothers were out of employment.

It is a little singular that no class of people in Chicago fear the competition of
the handful of blacks here, except the Irish. The Germans never mob colored men
for working for whoever may employ them. The English, the Scotch, the French,
the Scandinavians, never molest peaceable black people. Americans never think of
doing such a thing. No other nationality consider themselves "degraded" by seeing blacks earning their own living by labor. If it puts negroes on an equality with
Irishmen to labor, and thereby degrades the latter, we see no way to help it except
to keep the blacks in idleness by taxing the balance of the community for their
support. The reason given in justification of the assault—that "the brothers of the
mobocrats were thrown out of employment by the blacks"—has a lie for a basis.
Work is not so scarce in Chicago, and the few blacks here are not depriving the
Irish of employment. There is far more work than workmen. There is abundance
of employment for thousands more men then are here. If all the black people in
this city should leave Chicago to-morrow it would not benefit the condition of
the Irish a single dime. Their hostility to the colored people is a miserable blind
prejudice which the Irish ought to be ashamed to harbor.

But there is another view of this matter. Almost every Irishman, we are sorry
to say, is literally pro-slavery. They want the black to be slaves and are opposed to
their emancipation from bondage.

Chicago Tribune, 15 July 1864

IRISH AND GERMANS

Irish hostility toward emancipation of slaves led to growing disillusionment with the changed war aims of Lincoln and his administration. This resulted in their growing resistance to the draft, for they felt that it unduly burdened the working poor, who could not afford the $300 payment to avoid military service. Although Chicago avoided the violence and destruction of the New York Draft Riots, in which working-class New Yorkers, especially Irish Americans, reacted to demands for their enlistment by embarking on a rampage from July 13 to 16 that killed at least 120, wounded over 2,000, and resulted in the lynching of 11 African Americans. In this article published in the Chicago-based Illinois Staats-Zietung, German Americans announce the formation of a militia to maintain order in Chicago. The statement indicates German liberals' qualified support for the Union draft policy and their uneasiness with the Irish and the Catholic Church, as well as their lingering fear of European-style despotism.

THE CHICAGO ARBEITERVEREIN DEFENSE CORPS AND A GERMAN VOLUNTEER PRESIDENT SPEAKS FOR SOCIETY

The New York riots have shown that this Republic is headed for an abyss if its citizens, the people, are not able to check perversive activity and thus avert the ruin of our nation. We do not agree with those who are inclined to shut their eyes to the injustice of the Conscription Act. Say what you will, the fact remains that the three-hundred dollar clause is not in keeping with the ideals of equality, one of the fundamental principles upon which this Democracy is founded.[9] Senator Wilson [Republican, Massachussetts], the author and sponsor of the Conscription Act may boast that it is an exact replica of the French law, yet we must sustain the objection that we are living in a Republic, in which all citizens are equal before the law, in which no one has preference on account of social standing, financial status, color, race, or creed, in which each and every citizen has the same privileges and the same duties toward the country and its Government. In France, however, the people are under the rule of despotism—a reign that ignores and tramples upon the rights of the governed and serves the interests of stockbrokers, Jesuits, and inhuman ruffians who traffic in souls.

Yet, although we are opposed to the manner which the law prescribes for conscription, we firmly believe that conscription itself is necessary. Or is the Rebellion to gain in extent and strength because the Free States lack sufficient men? Shall our victorious Army stop fighting? Or is it to be halted on its successful course? Or shall we give the French Emperor, who is controlled by the Jesuits, time to carry out his pernicious plans against our Republic? No, a thousand times! No!! So, whoever wishes to attack conscription itself, will have to be looked upon as a friend of the Rebels.

However, the citizens of New York who incited men to riot must also be classed as friends of the Rebels.

The atrocities committed against defenseless people, the murders, robberies, the looting, and the arson must convince every loyal citizen of the Republic, every true Democrat, as well as every true Republican, that the Conscription Law, despite its evident and deplorable deficiencies, is the lesser evil. And why? Because mob activity is always followed by martial law. . . .

The June Battle in Paris in 1848 was mob activity on a large scale and resulted in rule by the military authorities. The fights in which Lichnowsky and Auerswald lost their lives (1848, at Frankfurt on the Main) were nothing but riots, and it was through these riots that the reaction in Germany gained power.[10] Not only the Philistines (a revolutionary faction that took part in the German uprising of 1848) but also many others sided with the Government. They decided it was better to be ruled by soldiers than by the kind of Democrats who resort to murder, robbery, and arson, and thus the hope that they would be governed by a German Parliament was destroyed, and all other "golden dreams" vanished in thin air.

The New York riots will serve the Republic no better. All the people who participated in them were not worthy to be citizens of a republic. If this statement needed further proof, it is furnished by the fact that the persuasive eloquence of an Archbishop was required to quiet the rioters, and that they bowed to this Prelate. This immaturity of the people is their strongest invitation to tyranny, and if all citizens of America were as incapable of governing themselves as those New York rioters, the fate of the Republic would be sealed!

Who, for instance, will guarantee that the same mob will not act on request of those who do the thinking for the "minors," (at the request of political or religious leaders, or rather seducers) and create a riot in favor of a monarchy? People who are not able to form their own convictions, who cannot think, who have no will of their own, are as unstable as the waters of the ocean, as a straw in a storm, and constitute the greatest danger that can beset a republic. The mob rule in the South was responsible for the Rebellion of the slaveholders. Only through rioting did the leaders of the Rebellion succeed in overpowering the Union element.

However, in the North, in the Free States, there is another element, and that is very fortunate. We refer to those Germans who immigrated to this Republic because they love liberty more than the land of their birth, yea, even more than life itself. At their side you will find those Americans and Irish who have attained political independence, because they are able to form their own convictions and do their own thinking—people who want neither mob rule nor sword rule.

The question is, what they must do. The answer is simple: They must permit no rioting, so that military rule is unnecessary.

The citizens themselves must preserve order. Germans, Americans, and Irish must stand together and everyone who attemps to sow the seed of discord, mistrust, or dissatisfaction among our citizens, everyone who awakens internal strife by creating prejudice, whether it be against Americans, or Irish, or Germans, whether it be of a political or religious nature, must be looked upon as an enemy of the Republic.

Everywhere we must establish citizens' defense organizations, so that our military authorities will have no reason to interfere with, or take charge of, the administration of our political affairs; for it is far easier to bring about sword rule than to remove it.

But how about the three-hundred dollar clause? Well, if the Republic perishes, will only the rich be affected, and not the poor? We think the poor will suffer more than the rich. Rich people can live anywhere, but poor people need the Republic too much to permit it to be destroyed or its privileges curtailed. And many of the wealthy will not purchase substitution, but will fight themselves. The Rebellion must be suppressed, and suppressed now, and at any cost. If our people hesitate, old Sybil will cast another book of the history of the world into the fire, and only because our people and Government were ignorant; and we will be troubled and harrassed not only by the Rebellion, but also by the intervention of the "Jesuit Emperor" of France. That must not happen. So let us prevent any mob violence; for who can guarantee that agents of the "French Scoundrel" will not take advantage of the confusion of our Government to create these riots? And friends of the Rebellion who incite to rioting in the North are no better. So down with them! Or shall we wait until a riot is in full sway and intervention by the military authorities is necessary? Then it will be too late. Martial law will put an end to the people's liberty. Freedom of speech, freedom of the press, freedom of lawful assembly—all these cease to be when the sword takes up its rule.

Therefore the Chicago Arbeiterverein[11] resolved to take up arms against any and everyone who makes any attempt to incite a riot. Someone, some organization, had to take the initiative. However, any friend of the Republic is invited to join our organization for the preservation of law and order. They need not be of German descent; they need only be loyal patriots—Americans in the true sense of the word.

Theodore Hielscher, President.[12]

Illinois-Zeitung, July 30, 1863.

~

The Civil War exacerbated tensions between Chicago's ethnic groups where these groups intersected in neighborhoods on the North and South Branches of the

Chicago River. *The Germans and the Irish, one-time political allies, drifted further*
apart when Lincoln and federal policy moved toward emancipation. In July 1862,
what was called the Tenth Ward Riot erupted between the Irish and Germans. Two
days later another brawl ensued at a German picnic.

RIOT IN THE NORTH DIVISION.

Yesterday afternoon was signalized by a riot in the North Division of more
than ordinary violence. About noon, a German named Charles Hitman, better
known by the *soubriquet* of "Peanut Charley," and an Irishman whose name has
not transpired, engaged in angry discussion on the corner of Clark and Kinzie
streets, which soon resulted in a pitched fight. A crowd of people quickly gathered
and a general row, in which the friends of both combatants participated, was soon
progressing. At this time Officer Nixon, who was coming over Clark street bridge,
seeing the crowd, ran to discover the cause of the trouble. He arrested the Irishman and was immediately knocked headlong by a comrade of the prisoner. Nixon
let him go, and when he recovered from the effects of the blow, attempted to
arrest the party who struck him. He had hardly laid his hand upon the man when
he was again floored. Again he sprang to his feet only to find himself a third time
lying in the gutter. The arrest was made a fourth time with a like result.

About this time the officer began to think the proper time for the use of fire-
arms had arrived, and attempted to draw his revolver, when his arms were seized
and he was prevented from discharging it. With considerable exertion, he managed to free himself from their grasp and succeeded in arresting the offender for
the fifth time, and handed him over to officer Ludwick, who had hardly placed his
hand upon the prisoner when the crowd set upon *him* and took the prisoner from
his custody. The crowd increasing, the officers thought best to beat a retreat, and
came to the South Side for assistance. When this arrived the crowd had dispersed
and Kilgubbin subsided into its pristine condition of peace and quietude. The ringleaders are known, and we hope to chronicle their speedy arrest.

Chicago Tribune, July 22, 1862.

∿

Riot at a German Pic Nic [*sic*]—A serious riot occurred at a pic nic of the Tenth
Ward Workingmen's Society, at the foot of Reuben street, Sunday afternoon.
About seven o'clock, and after all but the committee had left the grounds, an
Irish boatman came among them, and after offering various insults to the com-
mittee, attempted to snatch the money from the hands of the treasurer. He was
resisted and driven off. He returned almost immediately, reinforced by about fifty

Irishmen, who attacked the committee of fifteen, with clubs and stones. Louis Shorr, had an arm broken, John Prechtel had his head terribly smashed.

Chicago Tribune, July 23, 1862.

~

The competition between the Irish and Germans is reflected in this selection in which an Irish reader of the Tribune *challenges the paper's reporting that Chicago Germans enlisted in greater numbers than the Irish. The* Tribune *incorrectly replied that the Irish population was larger and that they had not shown the same level of devotion to the Union as the Germans.*

IRISH AND GERMAN ENLISTMENTS.

EDITORS TRIBUNE:—In your issue of to-day you say in an item in your locals, that "it would be well for other nationalities to imitate the patriotism of the Germans," in getting up a war fund of their own, to encourage enlistments. Now, sir, would it not be more patriotic for the Germans to imitate the Irish, in enlisting without the patriotic fund? You will not deny but the German population of Chicago is twice that of the Irish, and you will not deny that the Irish have volunteered more than the Germans, since the last call of the President, in this city, as witness the Provost Marshal's report up to the 13th inst., viz:

United States 218	England 27
Germany 108	Scotland 7
Canada 21	Colored 121
Ireland. 132	

You will see that the colored men have beat your "patriotic Germans" by thirteen men. Will you insert the above for the benefit of your Irish readers? Perhaps the reason the Irish enlist more freely than the Germans is that the former are Democrats and the latter Republicans.

AN IRISH SUBSCRIBER.

REMARKS.—Our correspondent is greatly mistaken in say that the German population of Chicago is twice as large as the Irish. The latter is the largest. There are several thousand more Irish in this city than Germans.[13] Nor do we know that the table of nationalities in our correspondent's letter is accurate; we are preparing a later and more complete one, and will know just how many men each class has furnished. But assuming the above figure to be correct, it gives us great pleasure to see that the Irish are being emancipated from the disloyal influences that have heretofore kept them from contributing their proper quota to the National defense. Better late than never. We have no fears of the Germans holding back, or failing to perform their duty; they have been among the foremost in fighting for Liberty and Union since this war began, and we will not ask the Irish to put more men in the field to a given population than the Germans. If they do as well, the country will not fail to recognize their services and award them the credit they deserve. In regard to the last sentence of our correspondent, we have only this to remark, that Democrats have, and should feel, as deep an interest in the preservation of the Union as Republicans, and should make as many sacrifices and contribute as many men for its salvation as the latter, no matter what Copperhead demagogues may tell them to the contrary.

Chicago Tribune, January 17, 1864.

~

The Germans are Loyal.

It does not often accord with our privileges—if it frequently agrees with the fact—to single out one class of citizens to praise them, at the expense of another class. But the recent atrocious riots in New York have established for that city, what was before apparent to Chicago and other cities, namely, that of two classes of foreigners in our midst, one is loyal, and the other is disloyal. The Germans are true; there are individual exceptions, but such is the rule. The Irish are in the snares of the Copperhead faction of the Democracy, and are false to the country of their adoption. This charge needs some modification. Thousands of Irishmen are now in the ranks, and have fought with a bravery equal to the bravest; and thousands who are not in the army, give all their sympathies to the Government. The great majority, however, of that class, have resolved that they will aid no man but a Copperhead, and no cause but the rebellion. They are criminal; but they, deluded men, are not by many shades as black criminals as their intelligent leaders. But upon their heads has fallen in New York, and will fall elsewhere, if riots are attempted, the full vengeance of the outraged country.

Chicago Tribune, July 22, 1863.

THE FEAR OF BLACK IMMIGRATION

As Union armies in the West successfully invaded the Deep South, a large number of enslaved people seized the opportunity for freedom and fled to federal forces. Union troops refused to return these people, known as "contrabands" even before the Emancipation Proclamation, to bondage. Eventually camps with thousands of the refugees from slavery were maintained by the army. One of the largest was at

Cairo in far southern Illinois. The prospect of some of these newly freed people coming to Chicago excited the racial and economic fears of Chicago Democrats. In August 1862, Chicago Republican congressman Isaac Arnold was renominated for his seat in the House of Representatives by his party. When Lincoln announced the Emancipation Proclamation on September 1, 1862, Chicago Democrats and their organ, the Chicago Times, *voiced concern that Arnold and Lincoln did not reflect the sentiments of the Union on the issue of abolitionism and emancipation, as well as the fact that the Lincoln Administration attacked constitutional liberties of free speech and a free press. Democrats nominated Mayor Francis Sherman to challenge Arnold. Although a Democrat, Sherman was not a copperhead. While loyal to the Union, he was also loyal to Chicago's white working class, and he used fear of black migration to Chicago to rally support. Although Sherman won overwhelmingly in Chicago, rural Cook County voters tipped the election in favor of returning Arnold to the House. Below is an exchange between city officials and federal authorities regarding the contrabands.*

Telegram, September 22, 1862
To Mayor Sherman from J.N. Tuttle, Brig. Gen. (Cairo)

I have large numbers of applications from your city for negro servants. Will you appoint a committee to see they are properly put out to work, will send as soon as committee is appointed and I am notified, answer.

～

In his reply to this request, Mayor Sherman cited Illinois law of 1853 and the state constitution, which prohibited migration of blacks to the state. His position was strongly supported by the city council.

MAYOR SHERMAN'S REPLY

Your proposition to send imported negroes to Chicago to work would be in violation of the laws of this state, and a great injustice to our laboring population. I cannot give it any sanction, by appointing a committee as you propose, or in any other way.

John Jones, Papers, Research Center, Chicago History Museum.

～

Mayor Sherman's strong stand against allowing former slaves to work in Chicago inspired the Democratic Party to nominate him to run for Congress against the incumbent Lincoln supporter Isaac Arnold. Quoted below are Sherman's remarks upon accepting the nomination. Sherman, a conservative Union man with a son in the army, ran as a champion of the white working class. He carried Chicago voting that fall but lost because of strong Republican returns in the collar counties.

. . . My sympathies have always been and still are, with the laboring classes of our community. . . . I have always been for elevating labor. . . . But we have now a new issue forced upon us and every man and every woman has an interest in that issue. It is the great question as to whether the white labor in the North shall be elevated or degraded. Are you willing to see the mechanics, or the laborers in the workshops, or on the streets, or in the fields supplanted by a Negro population, imported into this state in violation of law?

Chicago Times, October 15, 1862.

~

SHALL ILLINOIS BE AFRICANIZED?

It is the policy of abolitionism to Africanize all the States. It is the policy of abolitionism to make all men free, and then to make all men equal,—that is, to elevate negroes to the level of white men at the polls, and to degrade white men to the level of negroes in the workshops and fields of labor.

Chicago Times, October 26, 1862.

~

Chicago politicians, empowered by the State of Illinois's infamous Black Laws, worked to keep the races apart in education. What might appear as an enlightened step to create schools for black children by the Chicago City Council actually established the pattern of de facto segregation. Below, the Committee on Schools reports to the mayor and city council on its recommendations.

. . . Consolidation Act for Chicago Ordinances . . . February 13, 1863

It shall be the duty of the common council and board of education to provide one or more schools for the instruction of negro and mulatto children, to be kept in a separate building to be provided for that purpose, at which colored pupils, between the ages of five and twenty-one years, residing in any school district in said city, shall be allowed to attend; and hereafter it shall not be lawful for such pupils to attend any public schools in the city of Chicago, at which white children are taught, after a school for the instruction of negro and mulatto children has been provided.

⌒

Order of the Committee on Schools Providing for Segregation
March 23, 1863
To the Mayor and Alderman of the City of Chicago, in Common Council
    Assembled:
Your Committee on Schools
to whom was referred on the 27th of June last an ordinance entitled "an ordinance in relation to public schools" . . . beg leave to report that the General Assembly of the State have by Sec 16 Chapter 13 of the revised charter approved Feb 13th 1863, made it the duty of the Common Council & Board of Education to provide one or more schools for the instruction of colored & mulatto children—They would therefore recommend the passage of the following order as a substitute for said proposed ordinance—

Ordered

That the Board of Education be authorized, and directed to hire a suitable building or rooms in the South Division, and provide requisite teachers and conveniences, for a school for the instruction of colored children, in accordance with, and to be conducted in conformity to the provisions of the amended charter of 1863. and that the Mayor & Comptroller be and they are hereby authorized to draw their warrant on the Treasurer, for the payment of such expenditures as may be incurred in connection with said school, when duly certified by the Board of Education, payable out of the School Tax Fund—

John Q. Hoyt,   ⎫ Committee on Schools
W T Shufeldt   ⎭

Report Concurred in and order passed

AFRICAN AMERICANS BUILD A COMMUNITY

Recognizing the need for adult education, Chicago's African American community formed their own evening school. The Tribune *championed their cause and extolled their achievements in an attempt to educate their readers on the intelligence and humanity of black community.*

A COLORED SCHOOL.—

The most persistent believer in "negro want of energy" views, would have acknowledged that his opinions were fallacious had he been present at a meeting held last evening at No. 640 West Lake street. It was the last meeting for the season of a colored evening school which has been in session during the past winter. The school was commenced two years ago by the *colored people themselves*, who, feeling their total ignorance, determined to secure the services of a competent white instructor. They were fortunate in obtaining as a teacher Mr. Theodore J. Ellmore, under whose tuition they have progressed wonderfully in the rudiments of a thorough English education. The first winter the school was only open for eighteen weeks, but this year it has been in session for more than six months. It has been held in rooms provided by the 'scholars' themselves, who also find their own books. When the school was first organized, the pupils were all totally ignorant of the very meaning of letters; now they can all read fluently and write better than a great number of their white brethren, besides which, they have a good idea of the country and its history.

Chicago Tribune, April 1, 1864.

AFRICAN AMERICANS FIGHT FOR THEIR FREEDOM

On April 16, 1862, Congress abolished slavery in the District of Columbia. In Chicago, African Americans gathered to hail Lincoln's and the government's actions as well as address the pervasive prejudice and anxiety that many white Chicagoans had regarding a world with free blacks. These fears ranged from the belief that blacks would be unable to conduct and govern themselves as free people to the prospect of mass migration of former slaves to the North. African American Chicagoans also argued that emancipation of slaves was key to success in the war effort and expressed their thanks to the white soldiers in the field who fought for freedom for all.

MASS MEETING OF THE COLORED PEOPLE OF CHICAGO.

Last night a numerously attended mass meeting of our colored citizens was held at the African M.E. Church . . . to give expression to their feelings and take some public action in relation to the recent act of Congress abolishing slavery in the District of Columbia. . . .

On motion, a committee of twelve was appointed to prepare and present a report expressive of the sentiments entertained by the meeting. . . . The preamble and resolutions . . . were adopted by a unanimous vote:

WHEREAS, Certain journals in the city of Chicago, and elsewhere, having assailed, vilified, and unjustly misrepresented the colored people in this country, charging them as being worthless, indolent and incapable of self government or control, unfit to enjoy the blessings of *freemen* in common with their white brethren, repudiating also the recent act emancipating the slave in the District of Columbia as well as in the States now in open rebellion against the Government, and

WHEREAS, An impression prevails throughout the Northern loyal States that in the event of emancipation the influx of the freed slaves to the North would be great, and as this impression is not confined to those who are opposed to emancipation or confiscation; and

WHEREAS, This fear is calculated to retard the consummation of such measures as would otherwise by adopted for bringing the present war to a speedy close, besides the enacting of laws by Legislatures and even State Constitutional Conventions, debaring migration to Northern States of persons of African blood; therefore,

Resolved, That we consider it a duty which we owe to ourselves and our race, to repel the charges made against us; also against a government which is gradually wiping from her escutcheons the foul stain of slavery.

Resolved, That as colored Americans, who have been enslaved for over eighty years, and suffered much from the unceasing scourge of our political enemies, we are now and ever have been *loyal* to a government oppressing us, and that we heartily approve the recent act of Congress in emancipating the slaves in the District of Columbia.

Resolved, That the States now in rebellion are Slave States, the rebels being the white inhabitants of those States; nine-tenths of the colored people of the United States, are natives of those rebel States, yet not one colored man can be found whose sympathies are with the rebellion.

Resolved, That though we have been denied permission to aid in defending our country, we nevertheless thank our soldiers for their valor in her defense and the cause of human liberty.

Resolved, That we regard Abraham Lincoln, that honest man, (which is the noblest work of God) as standing above any President which has ever filled the Executive Chair, and more especially in signing the act emancipating the slaves in the District of Columbia. This we consider the noblest of deeds. May he ever live in the affections of our people, throughout the land to the latest generation, and when he shall be called to rest from his labors of love and good deeds, may this act ever be an angel by his side.

Resolved, That in the opinion of this meeting (and we speak advisedly for the masses of our people) that the abolition of slavery in the Southern States will result in the general migration of the colored people of the North to the South.

Chicago Tribune, March 22, 1862.

CHICAGO'S AFRICAN AMERICANS ENLIST

The first African American Chicagoan to fight in the Civil War was H. Ford Douglas. Before the war he was an abolitionist speaker and for a time owner of a pro-emigration newspaper. On September 4, 1862, even before the preliminary Emancipation Proclamation was issued, this light-skinned, Virginia-born mulatto enlisted in the

Ninety-Fifth Illinois Infantry, where his comrades treated him as an equal in the
fight against the slaveholders' rebellion. Douglas later served as a captain of colored
infantry in Louisiana and raised a colored artillery unit in Kansas. In this January
1863 letter he explains to his mentor, Frederick Douglass, his decision to enlist.

. . . I enlisted six months ago in order to be better prepared to play my part in
the great drama of the Negro's redemption. I wanted its drill, its practical details,
for mere theory does not make a good soldier. I have learned something of war,
for I have seen war in its brightest as well as its bloodiest phase, and yet I have
nothing to regret. For since the stern necessities of this struggle have laid bare
the naked issue of freedom on one side and slavery on the other—freedom shall
have, in the future of this conflict if necessary, my blood as it has had in the past
my earnest and best words. It seems to me that you can have no good reason for
withholding from the government your hearty cooperation. This war will educate
Mr. Lincoln out of his idea of the deportation of the Negro quite as fast as it has
some of his other pro-slavery ideas with respect to employing them as soldiers.

Hitherto they have been socially and politically ignored by this government,
but now by the fortunes of war they are cast morally and mentally helpless (so to
speak) into the broad sunlight of our Republican civilization there to be educated
and lifted to a higher and nobler life. National duties and responsibilities are not to
be colonized, they must be heroically met and religiously performed. This mighty
waste of manhood resulting from the dehumanizing character of slave institutions of America is now to be given back to the world through the patient toil and
self-denial of this proud and haughty race. They must now pay back the negro in
Spiritual culture in opportunities for self-improvement what they have taken from
him for two hundred years by the constant over-taxing of his physical nature. This
law of supply and demand regulates itself. And so this question of the colonization
of the negro; it will be settled by laws over which war has no control. Now is the
time for you to finish the crowning work of your life. Go to work at once and raise
a Regiment and offer your services to the government, and I am confident they
will be accepted. They say we will not fight. I want to see it tried on. You are the
one to me of all others, to demonstrate this fact.

I belong to company G, 95th Regiment Illinois volunteers—Captain Elliot N.
Bush—a Christian and a gentleman.

Frederick Douglass' Monthly, February 1863.

∽

In March 1863, two months after the Emancipation Proclamation effectively freed
slaves in the states in rebellion, Massachusetts authorized the formation of the

Fifty-Fourth Massachusetts Volunteer Infantry Regiment as the first official African American unit raised in the North. Both the proclamation and the prospect of a chance to fight for their freedom thrilled and energized Chicago's African American community. Illinois had thus far denied its black residents citizenship and the opportunity to volunteer to fight. Twenty-one black Chicagoans left behind work as sailors, porters, or laborers and joined the Fifty-Fourth Massachusetts as an opportunity to claim their rights as equals and strike a blow against the Confederacy. They also felt it was their responsibility to carry the news of emancipation to slaves throughout the South.

THE COLORED PEOPLE ON THE WAR

The colored people of Chicago, and in fact of Illinois, are becoming fully aroused upon the question of enlisting in the colored regiments of Massachusetts. Several enthusiastic meetings have been held in this city, and a large number of men have been mustered in for a chance at their old southern masters. At a meeting of this kind, held at Quinn's Chapel, Monday night, Joseph Stanley in the Chair, a series of resolutions were adopted, and a spirited audience in the colored people of the State was prepared, which would do honor to the authors, even though the proud blood of the Caucasian leaped through their veins.

THE ADDRESS

Colored men of Illinois! This appeal to your! Give ear but for a moment. Over the country, the beloved land of our birth, is now in the midst of civil war, caused by the infamous rebel that ever distracted a people, or threatened a nation's existence. This rebellion, infamous in itself, is rendered doubly so when it is remembered that the sole object is to establish the godless bondage of our race by a constitution which declares—as expressed by Alex H. Stevens, the vice president of the "so-called" Southern Confederacy—that African slavery is, and shall be, the cornerstone of the Southern social system. What shall we do under such circumstances? . . . it requires no argument as our duty is plain.

We have long petitioned, prayed, and labored that justice be done us as part of the American people. We have asked that the General Government [abolish] all legal distinctions between us as a race and the whites. We are now beginning to realize our hopes and expectations so far as the present Government is concerned. Under President Lincoln, great things have been accomplished in the providence of God, for the oppressed and downtrodden. Slavery has been abolished in the District of Columbia, the black republic of Haiti and Liberia have been recognized. We have been declared citizens of the United States, black soldiers have been called into the ranks of the army; representatives of a black garrison now reside near the Government and attends as a diplomatic member of the American court.

And lastly, by a general proclamation of the President, the slaves of the rebellious States , and those of all rebels have been declared free, and compensation offered by the Government for the freedom of all persons in bondage by loyal slaveholders.

In the Revolutionary War, it required seven years struggle to establish the Declaration of Independence. It may require a longer struggle to enforce the Emancipation Proclamation. In this war the liberty of slaves is at once established, as soon as the Proclamation is carried to them.

Who is to bear to our brethren of the South this good news—this glorious, heavenly tidings of great joy—thousands of whom have not yet heard it. It is our duty—the duty of the black man to bear that proclamation, which can only be effectively accomplished by entering the army as soldiers supporting the arms of the Government, and thus carry it by fire and sword, not only into the heart of the South, but into the hearts of the rebels.

We need not remind you that, while this State denies us the right of volunteering as freemen, with the privileges guaranteed to other citizens, you are subject to the draft the same as whites. To you Massachusetts now offers this opportunity as black volunteers, with the rights, immunities and benefits of citizen as well as soldiers. You are invited to enter that State's service on terms of equality, with the same pay, rations, clothing, term of enlistment, and land bounty as in all other regiments of volunteers. The enlightened policy of the people, Legislature and Governor of the state, fully welcome you as full equals in the body politic.

As inhabitants of Illinois, politically degraded by a cruel system of black laws at variance with the progress of the age, you are now offered the opportunity honorably to enroll your names on the list with the brave and patriotic heroes who are now fighting to maintain the Government, reestablish the freedom . . . and extend liberty and political equality on the list with the brave and patriotic heroes who are now fighting to maintain the Government . . . and extend liberty and political equality to all the inhabitants thereof."

Chicago Evening Journal, March 30, 1863.

~

The Chicago Tribune *attempted to sway public opinion to accept African American volunteers into Illinois military units with an ironic argument that it was unjust for white men to bear the burden of military service while negroes were protected "from the hardships and privations of military service. . . ."*

SUBSTITUTES FOR NEGROES.

Every white man drafted into the army, while a negro volunteer is rejected, or exempted, *goes to the war as that negro's substitute, without bounty.* A full regiment of colored men from Chicago were tendered to Governor Yates yesterday. If the Governor is not allowed to accept them, a full regiment of white men must be drawn from the pursuits of business and the society of their families, to fill the place of this colored regiment. Is this the President's decision? If so, we suppose it can be endured until the force of public opinion shall overbear it, which will not be a long time. If such be his decision, it exhibits a tenderness toward the colored race, and a disposition to shield them from the hardships of warfare, which we were not prepared to expect.

It behooves every man who does not wish to be turned into a private soldier, as a substitute for a negro, without bounty, to make his voice heard in this crisis. The country must be saved through its lawfully constituted machinery. President Lincoln must be told by so many voices, and in such decided tones, that his policy is unjust to his own kindred and race, that he cannot fail to hear. There is neither sense nor decency in compelling a man doing a business of $50,000 a year, with a hundred laborers and their families dependent on his enterprise and success, to leave all and shoulder a musket while a thousand colored men around him would gladly take his musket and step into his place in the ranks. When that *necessity* comes—when the man of large business and great value to the community can find no one black or white to go in his place, then he will go, and go cheerfully if he is a patriot, and serve his nine months, trusting the consequences to God, his Father. . . . We have argued long and earnestly for justice to the black man. *We now appeal for justice to the whites!*

We understand this hesitation at Washington to employ negroes in the military service. It is a part of the Kentucky policy, which fears that slavery may somehow suffer in the Border States by contact with colored regiments. So we are not saving the Union with our anguish so much as we are saving slavery for the Border States, or rather pandering to a haggard fear which has no foundation. The country is sweating, as it were, great drops of blood. It demands the firm nerve, the un-shrinking spirit, the iron will, to direct its energies.

Chicago Tribune, August 7, 1863.

~

Illinois finally formed its own colored regiment, the Twenty-Nine Illinois Volunteer Regiment of Colored Soldiers, in January 1864. Their commanding officer, Colonel John A. Bross, was the brother of a co-owner of the Chicago Tribune. *Before* embarking for training camp, Chicago African American enlistees paraded down Clark Street, and then after "saluting the office of the Tribune," which championed their cause, they boarded trains for Quincy, Illinois.

FROM QUINCY, ILL.

There are now in camp at this place three full companies of the First Regiment Illinois Colored Volunteers. Ample arrangements have been made to clothe and subsist recruits as fast as they report here. The regiment occupies the barracks erected here by the Government and with some improvement as the regiment grows will be all that can be desired. A regular system of drill and discipline is already in successful operation. A regular camp guard is established and a large portion of the day is occupied in the instruction of recruits.

The aptitude and desire of the men to learn the rudiments of the military art is quite remarkable.

Today about two hundred of the men paraded the streets with martial music, carrying with them the old flag. The regularity and precision of their marching received the unqualified approbation of many military men and thousands of civilians.

Chicago had a magnificent representation in the physique of the company of which she may well be proud. Will she not have to honor a draft for three full companies of the maximum number for this regiment?

The Government officials here and the citizens are working energetically for the success of the regiment, and its officers desire to carry out your own expressed wish to be ready for the field for the Spring campaign.

Chicago Tribune, January 14, 1864.

∼

THE ILLINOIS COLORED REGIMENT.

ITS ARRIVAL IN CHICAGO—RECEPTION— ITS DEPARTURE TO JOIN BURNSIDE.

The Illinois colored regiment, 29th U.S. Colored Volunteers, Col. John A. Bross commanding, reached this city from its camp of rendezvous at Quincy, yesterday morning at 8 o'clock, en route to join Burnside's movement of the 9th Corps from Annapolis, Maryland. The patriotic and generous ladies of the Soldiers' Rest had in readiness a bountiful repast to which the regiment did full justice. The regiment is the first colored regiment organized in this State, and elicited high encomiums yesterday from all observers, by their soldierly appearance.

Chicago Tribune, March 28, 1864.

AFRICAN AMERICAN WOMEN

The African American women of Chicago recognized the need to help the displaced slave population caught in the path of war. Mary Jones and Sattira Douglas, wives of the city's leading black abolitionists, were also formidable leaders in their own right. Sattira Douglas later moved to Kansas to work as a teacher in a freedmen's school, while her husband, H. Ford Douglas, recruited and led former slaves in military service. In 1864, Mary Ann Shadd Cary, the tireless black abolitionist and newspaperwoman, moved to Chicago to become the fundraising agent for the society.[14]

COLORED LADIES' FREEDMEN'S AID SOCIETY.—

The Secretary of the Colored Ladies' Freedmen's Aid Society has handed us the following report for publication:

This Society having been in existence since September 15th, 1863, a period of nearly seven months, has, during that time, sent South a large quantity of clothing and cooking utensils, together with several barrels of vegetable supplies for the freedmen. They also contributed liberally to the relief of the Kansas refugees, besides having appointed a permanent committee to act as city missionaries among the freed people, and report all cases of destitution that come under their notice. Since the organization, the receipts of accruing from lectures, festivals, donations, etc., amount to $321.40; disbursements, $149.53; leaving a balance in the treasury $171.87. The members are confident that their goods reach the desired destination, as all boxes are sent through the efficient agency of the Northwestern Freedmen's Aid Commission. The Society meets regularly and continues to prepare clothing, and, with other necessaries, to ship them South, besides endeavoring, to some extent, to alleviate the condition of the sufferers who come in our midst.

Mrs. John Jones, President.

Mrs. H. F. Douglas, Secretary.

Chicago Tribune, March 15, 1864.

THE SUFFERING OF SOLDIERS' FAMILIES

As the war stretched on, year after year, the families of poor soldiers faced greater and greater difficulty in making ends meet. There was no formal government means to help destitute women and children. The Northwest Sanitary Commission and soldier's aid societies tried to step into the breach. Here Mary Livermore recounts a day of visiting needy soldiers' families.

On one occasion the week had been so crowded with work that I was obliged to devote Sunday morning to visiting some half-dozen soldiers' families, concerning whom I was feeling great anxiety. Chaplain McCabe, of the Christian Commission, who had been a chaplain in the army, and was captured at the battle of Bull Run, spending months in Libby Prison, wished to accompany me in these visits. He desired to witness for himself the poverty and distresses of the families of men in the field. With one exception I had visited every family on which we called for a year or longer, and knew their circumstances intimately, so that there was no chance for imposition. I transcribe from my journal the details of the visits made that morning, as they were written Out on my return:—

"Visit number one was made to a German woman, whose husband is in the Twenty-fourth Illinois, now before Atlanta, Ga. She has seven children, the two youngest of whom cannot walk,——one from paralysis, and the other from its babyhood. Her husband left her eighteen dollars when he went away, and he has sent her money but once since, as he has been most of the time in the hospital. They own a little house with three rooms, built on leased ground; but the lease expired the first of this month and the land has been sold to an Irishman, who wishes the house moved off. What to do, she is unable to decide. Where she can lease a new lot, or obtain the money for leasing, and for moving the house, she does not know. If her husband were at home, all would be well; for his neighbors with one voice testify to his industry and sobriety. 'He is too much patriot,' they cry; 'he fight too much in the army.' And to prove their assertion they tell you he went into the revolutionary war of Europe in 1848, leaving his family then in distressing circumstances.

"Three times in a year the poor woman has been to me, weeping bitterly because she had not a mouthful of food for herself and children. On one occasion she brought three of her younger children into my kitchen. Ordinarily they are exceedingly quiet and well behaved; but this time they were so hungry that they were fierce and wild, and caught at food like animals, eating so rapidly and voraciously that I had to interfere lest harmful results would follow in the matter of digestion. To feed, clothe, and warm her family this winter, she has only her own labor to depend upon, and the irregular and small remittances from her husband. She washes, cleans house, and picks rags. Both the house and children were scrupulously clean, although indicative of extreme poverty; and the mother, though worn with care and labor, says she does not regret her husband's enlistment. 'It was right,' she says."

"Number two was an American family. The father is in the Ninety-first Illinois, and is in Vicksburg, guarding the prison. He is a carpenter, and could earn two and a half to three dollars per day if he were at home. His wife is a lovely, delicate woman, with three children. The husband is a noble fellow, and has only expended five dollars at the sutler's in two years; and that has been for stationery. He has drawn as little clothing as possible, and sends all his money home. It has reached his wife with unusual regularity. She owns a sewing-machine, gets plenty of work; for she is a most skilful needlewoman, aside from being a good operator on the machine. She is able, with the assistance of her husband's pay, to get along comfortably. But the last hundred dollars from her husband, brought up by one of his discharged lieutenants, was gambled away by the latter when coming up the Mississippi.

"She has lately fallen ill and been confined to her bed by sickness. The loss of this money plunged her into poverty, which, with the instinct of American women, she kept to herself. At last the unpaid rent had accumulated to thirty dollars, and she was in imminent danger of being turned out of doors. Food and fuel were gone, and starvation stared her in the face. All the while she wrote brave, cheerful letters to her husband, hiding the truth from him, and assuring him all was well. She would not distress him with the narration of troubles he could not remedy, she said; and so suffered and kept silence. I learned accidentally of her destitute circumstances. It is needless to say that speedy relief was carried to her and her weeping children.

"Her husband also learned accidentally how sad was the plight of his family, and besought his commander so earnestly for a furlough, that three weeks' leave of absence was given him. That visit brought the wife back from the verge of the grave; and, when her husband returned to his regiment, leaving her the money he had earned at his trade during his furlough, which a few generous people had largely increased by donations that they compelled him to accept, she again took up her burden of life, a little stronger to bear it. She cannot work yet; but she is not forgotten by the generous and patriotic, and will not be.

"Visit number three was to an underground room, in an old tumble-down building, on Wells Street, which is inhabited by nine families, one half of whom live in cellars, below the level of the street. Here, the wife of a soldier in one of the Ohio regiments, an American woman, died some two months since. I only learned of the case after she was dead. I went in the morning to the apartment, and found her aged mother, over seventy, with two children, two and four years of age, her only surviving relatives. They were so poor that they had not even a bit of candle, nor a drop of kerosene, nor a stick of fuel with which to make a light during the night, when the dying woman asked her mother to read some verses from the Scriptures, as she was passing away. The dreadful underground room is infested with rats, and during the remainder of the night the aged mother stood by her daughter's bedside, fighting the rats from the lifeless body.

"A few weeks after the mother's sorrowful death, the youngest child died. There remain now only the aged grandmother and the boy of four years. The husband was killed in the army some eight months before. They have no acquaintances, except among those who are in such abject poverty that affection is killed by it. They have no near relatives. The aged grandmother clings to her little grandson, who is her only tie to life. The sufferings of the dead mother and the entire family have been fearful; and the attenuated-figure of the little boy and of the aged woman tell a story of starvation. No one knew them until suffering had done its dread-nil work on the young soldier's widow, and laid her at rest from the sorrows of life.

"The poor grandmother is an object of the deepest commiseration. I never go to her comfortless home that I do not surprise her in tears. She is afraid her dead daughter has failed of heaven; and I am always compelled to go over my grounds of assurance that all is well with her. Chaplain McCabe, who listened to the poor woman's story, prayed and sang with her, and bade her be comforted with the confident assertion that her daughter was with the blessed. Arrangements are nearly completed to place the grandmother in the Old Ladies' Home, and to take the little boy into the Home of the Friendless.

"Number four was a soldier's family whose heaviest burdens have been removed by the return of the husband and father to his family. He has been discharged from the service, in consequence of serious injuries received in the left hand, arm, and side, from the bursting of a shell. He has found a little light employment, which, with the work of his energetic American wife, renders them comparatively independent of charity. She has toiled, suffered, and endured patiently, in his long absence, to support herself and child. Since the return of her crippled husband, the pinched look has left her face, and the pallor of death has been supplanted by a healthy hue. 'If I could only get plenty of work,' she says, 'I should be so happy that a queen might envy me!'

"Number five was the wife of one of the men who are forcing their way into Mobile under Admiral Farragut. She is one of the better sort of Irish women; and, though she rarely receives money from her husband, she earns enough to support herself and little daughter. When well, she needs no assistance; but a week's sickness or the loss of a week's work puts her in a tight place.

"Number six is a woman whose husband is in the Seventy-second Illinois. She has three children to maintain, whom she has to neglect in order to earn bread for them. Almost every day, week after week, she leaves the two younger in the care of the older, a little girl of nine years, and goes out to work, washing, scrubbing, and cleaning, from seven in the morning till six in the evening. Last week, when her children were locked up in the room in her absence, the baby, eighteen months old, fell out of the second-story chamber window, and was taken up for dead. It did not kill the child immediately, but he may yet die from the effects of the fall. He was taken to the children's ward of the hospital, where he can receive the care and nursing that his mother cannot give him. She is worn to a skeleton with hard work, but rarely complains, or asks for help. These last two women occupy three miserable attic rooms together, paying ten dollars per month for rent; and they render each other all the assistance in their power. Poor as they are, they are very helpful to one another.

"Number seven was a colored woman, whose husband has been in the Fifty-fourth Massachusetts, under Col. Robert G. Shaw, from its organization. Not a cent has yet been paid by government to any colored soldier who has gone from Chicago. This woman was a slave when the war began,—is still, as far as any manumission by her master is concerned. Since her husband's absence, she has passed through hunger, cold, sickness, and bereavement. Her landlord, a rich man of the city, a German, put her out of her house on the sidewalk, in a cold rain storm, because she owed him five dollars for rent, and could not then earn it, as her child was sick unto death with scarlet fever. One of her colored neighbors, as poor as she, took her in; and the baby died on the next Sunday morning. She came to me to get the baby buried, without going to the poor master. 'It don't seem right for my child to be buried like a pauper,' she said, 'when her father is fighting for the country.' And I agreed with her.

"A way was devised to give the little one decent burial; and the mother's heart is comforted by the thought that her child will never have to pass through what she has. The woman's husband was born a slave in Beaufort, S. C., and thither his regiment was first ordered. He has learned to read and write, and wrote me a most graphic account of the battle in which his heroic colonel, the brave Robert G. Shaw, was killed. I made the poor woman supremely happy by reading to her a letter from Governor Andrew of Massachusetts, giving me carte blanche for the relief of the families living in Chicago whose husbands and fathers have enlisted in the Fifty-fourth. I promised to help her to house-keeping again, as soon as she can collect her scattered household goods.

"Number eight was the wife of another colored soldier of the Fifty-fourth Massachusetts She has four children, and has not received any of her husband's earnings. Government has not paid him. She is lying very sick with typhoid fever. I gladdened her by telling her of Governor Andrew's letter, which will immediately procure her a physician and nurse, medicine, and food for her children. Chaplain McCabe sang her a beautiful hymn, in his melodious and expressive style, and then prayed with her. The colored people in the neighborhood, whom music always attracts, silently flocked into the room, as he sang and prayed; and, as they stood weeping and listening, I found it difficult to repress my own tears for the friendless and feeble wives of the soldiers, of whose sad condition I know so much. They are not remembered, nor ministered to, nor sympathized with, as they should be."

If the history of this war shall ever be written in full, whatever else the historian may forget, he will not fail to chronicle the sublime valor manifested at the hearthstone, all over this struggling land.

Mary A. Livermore, *My Story of the War* (Hartford, CT: A. D. Worthington, 1888), 580–86.

EIGHT

~

The Long Shadow of War

*T*HE NEW YEAR of 1865 began optimistically with the war's end in sight. Buoyed by their city's growth and prosperity, Chicagoans viewed the future of the nation and their city in expansive terms. With the Pacific railroad finally beginning to make progress, they envisioned a time when Chicago's commerce would reach beyond the fabled South Pass in the Rockies to the blue Pacific. Chicago's interest in war news reached a fever pitch when Grant's army captured Richmond and Lee's army was out of its entrenchments and on the run. Chicagoans greeted the news with restrained joy. Businesses were closed, people rushed into the streets, American flags were draped on buildings, and impromptu parades formed. But not until Lee surrendered on April 9 was the tension that had built up over four awful years finally broken. The people of the city did not need any leaders to organize an official celebration, as they quickly and spontaneously formed the "People's Procession," which wended its way through the city for miles. This was the first of many parades, as others were organized to greet soldiers as they returned from the battlefields in the weeks to come.[1]

The news of Lincoln's death on April 15 came as a personal blow to many Chicagoans. Scores of people in the city had worked with him professionally, nominated him for the presidency, helped elect him, and supported his administration throughout the dark days of the war. Therefore, it was critical for Chicagoans to greet the return of his remains with all the dignity and ceremony possible. In elaborate detail, plans for his funeral procession through the streets of the city and to lay the president in state at the courthouse were worked out. On May 1 a hushed crowd received Abraham Lincoln at the railroad depot at Lake Park, and a crowd, estimated by some to be nearly five hundred thousand, escorted the procession or lined the streets as Lincoln's black-draped hearse pulled by ten black horses make its way to the courthouse. In a fitting tribute to the nation Lincoln helped forge, city dignitaries processed with the United Sons of Erin, a deputized group of "Colored citizens," the Chicago Board of Trade leaders, and the Laborer's Benevolent Association. The entire procession of thirty-seven thousand took nearly four hours to complete its journey.[2]

Despite their grief at the loss of their leader, the sanitary fair commissioners continued to carry out their plans for a Second Sanitary Fair in June. Soldiers still needed nursing and care at the Soldiers' Home, and returning veterans needed a place to stay at the Soldiers' Rest as they passed through Chicago. Generals Ulysses S. Grant, William T. Sherman, and Joseph Hooker honored the event through their attendance and generous words of praise for the work of the Sanitary Commission. Even Tad Lincoln attended the fair. The event lasted for three weeks and raised $85,000.[3]

The return of several regiments during these weeks added to the celebratory mood of the city. Chicago held its own "grand review," which included the Eighty-Eighth Illinois ("Second Board of Trade Regiment"), the Ninetieth Illinois ("Irish Legion"), and the Eighty-Ninth Illinois ("Railroad Regiment") on the fairgrounds. They were cheered by Chicagoans of all walks of life and feted by the city's elite. Amid the exuberant celebration was also a tone of somber remembrance. Cook County had sent 22,436 men into the Union army. Chicago contributed about 15,000 of those soldiers, and nearly 4,000 of these men never returned. Many disabled veterans languished for years after in the Soldiers' Home. These losses were painfully obvious when the regiments formed their much-reduced ranks for the review parade. The black crape of mourning decorated many a Chicago home.[4]

Not all returning soldiers arrived in time for honors or parades. As the weeks went by, those who straggled into town unannounced were greeted by a growing indifference. Exhausted by the war years, many Chicagoans were ready to put that chapter in the city's history behind them and get on with their lives. The city draped in sable crape had also greatly prospered during the conflict. Men shedding their tattered blue uniforms found themselves forced to scramble to catch up with the stay-at-home entrepreneurs who had cashed in on war's opportunities. Riches and bitterness were part of the war's legacy to Chicago.

The impact of the Civil War on Chicago was immediately evident to returning soldiers upon their arrival in a city vastly transformed from the one they had left in 1861. Chicago's population had climbed throughout the war, and after peace was made, newcomers streaming out of the railroad stations hustled to find new jobs in this burgeoning city. By 1870, the city's population had increased nearly threefold over the war decade. Its geographic boundaries had also expanded. In 1863 the city annexed two budding industrial districts—one thick with distilleries and iron makers on the North Branch of the Chicago River and another on the South Branch of the River that included the new Stockyard district and the immigrant-rich Bridgeport neighborhood. While eastern cities such as Philadelphia closed down their war manufacturing and plants returned to their prewar economic activities, Chicago's new industries, built on the foundation of its prewar economy, surged forward. The city had laid the foundation for its transition from being merely a commercial hub to becoming an industrial giant. Chicago's iron rails and steamship lines reached like tentacles north and west, transforming forest and prairie into a hinterland supplying raw materials and foodstuffs to be processed for markets throughout the nation and even the world. Civil War Chicago had beaten out St. Louis and Cincinnati as the unquestioned capital of the American heartland. Returning veterans were eager to make up for their absence from this economic expansion and embraced the unofficial motto of the city's rising business and political leaders—"What's in it for me?" They eagerly shed their uniforms, tried to forget the war, and joined the scramble for upward mobility.

The postwar years were the era of Reconstruction, when a reunited nation tried to come to terms with the end of slavery and the reintegration of wayward states. While the most famous issues of Reconstruction dealt with the defeated Southern states and the rights of the freed African American men and women, historians have of late become more sensitive to the need to look at how Reconstruction also played out in the West and North. In Chicago, Reconstruction was manifested in the contest for African American civil rights, an acceleration of the class antagonisms that had first emerged during the war, and finally an impulse to honor the fallen and cement the restored Union through reconciliation with former enemies.

For Chicago's African American population, this meant working to secure their future as equal citizens in the city and state. Prewar Black Laws prohibited their entrance into Illinois and denied African Americans basic civil rights. After the Emancipation Proclamation clarified war goals, black Chicagoans organized the Chicago Repeal Association and collected signatures on petitions that pushed the Illinois General Assembly to act. Just a week after Congress passed the Thirteenth Amendment formally ending slavery, Illinois expunged its Black Laws. This was a significant victory, although an incomplete one. African Americans would have to wait until 1870 for the right to vote, and then Illinois acted only under the spur of the Fifteenth Amendment. John Jones, who had spearheaded the Black Laws fight, was the first of his race to be elected to public office when he became a Cook County commissioner in 1871. With the end of the long fight over slavery, blacks lost their status as a symbol in a moral crusade. A new nuance emerged even among some of the Republican press: they were vocally in support of freedmen's rights for the South, yet not anxious to have more African Americans move to the city. The Methodist, antislavery newspaper *Northwestern Christian Advocate*, edited in the suburb of Evanston, went so far as to encourage African Americans in the city to migrate to Haiti. In the wake of the war, young black students remained segregated in the "Negro School," removed from even superficial equality with white neighbors. Having seen slavery fall, black families attacked this symbol of secondary status. Many began to boycott the "Negro School" and send their

children to local public schools. Eventually, this strategy wrangled a gradual acquiescence from city leaders to school integration, although de facto segregation
of schools would endure long into the future.

The October 1871 fire that swept away Chicago's business district and much
of its North Side residential neighborhoods played an important role in the city's
memory of the Civil War. The Chicago Historical Society had amassed a large
collection of war memorabilia and records, only to see it destroyed in their "fire
proof" vault. With that, the voices of many Chicagoans who had experienced the
war years were silenced to history. At the time of the fire, some commentators
drew a parallel between the war and the Great Fire. More commonly, Chicagoans interpreted the experience as a moment of rebirth for the city, a rebirth that
tended to eclipse the history that came before.

Although veterans were anxious to get on in the world of work and embrace
the simple joys of home life, war experiences and memories inevitably lingered for
the Civil War generation. In the immediate wake of the war, organizations like the
Grand Army of the Republic (GAR) and other veterans' groups elicited a weak response from young men anxious to catch up with their fast-moving city. However,
by the mid-1870s, both veterans and civilians were ready to reflect on the meaning
of the war in both their private and their civic lives. By 1882 the city boasted ten
GAR posts, and Decoration Day (Memorial Day) celebrations grew in size and
scope. Only after a decade or more of peace did most Chicago veterans began
to organize with fellow former soldiers. With family and work lives established,
they found that they craved the camaraderie of those who had shared the years of
bitter conflict, men who understood what they had been through. Veterans also
felt it was important to teach their children the legacy of the Civil War generation
and what historian Ray Ginger aptly termed "the Lincoln ideal." That idealism
was based on self-sacrifice, individual rights, vibrant democracy, and an embrace
of the common man. Every year the city's schoolchildren were trotted out to visit
the city cemeteries and the sixteen thousand graves dedicated to those who fought
in the war.

Jane Addams, cofounder of Hull House, is the most notable example of
a Chicagoan embracing the "Lincoln ideal." Her first memory of Lincoln as a
young girl dated to his assassination, when her father, with tears streaking his face,
put his arm around her and said, "The greatest man who ever lived has died." The
inspiration for her settlement house serving the squalid immigrant population
of Chicago's West Side was the fact that Lincoln had come from a humble background. His parents were illiterates. Yet American democracy and opportunity
had provided him the means to rise to the presidency, where he rescued those
republican ideals. That was her mission at Hull House—to provide the common
man and woman the opportunity to fully participate in American life. When

doubt or trials caused her to despair, "the memory, the mention of his name" acted like a "refreshing breeze from off the prairie."

Chicago became the perpetual home for at least 4,457 Confederate dead, and their physical remains forced Chicagoans to confront national issues of reconciliation in a way most other Northern cities did not. The healing process was made possible through the efforts of former Union and Confederate veterans, who with their unique ability to identify with the common experience of sacrifice and death provided the moral authority for this emotional reunion. In 1887 in a Memorial Day ceremony, Union and Confederate veterans joined together to honor the rebel dead buried in the city with Northern flowers and Southern moss. Such ceremonies required a carefully negotiated rhetoric of reunion. Northern and Southern men each gained honor from the recognition of the other's valor. Only by reconciling with their former enemies could aging Chicago veterans rest easy in the knowledge that they had indeed saved the Union. Left unstated when white men shook hands was the fate of African Americans, most of whom resided in the South and after Reconstruction were left to the tender mercies of racists and segregationists. The climax of a series of staged reconciliations came in 1895 when Union and Confederate veterans assembled in Oak Woods Cemetery at the site of one of the nation's largest mass graves to dedicate a memorial to those men who had never escaped Camp Douglas. Yet lest the spirit of reconciliation be taken too far, a second, and much smaller, monument was erected with much less fanfare near the Camp Douglas memorial. It was dedicated to Southern Unionists, and it condemned the Confederates as "traitors to the Union" and "ruthless enemies."

The impact of the Civil War on Chicago is still visible today in the many parks, memorials, and boulevard dedicated to war heroes. The most notable is Lincoln Park on the near North Side, dedicated immediately after the war on June 12, 1865. Twenty-two years later, Chicago dignitaries and city residents gathered at the unveiling of the Lincoln statue designed by the distinguished artist Augustus Saint-Gaudens. Other memorials followed for General John Logan in Grant Park, and Grant himself was honored in 1901 with a vast park of his own on the city's lake front. A decade earlier, a quarter of a million Chicagoans assembled for the unveiling of a Grant statue in Lincoln Park. Sheridan Road was built and dedicated to General Philip Sheridan in 1889. In 1924 the diminutive Irish American hero of the Shenandoah was honored with a gigantic equestrian bronze statue.

Civil War memories, however, were painful for many Chicagoans. Despite the eagerness of veterans to get on with their lives, they quickly encountered the realities of a society that had become both more wealthy and less equal. A new class of industrialists arose during the war to assume the mantle of civic leadership. Prewar elites had rallied to the cause of the Union and paid an awful price in sons and brothers. Gurdon Hubbard, who had come to Fort Dearborn at age sixteen and had been a pioneer in meatpacking and grain trading, enlisted in the army at age sixty-two. In his regiment were the sons of three Chicago mayors, one of whom died at Chickamauga. *Tribune* owners Joseph Medill and William Bross both lost brothers in combat. John H. Kinzie, heir of Chicago's oldest family, died fighting on a Union gunboat. Gradually, in the 1870s and 1880s, prestige and influence passed to those who had stayed home and established their fortunes, such as Philip Danforth Armour, Potter Palmer, and Gustavas Swift.

For decades after the war, the new captains of industry violently clashed with common laborers over meager wages and long hours—most notably in the 1867 eight-hour-day fight and later during the Great Strike of 1877. Civil War veterans, who were still trapped in the working class, grew to resent the "big bug capitalists." The last years of the Civil War brought to Chicago a crisis in the ideology of free labor. Republicans like Lincoln had trumped a "free labor ideology" that was based on fluid social mobility with hard-working white men moving from wage labor to ownership of businesses. Yet it became painfully clear to working-men that the highly capitalized industries that grew in Chicago during and after the Civil War—meatpacking, manufacturing, and steel production—operated on a scale that swamped the efforts of small producers and pushed those men into the ranks of the wage laborers. During the late 1860s and 1870s, this growing and increasingly self-conscious class redeployed the language of the prewar antislavery movement to fight for the right to organize against capital and to achieve an eight-hour workday. This development, like previous service in the Civil War, was an important event in the movement of the foreign-born from immigrant to American. The conflict necessarily inflamed class tensions. The business elites and the middle-class professionals allied with them saw in labor actions the potential for the disorder and violence of the Civil War, and they called for a revival of the masculine order and discipline that many had known in the wartime military.

For the poor, the loss of a loved one in the war, whether it was a husband or son, was a blow from which few could ever recover. One of the few places these postwar traumas were recorded was in the works of Finley Peter Dunne, an Irish American newspaperman with roots in St. Patrick's parish on Chicago's Near West Side. In the 1890s, he opened a fictional Irish saloon on Archer Avenue in Bridgeport in the pages of the *Chicago Evening Post*. The main character was an Irish bartender—Mr. Dooley. Dunne brought to life the trials and travails and simple joys of Chicago's Irish American community as it navigated its way from immigrant alienation through the challenges of working-class life to the dream, perhaps for the next generation, of middle-class respectability. Never far from the surface of Dunne's sometimes comic columns were the scars of the Civil War generation, which were poignantly recounted in the details of political wrangles, heroic memories, and Memorial Day observances.

For soldier and civilians, every war begins as one struggle and becomes two. The trauma of combat shapes dramatically the way soldiers experience war from the way it is lived by those on the home front. The wealth generated by the Civil War, the city's rapid population growth, and the bitter political and class divisions fostered by the conflict all made Chicago a changed place for the veterans who returned home in the spring and summer of 1865. Like the men and women who would later return from the nation's foreign wars, the Civil War veteran found himself immediately caught up in a new struggle—one in which patriotism and comradeship were initially replaced by greed and isolation. While not all veterans could emerge victorious in this new struggle, the men and women who had devoted themselves to the Union cause could win the war over memory. They became one again with the city they had left by creating in Chicago an elaborate memorial landscape that proclaimed to subsequent generations that it was not the making of money or the building of marbled mansions that defined their generation but the part they had played in giving a nation "a new birth of freedom."

CHICAGOANS CELEBRATE THE WAR'S END

The tumultuous events of the war's end in Chicago were recorded in the diary of a twenty-one-year-old woman whose middle-class life normally revolved around family, music lessons, and the Methodist Episcopal Church. This routine was broken by the news of the fall of Richmond, the Lincoln assassination, the return of the president's body to Chicago, and finally by her visit to the second Northwest Sanitary Fair.

April 3, 1865

Hail to America, hail to the North! Richmond has been taken by Union forces! The capital of the Southern Confederacy has fallen from their hands. May God surrender the whole for His glory. The news has created a great deal of emotion. The bells have & are still ringing, cannon being fired, bonfires have illuminating. The bands have been parading the streets giving strains of music to gladden & brighten the scene. Men are (alas! That it is so) reeling in the street.

April 16

Sabbath, Apr. 16th. This bright warm beautiful day the <u>Nation</u> is <u>mourning</u>. President <u>Lincoln</u> is <u>dead</u>. Dead. There is, as it were, one loud continued wail of mourning in which almost every man, woman & child joins. The great & noble man…was shot through the head while sitting in an easy chair in a private box in the theater at Wash. at eleven o'clock P.M.; he lingered, unconscious, nearly, or quite all the time until his death which was about seven o'clock A.M. The next morning (Saturday Apr. 15th, 1865) he sank away gradually. The assassin was an actor in the [?] and has since been captured.

At about the same hour the same night a villain entered the sick room of Secretary Seward stabbed him two or three times, wounded his son, & injured some others and then the murderer made his escape. He has been identified but not found. Seward and son lie at the point of death. It is hoped he will recover but fears are entertained. The nation feels that it has lost its father, lost its leader, and best friend. Streets of the city are draped in mourning, men & some women wore badges of mourning. Almost every family circle seems to be broken. Men who have been, & are, strong Democrats now mourn with the rest. It is pronounced the greatest or saddest event that ever happened to the Country. His name will stand next to Washington on the roll of honor.

The country, only two weeks ago was rejoicing over the possession of Richmond, the rebel Capitol, and the capture of Lee & army and one week ago they were rejoicing because of this surrender of Johnson's army. With the great divisions of confederate army ever conquered, the prevalent opinion of the people was that fighting & bloodshed were almost over. God only knows what will become of us now. But surely there is a God that rules yet. Bro. Read expressed my feelings this morning on the pulpit. His text was the following: Blessed is the nation whose God is the Lord." Bro. R. thinks that Providence will direct this sad circumstance so that it will result in great good to the nation. It will make all to feel more dependent, all will feel weaker & if they but seek help from God they will be stronger. The nation had trusted too much in human instrumentality, now God was chastizing them.

The church was well filled, strong men wept, some were there who seldom come to church. This eve. Bro. R. preached from this passage: Whosoever shall give to you a cup of water to drink etc.," the object was to show that little things are important. Verily "vast is the mighty ocean, but drops have made vast [sic]." He exhorted us at the close of this discourse not to indulge in a vindictive spirit, and to be careful of their speech, may God grant grant [sic] great good may come out of this evil.

P.S. It has been learned that the assassin of the President has not been found, but there is an investigation being made. It has already been found that a plot was made to assassinate at the same time Gen. Grant, Stanton & others, but some of the murderers backed out. Reports say that investigators can make a case that will implicate some whom the public least expected.

May 1st

Ma, Clara, and myself went to Chicago partly to witness the scene that presented itself to the thousands who thronged the streets. . . . The remains of Pres.

Lincoln were to be exhibited forty-eight [hours] or more. An elegant mahogany coach richly draped with black alpaca & silver fringe & baskets on the outside. (we did not see the outside), brought the body from Washington, with it were other coaches draped which conveyed many prominent men, distinguished officers of the Government & army & some friends of the deceased. The train arrived at C.[hicago] about eleven A.M. it stopped at Hyde Park where a large arch had been erected & beautifully draped after the landing of the company some ceremonies were performed there such as: a company of young ladies from the High School draping bouquets of green & white upon the funeral car & coffin, etc. A procession formed there made up of soldiers, every organized association in the city, clergy, the young, the school children, etc. The procession was of such length it was about four hours passing a given point. It was escorted by many Bands of Music. They marched down Mich. Ave. then up Lake St. to Clark St. & up that St. to the Court House through the yard & through the house. The funeral car in which was placed the funeral coffin richly covered was drawn by ten horses each led by a black groom. After reaching the door of the Court House the catafalco was placed in the large hall the walls of which were draped or covered in black, the ceiling was ornamented with black & white nicely & carefully arranged. Everything seemed solemn & impressive. After the original procession had passed through the hall some of the mass went through, the doors were left open all night; in the evening the rain began to fall, not withstanding that people continued to frequent the place of the Honored Dead. One prominent Gen.[eral] was stationed at the head, others at different places but not a word was spoken by any one. The corpse lay there until the following morning when it was taken to Springfield the place of its internment, where it was kept for a number of days before [a] final funeral ceremony. While in the Court House in Chicago there were many singers that chanted mournful requiems.

The war is at last pronounced ended. The main armies of the Confederacy have been conquered, the leading Gen[erals] taken by soldiers of the Union, & last but not least, the Pres[ident] of the Confederacy has been captured & in such a manner as to bring shame and disgrace to his already ignoble name. When he saw they were conquered himself & family & others fled from Richmond but before many weeks elapsed our "brave boys" had traced them to their encampment. When the inmates knew they were surrounded Jeff Davis dressed himself in women's clothes & tried to pass himself off as a woman . . . but the "boys" detected the boots & beard & captured him forthwith. It seems remarkable that the Pres[ident] of the C.S.A. would be publically disgraced thereby making even his supporters blush with shame.

I pass over many interesting events which have now passed from my mind to speak, or write of the "Great Sanitary Fair" that was opened the last of May. Very extensive preparations have been made. Buildings have been erected that cover a block in the city (Chicago). The largest one was the Union Hall was filled with innumerable fancy, beautiful, & elegant articles. The very first view was magnificent. The Floral Hall was very artistically arranged. There were streams of water, fountains, springs apparently gushing from the side of a hill. There was a well, said to be Jacob's well, Rebeckah & Isaac at the well dressed in ancient costume. There was a Highlander with a bagpipe on which he played. Oh! so many things to admire and wonder. Another building was the Farm House, an old fashioned family all dressed in ancient style (where has been at least one genuine wedding). Beside those mentioned there were other buildings. An Art Gallery for which Bryan Hall was used, there were grand, superb pictures. . . . I cannot describe, cannot imagine all, or half the beauties & excellences which were there. I think this Fair surpasses anything ever known in the West. The receipts on this day June 23 have already been $257,000. It has been open commencing this week & it is to close next week.

Mattie Smith Diary, 1862–66, Manuscripts Collection, Research Center, Chicago History Museum, Chicago, IL.

MOURNING LINCOLN

In the wake of the assassination, Chicago Times *editor Wilbur Storey quickly changed tacks on Lincoln, from condemning his policies to mourning his passing. Ever the partisan warrior, however, Storey immediately began to try to undermine the creditability of Andrew Johnson, who succeeded Lincoln in the White House.*

THE ABSORBING EVENT.

It is hard to conceive of the occurrence of any event which would be so shocking to the sensibilities of the country, occasion sorrow so profound, and create apprehension and forebodings so painful as the event which to-day absorbs all minds and agitates the public heart to its lowest depths. Since the 4th of March last a higher estimate has been put upon Mr. Lincoln's life, and more voices have ascended to Heaven that it might be spared, than before. Since that time all men have realized something of the magnitude of the concerns involved in his lease of existence, and have shuddered at the thought of the possibility of his death. It is not chiefly the manner of his death—awful as that was—that so moves the national mind. It is not this, but it is that at this present crisis of the country—more important and critical than any through which it has passed—the presidential mantle falls upon the shoulders of a man in whom nobody feels confidence. It is that the future, the darkness of which was just beginning to yield to a glorious light, is again enveloped in utter night. It is this that so magnifies a calamity that would be terrible at any rate and which so intensifies the national morning. . . .

FIGURE 20. The Lincoln funeral in Chicago, April 1865. Courtesy of the Library of Congress.

There are not on this day mourners more sincere than the democracy of these northern states. Widely as they have differed with Mr. Lincoln,—greatly as their confidence in him had been shaken,—they yet saw in the indications of the last few days of his life that he might command their support in the close of the war, as he did in its beginning. These indications inspired them with hope, and confidence, and joy, which are now dashed to the ground. The democracy may well mourn the death of Abraham Lincoln.

Chicago Times, April 17, 1865.

THE CHICAGO SANITARY FAIR CARRIES ON

The work of the Sanitary Commission continued with a Second Sanitary Fair to raise funds to continue their work ministering to veterans.

THE SECOND SANITARY FAIR

The death of the President was a severe shock to the Fair, and robbed it of its crowning glory. . . .

But the work went on. The buildings were completed, the thirtieth of May arrived, and the Fair opened brilliantly. The procession was a pageant, such as the Northwest had seldom seen, but all remembered that the funeral cortege of the President had just preceded it, and an undertone of sadness breathed through all the festivities. The ladies were arrayed in mourning badges, and a picture of the dead President, draped in black, adorned every booth. . . .

Many buildings were needed to accommodate the huge proportions of this Fair. The main structure raised for this purpose covered the whole of Dearborn Park—more than an acre of ground. It consisted of a central edifice and two, parallel wings, each 385 feet long. The central portion was sixty feet wide and fifty feet high; the wings were forty feet wide. This large structure, was christened Union Hall. Various other Departments were respectively denominated Floral Hall; Trophy Hall; The Art Gallery; and Monitor Hall; while the Soldiers' Rest served for a Dining Saloon.

A beautiful little specialty of Floral Hall was its Jacob's Well—a happy idea, most happily carried out. On an eminence in the center of the hall was a rustic arbor, roofed with evergreen. Within was the mimic well, over which presided a lovely Rebecca, with her bevy of handsome maidens, assisted now and then, especially in the evening, by a few grave, male attendants—all in most brilliant oriental costumes. The bucket that went down into the well brought up a variety of beverages that would have astonished the ancient Syrians, not to speak of their flocks and herds—under the circumstances, a pleasing anachronism. . . .

On peculiar feature of this Fair was found in its "Denominational Departments." Each religious sect held here its fair within a fair, and all provoked one another to generous giving. The Christian Commission had also joined in the enterprise. The spectacle was therefore presented of a last great effort in behalf of the army, which united the Sanitary and Christian Commissions, and all interests, sects and classes of the northwest. . . .

A very original mode of raising money for the Fair, was devised by Mr. Alfred L. Sewell, a publisher in Chicago. Upon the history of "Old Abe," an eagle that had accompanied a Wisconsin regiment throughout the war, he based the idea of forming, for children, what he called the "Army of the American Eagle." Colored pictures were struck off, of this noble specimen of the bird of Jove. The child who paid ten cents for one of these was to be considered a private, while the investment of certain other small sums was graduated so as to secure the dignity of different commissions in the Army of the Eagle. The children were charmed with the ingenious device, and gave such evidence of their desire to aid the cause, that this little instrumentality alone netted the Fair the sum of $16,308.93; which was more than was paid by any other department, and was nearly one-tenth of the entire profits of the Fair.

Large numbers of military and political dignitaries assembled on this occasion, giving to it its chief éclat. The army was fast disbanding, and this was plainly the last Sanitary Fair. Many officers, therefore, made a special effort to visit it. Thousands of returning soldiers, in their passage through Chicago, looked on at its bewildering beauty. Generals Grant and Sherman, the Hon. Richard J. Oglesby, and the Hon. Richard Yates were its honored guests. With their presence the interest of the Fair culminated. General Grant was welcomed by General Hooker, at a public reception which called out thousands of spectators. General Sherman received similar honors. . . .

The youngest and much loved son of President Lincoln, "Little Tad," was present at this Fair. He wandered form booth to booth, and finally was found by a lady, sitting apart in bitter weeping; to her enquiries he replied, "I cannot go anywhere without seeing a picture of my father." "You did love your father very much," said the lady, her own eyes humid with sympathy. "O yes," exclaimed the child, "nobody ever had such a good father! He was always kind and there was *one* thing that he never forgot—*never!*" said the child, with loving emphasis. "And what was that?" inquired his interested auditor. "Every day, no matter how busy he was, he never forgot to say a prayer with me. If he had time for only four or five words, he would put his hand on my head and say them."

The Fair lasted three weeks, and netted nearly $85,000.00. Fifty thousand dollars of the proceeds were given to the Christian Commission, and the remainder was equally divided between the Sanitary Commission and the Soldiers' Home. . . .

. . . Treasuries were filled, if they were not running over, and the whole creation passed swiftly away, and "left not a wreck behind." Chicago woke up as if from an absorbing dream, and returned to her everyday existence. . . .

. . . "The Commission," said a correspondent, "is going out in a blaze of glory."

Sarah Henshaw, *Our Branch and Its Tributaries: A History of the Work of the Northwest Sanitary Commission* (Chicago: Alfred L. Sewell, 1868), 295–302.

WELCOMING THE TROOPS HOME

When General U. S. Grant arrived in Chicago, he received a hero's welcome. However, when the 105th Illinois Infantry came to Chicago late on a rainy night, they found the Soldiers' Rest closed. They finally marched to an empty train depot and slept the night on a cold floor with empty stomachs. The volunteers of the Soldiers' Rest were deeply disturbed when they heard the news and did all they could to make amends to the soldiers.

FIGURE 21. Chicago veterans pose for a last picture before mustering out of the service. Courtesy of the Chicago History Museum.

THE BOYS IN BLUE.

We have seen brilliant pageants where the stately processions were as rich in coloring as if they had walked out of a kaleidoscope, or gotten into a rainbow, and the flash of arms mimicked the flash of sunshine. But we never saw so impressive a demonstration as that given to the Lieutenant General [Grant] on Saturday. To be sure, that veteran battery, the 24th Ohio, gave him a roaring welcome of fifteen syllables at the Depot, as he landed, in the old dialect of Shiloh and the Wilderness. To be sure, that beautiful battalion of "coming men"—the young Zouaves—were borne on before, like a bouquet of red blossoms, but that was all. No bristling ranks were ordered out to do him honor; no swords flamed out of the scabbard with the word of command. That broad and solemn column of civilians without badge or banner moved down the street on foot, and after them, with no brilliant staff encircling him like a halo, quietly rode the Lieutenant General. It was the power that beat the plowshare into the sword; it was the man that wielded that sword so grandly, and was bringing it back to be made ready for the furrow again. It was: the People to the Soldier, greeting!

Down the lanes with their dense hedges of living souls, that blossomed like the hawthorn with the waving of white welcome, he rode; cheers burst out along the lines as he came; the multitudes surged along the intersecting streets like the rolling in of a heavy sea: there was no plot to the drama; there was no drama to plot; it was only the irrepressible utterance and action of an hundred thousand hearts. It was a Western welcome. . . .

Some of them [returning Illinois regiments] have gone unheralded. Thus the gallant 105th regiment surprised us in the small hours of the morning. They landed at the depot of the Pittsburgh and Fort Wayne Railroad, and not a breath of welcome; not even "the cup of cold water." They marched through the storm—it was nothing but rain—to the Soldiers' Rest and found New England in it. They summoned the watch of the Great Central Depot, were admitted to its cavernous hospitality, and hungry enough "to eat a horse behind the saddle," they gave three cheers for the good cheer of the ladies of Pittsburgh—the last pleasant thing they had to remember—then it was upon the bare floors and so passed their first night in dear old Illinois.

We deeply regret all of this; and whoever reads these lines will bear as company. But we have only written as it *seemed* to them. The ladies of the New England Farm House are as far from blame as Mercy's own angel. They do not occupy one square foot of space ever assigned to soldiers at the Rest. They extended the hospitalities of their tables to returning regiments last week, till the shelves of their pantry were as bare as the boards whereon the 105th lay the night out. Had Mr. Bryan, the President of the Fair, gained the faintest hint of their coming, he would have made it "as merry as a marriage bell" for them. The moment he learned of their arrival, he hastened with all the warmth of his self-forgetting devotion to make them honored guests, but the night had passed, and the regiment had gone to Camp Fry. It is a thing to be deeply regretted, and all the more, that it belies the heart and spirit of the Officers of the Fair, of the Soldiers' Rest, of the whole Northwest. . . .

Chicago Evening Journal, June 12, 1865.

CLASS RESENTMENTS FESTER

Amid the parades and praise for the returning troops, there also was tension. Chicago, because of the Times, *had a reputation as a copperhead center. It had a business community that had profited mightily while soldiers had suffered and sacrificed. Returning veterans were sensitive to any perceived snub. For example, when a policeman ordered one returning regiment off the sidewalk and into the muddy street, a riot nearly ensued. High spirits mixed with bitterness over the deprivations of many soldiers and their families boiled over one evening at a North Side beer garden.*

A SERIOUS RIOT.

A serious riot occurred yesterday at a beer garden in the vicinity of Camp Fry. The keeper of the place, after violating General Grant's order relative to selling liquor to soldiers, got into an altercation with sundry veterans who were intoxicated. It is said that he pronounced General Sherman and his soldiers to be copperheads, whereupon a row ensued. The police interfered and a general fight took place, the soldiers putting the police here *hors de combat* and destroying the establishment of the indiscreet proprietor. Windows and furniture were smashed and the liquors turned loose. A great many were hurt on both sides. Policeman Kelly was very seriously wounded. We know nothing as to the merits or demerits of the quarrel as a great variety of opinion prevails in regard to the offending parties.

Chicago Evening Journal, June 12, 1865.

~

A veteran explained that the reason for the riot in Chicago was because the city failed to receive them with the honors they felt they were due.

Letter from a Returned Veteran—
Complaints of the Cold Reception the
Returning Regiments Received in Chicago.

To the Editors of the Chicago Evening Journal:

. . . After we sat around our camp fires after Lee had been captured and Johnston surrendered to Sherman, we discussed the manner in which the people of our beloved Prairie State would receive us. Some of the boys said they intended to doff their blue uniforms just as soon as possible while others decided they would wear them home, and it would be respected more than any other dress they could procure. Well, we started home, just passing through Richmond, where we were paid all the honors we could expect—simply a great crowd to stare at us as we passed through the burned city. At Washington we passed through a grand revue, and the word "WELCOME" worked by fair hands greeted us. . . . We were satisfied, pleased. As we rode through the valley and over the mountains of Maryland and Pennsylvania, we were greeted at every village, and from every farm cottage, as if they all loved us and had an interest in us. At Pittsburg we received a welcome that filled every soldiers' heart with happiness. They had received no "telegraph dispatch" about our coming, but they have a "Subsistence Committee" there that is every ready to welcome the homeward bound boy in blue. Fair hands dealt out to us hungry and weary soldiers coffee, rasks [*sic*], crackers and meat, and we all left Pittsburgh with a God bless you. We really expected much from Chicago: this metropolis of our loved State, a city that has grown rich while our families and everything dear has been suffering. We find your people nearly crazy over General Sherman and Grant, and the Sanitary Fair. We love these men more than you can, and we have done more for them than you, but we cannot help feeling that we deserve a very small portion of the money and time so willingly lavished upon these great men and the Fair.

Among the five thousand men of this camp, not one speaks a word in praise of Chicago; but everyone is anxious to get his pay and leave the city. We well know that many of the citizens of Chicago would gladly do all in their power to render our return happy, yet we cannot help believing that Chicago has disgraced herself by neglecting, to such an extent, the homeward bound soldiers. This neglect is the cause of the bad conduct of our soldiers and not a desire for liquor, as one paper states. . . .

Chicago Evening Journal, June 14, 1865.

CHICAGO TRIES TO HEAL WOUNDS

At the sanitary fair, General William T. Sherman walked among the returning troops, personally shaking their hands and thanking them for their service, as well as gently reminding them not to treat Chicago like Atlanta or like Columbia, South Carolina. His remarks reveal that there was an undercurrent of fear that soldiers might bring the violence of war back to the city.

OUR VETERANS AT HOME.

The 88th and 89th Illinois Regiments—Reception in Chicago—

March through the Streets—In Union Hall—The Boys on 'Change Addresses of Welcome, &c., &c., . . .

"Welcome Home!" Sweet words are these to the toil worn wayfarer; sweeter still to the battle scarred veteran. Our boys are coming home, and they are receiving a hearty welcome—one which albeit is not an equivalent to the toils and dangers they have undergone, the sufferings they have endured, is still a grateful acknowledgement of their deeds and worth, and will go far to cheer them after all their privations, and make them feel that their suffering have not been for naught, nor underdone in an unworthy cause. They do receive a hearty welcome, not one of words merely, but one of something more substantial. 'True, the first comers were not received as was their due; they came unheralded, unannounced, and the people were not prepared to receive those whom they delight to honor. But now that their coming is known, none can find fault with the enthusiastic reception the brave boys meet with. . . .

. . . Shouldering arms again, resumed march, followed on either side by hosts of small boys and big men, all enthusiastic and anxious to do honor to the heroes... When the regiment reached the Fair building, they were permitted to break ranks and receive the congratulations of friends, which opportunity was not lost. Mothers and sisters, fathers, brothers, and sweethearts, rushed forward in embrace and welcome back the heroes of a hundred battles. . . .

Major General Sherman

General Sherman, who, while the speaking was going on, had been passing along through the line of troops shaking hands with his old comrades, was called for, . . . and was received with such cheers as only soldiers know how to give. The General then addresses them substantially as follows:

"I think I see more soldiers here than citizens; whatever words, therefore, I may say I shall address to the old soldier boys of the 4th corps. Boys, I parted with you at Gaylesville; I saw the game that was to be played; I saw that I could do two things at the same time; I went to Savannah, and you turned back with General Thomas to follow the retreating Hood, and whipped him terribly at Nashville. [Cheers.] Fortunately, we had no newspapers down where we went to tell us what do to. [Laugher.] . . . I believe there is no one more gratified to see you, and to welcome you home to your wives, children and sweethearts than I am. If you have no sweethearts where you live, you will find plenty of them here. [Laughter.] Boys, I want you to go to your homes and behave yourselves. [Laugher.] Should your country ever again need your good right arms to defend her from foreign foe or internal enemy, I know you will not stand aloof. You will go at them with the same yell that I have so often hear on your skirmish lines. [Cheers.]...Once more boys, I say, go home and behave yourselves. I place myself as a hostage to Illinois for the good behavior of Sherman's army—and I know you will not betray me. [No! no!] You will come and see me in the woods—in my tent—in my house—you are always welcome. Good bye."

The Irish Legion—A Salute

As they filed into the street, to take up their arms and march to the Board of Trade rooms, the gallant old 90th regiment—the Irish Legion—one of the oldest regiments in the field, having entered Sherman's army at Vicksburg, came marching into the Washington street entrance of Union Hall, having come from Camp Fry where they are stationed. The 90th and the 88th and 89th exchanged congratulations as they filed passed each other, some of the remarks being funny and quaint. The 90th made a detour of the main Hall and halted in front of the platform, and were greeted with hearty cheers. . . . The boys of the 90th remained at the Fair till late in the afternoon, and then returned to Camp Fry.

About twelve o'clock the rain poured down in torrents, but the boys of the 88th and 89th had been living under no canopy but that furnished by Heaven for four years past, and did not seem to mind the storm in the least. They formed and took up lines of marching for the Board of Trade rooms. . . . Along the line of march the people turned out in the rain and welcomed the boys by shouts and waving flags, handkerchiefs, etc.

Chicago Tribune, June 14, 1865.

SOLDIER-CIVILIAN VIOLENCE

The most tragic clash between returning soldiers and Chicago civilians was naturally enough triggered by a mixture of strong drink and resentment of the city's copperhead reputation. The incident related below came about when several Iowa troops stopped at a saloon for a last drink before boarding the train for home. They resented the German saloonkeeper, accused him of not being a Union man, and tried to leave without paying. In the struggle that followed, twenty-year-old Edward Kehoe, a veteran who had survived three years of war, was shot and killed.

SCENES OF TERROR
A FRIGHTFUL RIOT IN THE NORTH DIVISION

A riot of the most serious kind occurred at 11 o'clock yesterday morning near the corner of Wells and Kinzie streets, in the North division. The 9th Iowa regiment, which arrived in the city yesterday morning, was proceeding from the Soldier's Rest to the depot of the Galena division of the Chicago and Northwestern railroad, when the members of Company I went for liquor into a saloon at No. 27 Wells street. They had not been inside the building more than five minutes when citizens heard the rapid reports of the different barrels of a revolver following each other in quick succession. Immediately there ensued an unearthly uproar, and the soldiers were seen rushing violently to and fro about the premises and on the sidewalk in front of the saloon. First the whole front of the building was demolished, and then fragments of furniture were flying through the air, making it dangerous to go in the vicinity. Cries of "Murder," and "He has killed him," were heard and the utmost confusion followed. Policemen rushed to the spot, but were driven back by the infuriated soldiers, who seemed to have the whole thing their own way.

The noise attracted attention, and an immense crowd thronged to the scene now fast becoming a wild one. Fearing for their own bodily safety, citizens kept aloof, and the crowd surrounded the saloon, forming a large circle within which the rioters held carnival. Fiendish yells of rage rent the air, and fragments of demolished furniture went whizzing by the heads of everybody. Keepers of stores and saloons hurriedly put up their blinds and fastened their doors, fearing that the riot might become general, and themselves fall victims to the infuriated mob. The early days of the war seemed to be repeating themselves and apparently the great Baltimore riot was finding its counterpart. The police force of the third precinct were promptly on the spot but they were powerless to quell the hundreds of enraged veterans, to whom riot and bloodshed were pastime. . . .

. . . With an unearthly volley of yells, which told of pent up rage, the rioters dragged the body of the saloon-keeper into the street, pounding him and swearing that they would hang him. At this instant the police made a masterly dash into the crowd, seized the saloon-keeper, and, throwing him into a wagon, drove rapidly away before soldiers could react. . . .

[The soldiers vented their anger by completing the demolition of the saloon building.] It was scientific destruction, accomplished by men who have learned in the school of war how to demolish buildings and their contents. . . .

. . . The dead body [of a fallen comrade] was borne to the railroad depot, where the remainder of the regiment were awaiting the departure of the train. As it was carried into the gentlemen's room of the station, a scene ensued that beggars description. One soldier threw himself upon the body of his fallen comrade and wept tears of bitterest anguish. Instinctively the click of ramrods was heard, and the next moment several hundred battle-scarred veterans were prepared to avenge the death of their comrade. . . . [T]he soldiers rushed into the street and made for the scene of the affray, leaving the body in charge of a sergeant and some friends of the deceased. [The troops marched on the police station and would have assaulted it had the police not prudently sent the saloon-keeper out of the city. The officers of the 9th Iowa were then able to regain control of their men and return them to the depot, whence they left Chicago without further violence.]

Chicago Times, July 22, 1865.

BITTER MEMORIES OF WAR

While welcomed home as heroes, veterans gradually became embittered when they realized the unequal sacrifices between those who went to war and those who reaped the profits in the rear. Historian Joseph Kirkland was one of those veterans, and he wrote from personal experience.

. . . A soldier's family, trying to get along on the money sent back by the absent bread-winner—only thirteen dollars a month, even when he sent every penny home, as many did,—and the thirteen dollars dwindling month by month as the price of the necessaries of life climbed out of reach; the thought of such sufferings and sacrifices brings a swelling of the heart and dimming of the eyes which makes it hard even to dwell upon them! The relief societies of the rich did large and noble work; the neighborly help of the poor did ten times as much in unmarked ways; all this was well, but, after all, the stay-at-home givers grew rich and the absent fighters and their families grew poor, and so, to this day, the respective classes have, on an average, remained. There was always plenty of work and wages at the rear—and plenty of room at the front. . . .

Joseph Kirkland, *The Story of Chicago* (Chicago: Dibble Publishing, 1892), 287.

THE LAST TO LEAVE CAMP DOUGLAS

Rebel prisoner John Copley recalls his exit from Camp Douglas.

The papers began to be filled with news of all sorts of defeat and capture of our armies, which would be greeted by the Federals with the booming of cannon firing salutes. Telegrams were also frequently coming in at headquarters, announcing new victories for the Federal armies on the front, which was made known publicly to the privates of their army stationed at Camp Douglas, upon the receipt of which they would send up such a yell and shout as would almost shake the earth. Such demonstrations of joy from our enemy proved to us beyond a doubt that there was some truth in these rumors, and ere long we received more definite news of the surrender of the Southern armies. The authorities notified us that we would be permitted to take the oath of allegiance to the United States government, be released and return to our homes; but it was not until the first squad of five hundred prisoners marched out of the prison square to headquarters and took the oath, that we could realize the extent of the news.

The prisoners were released in squads of five hundred each day; those at the hospital had to remain and go with the last squad who left the prison. Early on the morning of the 20th of June, 1865, we received orders to vacate the hospital, fall into line, march to headquarters, to take and subscribe the following oath of allegiance to the United States Government of America, to wit:

"UNITED STATES OF AMERICA.

"I, J. M. Copley, of the county of Dickson, State of Tennessee, do solemnly swear that I will support, protect and defend the Constitution and Government of the United States against all enemies, whether domestic or foreign; that I will bear true faith, allegiance and loyalty to the same, any ordinance, resolution or laws of any State, convention or legislature to the contrary notwithstanding; and further, that I will faithfully perform all the duties which may be required of me by the laws of the United States; and I take this oath freely and voluntarily, without any mental reservation or evasion whatever.

(Signed), J. M. COPLEY."

"Subscribed and sworn to before me at Camp Douglas, Chicago, Illinois, this 20th day of June, 1865.

E. R. P. SHURLY,
Captain and A. A. A. General.". . .

We were also furnished with three days rations, consisting of pickled beef and hard-tack. The guards then discharged us, informing us that we were now free and could take the train for our homes as soon as we saw proper to do so.

"Of all the joys within that reign,
There's none—like getting out again!"

John M. Copley, *A Sketch of the Battle of Franklin, Tenn., with Reminiscences of Camp Douglas* (Austin, TX: Eugene Von Boeckmann, 1893), 204–6

END OF THE BLACK LAWS

From 1818 to 1865, Illinois had laws that prevented African Americans from exercising civil rights. These laws included statutes that required African Americans entering the state to post a $1,000 bond to ensure they would not be a burden to the state and offered large rewards to citizens turning in illegal blacks. Nor were African Americans allowed to give testimony in a court of law against a white person. Gatherings of three or more blacks were subject to police action and jail. John Jones, a former slave and a successful businessman in Chicago, lobbied against these laws in his pamphlet Black Laws of Illinois and a Few Reasons Why They Should Be Repealed, *published by the* Tribune *in 1864. A year later, Jones successfully appealed for legal equality. Below are the introduction and conclusion from his pamphlet.*

People of the State of Illinois, I appeal to you, and to your Representatives, who will assemble in the city of Springfield in a few weeks, to legislate for a noble and generous people. We ask you in the name of the Great God, who made us all; in the name of Christianity and Humanity, to erase from your statute book that code of laws commonly called the Black Laws. . . .

You ought to, and must, repeal those Black Laws for the sake of your own interest, to mention no higher motive. . . .

. . . For I do assert, without the fear of successful contradiction, that the colored people of America have always been the friends of America, and, thanks be to God, we are *to-day* the friends of America; and allow me to say, my white fellow-citizens, God being our helper, we mean to remain on American soil with you. When you are in peace and prosperity, we rejoice; and when you are in trouble and adversity, we are sad. And this, notwithstanding proscription follows us in the school-house, and, indeed, drives us out; follows us in the church, in the lecture-room, in the concert-hall, the theatre, and all places of public instruction and amusement; follows us to the *grave;*—for I assure you, fellow-citizens, that to-day a colored man cannot buy a *burying lot* in the city of Chicago for his own use. . . . Then, Fellow-Citizens, in the name of the great Republic, and all that is dear to a man in this life, erase those nefarious and unnecessary laws, and give us your protection, and treat us as you treat other citizens of the State. We only ask evenhanded justice, and all of our wrongs will be at an end by virtue of that act. May God in his goodness assist you to do the right. Will you do it?

John Jones, *Black Laws of Illinois and a Few Reasons Why They Should Be Repealed* (Chicago: Tribune Book and Job Office, 1864), 1, 16.

~

Chicago African Americans gathered to celebrate the repeal of Illinois Black Laws.

Repeal of the Black Laws
Colored Jubilee at Metropolitan Hall
Address—Refreshments

Under the auspices of the Chicago Repeal Association, a jubilee over the repeal of the Black Laws was last evening held by our colored citizens at Metropolitan Hall. The room was well filled—a small number of whites being present. The audience was enthusiastic, and their hearts seemed to overflow with gratitude for their success in securing the consummation they assembled to celebrate.

The exercises were commenced with prayer by Rev. A. T. Hall, after which J. B. Dawson, Chairman of the Association, delivered an address, of which the following is an abstract:

He congratulated the colored citizens of Chicago upon the repeal of the Black Laws. A sense of their forced degradation impelled them some months since to form a society called "The Repeal Association." They obtained several thousand signatures to their petitions and delegated to Mr. John Jones the duty of laying them before the Legislature. Their confidence had not been misplaced. The Legislature were the instrument in the hands of God of wiping out the records of injustice. The status of the colored race had become materially changed.

John Jones announced himself as a representative of the African and European races. He asked his fellow-citizens if they were ready for the proper appreciation of the boon recently conferred. Should they use these rights without abusing them, others still greater were in store. Previous generations had conceded but little to the negro, and in return had asked but little. With augmented rights would come augmented duties. Education was the only safeguard. The right of suffrage was yet to come. It would, however, be based upon an educational qualification, and they must prepare for the duty. They would wage eternal war upon all proscription of color. The war would have a radical effect upon the southern colored population. If miscegenation produced a superior race, we should look for an improved bred of the negro.

Rev. E. G. Lett hoped the audience would excuse him if he did not address them as "fellow citizens." He was so recently made a citizen that he did not know how to use the word. He thanked God, John Jones and the Legislature for the repeal of the Black Laws. He hoped the colored people of Illinois would be found worthy of the trust reposed in them. The first great step to be taken was to educate the race. One intelligent, upright man would educate ten others through his moral influence.

Chicago Tribune, February 14, 1865.

SPORT AS A MORAL EQUIVALENT OF WAR

In September 1866, a grand baseball tournament was held on the grounds of the Camp Douglas former prisoner of war facility. Not only did the games signal an end to the grim wartime use of the site, the two thousand fans in attendance were an indication of the emergence of baseball as Chicago's first mass popular culture amusement. Baseball would thrive in post–Civil War Chicago because, as this Chicago Tribune *editorial indicates, it was seen as an activity that could maintain the teamwork and the manly vitality of wartime service. The link between the game, the players (many of who were veterans), and the war is seen in the prize possession of the Excelsiors, the city's elite team: a baseball bat with a silver plaque indicating that it came from a tree shattered on the Chickamauga battlefield. By the 1870s, there were scores of teams playing the game, and in 1876 the National League was headquartered in Chicago.*

THE AGE OF BASE BALL.

Why have we gone so from our war into play? We used to be satisfied with our agricultural fairs, where the sights of great pumpkins and wonderful reapers refreshed our spirits after a year of work. We begrudged the time lost by the Sabbath, or reconciled ourselves to it by the consideration that we needed it for rest, and really lost no money by it. But now this great nation, in the greatest intensity of its business activity, as well as of its political earnestness, is breaking out in downright play. Men leave their business and go hundreds of miles, and spend day after day in playing ball. What does it mean?

We think that the answer is the same with the answer to the question, why the business activity of the people went on so mightily through the war, and so much more mightily now that the war is over. It is the superabounding vitality and elasticity of the nation, which the crisis has called, as we say, into play. We are no longer a nation at work, its great powers steadily moving by an outward compulsion, but a nation at play, driving business as we drive a ball, for the luxury of the activity, and because life must have vent. Because the power is within, the engine still plays, and the balance wheel gathers momentum instead of inertia in the intervals of work. . . .

There is nothing better than a game of ball to train the attention and alertness at once of mind, eye, and nerve, to eagerness, always obedient to exact law, to enthusiasm for one's own cause, always controlled by principles of a larger loyalty; in general, to a generous playing together of faculties of body, mind and spirit; from which we may come back to daily duty, with a freer breath and a freer hand.

Let us learn to play, that we may keep alive the heroism of the age. Such sports are worthy to be called re-creating. When we subside from them into the languor of amusement, or lose ourselves again in the incessant toil of business, we may expect that the generous pulse of our business and public life will begin to be languid or corrupt, or famish again.

Chicago Tribune, July 23, 1866.

THE GREAT FIRE

On Sunday, October 8, 1871, Chicago was swept by a fire that leveled the central business district and much of the North Side of the city. More than one hundred thousand residents were rendered homeless, and about three hundred were killed. The Civil War hero General Philip Sheridan was in the city at the time, and he took command of a group of war veterans and called in several companies of regular troops to help keep order. Relief supplies for the people and material for rebuilding quickly flowed into Chicago after the fire, prompting many observers to note how the sectional divisions that had sparked the Civil War had passed. That sentiment, however, was not universal, as memories of the war still evoked bitterness, as the editorial below indicates.

WHY SHE WAS BURNED—A REBEL VIEW.

Near one-half the city has been laid in ashes, and a hundred and fifty thousand people rendered homeless.

The announcement, at first, seemed incredible. When the telegraph confirmed the facts, a thrill of horror and sympathy pervaded the universal heart. This fact presents a palliative for many of the outrages and cruelties of the past ten years, and shows that human nature has, after all, some redeeming traits. It was far different when Sherman's army desolated and destroyed the fairest region of the South, robbing and plundering, and burning as they went, leaving the people to starve; or, when Sheridan, a monster of cruelty, overran and destroyed the valley of Virginia, afterward boasting that a crow would have to carry its provisions under its wings, if it should attempt to fly over it; and thus he brought starvation on the old men, women, and children of that region, so that thousands perished of famine. More property, and more lives were destroyed in these raids than all Chicago put together, and what was the sentiment of the North? One of exultation and rejoicing. These acts of vandalism were paraded as victories, and the heroes were met on their return with ovations of men and oblations of kisses from many of the gentle damsels of the North, carried away by the military glory that settled around the heads of these vandal chiefs, that was degrading, sickening, disgusting! What cared these women for the homeless, houseless, starving mothers and children of the South? Nothing. They exulted in their sufferings; laughed at the story of the ravishment of the daughters of the South, the burning and robberies of their dwellings, and slaughter of her strong men; shouted hosannahs and threw from the tips of their fingers kisses to the perpetrators of these acts of vandalism.

That was then! Now, that which is not half so horrible, thrills their bosom with sympathy, and their hand is quick and liberal to the relief of the sufferers. These things prove that man is a good deal lower than the angels, and sometimes, at least, a little higher than the devils. Chicago has lost, perhaps, three hundred million dollars by the fire. The property destroyed in the South is estimated at over one thousand millions. The fire in Chicago was the result of accident. The destruction of property in the South was done purposely, by Northern soldiers, and compares exactly with the acts of the Goths and Vandals, savages that overran and subjugated the Roman Empire. But we are living under a higher civilization. Chicago did her full share in the destruction of the South. God adjusts balances. Maybe with Chicago the books are now squared.

Rushville (IN) American, quoted in Elias Colbert and Everett Chamberlain, *Chicago and the Great Conflagration* (Chicago: J. S. Goodman, 1871), 521–22.

VETERANS FIGHT FOR JOBS

*After Chicago's labor movement came together across ethnic lines in 1864, workers'
central demand was for the establishment of an eight-hour workday. At the time,
most workingmen labored six days a week, putting in ten to twelve hours per*

day. In 1867 they appeared to have won a signal victory when the Illinois state legislature passed an eight-hour-day bill, but unfortunately it had a clause that allowed employers to opt out of compliance. In May 1867, Chicago workers staged a citywide strike in support of the eight-hour day. Eduard Schlager was a left-wing German Republican who came to Chicago in the wake of Europe's unsuccessful 1848 revolutions. He was a follower of the German socialist Ferdinand Lassalle, who advocated that labor use the ballot to cure the ills of capitalism. Schlager advocated creating a labor party. P. W. Gates was a Chicago manufacturer who owned the Eagle Works foundry. In 1867 he offered to give each workman a 5 percent annual dividend on wages earned. Some labor activists resented this, as it tended to kill off interest among workers in labor unions. After two weeks, the Chicago workers' eight-hour-day strike was lost, although the issue remained central to the labor movement for the rest of the century.

THE STRIKE

Aurora Hall

Mr. Schlager being called upon came forward. He said systematic action was the great want of the workingmen. Formerly their only work was once in four years to a choice by their votes between two evils. They had settled the black labor question, and now they were going to settle the white labor question. In ten years this question would overshadow all others. They must know the philosophy of their movement before they could reap its benefits. Only three years ago a London paper had said that labor needed no vote. Now London was in terror of the movements of the reformers. He asked only the people—the laboring men did not appoint the police—why did they not rule the city. It was due [to] the Anglo-Saxon superstitious respect for law. This was shown in the late riots when, the white staff of the policeman appearing, rioters stood back in awe, and the riot was at an end. Ere long the workingmen would appoint the policeman, and then the latter would doff their hats to themselves and not to the [face of] P.W. Gates and the like. The working man has been stupid enough to believe there was something terrible in law and its defenders. The late rioters should open their eyes in this regard. The Tribune has said the law [eight-hour-day law] was passed by demagogues, and he did not doubt it. They had expected to gain popularity by the act, hoping that it would only be an addition to the list of dead-letter statutes. The course of the Tribune and the Times showed them [workingmen] that they had nothing to hope for from the old parties. They would both join when capital was endangered. Both were cat paws of the same power—capital. . . . The press had by its course shown that the law-power is but an agency to enact the interests of a class into law. The people were used by capital and drained of their money like a squeezed lemon. Law is nothing but a machinery to rob workingmen. . . . Now when you have the semblance of law on your side, a general howl is raised by capital. The press and capital ask you what will you do with your two hours, and say there will be 4,000 saloons in the city instead of 2,000. They ask if you have lyceums, libraries, and institutes.

Chicago Times, May 10, 1867.

~

In the summer of 1877, the nation was suffering through its fourth year of a vicious economic recession. A large number of Chicago workingmen and women were out of work, including many Civil War veterans. Responding to reports of strikes in West Virginia and Pennsylvania, Chicago workers, particularly railroad men and dock workers, stormed into the streets, determined to stop rail traffic. In a panic the Chicago Times *proclaimed, "Terrors Reign: The Streets of Chicago Given Over to Howling Mobs of Thieves and Cutthroats." The mayor organized a vigilante corps composed of middle-class Chicago veterans to break up the strike, and in clashes that followed, men on both sides who in the war may have been comrades fired on each other in an ugly class war. Nearly twenty people were killed, and many were wounded. The "Great Strike of 1877" demonstrated the widening class gulf that would lead to even more serious urban violence in the decades ahead.*

"I'M TOM GILLEN, AND I DON'T CARE WHO KNOWS IT;

["]I'm not afraid to show myself to anyone, or all of you," and with that he turned about and showed the results of fifty years upon an original Hibernian. He began by saying that his sympathies were with the workingmen in all cases in the present or prospective fight with labor; they had been ground down and compelled to accept a smaller wage than their due for a day's work. It was impossible to secure a living for a working man off less than $2 per day, and to this figure he wanted all the lowest salaries to come; it was impossible for a man to support a wife and family on less, and why should they suffer themselves to be cut down below that point? No answer being vouchsafed, the speaker proceeded to ask for the enfranchisement of the workingmen; the black man had been fought for, and upon him had been bestowed the ballot; the people had shown an interest in him, and had done all they could to raise him up to where he could compete with the white man. Now, why not doing something for the workingman! Why not help him along so that he could get a fair day's wages for a fair day's work! The speaker had fought at Shiloh, and had been through the War, and had fought for the big-bugs,—the capitalists,—and many other of his hearers had done the same. Now, what was their reward? What had the capitalists done for them? The answer was a furious howl from the crowd, which encouraged the speaker to add that these

FIGURE 22. The Great Railroad Strike of 1877 pitted Civil War veterans among the workers against police and U.S. cavalry protecting some of Chicago's most powerful businesses. From *Frank Leslie's Illustrated News*, August 11, 1877.

capitalists must be brought to understand the matter as it was, and the best way to bring them down to [where] their level was.

With Powder and Ball.

A great shout of approval went up at this, and the speaker twice repeated his words "powder and ball," twice meeting with return cries of, "We are the boys to give it to them," "Yes, yes, powder and ball; that's what will fix them." But the peculiarity of the dissatisfaction was in the fact that not more than a quarter of the people cried out at all, the others shaking their heads doubtfully and quietly skipping out to join some other party. Encouraged by the shouts, Mr. Gillen went on to say that the rights of the workingmen could never be gained by talk alone. They might remonstrate and protest till they were hoarse, but they would do no good; what they needed was to take action;—not one, not two, or half a dozen, but plenty together. "Why," said Mr. Gillen, "if 5,000 of you will march out to take your rights I will be in front, and that by God I swear." The cries of approbation which met this sentiment and proffer were so loud as to drown the speaker's voice for a moment, and the chief cry of all was "Pittsburg[h]!" Mr. Gillen then continued, but in a slightly lower tone; he thought that the capitalists must be brought to terms, and he asked the crowd to help him in this attempt. This was the last appeal,—an appeal, as he phrased it, "to the court of the last appeal; to the riff-raff of Chicago;" they must decide the matter.

Chicago Tribune, July 24, 1877.

MEMORIALS AND RECONCILIATION

On Memorial Day in 1887, Union and Confederate veterans joined together to honor the Confederate dead buried in the city. This was the first of a series of events that used the large number of rebel graves in Chicago to bring veterans of both blue and gray to meet in reconciliation. A second event in 1895 prompted former Confederate general M. C. Butler of South Carolina to comment, "I do not believe there is another city on the face of the earth that would have had the audacity to have done what Chicago has done in inviting us rebels." Another former Confederate general complimented the city, saying "Chicago knows no sectional lines." Why and how more than four thousand Southern soldiers came to be buried in the city was left unstated.

NOT A REMINDER OF WAR.

The memorial parade in Chicago yesterday was worthy of the day. The procession was one of the largest ever called out by such an occasion in this city, and the organizations participating made it representative and significant. The solid column of police, the picked men of the fire department, and two regiments of National Guard, and the other military organizations, the several civic societies, and the members of the Grand Army of the Republic and the Sons of Veterans, taken in connection with the immense crowds of interested spectators, made a memorial picture worth remembering. The music of the bands, the legends on the flags and banners, the grouping of the old veterans, and the soldierly bearing of young men and old, of the police as well as the military, were well calculated to stir the blood, and yet there were no reminders of war that opened up old wounds or fanned to new life old resentments.

The unique cross of Southern moss, an offering from a Southern city to the ex-Confederates living in Chicago, stood for two days in the window of THE INTER OCEAN office, the uncompromising Republican paper of the Northwest. This was a reminder, not of the war, but of what followed the war. The ex-Confederates went quietly to Oakwoods to decorate with Southern moss and flowers the graves of those who wore the gray, and as they stood in seeming isolation, the sudden roll of drums marked the approach of three detachments of men who still wore the blue, each with a testimonial of their simple respect for the men who fought against them. This mingling of Southern moss and Northern flowers, this marching down of Union Veterans on ex-Confederates, who now carried the same flag as themselves—these were not reminders of the war so much as what came after the war.

There occurred yesterday a good many things to stir the blood, to touch the heart, to turn the thoughts of young and old in the right direction. Even the ex-Confederates at Oakwoods confessed to a feeling of unwonted tenderness when the men in blue bared their heads in silent, soldierly fashion in the presence of the Confederate dead, and afterward, as the heavy columns moved through the streets, these same ex-Confederates were free to say they liked to see much made of the day and what it represented. They did not regard the display as a reminder of the cruelties of war, but as a vivid illustration of what had come to the Nation through war.

Daily Inter Ocean, May 31, 1887.

～

The dedication of the first of six Lincoln statues in Chicago was a major milestone in Civil War memory in the city. Unlike statues of Lincoln unveiled shortly after his death, none of the Chicago statues make an overt reference to his role in ending slavery. In fact, prominently displayed adjacent to the statue was a phrase from Lincoln's 1862 letter to Horace Greeley that discounted his commitment to abolition of slavery. This memorial demonstrated the increasing marginalization of African Americans in the way Chicagoans remembered the Civil War.

THE MARTYR PRESIDENT.

UNVEILING OF HIS STATUE AT LINCOLN PARK YESTERDAY.

A Large Assemblage Braves the Wind from Lake Michigan to Witness the Ceremonies—Old Abe's Grandson Draws Aside the Flag and Exposes the Great Work of Art to the Public View—Leonard Swett's Oration Upon the Life of the Great Emancipator.

Since the night of the great fire Lincoln Park has never contained within the same area so many human beings as thronged its plains, clustered under its trees, and in every variety of vehicle crowded its roadways yesterday afternoon. A grand stand had been hastily thrown up to the east of the Dearborn avenue entrance. Seats were also arranged around the terrace leading to the pedestal upon which stood the veiled figure of Abraham Lincoln by Augustus Saint-Gaudens in accordance with the will and bequest of Eli Bates. A military band played a spirited prelude of airs appropriate to the occasion, among them "My Old Kentucky Home." All the seats were filled, and tremendous pressure was made by the multitude outside the frail barriers protecting the inclosure [sic] for the sake of order of procedure. The statue itself, rising twelve feet above the terraces, was visible from Clark street to the lake. . . .

The intense feelings of the thousands who had assembled to witness the ceremony were divided between a disposition to hail the splendid triumph of the sculptor and eager curiosity to examine its merits in detail. There could be only one opinion: that the counterfeit presentment was indeed Abraham Lincoln. The idealism of the artist's scheme had been perfectly embodied. Dignified, as becomes the head of a great nation; majestic, as becomes the emancipator of 4,000,000 human beings; tender, as was the heart of the gentlest of men; sad, as he must have been throughout the whole of his official life; tall and lithe, but neither muscular nor sinewy, he stands forever, his rugged, deeply seamed countenance stooping, as it were, a little over the people, as his mind must have stooped upon them all, North and South, with pity, attention, and compassion, to the close of his consciousness. . . .

. . . When scientists shall have uncovered the principles that still secrete the evolution of species; when philosophers shall have unraveled the riddle of the antiquity of man; when the rocks shall have told their ages and the sea shall give up the clew to its tidal throbs, men will continue to marvel over the evolution of this majestic mortal out of literal dirt and ignorance and penury; and when they shall approach the truth it will be found in a revelation of the power of humanity in an honest heart resolved to insure to all men the sole gift to which they are equally entitled at their birth—liberty.

Chicago Tribune, October 23, 1887.

THE LINCOLN IDEAL

Lincoln lived on in Chicago as an inspiration to idealism, a counterforce to the city's crass materialism and self-serving politicians. Jane Addams recounts her experience at the Chicago settlement house on the Near West Side, which teemed with newly arrived immigrants whose lives were lived in abject poverty. Like others who worked with newly arrived immigrants, Addams used the life of Lincoln to encourage and uplift struggling new Americans.

I suppose all the children who were born about the time of the Civil War have recollections quite unlike those of the children who are living now. Although I was but four and a half years old when Lincoln died, I distinctly remember the day when I found on our two white gateposts American flags companioned with black. I tumbled down on the harsh gravel walk in my eager rush into the house to inquire what they were "there for." To my amazement I found my father in tears, something that I had never seen before, having assumed, as all children do that grown-up people never cried. The two flags, my father's tears, and his impressive statement that the greatest man in the world had died, constituted my initiation, my baptism, as it were, into the thrilling and solemn interests of a world lying quite outside the two white gateposts. . . .

My father always spoke of the martyred President as Mr. Lincoln, and I never heard the great name without a thrill. I remember the day—it must have been one of comparative leisure, perhaps a Sunday—when at my request my father took out of his desk a thin packet marked "Mr. Lincoln's Letters," the shortest one of which bore unmistakable traces of that remarkable personality. These letters began, "My dear Double-D'ed Addams," and to the inquiry as to how the person thus addressed was about to vote on a certain measure then before the legislature, was added the assurance that he knew that this Addams "would vote according to his conscience," but he begged to know in which direction the same conscience "was pointing." As my father folded up the bits of paper I fairly held my breath in my desire that he should go on with the reminiscence of this wonderful man, whom he had known in his comparative obscurity, or better still, that he should be moved to tell some of the exciting incidents of the Lincoln-Douglas debates. There were at least two pictures of Lincoln that always hung in my father's room, and one in our old-fashioned upstairs parlor, of Lincoln with little Tad. For one or all of these reasons I always tend to associate Lincoln with the tenderest thoughts of my father. . . .

In our early effort at Hull-House to hand on to our neighbors whatever of help we had found for ourselves, we made much of Lincoln. We were often distressed by the children of immigrant parents who were ashamed of the pit whence they were digged, who repudiated the language and customs of their elders, and counted themselves successful as they were able to ignore the past. Whenever I held up Lincoln for their admiration as the greatest American, I invariably pointed out his marvelous power to retain and utilize past experiences; that he never forgot how the plain people in Sangamon County thought and felt when he himself had moved to town; that this habit was the foundation for his marvelous capacity for growth; that during those distracting years in Washington it enabled him to make clear beyond denial to the American people themselves, the goal towards which they were moving. I was sometimes bold enough to add that proficiency in the art of recognition and comprehension did not come without effort, and that certainly its attainment was necessary for any successful career in our conglomerate America. . . .

Is it not Abraham Lincoln who has cleared the title to our democracy? He made plain, once for all, that democratic government, associated as it is with all the mistakes and shortcomings of the common people, still remains the most valuable contribution America has made to the moral life of the world.

Jane Addams, *Twenty-Five Years at Hull House* (New York: Macmillan, 1910), 23–24.

BRIDGEPORT REMEMBERS THE WAR

The Irish American community's reflections on Civil War experiences at the century's end include the heartbreak of Decoration Day memorial services for the mothers and widows of those killed in battle. Through his newspaper columns, Finley Peter Dunne portrayed the memories of the Irish for those who never came back from war or came back broken men. The political and racial tensions of the war years tended to be forgotten while a strong memory remained of the start of the war and pro-Union beliefs and the enthusiasm of joining with Colonel Mulligan and the Irish Brigade; and pride in other distinguished Irish generals. This memory of the Chicago Irish community's service to the Union quieted charges of disloyalty in the years that followed the war.

BRIDGEPORT IN THE CIVIL WAR

[Colonel James Mulligan led Chicago's Irish Brigade of 900 men off to the Civil War in July, 1861. "Calv'ry" is Calvary Cemetery, just north of Chicago, where most Irish Catholics buried their dead, and Gavin was a real Bridgeport undertaker. [Thomas Francis] Meagher (a veteran of the 1848 Rising in Ireland) and "Shur'dan" (Philip H. Sheridan) were Union generals of Irish descent.]

"Jawn," said Mr. Dooley the other evening, "did ye see th' p'rade yesterday?"

"Yes," said Mr. McKenna.

"Was it good?"

"Fine."

". . . I've made it a rule niver to go out on Dec'ration Day. It turns the hear-rt in me gray f'r to see th' women marchin' to Calv'ry with their veils over the heads an' thim little pots iv gyraniums in their hands. Th' sojers has thim that'll fire salutes over their graves an' la-ads to talk about thim, but there's none but th' widdy f'r to break her hear-rt above th' poor soul that died afther his hands had tur-rned to leather fr'm handlin' a pick. . . .

"Ye was a little bit iv a kid, Jawn, durin' th' war. . . . But to me th' mim'ry iv it is as fr-resh as paint. I wint through it all. I mind as well as if it happened yisterday whin Thomas Duggan came up th' r-road wan afternoon an' says he: 'Barrygard,' [Beauregard] says he, 'is firin' on Sumter.' . . . But he was half crazy with th' news an' whin others come in ye scarce could hould him. 'I'm a dimocrat,' says he, 'that's voted th' ticket,' he says, 'iver sence I put fut in this counthry,' he says. 'But whin anny man fires on that there flag,' he says, 'I'm a dimocrat no longer,' he says. 'I'm goin' into th' ar-rmy,' says he. . . . That shtarted Duggan, an' before two weeks was out he had gone up an' down th' r-road an' enlisted fifty men, an' they wint off with Mulligan. . . .

"I heerd no more about th' war f'r a long time, f'r I didn't r-read th' pa-apers in thim days, an' bedad, I wisht I'd niver started to r-read thim. There's nawthin' in thim but hell an' horrors. But in th' coorse iv a year we heerd tell iv what th' A-archy road lads was doin'. Poor Duggan died iv th' fever an' Dorgan, th' plumber, was made a sergeant an' ye cuddent walk on th' sa-ame side iv th' shtreet with Mrs. Dorgan. Thin wan day a lad with a leg gone an' a face as white as a ghost's came into me shtore. 'Do ye know me?' he says. 'No,' says I. 'I'm Larry Hinnisy,' said he, an' he tould me all th' news iv th' war—how th' south was lickin' th' divvle out iv the north, an' how th' throuble was they didn't make Thomas Francis Meagher gin'ral iv th' ar-rmy. . . .

"Th' la-ads that had gone out so brave an' gay come back wan be wan an' iv'rybody talked war talk. I raymimber th' battle iv Gettysburg well. . . . Wan night there was a free fight up an' down Archey road because Dan Dorgan said Shur'dan was a betther gin'ral thin Thomas Francis Meagher. Thim was th' only two afther Mulligan was kilt that th' A-archey road cared f'r. Nearly all th' Mayo men was f'r Shur'dan. Well, sir, thin th' first thing we knowed th' war was over. Father Kelly comes in wan day an' says he: 'Praise be to Gawd,' he says, ''tis inded.' 'Th' war?' says I. 'Yis,' says he. 'Well,' I says, 'I'm glad iv it,' I says, 'an' Jawn, I was that." (June 2, 1894)

Finley Peter Dunne, *Mr. Dooley and the Chicago Irish: An Anthology*, ed. Charles Fanning (New York: Arno Press, 1976), 30–34.

NINE

A Guide to Civil War Chicago Sites

Rosehill Cemetery (5800 North Ravenswood)

Rosehill Cemetery holds the largest number of Civil War dead in the city, including 230 enlisted men, 14 generals, and 6 drummer boys. This Victorian landscaped burial ground was founded in 1859 by William B. Ogden, Chicago's first mayor and a leading businessman. Its dramatic Gothic gate was designed by William Boyington, who later did the famous Water Tower. As the carnage from the war grew with no end in sight, the cemetery's managers voted in April 1862 to establish a "a lot at Rosehill for the burial of all volunteers who might die or be killed while in the service of their country, together with the services of the Superintendent of the Cemetery to take charge of any bodies to be buried, and see that they were properly interred without charge."[1] That plot is directly inside the cemetery's main gate.

Among the soldiers buried in this Civil War section are General Thomas E. G. Ransom, who sustained four wounds while leading the Eleventh Illinois Infantry, before finally dying of dysentery during the Atlanta Campaign in 1864, and Edward Kirk, who fell at the Battle of Stones River while leading the Thirty-Fourth Illinois Infantry. The most notable of the monuments in this section is for Colonel John Wyman of the Thirteenth Illinois Infantry, who was killed at the Battle of Chickasaw Bayou in December 1862 as part of the ill-fated first attempt by the Union army to capture Vicksburg.

Most enlisted men who died in the war were buried in national cemeteries near the sites of major battles. The soldiers whose graves are marked at Rosehill are largely men who died while being trained at Camp Douglas in Chicago. Among those is Charles Miller. His passing was recorded in a comrade's journal and can fairly stand for the many thousands of Civil War soldiers who died for their country without ever seeing combat. "My chum Charley Miller, who was sent to the Post Hospital a few days ago, having caught a severe cold, which developed into a raging fever died last night unexpectedly, which caused me much sorrow, as we had become very much attached to each other. The funeral took place this afternoon; he was buried with military honors, a salute being fired over his grave, and the regimental band playing a dead march. He is the first member from our company to cross the line over into the great beyond."[2] Among the important figures in Civil War Chicago who rest elsewhere in the cemetery are Mayor and Congressman "Long John" Wentworth; *Chicago Times* editor Wilbur Storey; Levi Boone, leader of Chicago's Know-Nothing Party; Camp Douglas commandant Benjamin Sweet; and sculptor Leonard Volk.

In 1870 Volk designed the most prominent monument in the cemetery, the forty-foot-high column topped with a Union soldier holding a furled national banner. Titled *Our Heroes*, the monument honors the fifteen thousand Chicago-area men who fought in the war and the nearly four thousand who died to save the Union. For two generations after the Civil War, and continuing in recent years, this monument was the centerpiece of Memorial Day services at Rosehill.

Near *Our Heroes* are numerous regimental memorials. Perhaps the most beautiful of these is an 1874 sculpture of a flag-draped cannon that honors the men of the Chicago Light Artillery—Battery A, who fell in the war. This unit served heroically at the Battle of Shiloh, where it fired 838 rounds to beat back the Confederate attack. The unit lost four men killed and twenty-six wounded in the two days of heavy fighting. At the conclusion of this awful baptism of fire, James Milner wrote home to his father, "We have at last had our wish for a hard battle gratified and never again do I expect to hear the same wish from the lips of our men. We are just as ready to do our duty as we were, but to desire another hard battle, with the same chances of loss to our company, is quite a different thing."[3]

A sister unit, Battery B of the Chicago Light Artillery, has a monument across the lane from Battery A. The granite memorial is topped by a sculpted cannon barrel and has the names of the men of the battery who died during the war. An inscription quotes a comrade mortally wounded at the Battle of Fort Donelson—the first great victory won by Chicago troops. "I die for liberty boys. Go back and man the gun" were his last words. The unit saw hard service throughout the western theater of operations, culminating at the Battle of Franklin in Tennessee, where their guns contributed to the withering Union fire that broke a rebel attack and killed six generals in gray.

A third artillery unit honored at Rosehill was the Board of Trade Battery raised in 1862 with the sponsorship of the Chicago Board of Trade. Veterans of more than twenty-five battles, the unit played an important role in the vital Union victory at Stones River. The monument was erected in 1901.

The last of the artillery units from Chicago to answer Lincoln's call for troops was Bridges Battery, authorized in January 1863. A total of twenty-nine members of the unit died of disease or wounds during their service, which spanned the Tullahoma Campaign, Chickamauga, Chattanooga, and the grueling Atlanta Campaign and concluded at the Battle of Nashville. Their monument, topped

FIGURE 23. Bridges Battery Monument, Rosehill Cemetery, surrounded by the sunken barrels of captured Confederate cannon. Photograph by the author.

by the allegorical figure of Hope, is triumphantly surrounded by the barrels of ten captured Confederate cannon sunk into the earth. Unfortunately, the marble memorial has suffered considerably from erosion.

North of the Civil War section near the entrance to Rosehill Cemetery are monuments to several Grand Army of the Republic chapters. This organization of Union army veterans established burial plots so their members could, in death, lie in rank with comrades. The John A. Logan post has a simple granite memorial, while the George A. Thomas post fittingly marks the plot with a giant rough-hewed granite boulder in memory of a Union general known as the "Rock of Chickamauga," for his determined rearguard action that saved the Army of the Cumberland.

General Philip Sheridan Statue
(North of Belmont Avenue and West of Lake Shore Drive)

The last of Chicago's grand lakefront memorials to the Civil War to be erected is the dramatic memorial to the popular Irish American hero who was known to his troops as "Little Phil." Designed by Gutzon Borglum of Mount Rushmore fame, the statue was not dedicated until July 1924. Sheridan, who for a time commanded the Army of the Potomac's cavalry, took great pride in being a good rider. Before his death, he asked his wife to ensure that he would never be depicted in a statue like a "clothes pin" on a horse. Borglum honored that request by depicting the general at full gallop in a moment of high drama. On October 19, 1864, Sheridan, then commander of the Army of the Shenandoah, was returning to his troops from a conference in Washington, DC. From twenty miles away he heard the sound of gunfire and surmised that his men were under attack. The Confederate assault drove the Union men from their camp in panic. Riding "hell for leather" on his favorite horse, Rienzi, Sheridan arrived in time to rally his men and organize them into a counterattack that broke rebel power in western Virginia for good. The Battle of Cedar Creek was a welcome piece of war news that helped sweep Abraham Lincoln into the White House for a second term.

To schoolchildren in post–Civil War America, the poem "Sheridan's Ride" by Thomas Buchanan Read was well-known and frequently memorized, making Sheridan and Rienzi famous. Read's poem concludes with this stanza:

> Hurrah! Hurrah for Sheridan!
> Hurrah for horse and man!
> And when their statues are placed on high
> Under the dome of the Union sky,
> The American soldier's Temple of Fame,
> There, with the glorious general's name,
> Be it said, in letters both bold and bright:
> "Here is the steed that saved the day
> By carrying Sheridan into the fight,
> From Winchester—twenty miles away!"

Rienzi was so famous for that twenty-mile ride that upon his death in Chicago, his remains were mounted by a taxidermist and today are in the collections of the Smithsonian Institution. When Borglum's Sheridan monument was dedicated in 1924, the *Tribune* noted, "Thousands of motorists, to whom twenty miles is a mere trifle to travel, will pass it daily."[4]

Sheridan played a prominent role in Chicago life during the postwar period. The city was the headquarters for the U.S. Army's western forces during the Plains Indian wars. At the time of the Great Fire in October 1871, Sheridan was asked by city authorities to establish martial law. Acting quickly, he called for six companies of regular troops to come to Chicago while he led volunteers and Civil War veterans in setting several firebreaks that partially restricted the spread of the blaze.

By the late twentieth century, Rienzi and "Sheridan's Ride" had long been forgotten, and the statue became the prop for one of the more notorious pranks that major league baseball players used to haze rookies. Team buses heading from downtown hotels to Wrigley Field to beat the lowly Cubs passed behind the rear of the statue, where Rienzi's testicles are rather prominently displayed. For several decades, San Francisco Giants players and Cincinnati Reds rookies were sent at the midnight hour to spray-paint team colors on the poor horse's genitals.⁵ The tagging of the testicles is a reminder, as the heroes of the ancient Greece and Rome were warned, that "all glory is fleeting."

Ulysses S. Grant Statue (West of Cannon Drive between Fullerton Avenue and North Avenue)

One of the largest crowds in Chicago history, more than 250,000 people (one in four Chicagoans), gathered in 1891 to dedicate this statue of the Civil War's most famous soldier. Hailed as one of the saviors of the Union, elected twice to the

FIGURE 24. Statue of General U. S. Grant in Lincoln Park, Chicago. The statue by artist Louis Rebisso was dedicated in 1891. More than 250,000 people attended the dedication, including hundreds of Grant's former soldiers in the Army of the Tennessee. Courtesy of the Library of Congress.

presidency, Grant was particularly beloved in Chicago because he was an "Illinois man" and the general who led both the Army of the Tennessee and the Army of the Cumberland—the two armies most Chicago soldiers fought in—to victories.

The eighteen-foot-high equestrian bronze was the work of Louis T. Rebisso, an Italian immigrant who fled the suppression of the Revolution of 1848. Rebisso's most famous works were all equestrian statues of Civil War generals, including the statue of General James McPherson in Washington, DC. Almost as prominent as Rebisso's statue is its massive Romanesque-style granite base. The idea for this distinctive feature has been credited to William LeBaron Jenny, the father of the modern skyscraper. During the Civil War, Jenny served as a military engineer and designed fortifications for Grant. This arched feature provides Grant with the grandeur and epic scale that Chicagoans felt befitted the beloved general.

Abraham Lincoln: The Man Statue *(South End of Lincoln Park near Clark Street and North Avenue)*

This memorial to the sixteenth president is in fame second only to the Lincoln Memorial, in Washington, DC. Dedicated in 1887, the statue was hailed by the *New York Post* as "the most important achievement American sculpture has yet produced." The twelve-foot bronze statue is the work of Irish-born Augustus Saint-Gaudens, perhaps America's greatest sculptor. Saint-Gaudens depicted Lincoln as if he was rising from a chair to give a speech. The limestone backdrop for the statue was the work of Stanford White.

The statue is notable for being the first Lincoln statue that made no reference to the Emancipation Proclamation, the action that had long been considered the president's singular achievement and the action that he himself thought would be the basis for his historical reputation. The date of the statue helps explain this omission. By the late 1880s, the country was moving toward sectional reconciliation. No longer did the federal government enforce the rights that African Americans in the South had won during the war and Reconstruction. Northern and Southern politicians came together as white men and tried to avoid the divisive issue of racial justice. This political posture is graphically revealed in the selection of two Lincoln texts inscribed on two bronze globes that flank the statue. One quotes from the Gettysburg Address, artfully emphasizing the importance of saving the Union and leaving out the reference to a "new birth of freedom." The other globe's inscription misleadingly quotes from Abraham Lincoln's August 1862 letter to journalist Horace Greeley, which gives the impression that Lincoln's sole goal was to save the Union and ending slavery was a secondary concern.

The statue was funded through an 1881 gift to the people of Chicago from lumber merchant Eli Bates. In 1884 Saint-Gaudens began to work on the statue.

FIGURE 25. *Abraham Lincoln: The Man.* Better known as the "Standing Lincoln," this statue by Augustus Saint-Gaudens was dedicated in 1887. Photograph by the author.

He used a 6-foot-4-inch farmer who lived near his New Hampshire studio as a model. However, the statue's extremely realistic depiction of Lincoln's appearance was in large part a result of the work of a Chicago artist. In 1860 Leonard Volk, who later designed the Cook County Civil War memorial in Rosehill Cemetery, persuaded Lincoln to sit for a plaster life mask of his face and another cast of his hands. Saint-Gaudens used these casts, as well as his memory of seeing Lincoln at his inauguration and later as he lay in state after the assassination, to craft his depiction of the president. Daniel Chester French later used these same casts when he sculpted the model for the Lincoln Memorial in Washington, DC.

Chicago Cultural Center (77 East Randolph)

The Chicago Cultural Center is a magnificent classical revival building. Completed in 1897, it was designed to serve the dual purpose of being the home to Chicago's central public library and a memorial and local headquarters for the Grand Army of the Republic—the Union army veterans' organization. From 1897 to 1948 the veterans met in an ornate meeting room on the second floor of the building. When mortality and old age took the last of the veterans, their space became the site of a marvelous Civil War museum that contained many notable artifacts from the war, including items associated with U. S. Grant, William T. Sherman, George A. Custer, and Phillip Sheridan as well as uniforms, swords, drums, and cannon from local Civil War units. Unfortunately, the public library closed the museum in the early 1980s when a new central library was planned. Today the artifacts and many documents are housed in the Special Collections Department of the Harold Washington Library (400 South State Street), but they are only rarely on display.

The Memorial Hall of the Grand Army of the Republic is still open to visitors in the Cultural Center. Enter the building from its north side (Randolph Street), ascend the curving marble staircase to the second floor. Above is the large Grand Army of the Republic Rotunda; the forty-foot-wide stained glass dome is surrounded by plaster casts of swords, shields, helmets, and flags. The beautiful, multicolored floral patterns of the dome signify new life flourishing in the wake of war's devastation. The splendid dome was the work of the Chicago firm of Healy-Millet. At the top of the stairs is the Grand Army of the Republic Memorial Hall. The Vermont marble shrine is fifty-three feet wide, ninety feet long, and thirty-three feet high. The walls bear the gold-embossed names of more than thirty Civil War battles in which Chicagoans fought. This was the impressive space formerly occupied by the Civil War museum. Today it is largely unused save for the occasional corporate or matrimonial function. Adjacent to the hall is a second, less grand, space once used by the veterans for their meetings. It is today the Claudia Cassidy Theater. If you exit via the south side of the building, the marble stairs will take you past a second rotunda, which contains the largest Tiffany stained glass dome in the world.

Abraham Lincoln, Head of State *("The Sitting Lincoln," North President's Court, Grant Park)*

In 1889 the philanthropist John Crerar left a $100,000 bequest to the City of Chicago to erect a statue of Abraham Lincoln. This was only two years after the "Standing Lincoln" statue had been dedicated in Lincoln Park. Augustus Saint-Gaudens, the famed sculptor who had won renown for that depiction of the sixteenth president, was selected to create the second Lincoln statue. Saint-Gaudens's deep respect for Lincoln emerges in this more somber depiction of the martyred president. He is seated on the flag-draped chair of state, his head bowed under the strain of trying to heal a divided nation. The face of Lincoln is furrowed in deep thought or worry. Saint-Gaudens was a meticulous craftsman. He first worked with small clay figures, usually a nude of the subject to get all the physical proportions correct, then experimenting with different poses and with fully clothed models. The final step was the creation of a full-size plaster mold that could then be cast in bronze. He worked for many years to get each detail right for this commission; then in 1904, when it was nearly complete, a fire broke out in his studio and destroyed the statue. Deeply discouraged and suffering from the cancer that would eventually take his life, Saint-Gaudens, with the help of two gifted assistants, re-created the figure. It was finally cast in 1906. The statue, however, did not come to Chicago for many years. Lawsuits by Aaron Montgomery Ward, who wanted Chicago's lakefront to be clear of all structures, prevented the city from completing its plans for what became Grant Park. The statue meanwhile was exhibited at the San Francisco Exposition in 1915 and for many years at the Metropolitan Museum of Art in New York.[6]

The setting for the statue was designed by Stanford White, who had worked with Saint-Gaudens on the Lincoln Park statue also. Unfortunately, neither man lived to see their work completed. In 1906 White was murdered in a sensational crime that led to the first "Trial of the Century" and was featured in the novel and movie *Ragtime*. Saint-Gaudens died in 1907. It was White's son Laurence who finished the design of exedra that frames the statue. This feature is a 150-foot-wide curving marble bench flanked on each side by Doric columns topped by the flame of liberty.

Not until 1926 were the statue and exedra formally installed in Grant Park. Even after the installation and for the half century that followed, difficulties continued to stalk the beautiful statue.. Chicago dubbed the area of Grant Park where the statue was placed as "Presidential Court," with the intention of having statues of other great presidents join Lincoln in a grassy court of honor. No others were ever erected, however, and hidden from view from the city streets, away from the normal flow of foot traffic in the park, the "Sitting Lincoln" was gradually forgotten by all save the pigeons. A brief moment of rediscovery occurred in 1969 when the radical antiwar group the Weathermen launched their "Days of Rage" against the City of Chicago. At one point the group's "Women's Militia" rallied near the statue, and one nimble protester climbed atop the president's shoulders and draped her bra across his face. Such disrespect was invited by the trash and deterioration that marked the monument on a day-to-day basis with "wine bottles, beer cans, hamburger wrappers, and newspapers liberally scattered about." In 1983 a newspaper reporter lamented that "the grave countenance of Lincoln might well be meditating on the state of current society as reflected in graffiti, litter, and deterioration that his eyes have witnessed about his monument."[7]

Fortunately in 1985 the John Crerar Foundation, which had initially funded the monument, stepped forward with a matching grant to the Chicago Park District to clean and restore the monument. The statue has enjoyed a better fate since that time, although it still remains one of the finest but least known of Chicago's seven Lincoln statutes.

General John A. Logan Statue, Grant Park (Michigan Avenue near 9th Street)

Augustus Saint-Gaudens was also responsible for the most dramatic of Chicago's Civil War memorials. In 1897 more than 200,000 Chicagoans gathered to dedicate a statue of John A. Logan. Logan had been prominent in first Illinois and later national politics for better than a half century. In 1861 he was credited with personally keeping far southern Illinois, with its close geographic and family ties to Kentucky and Missouri, loyal to the Union. After the war he would win renown as the father of the Memorial Day holiday and as one of the founders of the Grand Army of the Republic veterans' organization. Such was his devotion to the memory of the war that at the first Memorial Day Logan swore an oath that "[i]f other eyes grow dull and other hands grow slack, and other hearts cold in the solemn trust, ours shall keep it well as long as the light and warmth of life remains."[8] After service in the U.S. Senate, Logan was the Republican vice presidential nominee in 1884. Upon his death the State of Illinois appropriated $50,000 to erect a bronze statue in his memory.

The moment that Saint-Gaudens chose to memorialize Logan came from the latter's distinguished service in the Union army. Actually, Saint-Gaudens sculpted only the figure of Logan; his associate, Alexander Phimister Proctor, sculpted the horse. Logan had begun his service in the conflict at the Battle of Bull Run

FIGURE 26. The General John A. Logan statue in Grant Park was dedicated in 1897 and famously saw service in anti–Vietnam War protests in 1968 and 1969. Courtesy of the Library of Congress.

as an unattached volunteer. He then rose to regimental command, and by the time of the Vicksburg Campaign, he led a division. Logan's grand moment came during the 1864 Battle for Atlanta. In an attempt to stem a furious rebel attack, the commander of the Union army of the Tennessee, General James McPherson, was fatally wounded. Logan took command and rallied the Northerners to a decisive victory. Saint-Gaudens's statue captures this moment with the fierce-eyed Logan holding aloft the fallen American standard behind which the Union men surged to the attack. The artist sought to capture in Logan's form the potent military power of the American volunteer soldier.

For many years the City of Chicago's Memorial Day parade began at the Logan statue, that is, until Chicagoans in the 1960s determined that the day was better spent attending backyard barbeques or shopping mall sales and the parade was discontinued.[9] The Logan statue endured a greater ignominy in 1968 when it became a battleground in the campaign by antiwar protesters to disrupt the 1968 Democratic Party convention. On August 26, after an unsuccessful attempt by a group of protesters to secure the release of one of their arrested leaders, a large mob gathered in the southern section of Grant Park—across the street from the Conrad Hilton Hotel where most Democratic Party delegates were staying. Suddenly several people in the group noticed the Logan statue, which Saint-Gaudens had artfully placed on a man-made mound some wags had dubbed "the highest hill in Chicago." A cry went up, "'Take the hill," and the group surged toward the Logan bronze. The mob crowded the base, and many scrambled atop the horse and the hapless general. From this perch they waved North Vietnamese flags in protest of the war. Eventually, a phalanx of baton-wielding police drove them away. Photographs of the incident became iconic images of America's political and cultural divisions in the 1960s. Unwittingly, although ironically, the protesters had used the statue of one war's greatest volunteer soldier to make clear their generation's unwillingness to serve in another conflict.

   In the wake of 1968 the Logan statue became a rallying point for antiwar protests, and it was the scene of clashes with police again in 1969, 1970, and 1972.[10] The statue of the general was also repeatedly vandalized. The bronze plaques at the base of the monument where Logan's major battles are named were damaged by individuals using them to climb atop the horse. The general's bronze sword that hung from his saddle was repeatedly stolen. Five times it was replaced before Chicago Park District officials gave up and the statue was left sans sword.[11] Finally, in the late 1990s General Logan found a much-needed friend. Lawrence Pucci, a Chicago tailor, dedicated the funds to refurbish the ill-used statue. He even succeeded in briefly reviving the Memorial Day parade, which, after twenty years of neglect, once again kicked off from the Logan statue. While the parade did not continue, the Logan statue in the twenty-first century is remembered with a brief dignified service each Memorial Day. It is a fitting if belated rededication to Logan's 1868 sentiment, "Let no vandalism of avarice or neglect, no ravages of time, testify to the present or to coming generations that we have forgotten, as a people, the cost of a free and undivided republic.[12]

Camp Douglas (31st Street to 33rd Street, Martin Luther King Drive)

   Between 1862 and 1865, 26,060 Confederate prisoners of war were housed on Chicago's South Side at one of the nation's largest military prisons. Today the area is the site of the Lake Meadows Condominiums and presents a decidedly unmilitary, unhistorical appearance. Nonetheless, it is the site of a critical aspect of Civil War Chicago.

   Originally, the camp was founded as a training center for Union army volunteers. The facility took its name from the fact that the land had formerly belonged to Senator Stephen A. Douglas. As with all Civil War prisons, Camp Douglas had a high mortality rate. One in seven of the rebels sent to Chicago died there. Poor sanitation at the camp, harsh weather conditions during the winter, the

FIGURE 27. The site of Camp Douglas in 2013. Open lawns and high-rise apartments sit on the site where between four thousand and six thousand rebel soldiers died. Photograph by the author.

unpreparedness of rural Southern men to survive the germs of an urban setting, and the poor diet of the soldiers before and after their capture all contributed to the death of more than four thousand rebels in Chicago. In June 1862, a U.S. Sanitary Commission agent decried the camp's "foul sinks," "unventilated and crowded barracks," and "soil reeking with miasmatic accretions" as "enough to drive a sanitarian to despair."[13]

Most of the buildings of the camp were quickly removed after the war. The camp parade ground was the site of one of postwar Chicago's first baseball games. The last structure remaining from the camp was an officers' barracks located outside the stockade. It remained until June 1940 before being torn down.[14] For many years the Griffin Funeral Home (32nd Street and Martin Luther King Drive) stood on a portion of the prison camp grounds. Ernest Griffin operated his establishment on the site for many years before he learned the history of the camp. Upon doing further research, he discovered that his grandfather had enlisted in the Twenty-Ninth U.S. Colored Infantry at Camp Douglas. In 1992 Griffin erected a memorial to the thousands of rebels who died on the site. To some controversy in the Bronzeville community, it included a Confederate battle flag flown at half-mast. Many times the flag was taken from Griffin's small memorial, but each time he replaced it. "The flag is not a symbol of hate," he said. "It is a symbol of respect for a dead human being." The funeral home closed in 2007, and the memorial wall Griffin created was removed.

The Soldiers' Home (739 East 35th Street)

This building was erected in 1864 to house wounded Civil War soldiers. Many men who were sick or wounded passed through Chicago while traveling from the front to their midwestern homes. Soldiers would sometimes suffer relapses or have their wounds reopen during their travels. The Soldiers' Home was originally created to give shelter and care to these men who were out of military control but still far from their loved ones. In 1863 the home began operations at a wood-frame house at Randolph Street and Wabash. The Northwest Sanitary Commission in Chicago raised funds for construction of a permanent structure through donations using the slogan "Let loyal hearts and willing hands, cherish, comfort and care for my wounded heroes." Later, surplus monies from the 1865 Sanitary Fair were dedicated to the home, which became very crowded with returning veterans who could not afford to stay in hotels as they passed through the city. The building was designed by William W. Boyington, Chicago's most prominent architect in the 1860s, in the Italianate style. The building continued to serve Civil War soldiers after the war, when it acted as a place of refuge and comfort for disabled or homeless Union army veterans. When the veterans had passed away, it became the St. Joseph Home for the Friendless, and the structure was enlarged. Today it continues to be administered by Catholic Charities. In 1996 it was selected as a Chicago Landmark, because it was the last building in the city directly associated with the Civil War.[15]

Stephen A. Douglas Memorial (636 East 35th Street)

Few Chicagoans have had a more profound impact on the history of the city and the nation than Stephen A. Douglas. While he is largely forgotten by Windy City residents of the twenty-first century, the energetic if diminutive politician was known across the country as "the Little Giant," because of his major role in American politics. Douglas had helped to save the nation from civil war in 1850 by engineering a great legislative compromise. He was a strong supporter of national expansion and a supporter of federal support for railroad construction that helped make Chicago the nation's rail hub. He is better known, however, for his two campaigns against Abraham Lincoln. While Douglas won the 1858 Senate seat, the race catapulted Lincoln to national fame and into the 1860 presidential race, in which Lincoln bested Douglas for the White House. Douglas died of typhoid fever in June 1861; he was only forty-eight years old.

FIGURE 28. The Chicago Soldiers' Home as it looked in 1864. The building
continues to be used for charitable purposes and is the only structure in Chicago still
standing that was directly related to the war. From Alfred Andres, *History of Chicago*
(Chicago: A.T. Andreas, 1884), 2:311.

The burial site is located on what was then Douglas's rural estate south of
the city. Although the cornerstone was dedicated in 1861, the monument was
not completed until 1881. The memorial is the work of Leonard Volk, who in
many ways owed his distinguished career to Stephen Douglas: Volk was married
to Douglas's cousin, and Senator Douglas provided Volk with funding to study
art in Europe for two years before the sculptor returned to Chicago and founded
the Chicago Academy of Design. Volk repaid Douglas with an impressive forty-
five-foot-tall white marble column atop which he placed a ten-foot statue of
the senator. At the base of the memorial is an octagonal mausoleum housing a
Vermont marble sarcophagus. Four allegorical statues decorate the corners of
the mausoleum: *Illinois, History, Justice,* and *Eloquence.* Volk also fashioned four
bronze bas-relief plaques that he placed upon the column. These represent scenes
from Douglas's life, such as his speaking in the Senate, as well as his notable
contributions to Chicago, seen in the train arriving in the city.

Oak Woods Cemetery (1035 East 67th Street)

This magnificent landscaped cemetery is among the oldest in the Chicago area.
Founded in 1853, Oak Woods has numerous important Civil War connections. The
most notable of these is in section K: a forty-foot-tall bronze and granite memorial to the more than four thousand Confederate soldiers who died at the Camp

FIGURE 29. The Stephen A. Douglas tomb in Chicago. Courtesy of the Library of Congress.

Douglas prisoner of war facility on Chicago's South Side. The bronze figure atop the column depicts a Southern soldier, hat removed, head bowed as if contemplating the fate of comrades. It is the work of artist Louis R. Fern and is based on a famous painting that captured the pathos of Confederate defeat—John A. Elder's *Appomattox*. The monument sits on an earthen mound that contains the remains

FIGURE 30. The Confederate Mound at Oak Woods Cemetery. The memorial is one of the largest mass graves in the United States. Photograph by the author.

of the prisoners. They were originally buried individually in pine coffins at the Chicago City Cemetery, in what is now Lincoln Park. After the war, it was noted that the lakeshore site was uncomfortably close to the city's water supply, and the city council voted to close the cemetery. Most bodies were then removed to new burial places. The rebel soldiers were reburied together in what is known as the "Confederate Mound," which constitutes one of the largest mass graves in the United States. In front of the monument are the headstones of twelve Union soldiers. They are believed to have been guards who died while on duty at the camp.

The erection of this elaborate memorial to rebel soldiers was an important moment in national reconciliation. One of the smallest veterans' organizations in Chicago, the Ex-Confederate Veterans Association, successfully made a general appeal to the citizens of Chicago to help them complete the project. Typical of Chicagoan's response was the GAR post commander who observed, "Our Union soldier dead cannot receive their need of praise without the fullest recognition of the most unqualified admiration of the magnificent bravery of their Confederate opponents." President Grover Cleveland, the first Democrat

FIGURE 31. Photograph of five Confederate prisoners in front of their Camp Douglas barracks. Courtesy of the Library of Congress.

elected to the White House since the Civil War, brought his entire cabinet to preside over the event. Amid appeals to the common Anglo-Saxon heritage of both sides, the monument was dedicated in the hope of forever "sealing the book of ill-will between the sections."[16]

While most Chicago veterans wanted to put the bitterness of the war behind them and bask in the glow of a heroic mission accomplished, there remained in the city a reservoir of animosity toward the Confederate cause that bubbled up to the surface at the time of the dedication of the Camp Douglas memorial. The night before the dedication, the thirty-foot granite monument was defaced by unknown vandals. A more permanent protest to the idea of honoring Confederates was erected a short time later. Adjacent to the mound containing the mass grave of dead rebel soldiers, Thomas D. Lowther, a Florida resident driven from that state in 1861 because of his Unionist and abolitionist sentiments, sponsored the erection of a large granite cenotaph. The text of the memorial honors Southerners who resisted secession as "martyrs of human freedom." For Lowther his cenotaph was meant to be "an inspiration to the youth of the country," who were in danger of

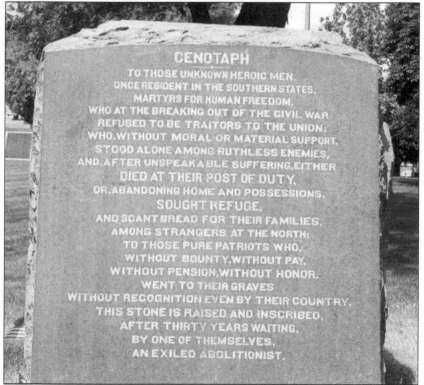

CENOTAPH
TO THOSE UNKNOWN HEROIC MEN,
ONCE RESIDENT IN THE SOUTHERN STATES,
MARTYRS FOR HUMAN FREEDOM,
WHO AT THE BREAKING OUT OF THE CIVIL WAR
REFUSED TO BE TRAITORS TO THE UNION;
WHO, WITHOUT MORAL OR MATERIAL SUPPORT,
STOOD ALONE AMONG RUTHLESS ENEMIES,
AND, AFTER UNSPEAKABLE SUFFERING, EITHER
DIED AT THEIR POST OF DUTY,
OR, ABANDONING HOME AND POSSESSIONS,
SOUGHT REFUGE,
AND SCANT BREAD FOR THEIR FAMILIES,
AMONG STRANGERS AT THE NORTH;
TO THOSE PURE PATRIOTS WHO,
WITHOUT BOUNTY, WITHOUT PAY,
WITHOUT PENSION, WITHOUT HONOR,
WENT TO THEIR GRAVES
WITHOUT RECOGNITION EVEN BY THEIR COUNTRY,
THIS STONE IS RAISED AND INSCRIBED,
AFTER THIRTY YEARS WAITING,
BY ONE OF THEMSELVES,
AN EXILED ABOLITIONIST.

FIGURE 32. The Cenotaph at Oak Woods Cemetery is a granite protest by Southern Unionists and abolitionists against the adjacent memorial to the Confederate dead in Chicago. Photograph by the author.

forgetting that "great principles" were at stake in the war. Lowther's remarkable editorial in granite was an increasingly rare expression of an emancipationist interpretation of the Civil War that was largely subsumed in the 1890s in the interests of sectional reconciliation.[17]

In 1911 the Confederate monument was altered with the addition of a six-foot base that held bronze plaques listing the names of 4,275 known Camp Douglas dead. Also planted about this time was a series of trees, all from Mississippi and planted in soil from the Vicksburg battlefield. Since that time the site has been used by the Sons of Confederate Veterans for services on April 26, Confederate Memorial Day.

Many Union army veterans are also buried and memorialized at Oak Woods. The oldest of those are found at the Soldiers' Home lot, located just west of the cemetery entrance (at the intersection of Harmony and Sunset Boulevards).

FIGURE 33. Chicago Soldiers' Home burial plot at Oak Woods Cemetery. Photograph by the author.

There a marble statue of a federal soldier at parade rest stands fifteen feet high over seventy soldier graves. These would have been either men who died in transit through Chicago during the war or veterans who lived out their days at the Soldiers' Home. The monument is terribly weathered, with the soldier's rifle missing and the text inscribed on the memorial all but illegible.

Just west of the Soldiers' Home plot is an impressive Abraham Lincoln statue. This marks the graves of 107 Civil War soldiers belonging to the Chicago Veterans Association. The statue was sponsored by the Abraham Lincoln Post 91 of the Grand Army of the Republic. It is the work of Charles J. Mulligan, an Irish-born sculptor who started his career as a humble stonecutter during the building of the village of Pullman, Illinois, and later studied at the Art Institute of Chicago with Lorado Taft. Mulligan went on to head the Columbian Exposition's massive sculpture workshop. Mulligan crafted several Lincoln statues. *Lincoln, The Rail-Splitter* is in Chicago's Garfield Park. The Oak Woods statue is a copy of a piece originally commissioned in 1903 for a cemetery in Pana, Illinois. Mulligan had a duplicate casting placed in Humboldt Park, and in 1905 it was brought by the Grand Army of the Republic to its current location. The statue, titled *Lincoln the Orator*, is mounted on a seven-foot tapered pedestal. The eleven-foot-high bronze Lincoln is shown gesturing with his arm to the sky. Mulligan intended this to show the president at the climax of the Gettysburg Address, but in its current setting, facing the graves of Union veterans, Lincoln appears to be gesturing to heaven on behalf of the men whose deeds gave America "a new birth of freedom."

FIGURE 34. *Lincoln the Orator* by Charles J. Mulligan seems to be gesturing to heaven on behalf of the Union army veterans buried before the statue at Oak Woods Cemetery, Chicago. Photograph by the author

Notes

INTRODUCTION

1. Robert Collyer, *Some Memories* (Boston: American Unitarian Association, 1908), 115–16; Lloyd Lewis and Henry Justin Smith, *Chicago: The History of Its Reputation* (New York: Harcourt, Brace, 1929), 113.

2. Carl Sandberg, "Chicago," in *Chicago Poems* (New York: Dover, 1994), 1; William Cronon, *Nature's Metropolis: Chicago and the Great West* (New York: W. W. Norton, 1991).

3. Theodore J. Karamanski, *Schooner Passage: Sailing Ships and the Lake Michigan Frontier* (Detroit: Wayne State University Press, 2000), 57–59. Davis also tried to circumscribe Chicago's western transportation links in 1855 when he refused to allow a Chicago-based railroad to use a federal island in building a bridge over the Mississippi River. Fortunately, the U.S. District Court overruled him. See David Young, *Chicago Maritime: An Illustrated History* (DeKalb: Northern Illinois University Press, 2001), 172.

4. Wyatt W. Belcher, *The Economic Rivalry between St. Louis and Chicago, 1850–1880* (New York: Columbia University Press, 1947), 65–74.

5. Justin W. Walsh, *To Print the News and Raise Hell! A Biography of Wilbur F. Storey* (Chapel Hill: University of North Carolina Press, 1968), 162–66.

6. Theodore J. Karamanski, *Rally 'Round the Flag: Chicago and the Civil War* (New York: Rowman and Littlefield, 2006), xi–xiv.

7. John L. Hancock and Jno. F. Beatty, Chicago Board of Trade, to President Abraham Lincoln, October 20, 1864, in *Official Records of the War of the Rebellion* (Washington, DC: Government Printing Office, 1880–1901), series 2, vol. 7, part 1, 1015.

8. John B. Jentz and Richard Schneirov, *Chicago in the Age of Capital: Class, Politics, and Democracy during the Civil War and Reconstruction* (Urbana: University of Illinois Press, 2012).

9. Ross Miller, *American Apocalypse: The Great Fire and the Myth of Chicago* (Chicago: University of Chicago Press, 1990), 58–59.

10. Theodore J. Karamanski, "Memory's Landscape: The Civil War and Public Memory in Chicago," *Chicago History* 26, no. 2 (September 1997): 54–72.

CHAPTER 1: A DIVIDED CITY

1. Frederick Francis Cook, *Bygone Days in Chicago: Recollections of the "Garden City" of the Sixties* (Chicago: A. C. McClurg, 1910), 171–82; Dominic A. Pacyga, *Chicago: A Biography* (Chicago: University of Chicago Press, 2009), 38–47.

2. Anthony Trollope, *North America* (Leipzig: Bernard Tauchnitz, 1862), 1:161. Ceres is the Roman goddess of agriculture. Karamanski, *Schooner Passage*, 59–64; Cronon, *Nature's Metropolis*, 111.

3. Marc Egnal, *Clash of Extremes: The Economic Origins of the Civil War* (New York: Hill and Wang, 2009). Egnal's thesis is that the economic development of the Great Lakes

region and its desire for internal improvements, as well as the simultaneous development of radical states' rights politics in the South, were what caused the Civil War.

4. *Historic City: The Settlement of Chicago* (Chicago: Department of Development
and Planning, 1976), 20.

5. *Historic City*, 35.

6. "Rough" men were those who were perceived by middle-class society to be prone
to disorderly behavior, which was usually associated with indulgence in drink and violence. Groups of men engaged in hard labor such as sailors, stevedores, construction
workers, and lumberjacks were frequently placed in this category. For more on the
perception of working-class male culture, see Peter Way, *Common Labor: Workers and
the Digging of North American Canals, 1780–1860* (Baltimore: Johns Hopkins University
Press, 1997); and Lorien Foote, *Gentlemen and Roughs: Manhood, Honor and Violence in
the Union Army* (New York: New York University Press, 2009).

7. Hartmut Keil and John B. Jentz, eds., *German Workers in Chicago: A Documen-
tary History of Working-Class Culture from 1850 to World War I* (Urbana: University of
Illinois Press, 1988), 151–56; Pacyga, *Chicago*, 30–32; Michael P. Funchion, "Irish Chicago:
Church, Homeland, Politics, and Class—The Shaping of an Ethnic Group, 1870–1900,"
in *Ethnic Chicago*, ed. Melvin G. Holli and Peter d'Alroy Jones (Grand Rapids, MI: W. B.
Eerdmans, 1995), 15; *Historic City*, 26, 36.

8. Edwin O. Gale, *Reminiscences of Early Chicago and Vicinity* (Chicago: Revell, 1902),
386; Robin Einhorn, "Lager Beer Riot," in *Encyclopedia of Chicago History* (Chicago:
University of Chicago Press, 2004), 451–52.

9. Christopher Clark, *Social Change in America: From the Revolution through the Civil
War* (Chicago: Ivan Dee, 2006), 205–6; David B. Danbom, "The Young America Movement," *Journal of the Illinois State Historical Society* 67, no. 3 (September 1974): 294–306.

10. Robert W. Johannsen, *Stephen A. Douglas* (Urbana: University of Illinois Press,
1997), 304–7, 335.

11. Harry V. Jaffa, *Crisis of a House Divided: An Interpretation of the Issues in the Lincoln-
Douglas Debates* (Chicago: University of Chicago Press, 2009), 294–301.

12. Alan Guelzo, "Houses Divided: Lincoln, Douglas, and the Political Landscape
of 1858," *Journal of American History* 94 (September 2007): 408–9.

13. Candidates for the state legislature who supported Lincoln won 54 percent of
the vote; candidates supporting Douglas won 45 percent of the vote. Because of recent
heavy immigration into Republican northern Illinois, however, those districts were not
apportioned the appropriate number of legislators, which helped Douglas prevail in
the face of Lincoln's overwhelming popular vote. For more on this, see Alan Guelzo,
Lincoln and Douglas: The Debates That Defined America (New York: Simon and Schuster,
2008). For Chicago-area totals, see *Chicago Tribune*, November 4 and 17, 1858.

14. Johannsen, *Stephen A. Douglas*, 759–73.

15. David Donald, *Lincoln* (New York: Simon and Schuster, 1995), 246–50; William E.
Baringer, *Lincoln's Rise to Power* (Boston: Little, Brown, 1937), 218–22; *Chicago Tribune*,
May 16, 1860; *Chicago Daily Journal*, May 16, 1860.

16. *Chicago Daily Journal*, November 17, 1860; Johannsen, *Stephen A. Douglas*, 803.

17. Doris Kearns Goodwin, *Team of Rivals: The Political Genius of Abraham Lincoln*
(New York: Simon and Schuster, 2005).

18. *Chicago Daily Journal*, November 21, 22, and 23, 1860; William E. Baringer, *A House Dividing: Lincoln as President Elect* (Springfield, IL: Abraham Lincoln Association, 1945), 63–71.

19. *Chicago Daily Journal*, April 8, 1861; *Historic City*, 24.

20. *Chicago Daily Journal*, May 2, 1861; Johannsen, *Stephen A. Douglas*, 871–72.

21. Johannsen, *Stephen A. Douglas*, 872–73.

22. The Wide Awakes were a Republican marching club used throughout the 1860 election campaign to escort candidates to rallies and to help build a crowd for speaking engagements. They wore distinctive black capes and hats and held large torches at night events.

CHAPTER 2: THE WAR SPIRIT

1. Mary A. Livermore, *My Story of the War* (Hartford, CT: A. D. Worthington, 1888), 112–19. For more on the reaction of midwestern states to the start of the Civil War, see Frank L. Klement, *Wisconsin in the Civil War* (Madison: State Historical Society of Wisconsin, 1997); Jack Dempsey, *Michigan and the Civil War: A Great and Bloody Sacrifice* (Charleston, SC: History Press, 2011); Kenneth Carely, *Minnesota in the Civil War* (St. Paul: Minnesota Historical Society Press, 2006); and Victor Hicken, *Illinois in the Civil War* (Urbana: University of Illinois Press, 1991). Statistics accessed September 22, 2012, in "The Midwest's Role in the Civil War," Kenosha Civil War Museum, July 14, 2011, http://www.kenosha.org/civilwar/midwest_role.html.

2. George Frederick Root, *The Story of a Musical Life* (Cincinnati: John Church, 1891), 130–31.

3. For more on Elmer Ellsworth, see Ruth P. Randall, *Colonel Elmer Ellsworth: A Biography of Lincoln's Friend and the First Hero of the Civil War* (New York: Little, Brown, 1960); and Adam Goodheart, *1861: The Civil War Awakening* (New York: Vintage, 2012).

4. *Chicago Tribune*, May 26, 1861.

5. Augustus H. Burley, "The Cairo Expedition," in *Reminiscences of Chicago during the Civil War*, ed. Caroline McIlvaine (New York: Citadel Press, 1967), 51–56; William Christian Memoir, May 29, 1911, Chicago History Museum, 4; M. Brayman, "Narrative of the Seizure of Cairo," n.d., Chicago History Museum, 6.

6. Hecker later formed a second regiment, the Eighty-Second Illinois Infantry, which had a large number of Chicago-area Germans. For more, see Marc A. Dluger, "A Regimental Community: The Men of the 82nd Illinois Infantry before, during, and after the American Civil War" (PhD diss., Loyola University Chicago, 2009).

7. William Kennedy to wife, August 23, 1861, William Kennedy Papers, Abraham Lincoln Presidential Library, Springfield, IL; William Scripps to brother, June 18, 1861, William H. B. Scripps Papers, Abraham Lincoln Presidential Library; *Chicago Tribune*, April 23, 1861.

CHAPTER 3: TIES BETWEEN THE HOME FRONT AND THE BATTLEFIELD

1. Only a small percentage of Chicago soldiers served in the eastern theater of operations, and none fought at the First Battle of Bull Run. Among the notable

exceptions who served in the East later in the war were the Eighth Illinois Cavalry, the German Eighty-Second Infantry, and the Irish Twenty-Third Illinois Infantry.

2. *Chicago Times*, June 23, 1861; *Chicago Tribune*, April 29, 1861.

3. William Onahan, "A Civil War Diary," *Mid-America: An Historical Review* 14, no. 1 (July 1931): 71.

4. Harold F. Smith, "Mulligan and the Irish Brigade," *Journal of the Illinois State Historical Society* 53, no. 1 (September 1960): 166–71.

5. Livermore, *My Story of the War*, 176–77.

6. *Chicago Tribune*, April 16, 1862.

7. For more on the role of women in the work of the Sanitary Commission, see Jeanie Attie, *Patriotic Toil: Northern Women and the American Civil War* (Ithaca, NY: Cornell University Press, 1998); and Nina Silber, *Daughters of the Union: Northern Women Fight the Civil War* (Cambridge, MA: Harvard University Press, 2005).

8. *Chicago Tribune*, April 18, 1862; Victor Hicken, *Illinois in the Civil War* (Urbana: University of Illinois Press, 1966), 74–80; *Chicago Tribune*, April 11, 1862.

9. Mark Grimsley, *The Hard Hand of War: Union Military Policy toward Southern Civilians, 1861–1865* (New York: Cambridge University Press, 1997). In this book Grimsley argues that the Civil War did not become a "total war" such as World War II but that Union commanders did gradually adopt policies of "hard war" that were designed to make the Southern population pay an economic price for secession through the confiscation of their food and strategic materials. For more on the Athens incident, see George Bradley and Richard Dahlen, *From Conciliation to Conquest: The Sack of Athens and the Court-Martial of Colonel John B. Turchin* (Tuscaloosa: University of Alabama Press, 2006); and Theodore J. Karamanski, "Soldiers, Civilians, and the Sack of Athens, Alabama," *Illinois History Teacher* 4, no. 2 (1997): 48–51.

10. *Chicago Tribune*, August 20, 1862.

11. Only a few weeks before, General Robert McCook was killed when rebel cavalry ambushed the wounded officer's ambulance.

CHAPTER 4: CONFINED CONFEDERATES

1. For more on Civil War prison camps, see Benjamin Cloyd, *Haunted by Atrocity: Civil War Prisons in American Memory* (Baton Rouge: Louisiana State University Press, 2010); Lonnie Speer, *Portals of Hell: Civil War Military Prisons* (Lincoln: University of Nebraska Press, 2005); and William Heseltine's classic study, *Civil War Prisons* (Kent, OH: Kent State University Press, 1997). For more on Camp Douglas, see George Levy, *To Die in Chicago: Confederate Prisoners at Camp Douglas, Chicago* (Gretna, LA: Pelican Publishing, 1999).

2. *Chicago Tribune*, February 14 and 22, 1862.

3. Levy, *To Die in Chicago*, 46–81.

4. *Chicago Tribune*, February 25, 1862; *Chicago Times*, March 6, 1862.

5. Otto Eisenschiml, ed., *Vermont General: The Unusual War Experiences of Edward Hastings Ripley, 1862–1865* (New York: Devin-Adair, 1960), 50–69.

6. Karamanski, *Rally 'Round the Flag*, 134–58.

7. Levy, *To Die in Chicago*, 96–146.

8. John Hancock and Jno. Beatty to Abraham Lincoln, in *Official Records of the War of the Rebellion* (Washington, DC: Government Printing Office, 1880–1901), series 2, vol. 7, part 1, 1015.

9. Karamanski, *Rally 'Round the Flag*, 141–58.

10. Dolores Gavin, Paul A. Hutton, and Carolyn Raine, *Eighty Acres of Hell* (Gary Foreman, Director, History Channel documentary, 2006); Kelly Pucci, *Camp Douglas: Chicago Civil War Prison Camp* (Chicago: Arcadia Publishing, 2007), 9.

11. Levy, *To Die in Chicago*, 273–74.

12. L. H. Pelouze, assistant adjutant general, to the Chicago Board of Trade, November 1, 1864, in *Official Records of the War of the Rebellion*, series 2, vol. 7, part 1, 1077.

13. A roorback was a fictitious acquisition made for political purposes. The term originated in the 1844 presidential campaign when opponents planted charges damaging to James K. Polk in a travelogue alleged to be by Baron von Roorback.

CHAPTER 5: THE POLITICS OF WAR

1. Megan McKinney, *The Magnificent Medills: American's Royal Family of Journalism during a Century of Turbulent Splendor* (New York: Harper, 2011), 19–31; Cecil Blair, "The Chicago Democratic Press and the Civil War" (PhD diss., University of Chicago, 1847), 55–68. Medill served as managing editor of the *Tribune* until 1864, when he passed those duties to Horace White. However, as owner of the newspaper and one of Chicago's leading Republican political figures, Medill continued to influence the *Tribune's* editorial policy.

2. Joel H. Sibley, *A Respectable Minority: The Democratic Party in the Civil War Era, 1860–1868* (New York: W. W. Norton, 1977), 124–28.

3. William T. Hutchinson, *Cyrus Hall McCormick: Harvest, 1856–1884* (New York: Appleton-Century, 1935), 61–62; Walsh, *To Print the News*, 150–67.

4. Walsh, *To Print the News*, 162–66; Karamanski, *Rally 'Round the Flag*, 188–90.

5. Karamanski, *Rally 'Round the Flag*, 105–6, 186–89.

6. Craig D. Tenney, "To Suppress or Not to Suppress: Abraham Lincoln and the *Chicago Times*," *Civil War History* 27, no. 3 (September 1981): 248–55.

7. Tenney, "To Suppress or Not," 257; Cook, *Bygone Days in Chicago*, 52–55.

8. *Chicago Tribune*, August 9, 1862, and July 2 and 9, 1863. For more on the draft, see Eugene C. Murdock, *One Million Men: The Civil War Draft in the North* (Madison: State Historical Society of Wisconsin, 1971) and *Patriotism Limited, 1862–1865: The Civil War Draft and the Bounty System* (Kent, OH: Kent State University Press, 1967); and Robert E. Sterling, "Civil War Draft Resistance in the Middle West" (PhD diss., Northern Illinois University, 1974).

9. Foote, *Gentlemen and Roughs*, 119–44.

10. Sterling, "Civil War Draft Resistance," 223–24; *Chicago Tribune*, July 2, 1863.

11. Ida M. Tarbell, *The Life of Abraham Lincoln* (New York: Harper and Brothers, 1909), 2:148–49.

12. *Chicago Tribune*, August 9, 1862; Affidavit of Joseph L. Heim, January 25, 1865, Provost Marshal, General Bureau, District 1, Letters Received, 1863–65, National Archives, Great Lakes Region, Chicago, IL, RG 110, Box 15.

13. *Chicago Times,* August 30, 1864; William F. Zornow, "McClellan and Seymour in the Chicago Convention of 1864," *Journal of the Illinois State Historical Society* 63 (Winter 1950): 283–90.

14. Thomas Hines and John B. Castleman, "The Northwest Conspiracy," *Southern Bivouac,* n.s., 2 (June 1886–March 1887); Stephen Z. Starr, *Colonel Grenfell's Wars: The Life of a Soldier of Fortune* (Baton Rouge: Louisiana State University Press, 1971), 165–75.

15. Mary Finn, *Chicago Democracy and Copperheads: An Analysis of the Party and a Quantitative Survey of the Voter* (MA thesis, Northeastern Illinois State College, 1969), 71.

16. Here Wilbur Storey seems to have invented a new word, accusing the president of foolish, frivolous, time-wasting behavior.

17. Karamanski, *Rally 'Round the Flag,* 217, 221, 233.

18. Karamanski, *Rally 'Round the Flag,* 208.

CHAPTER 6: THE BUSINESS AND POLITICS OF WAR

1. Albert D. Richardson, *The Secret Service: The Field, the Dungeon, and the Escape* (Hartford, CT: American Publishing, 1865), 157; *Chicago Democrat,* May 18, 1861; *Chicago Tribune,* April 1 and June 22, 1861, and January 30 and September 3, 1862; *Chicago in 1864: Annual Review of Trade, Business and Growth of Chicago and the Northwest* (Chicago: Daily Tribune, 1865), 1.

2. *Chicago Tribune,* June 15, 1861, and January 30, 1862.

3. *Chicago Tribune,* June 15, 1863; Wyatt W. Belcher, *The Economic Rivalry between St. Louis and Chicago, 1860–1880* (New York: Columbia University Press, 1947), 68–71; Robert M. Sutton, "The Illinois Central Railroad: Thoroughfare for Freedom," *Civil War History* 7, no. 3 (September 1961): 270–75.

4. Belcher, *Economic Rivalry,* 150–51; *Chicago Tribune,* April 10, 1862, and January 14, 1864; Louise C. Wade, *Chicago's Pride: The Stockyards, Packingtown and Environs in the Nineteenth Century* (Urbana: University of Illinois Press, 1987), 27, 33–34, 50–55, 61, 221.

5. Hutchinson, *Cyrus Hall McCormick,* 52–68. For a discussion of the difficult issue of political dissent in the wartime North, see Sibley, *Respectable Minority.* Historian Jennifer L. Weber portrays the copperheads as a dangerous threat to the Union war effort in *Copperheads: The Rise and Fall of Lincoln's Opponents in the North* (New York: Oxford, 2008). An older work by Frank Klement describes this group more as defenders of endangered civil liberties: see Klement, *The Copperheads in the Middle West* (Chicago: University of Chicago Press, 1960).

6. *Chicago Times,* February 3, 1864.

7. Karamanski, *Rally 'Round the Flag,* 101–7; Mary A. Livermore, *The Story of My Life; or, The Sunshine and Shadow of Seventy Years* (Hartford, CT: A. D. Worthington, 1899), 74–75, 126, 145; Silber, *Daughters of the Union,* 187–91.

8. Livermore, *My Story of the War,* 409–11.

9. J. Christopher Schnell, "Mary Livermore and the Great Northwestern Fair," *Chicago History* (Spring 1975): 42–46; Livermore, *My Story of the War,* 417–30; *Chicago Tribune,* October 28, 1863; *Chicago Times,* November 5 and 6, 1863.

10. Root, *Story of a Musical Life,* 132–34.

11. Root, *Story of a Musical Life,* 134; Dena J. Epstein, "The Battle Cry of Freedom," *Civil War History* (September 1958): 307–18; Cook, *Bygone Days in Chicago,* 118–20.

12. Root, *Story of a Musical Life*, 132–34; Epstein, "Battle Cry of Freedom," 312–18. In addition to writing many war songs, the firm of Root and Cady hired talented songwriters and published their work. The most successful of these writers was Henry C. Work, an ardent abolitionist who wrote "Kingdom Coming" and whose "Marching through Georgia" eventually sold a million sheets.

CHAPTER 7: THE WAR IN THE WARDS

1. Root, *Story of a Musical Life*, 127.

2. *Historic City*, 21–22, 35; Dominic A. Pacyga and Ellen Skerrett, *Chicago: City of Neighborhoods* (Chicago: Loyola University Press, 1986), 38; Lawrence J. McCaffrey, Ellen Skerrett, Michael Funchion, and Charles Fanning, *The Irish in Chicago* (Urbana: University of Illinois Press, 1987), 3, 62–63.

3. For more on the Irish famine and its impact on migration to the Midwest, see Arthur Gribben, ed., *The Great Famine and the Irish Diaspora to America* (Amherst: University of Massachusetts Press, 1999); and Mark Wyman, *Immigrants in the Valley: Irish, Germans, and Americans in the Upper Mississippi Country, 1830–1860* (Chicago: Nelson-Hall, 1984).

4. Tracey E. Strevey, "Joseph Medill and the *Chicago Tribune* during the Civil War Period" (PhD diss., University of Chicago, 1930), 87; *Chicago Tribune*, October 18 and November 3, 1860.

5. Keil and Jentz, *German Workers in Chicago*, 21–51.

6. Wyman, *Immigrants in the Valley*, 171–97.

7. *Historic City*, 25–27.

8. Larry Gara, *The Liberty Line: The Legend of the Underground Railroad* (Lexington: University of Kentucky Press, 1961), 102; James Davis, *Frontier Illinois* (Bloomington: Indiana University Press, 1998), 413; Karamanski, *Rally 'Round the Flag*, 181–82; Thomas Campbell, *Fighting Slavery in Chicago: Abolitionists, the Law of Slavery, and Lincoln* (Port Townsend, WA: Ampersand Press, 2009), 98, 113, 145.

9. The Enrollment Act of 1863 called for the enrollment of men between twenty-five and forty-five for a possible draft into the Union Army. However, those who were selected could pay a $300 fee or supply a substitute and thereby avoid military service. This led to the complaint that the policy made for "a rich man's war, poor man's fight."

10. The author here refers to two incidents from the 1848 revolutions in Europe. The first is the "June Days" violence by the Parisian working class that eventually led to the dictatorship of Louis Napoleon. The second incident refers to the murder of two conservative Frankfurt Assembly representatives (Felix Lichnowsky and General Hans von Auerswald) by a mob, which discredited an attempt at a republic.

11. The Chicago Arbeiterverein was a German workers' organization that sponsored social gatherings, political meetings, and educational programs. In 1862 the club had 389 members and a library of over 500 books.

12. Theodore Hielscher was a veteran of the 1848 revolution in the German states who thrived in Chicago as an educator and political organizer. He opposed Abraham Lincoln as not being radical enough in his opposition to slavery.

13. According to the 1860 census there were 22,230 Chicagoans born in Germany and 19,889 born in Ireland. During the war both groups increased in number. By 1870

the German population had grown to 52,318 and the Irish to 39,988. The *Tribune* had to have known that its statement was false, but as always, where the Irish were concerned it was determined to make its partisan point.

14. Ella Forbes, *African American Women during the Civil War* (New York: Garland, 1998), 43–45.

CHAPTER 8: THE LONG SHADOW OF WAR

1. *Chicago Tribune*, April 4, 1865.

2. Cook, *Bygone Days in Chicago*, 30; Livermore, *My Story of the War*, 468–71.

3. Sarah E. Henshaw, *Our Branch and Its Tributaries: A History of the Work of the Northwestern Sanitary Commission* (Chicago: Alfred L. Sewell, 1868), 297–99.

4. Cook, *Bygone Days in Chicago*, 30.

5. *Chicago Daily Tribune*, May 30, 1895.

CHAPTER 9: A GUIDE TO CIVIL WAR CHICAGO SITES

1. *Chicago Tribune*, April 21, 1862.

2. Benjamin T. Smith, *Private Smith Journal, Recollections of the Late War*, ed. Clyde C. Walton (Chicago: Lakeside Press, 1963), 17.

3. *Chicago Tribune*, April 18, 1862.

4. *Chicago Tribune*, July 15, 1924.

5. *New City* (Chicago), September 26, 1996.

6. National Park Service, *Lincoln Bicentennial, 1809–2009*, pamphlet (n.p.: Saint-Gaudens National Historic Site, 2009).

7. *Chicago Tribune*, October 23, 1969, and November 11, 1983.

8. John A. Logan, *Presbyterian Banner* 96 (May 26, 1910): 21.

9. *Chicago Sun-Times*, November 4, 1963.

10. *Chicago Tribune*, May 10, 1970, and April 23, 1972.

11. *Chicago Tribune*, August 27, 1972.

12. *Chicago Tribune*, February 15, 2004, and May 31, 2011; *Washington Times*, May 28, 2011.

13. Karamanski, *Rally 'Round the Flag*, 136.

14. John Drury, "The Barracks Being Razed: Housed Civil War Officers," *Chicago Daily News*, June 20, 1940, Camp Douglas File, Chicago History Museum.

15. *Organization, Constitution, and By-Laws of the Soldiers Home in Chicago, 45 Randolph Street* (Chicago: S. P. Rounds, 1863).

16. *Chicago Tribune*, May 31, 1895.

17. *Chicago Tribune*, June 9, 1896.

Index

abolitionists, abolitionism, 15, 26, 54, 61, 112, 121, 127, 135, 145, 146, 148, 149, 154, 205–6, 213, 220, 221, 223, 224, 230, 287, 288

Abraham Lincoln Post, GAR, 289

Addams, Jane, 238–39, 266–68

African Americans, 3, 15, 18, 43–44, 71, 78–79, 112, 143, 202, 204, 205, 206, 208, 219–30; abolitionists, 206, 224–25, 230; civil rights, 237, 239, 256–58, 275; colonization, 225; discrimination against, 209–10, 261; economic competition, 210–13; education, 221–23, 237–38, 258; enlistment, soldiers, 124, 206, 223–30; Lincoln's funeral, 235; migration to Illinois, 219–22; New York draft riot, 214; segregation, 221–22, 237; women, 230

African slave trade, 35

agriculture, 159, 164, 165, 166

American Party, 9, 12

Anglo-American Protestants, 202, 203, 204

anti-Catholicism, 19, 37, 205

Antietam, 88, 89, 181

anti-immigrant position, 9–10, 13

antislavery position, 8, 18, 60, 204, 237, 240

Appomattox, 91, 285

Archer Avenue, 240, 269

Armour, Philip Danforth, 230

Army of the Cumberland, 272, 275

Army of the Potomac, 159, 272

Army of the Shenandoah, 273

Army of the Tennessee, 274, 275, 280

Arnold, Isaac, 118, 220, 221

Athens, AL, 71, 85; sack of city, 79–80

Atlanta, GA, 83, 84, 85

Atlanta campaign, 270, 271

Baltimore, MD, 13

Baptists, 43

baseball, 38–39, 258–59, 273, 282

Bates, Edward, 14

Bates, Eli, 275

"Battle Cry of Freedom, The," 162, 193, 196, 198–99

Battle for Atlanta, 280

Battle of Cedar Creek, 273

Battle of Chattanooga, 271

Battle of Chickamauga, 101, 240, 258, 271, 272

Battle of Chickasaw Bayou, 270

Battle of Fort Donelson, 69, 74–76, 88, 92, 118, 271

Battle of Franklin, 271

Battle of Fredericksburg, 112, 113, 159

Battle of Gettysburg, 88, 108, 143–44, 145, 269. See also Gettysburg Address

Battle of Nashville, 271

Battle of Shiloh, 69, 70, 76–78, 89, 118, 248, 262, 271

Battle of Stones River, 90, 270, 271

Bean, R. T., 109–10

Bell, John, 14

Bismarck, Otto von, 1

Black Laws of Illinois, 256

Blatchford, Eliphalet Wickes, 167–68

Bohemians, 9, 205

Boone, Levi, 9, 18, 271

Borglum, Gutzon, 272, 273

Boston, MA, 3, 182, 186

bounty jumpers, 114

Boyington, William, 270, 283

Breckenridge, John C., 14, 40, 149

Bridgeport, 8, 113, 115, 133, 136, 138, 202–3, 204, 205, 236, 240, 268; poor, 208

Bridges Battery Monument, 272

Bross, John A., 228–29

Brotherhood of Locomotive Engineers, 189

Buchanan, James, 48

Buell, Gen. Don Carlos, 71, 79

Bull Run, 112, 159, 179, 231, 279

Burnsides, Gen. Ambrose E., 99, 113, 139, 142, 143, 146

Butler, M.C., 264

Cairo, IL, 49, 59, 62–64, 67, 69, 220

Calhoun, John C., 10

Calvary Cemetery, 268

Cameron, Simon, 14, 63

Southerners, 14, 62, 79, 111, 167

Southern prisoners. *See* Camp Douglas

Southern secession, 10, 15, 71, 216. *See also* secession, secessionists; secessionist crisis

Southern securities, 163, 165

Southern Unionists, 287–88

Springfield, IL, 63, 64, 151, 167, 172, 243

Stanley, Henry Morton, 100–101

Stanton, Sec. Edwin, 115, 127, 242

St. Joseph's Home for the Friendless, 283

St. Leger Grenfell, George T., 116

St. Louis, Chicago & Alton Railroad, 92–93

St. Louis, MO, 2, 13, 167, 173, 186, 237; capture of weapons, 49; Zouaves, 53

Stokes, James H., 49

Storey, Wilbur F., 112, 113–14, 115, 140–43, 145, 146, 150, 159, 191–92, 244, 271

St. Patrick's Church, 240

Sweet, Gen. Benjamin, 139, 271

Swedes, 9; enlistment, 49; poor, 208; population, 205

Swift, Gustavas, 240

Swift, Gen. R. K., 63–64

Tarbell, Ida, 155

Tennessee River, 77

Tenth Ward Riots, 217–18

Texas annexation, 10

Thirteenth Louisiana Infantry, 101

Thomas, George A., 272

"Tramp, Tramp, Tramp, the Boys Are Marching," 194, 195, 199–200

Tremont House Hotel, 12, 21, 32, 42, 68

Trollope, Anthony, 6

Trumbull, Lyman, 113, 142, 143

Tullahoma Campaign, 271

Turchin, Gen. John B., 3, 66; sack of Athens, AL, 70–71, 79–80

Turners Hall, 64

Underground Railroad, 43, 205

Union, 3, 22, 26, 34, 38, 45, 46, 49, 58, 111, 145, 149, 215, 237; army, 4, 69, 71, 77, 89, 100, 112, 131, 182, 219, 236, 241, 243, 255, 270, 273, 280, 281; cause, 80, 82, 116, 120, 122–23, 125, 126, 136, 161, 163, 220, 239, 241, 275; prisoners, 90, 94, 107–8; return home, 236, 237, 238, 247–49, 250–54; veterans, 238, 239, 240, 241,

248, 250, 251, 254–55, 258, 259, 262, 264, 265, 272, 283, 287, 288, 289; victories, 116; war effort, 56, 149, 150, 159, 189, 193

Union Defense Committee, 170

Union Hall, 246, 252

Unionists, 79, 287

Union Stockyards, 5, 158, 173, 174–75, 236

urbanization, 38

U.S. Congress, 7, 16–17, 18, 22, 26, 34, 36, 115, 124, 126, 144–45, 158, 162, 163, 201, 207

U.S. Constitution, 26, 27, 29, 34, 35, 45, 57, 61, 109, 126, 143, 144, 147, 148, 180, 207, 255

U.S. Navy, 99

U.S. Quartermaster's Department, 162, 168, 171, 172–73

U.S. Sanitary Commission, 5, 69, 80–81, 84–87, 159–61, 182–87, 235, 241, 282, 283; aid to families, 230–34

U.S. Senate, 279

U.S. Steel Corporation, 5

U.S. Supreme Court, 12, 23

U.S. War Department, 128, 155, 166, 167

"Vacant Chair, The," 194

Vallandigham, Clement, 113, 115, 150, 151, 152

Vermont troops, 95

Vicksburg, MS, 81, 160, 196, 231, 252, 270, 288

Volk, Leonard, 271, 277, 284

wage slavery, 206

Walker, W. E., 208

Ward, Aaron Montgomery, 278

war memorials, 5

Washington, DC, 53, 160, 167, 172, 182, 250, 268, 273, 275; abolition of slavery, 223–24, 226

Washington, George, 14, 20

waterways, 1, 2, 4, 6, 7, 16–17, 173, 182, 201, 205

Weatherman Days of Rage, 279

Wentworth, John, 271

West Point, 50

Wheaton College, 60

Whigs, 10, 12, 16, 26

White, Horace, 203

White, Stanford, 275, 278

"Who Will Save the Left," 194

Wigwam, 14, 16, 30, 31, 53, 54, 55–56